The Jewish Neo-Aramaic Dialect of Challa

Studies in Semitic Languages and Linguistics

VOLUME 54

The Jewish Neo-Aramaic Dialect of Challa

By

Steven E. Fassberg

BRILL

LEIDEN • BOSTON
2010

This book is printed on acid-free paper.

Library of Congress Cataloging-in-Publication Data

Fassberg, Steven E.
  The Jewish Neo-Aramaic dialect of Challa / by Steven E. Fassberg.
    p. cm. – (Studies in Semitic languages and linguistics ; Vol. 54)
  Includes bibliographical references (p.   ).
  ISBN 978-90-04-17682-9 (hardback : alk. paper)
  1. Aramaic language–Dialects–Turkey–Çukurca–Grammar. 2.
Jews–Turkey–Çukurca–Languages. 3. Çukurca (Turkey)–Languages. I. Title. II. Series.

  PJ5282.F37 2010
  492'.2–dc22

                                                                    2009046087

ISSN   0081-8461
ISBN   978 90 04 17682 9

PRINTED IN THE NETHERLANDS

For Teddy and Sarah

CONTENTS

    4.4.28.2. Verbs I-*y* and II-*w* 139

    4.4.28.3. Verbs I-*y* and III-*w* 139

    4.4.28.4. Verbs I-*y* and III-*y* 139

    4.4.28.5. Verbs II-*w* and III-ʾ 139

    4.4.28.6. Verbs II-*w* and III-*y* 139

    4.4.28.7. ʾ*rq* (ערק >)................................. 140

    4.4.28.8. ʾ*sy* (אתי >) 140

    4.4.28.9. ʾ*zl* (אזל >)................................ 141

    4.4.28.10. *b'y* (בעי >) 142

    4.4.28.11. *hnnl* (< *hənna*) 142

    4.4.28.12. *hwy* (הוי >) 142

    4.4.28.13. *hymn* (< הימן < *C* אמן) 143

    4.4.28.14. *mnx* (< נוח?; < עיני?) 143

    4.4.28.15. *mṣy* 'be able' (מצי >) 144

    4.4.28.16. *nbl* (יבל >)............................... 144

    4.4.28.17. *npl* (נפל >)............................... 144

    4.4.28.18. *xyy* (חיי >) 145

    4.4.28.19. *y'y* (ידע >) 145

    4.4.28.20. *yhw(l)* (< ל + יהב) 146

    4.4.28.21. *ytw* (יתב >) 146

   4.4.29. Modern Hebrew Verbs 147

4.5. Prepositions... 149

4.6. Conjunctions 152

4.7. Adverbs 154

   4.7.1. Interrogative Adverbs 154

   4.7.2. Temporal Adverbs 155

   4.7.3. Locative Adverbs 156

   4.7.4. Adverbs of Manner.................................... 156

4.8. Particles of Existence and Ability 158

   4.8.1. Particles of Existence 158

   4.8.2. Particles of Ability 159

4.9. Fillers 159

4.10. Exclamations and Expressions 161

V. Texts and Translation 165

5.1. The History of Jews in Challa 166

5.2. The Agha Takes What He Wants 172

5.3. Sufi Abraham, the Prayer Rug, and the Ḥajj 180

5.4. The Death of Mighty Qoto 188

5.5. The Murder of a Peddler 194

PREFACE

Like several other dialects of Neo-Aramaic, that of the Jews from Challa is now extinct. The last competent native speaker, on whose speech this grammar is based, died more than two years ago. Unfortunately, the few remaining Jews who grew up in Challa no longer speak this variety of Neo-Aramaic; their Aramaic speech has been supplanted by that of the related dialect of Jewish Zakho.

I am deeply indebted to several people for their hospitality, friendship, and generosity. The primary informant of this study, the late Shabbo Amrani, 'ilāha mānəxle, kindly and graciously welcomed me into his home in Bet 'Ajur on several occasions. He willingly told me of his life and family back in Challa before he immigrated to Israel and provided me with almost all of the data on which this study is based.

I was extremely fortunate to have met Shabbo through his relative, Ahiya Hashiloni. Ahiya, who is also from Challa, generously met with me over a long period of time and patiently went over all of the recordings. He also told me what he remembered of Challa and his relatives, and helped elucidate much of what Shabbo had told me. Without his friendship and kindness, this project would not have been possible.

Two members of the NENAFF colloqium in Jerusalem, Simon Hopkins and Hezy Mutzafi, went over an earlier draft of this book and offered detailed criticisms and corrections. I cannot thank them enough for their help and patience. I owe both of them an enormous debt of gratitude.

It is also a pleasure to thank The Hebrew University Jewish Oral Traditions Research Center and its director, Aharon Maman, as well as The Memorial Foundation for Jewish Culture, for their material support for this project. Finally I wish to thank Brill and the editors of the series *Semitic Languages and Linguistics*.

Jerusalem 2009

ABBREVIATIONS AND SIGLA

abstr.	abstract
adj.	adjective
adv.	adverb
Ar	Arabic
BiblAram	Biblical Aramaic
BiblH	Biblical Hebrew
c.	common
C	Classical Aramaic *hafʿel/ʾafʿel*
card. num.	cardinal number
CAradh	Christian Aradhin Neo-Aramaic
ClAram	Classical Aramaic (as reflected in the vocalization of Biblical Aramaic, Targums Onqelos and Jonathan to the Prophets, and Syriac)[1]
CPA	Christian Palestinian Aramaic
cst.	construct
CUrmi	Christian Urmi Neo-Aramaic
D	Classical Aramaic *paʿʿel*
dem.	demonstrative
denom.	denominative
det.	determined
dim.	diminutive
Dt	Classical Aramaic *h/ʾiϑpaʿʿel*
EgAram	Egyptian Aramaic
Eng	English
Eur	European languages
euph.	euphemism
excl.	exclamation
E-suffixes	enclitic pronominal suffixes
f.	feminine
Fr	French
G	Classical Aramaic *pəʿal*
GN	geographical name
Gr	Greek
Gt	Classical Aramaic *h/ʾiϑpəʿel*
H	Hebrew
Hert	Hertevin Neo-Aramaic
indef.	indefinite
indep.	independent

---

[1] For this term see Bar-Asher 1977:XVI.

interr.	interrogative
intr.	intransitive
inv.	invariable
IrAr	Iraqi Arabic
JAmid	Jewish Amidya Neo-Aramaic
JArbel	Jewish Arbel Neo-Aramaic
JAradh	Jewish Aradhin Neo-Aramaic
JBA	Jewish Babylonian Aramaic
JBetan	Jewish Benature Neo-Aramaic
JChalla	Jewish Challa Neo-Aramaic
JDohok	Jewish Dohok Neo-Aramaic
JGzira	Jewish Gzira Neo-Aramaic
JKoyS	Jewish Koy Sanjak Neo-Aramaic
JNaɣada	Jewish Naɣada Neo-Aramaic
JNeoAram	Jewish Neo-Aramaic
JNerwa	Jewish Nerwa Neo-Aramaic
JNerwa texts	Jewish Nerwa Neo-Aramaic as reflected in the 17th–18th texts published in Sabar 1984
JPA	Jewish Palestinian Aramaic
JSuleim	Jewish Suleimaniyya Neo-Aramaic
JZakho	Jewish Zakho Neo-Aramaic
K	Kurdish
KAI	H. Donner & W. Röllig, *Kanaanäische und aramäische Inschriften*, Band 1; 5., erweiterte und überarbeitete Auflage. Wiesbaden 2002
L	Classical Aramaic *pāʿel*
LAram	Late Aramaic (according to Fitzmyer 1979)
Lat	Latin
LEAram	Late Eastern Aramaic (Jewish Babylonian Aramaic, Syriac, and Mandaic)
LWAram	Late Western Aramaic (Jewish Palestinian Aramaic, Christian Palestinian Aramaic, and Samaritan Aramaic)
L-suffixes	pronominal suffixes introduced by -*l*
LL-suffixes	pronominal suffixes introduced by -*ll*
m.	masculine
Mand	Mandaic
MidAram	Middle Aramaic (according to Fitzmyer 1979)
MishH	Mishnaic Hebrew
Mlaḥ	Mlaḥso Neo-Aramaic
ModH	Modern Hebrew
Mutz	Mutzafi 2008a
NeoAram	Neo-Aramaic
NeoMand	Neo-Mandaic
OAram	Old Aramaic (according to Fitzmyer 1979)
onomat.	onomatopoietic
ord. num.	ordinal number
P	Persian
pl.	plural

pl. tant.	plurale tantum
PNENA	Proto-Northeastern Neo-Aramaic
PrAram	Proto-Aramaic
prep.	preposition
prn.	pronoun
Q	Classical Aramaic quadriliteral stem *palpel*
QAram	Qumran Aramaic
Qaraq	Qaraqosh Neo-Aramaic
recip.	reciprocal
s.	singular
SA	Samaritan Aramaic
Sab	Sabar 2008a
SH	Samaritan Hebrew
suff.	suffix
Syr	Syriac
T	Turkish
TJ	Targum Jonathan
TO	Targum Onqelos
tr.	transitive
Ṭur	Ṭuroyo Neo-Aramaic
voc.	vocative
WNeoAram	Western Neo-Aramaic
<	developed from
>	developed into
*	unattested, reconstructed form
-	enclisis
–	anacoluthon or significant pause
(C/V)	uncertain if the consonant or vowel is realized or clipped phoneme(s)

CHAPTER ONE

INTRODUCTION

1.1. Challa

The village of Challa, known today as Çukurca,[1] is located east of the Great Zab at 37° 15′ N 43° 37′ E in southeastern Turkey, about two kilometers from the Iraqi border and 100 kilometers from the Iranian border. Çāl in Kurdish means 'ditch, pit, hole, well' and the village is so named because it is located in a geophysical depression.

1.2. Jewish Presence in Challa

The earliest evidence for a Jewish presence in Challa is found in a 16th century letter asking for support sent from a schoolmaster in Mosul to different Jewish communities in Kurdistan:[2]

---

[1] For a short description of the village and the livelihood of its inhabitants see *Türk Ansiklopedisi* (Ankara: Milli Eğitim Basımevi, 1964), 12:146a.

[2] Mann 1931, 1:507, letter 3. See also pp. 482–483. Rivlin (1959:21–22 n.58) wondered if גילן mentioned in connection with Amidya by Benjamin of Tudela in the 12th century is Challa:

משם חמשה ימים לעמאריה ושם כמו כ״ה אלף מישראל. והיא תחלת הקהלות הדרים בהרי חפטן כי שם יותר ממאה קהלות מישראל. והיא תחלת ארץ מדי והם מן הגלות הראשון שהגלה שלמנאסר המלך. והם מדברים בלשון תרגום וביניהם תלמידי חכמים והם חונים ממדינת עמאריה ועד מדינת גילן מהלך כ״ה יום עד מלכות פרס.

Thence it is five days to Amadia where there are about 25,000 Israelites. This is the first of those communities that dwell in the mountains of Chafton, where there are more than 100 Jewish communities. Here is the commencement of the land of Media. The Jews belong to the first exile which King Shalmanezar led away; and they speak the language in which the Targum is written. Amongst them are learned men. The communities reach from the province of Amadia unto the province of Gilan, twenty-five days distant, on the border of the kingdom of Persia. (Adler 1907:נא, §עז; English translation p. 54).

The ר of עמאריה is taken by all to be an error for ד and עמאדיה (Adler 1908:54 n. 2). Challa is not, however, a twenty-five day walk from Amidya nor is it thought that there were ever 25,000 Jews in Amidya. The name גילאן (Challa? Jilan in Iran?) is also attested

ומבטח אני באלקי אבי ואדוני שכל מי שיקפח פרנסתי ומחיתי יקפח בניו ויראו עיניו פידו
גם מענין ביתנורי לא שלח לי שום דבר ואשתקד דאשתקד כתבתי ושלחתי להם ולגלא
ולנירוא ולכאכא

and my trust is in my God, my Father, and my Lord, that whoever deprives
my sustenance and livelihood, may (God) deprive his sons and may his
eyes see his (own) disaster. Also concerning the matter of Betanure he
didn't send me anything and two years ago I wrote and sent to them, and
to Challa, and to Nerwa, and to K'K'.

Challa (גלא) is mentioned in this letter together with Betanure and
Nerwa, two other nearby villages with Jewish communities. *K'K'* could
be an error for nearby *Kāra*.[3] Of the two, Nerwa was the closer village[4]
and the distance between the two could be covered on foot in about three
hours.[5] Another important Jewish center, Amidya, was a one day journey
on foot.[6]

Other letters that mention Challa (גלא, גאלא, and גילה)[7] come from the
18th century. In the first letter Rabbi Mordechai ben Simeon of Amidya
informs the communities of Nerwa, Challa, and Sindu of the arrival of
the religious judge (דַיָן) R. Aaron Ashkenazi from Tiberias, who has
sent the local Rabbi Sasson in his place to collect contributions from the
communities:

קהלא קדישא. ואבן הראשה לכל דבר שבקדושה. ה׳׳ה (= והחכם הגדול) עמי ועדתי
ק׳׳ק נירוא וגלא וסינד יע׳׳א (= יבנה עירנו אמן) ועילא מנהון החכמים הרמים

───────────

in a document written by the head of a yeshiva in Amidya, who writes to the community
of מראגא asking for financial support for his yeshiva:

...והרבה טובות עשיתם עם כל ישראל, כי לא לבד עמי עשיתם הטובות והמצות, שאלו כמה שנים
החזקתם ידי לתורה, כ׳׳א לכל אלו ישראל שבאילו הקהלות והגליליו, שלמדו תלמידים הגרים
במדרש שלי מד' פאות העולם, עשיתם עד אשר יש לי במצרים תלמידים ובקושטנטינא ובא׳׳י
ובגילאן ובאשר הקהלות...

... and many kind deeds you have performed with all of Israel, for not only
with me have you performed kind deeds and religious work, for several years
you have encouraged me in Torah (study), but for all those of Israel in different
communities and regions, students who have studied in my *(bet) midrash* from the
four corners of the earth, you have done so that I have (now students) in Egypt,
and in Constantinople, and in גילאן and other communities ... (Assaf 1934: קו,
who wonders if ובציילאן = ובגילאן, though he doesn't explain the latter).

[3] So according to Hezy Mutzafi (p.c.).
[4] See the map in Mutzafi 2004:13.
[5] See § 5.11.1.
[6] Ben-Yaacob 1980, supplement p. 47.
[7] Assaf 1943:141 n. א122.

The holy community. And the headstone for everything concerning holiness, the great Rabbi with me and my congregation, the holy communities of Nerwa, and Challa, and Sind(u), may the Lord build our cities amen, and above them the distinguished Rabbis...[8]

In a second letter the same Rabbi Sasson writes to Challa asking that they send contributions to Amidya, since he is afraid that if he goes himself to collect, he will be robbed on the way:

שלומות רבות וישועות קרובות לאלפים ורבבות יבואו ממזרח שמש וממערב אל ק״ק
גאלא...

Many greetings and may thousands and myriads of salvation soon come from the east and west to the holy community of Challa...[9]

A third letter was sent (apparently from Amidya) by an emissary from Jerusalem, Samuel Benjamin, to Nerwa and Challa:

אחינו אנשי גאולתנו גומלי חסדים טובים וחכמים וגבוהים ורמים אשר בק״ק נירוה יע״א
ואשר בק״ק גילה יע״א... וענין ק״ק גילה עליכם לגמור המצוה הזאת...

Our brethren, the men of our redemption, the charitable, and learned, and lofty, and distinguished, who are in the holy community of Nerwa, may the Lord build our city, amen, and concerning the holy community of Challa, may the Lord build our city, amen... and concerning the holy community of Challa, you must fulfill this religious duty...[10]

Another letter was sent by a religious judge of Amidya, Simeon ben Benjamin Halevi to the community of Challa concerning a ritual slaughterer (שׁוֹחֵט) for Challa:[11]

... הה (= והחכם הגדול) שלמה היו (= השם ישמרהו ויצילהו) והה יעקב היו ועכ כמֹ
קֹקֹ (= ועל כל כבוד מעלת קהל קודש) גלא כיבוֹש (=כן יבנה במהרה נוה שלום) כירא
(=כן יהי רצון אמן)... והרשיתי אותו שתאכלו משחיטתו...

and the great Rabbi Solomon, may the Lord protect him and save him, and the great Rabbi Jacob, may the Lord protect him and save him, and all the honorable holy congregation of Challa, may the Lord build speedily a dwelling of peace, so may it be, amen... and I empowered him so that you may eat from his ritual slaughtering...

Challa is also mentioned in oral texts from Betanure recorded by Hezy Mutzafi. It is noted that some Jewish families from Challa fled to Betanure because of Kurdish massacres during World War I and immediately

---

[8] Assaf 1943:142.
[9] Ibid.
[10] Assaf 1943:143–144.
[11] Mann 1931, 1:532–533, letter 14, line 7.

afterwards, while others went to Jerusalem and elsewhere.[12] The same Betanure speaker relates that Jews from Amidya, Zakho, or Challa would come to Betanure and offer a poor father of a bride a higher bride-price than the one offered by relatives.[13]

According to the *Kurdish Jewish Encyclopaedia*,[14] there were 30 Jews in Challa[15] in 1933, who engaged in weaving, trade, and agriculture. Some Jews left Challa for Palestine in the first decades of the 20th century; those who remained immigrated to Israel in 1951.

1.3. CHRISTIAN PRESENCE IN CHALLA

Christians also lived in the Challa area.[16] Today descendants of Christians from Chal (Čāl), as they refer to it, live in Tall Brej on the Khabur River in Syria.[17] They relate that their ancestors are originally from Belatha in Lower Tiari, and moved to Chal only after Belatha had been abandoned. Ahiya Hashiloni, who left Challa in 1929, remembers from his youth that the Christians lived outside of Challa.

1.4. MUSLIM (KURDISH) PRESENCE IN CHALLA

Ahiya Hashiloni and Shabbo Amrani relate that Kurds and Jews lived together in Challa, though Ahiya remembers that when he left in 1929 the Jews tended to live mostly towards the side of the hill (*ṭappá*) that overlooked Challa.

---

[12] Mutzafi 2008a:138–139. On the situation in and around Challa see Malik Yaqu 1964:81–82, who describes in some detail the capture, burning, and destruction of Nerwa, Challa, and nearby villages in September 1916, and mentions the deportation of villagers to Tehum. Jewish life in Challa changed after this.

[13] Mutzafi 2008a:192–193.

[14] Yona 2003, 1:185.

[15] For additional mention of the Jews of Challa, see Rivlin 1959:21; Ben-Yaacob 1980, supplement, p. 47.

[16] See, e.g., mention of a Christian from Chal in a text recorded by a speaker of Barwar (Khan 2008:297).

[17] Talay 2008:28,37. In 1940 there were 100 Christians from Chal in Tall Brej. Their language, which has been studied in Talay 2008, is considerably different from Jewish Challa and shares affinities, according to Talay, with Christian dialects from the Tiari dialect cluster (Talay 2008:48).

1.5. Jewish Challa Informants

The following grammatical description is based primarily on more than twenty hours of recordings made between 2001 and 2006 at the home of the one remaining competent native Jewish speaker from Challa, Shabbo Amrani (שבתאי עמרני).[18] Shabbo came to Israel in 1951 at the age of 30 and was settled in Moshav Ajur (עג׳ור; officially Agur) near the city of Bet Shemesh.[19] In Challa he was known as *Shabbo bron 'Ammo*, and belonged to the *Be Rubabči* clan. He took the name Amrani upon arriving in Israel. He spoke Neo-Aramaic, Kurdish, Turkish, Iraqi Arabic, and Modern Hebrew. He passed away in the summer of 2007 at the age of 86. Shabbo worked in agriculture in Challa with his father till he was drafted into the Turkish army, where he served as a hospital orderly from 1941–1945. He immigrated to Israel in 1951 leading a group of families from Challa; they travelled by rail to Istanbul and from there set sail for Haifa. After a period of time in the transit camp *Sha'ar Aliya* (שער עלייה) near Netania, he and his family were sent to Moshav Ajur. He initially worked for the Jewish National Fund in preparing land for agriculture. He then turned to agriculture himself and worked his own land. He later also worked as a security guard until his retirement.

A younger brother, who still bears the name by which the family was known in Challa, Dogumanchi (< Turkish *dokumacı* 'weaver'), no longer speaks the Jewish Challa variety of Neo-Aramaic, but rather that of Jewish Zakho, which predominates in the greater Jerusalem area.

I made the acquaintance of Shabbo through his cousin, Ahiya Hashiloni (אחיה השילוני),[20] who was born in Challa in 1920, the son of the well-known and respected local rabbi, Jacob Hashiloni.[21] Ahiya gave of his time freely and spent hours going over the recordings of his cousin, who was not always the most patient of informants. Ahiya took care to

---

[18] For this reason, one cannot always be certain what reflects Shabbo's idiolect as opposed to the dialect of Jewish Challa.

[19] For additional biographical details, see Yona 2003, 3:763–764.

[20] For biographical details, see Yona 2003, 2:274–275.

[21] For his obituary and stories about his ancestors, including miracles performed through קבלה מעשית ('practical Qabbala' = incantations and the like), see Yona 2003, 2:278–279; Hashiloni and Hashiloni 1985:129–132. Rabbi Jacob Hashiloni belonged to the *Be 'Ajamāye* clan in Challa. Two photographs of Rabbi Jacob Hashiloni taken in the 1930's or 1940's can be found in Brauer 1993 in the photographic section in the middle of the book under 'Man from Tchalla.' and on the following page, 'Man from Kurdistan' (he is photographed without a skullcap). For a photograph taken towards the end of his life, see Yona 2003, 1:185 and 2:279.

explain the events, persons, and background of the stories, and also aided in interpreting Shabbo's speech. Ahiya came to Palestine in 1934 after a stay of five years in Amidya. In Jerusalem he lived in the Neo-Aramaic speaking neighborhood of Zikhron Yosef. On occasion Ahiya supplied Jewish Challa forms that he remembered from growing up in Challa or from the speech of his parents in Jerusalem. These lexical items have been included when they show a divergence from the Jewish Zakho koine, which has greatly influenced his speech.

In addition, a few lexical items have been included from the tape recordings of Ahiya's father, Rabbi Jacob Hashiloni, which were made in 1964 at the Language Traditions Project of The Institute of Jewish Studies, The Hebrew University of Jerusalem. Rabbi Hashiloni recorded sections of the Passover *haggada* compiled by Rabbi Alwan Avidani, which was first published in 1959[22] together with a translation into the Jewish Amidya dialect,[23] though some features reflect an "all-dialectal Jerusalemite NA [Neo-Aramaic]".[24] Rabbi Hashiloni, when chanting from this *haggada*, sometimes substitutes Jewish Challa grammatical forms for those forms found in the printed *haggada*[25] and on occasion also replaces lexemes with entirely different lexical items.[26] The grammatical forms that deviate from the printed *haggada* are corroborated by Shabbo's speech. The lexical items that deviate from the printed *haggada* are included in this grammar since they provide evidence of where the Jewish Challa dialect differed from the Neo-Aramaic tradition of Rabbi Avidani. It should be kept in mind that these lexical items reflect a literary register.

---

[22] Avidani 1959. A second edition appeared in Avidani 1979. These recordings of the *haggada* have recently been digitized and have received the numbers 2534, 2535, 2536, 2537, 2538, 2539, 4356, 4360, and 4362. There are also recordings of Rabbi Hashiloni chanting in Hebrew from the Old Testament and the Mishna. For an older list of the recordings, see Fellman 1978:24–25,91,140,241,247.

[23] Hoberman 1989:11; Sabar 2002b: 75–76, 84.

[24] Sabar 1976:175.

[25] E.g., he consistently substitutes the JChalla form 2 pl. pronominal suffix -*exun* for the printed JAmid -*oxun*.

[26] I.e., the preposition *ṭla* 'to, for' is always replaced by JChalla *ta*. On some lexical points Rabbi Hashiloni agrees with the JZakho tradition of the *haggada* reflected in Alfiye 1986 as against the *haggada* of Avidani, yet because of the many divergences from the JZakho tradition, it does not seem likely that Rabbi Hashiloni was following the JZakho tradition.

CHAPTER TWO

JEWISH CHALLA AND THE
OTHER *LISHANA DENI* DIALECTS

2.1. DIALECTAL POSITION OF JEWISH CHALLA

Jewish Challa belongs to the dialectal cluster whose speakers refer to their language as *lishana deni* 'our language'.[1] The cluster comprises the Jewish speakers of Amidya, Aradhin, Atrush, Barashe, Betanure, Challa, Gzira, Dohok, Kara, Nerwa, and Zakho. According to Mutzafi,[2] two features that are shared by these dialects are

a. the independent genitive pronoun *did*- with pronominal suffixes in the singular, e.g., *didox* 'yours', but the possessive-relative particle *d*- with pronominal suffixes in the plural, e.g., *dexun* 'yours'
b. -*Vwun* in III-y pl. imperative forms, e.g., *sāwun* 'come!'[3]

2.2. SALIENT FEATURES OF JEWISH CHALLA

JChalla shares many features with other *lishana deni* dialects.[4] The following, however, is a list of salient features of JChalla that sometimes set it apart from some of the other dialects. Each feature is discussed in the appropriate place in the grammar or in the glossary.

a. Reflexes of the interdentals (§ 3.2.b): ClAram *ṯ* > *s* (*sele* 'he came'), *ḏ* > *d* ('*ida* 'hand')
b. Sporadic contraction of the triphthong *āya* > *ā* (§ 3.15): *qurdāya* 'Kurd' > *qurdǻ*; *xzāya* 'seeing' > *xzǻ*

---

[1] Sabar 2002a:5–9.
[2] Mutzafi 2002; Mutzafi 2008b:10–11.
[3] So too in JChalla *sāwun*. In other III-y verbs, however -*ūwun*, > *ūn*, e.g., *xzūwun* > *xzūn*.
[4] Of the *lishana deni* dialect group, JChalla appears to be closer in general to modern JNerwa (based on the fieldwork of Mutzafi) and to JBetan than to the other dialects.

   c. Independent pronouns (§ 4.1.1): 2 c.s. 'āhat (also 'āt), 3 c.s. 'āya ('ā; see [b] above), 1 pl. 'axnan

   d. Pronominal suffixes (§ 4.1.2): 2 pl. -exun

   e. Demonstrative pronouns (§ 4.1.7): c.s. 'iya 'this' (yā- only in the expression b-iya 'ida u-yá-'ida 'when it comes down to it'); c.s. 'ē 'that', 'āya ('ā) 'that (one)'; c.pl. 'anna ('an) 'these/those'

   f. Reflexive pronoun (§ 4.1.9): gyāna

   g. Reciprocal pronouns (§ 4.1.10): 'əǧdād(e), l-əǧdād(e), m-əǧdād(e); xa l-e-xeta/xet/xe

   h. Interrogative pronoun (§ 4.1.11): 'eni 'which'

   i. Indefinite Pronouns (§ 4.1.12): flān 'such and such' occurs before humans and flāna before non-humans.

   j. Preterite (§§ 4.4.23.4; 4.4.28.19): It is inflected with object affixes for all persons, e.g., xpiqənne 'he embraced me'. Unlike most lishana deni dialects, there is no construction of the type *qam xāpəqli 'he embraced me'.[5] There are no reflexes of *d in the Preterite of *ydʿ 'know', e.g., y'eli 'I knew'.

   k. Subjunctive based inflection (§§ 3.18.c; 4.1.6.c,f; 4.4.28.12): 1 f.s. E-suffix -an occasionally in place of 1 m.s. -ən; 1 c.pl. E-suffix -axin;[6] 2 c.pl. with L- suffix pronouns 'amrétūle 'you may tell him', dārétūle 'they may put it';[7] 3 f.s. of verb hwy—hūwa 'she may be', kūwa 'she is', pūwa 'she will be'

   l. Subjunctive particle (§ 4.4.7): mən/məl, e.g., mən hāwe 'let it be!', məl 'āzəl 'he may go!'

   m. Participle III-y f.s. (§ 4.4.27.9): xzeta 'seen'[8]

   n. Extensive Use of qym (§ 4.4.24): Though the construction qam xāpəqli is strikingly absent, it is noteworthy that qym is used widely to express ingressive action, particularly with participial forms that govern an object (like the qam xāpəqli construction), e.g., qāyəm xāzele 'he up (and) sees him', qemən gālənnu 'I up (and) reveal it', qemi mesele 'they up (and) bring him'.

   o. Preposition 'to, for' (§ 4.5): ta; ṭas when bound by suffixes and the independent genitive pronoun did-, e.g., ṭāsi, ṭāsox, ṭāsax, ṭas didi,

---

   [5] The construction is also absent from JNerwa texts (Sabar 1976:XXXIX) as well as modern spoken JNerwa (Hezy Mutzafi—p.c.).

   [6] Cf. -ax(ni) in other dialects.

   [7] Cf. modern J Nerwa qaṭlétunle (Hezy Mutzafi p.c.) and elsewhere in lishana deni dialects qaṭlə́tule.

   [8] As opposed to forms with medial i.

ṭas didox, ṭas didax; preposition 'to, with, by' *kəsəl, kəs,* and *kəl,* of which the last is attested only before nouns.

p. Particles of existence (§ 4.8): *'it, 'ítən(a)* 'there is'; *let, létən(a)* 'there isn't'.

q. Lexicon: *'áqqar(a)* 'so much', *'əl'uwwa* 'inside', *básbasər* 'right after' (cf. *basər* 'after'), *ḥál-u-masale* 'the upshot', *ḥil/ḥel* 'until', *plāṭa* 'go out' and *(m)palōṭe* 'take out', *plāxa* 'work', *qadōme* 'tomorrow', *bəšṭor* 'better', *qamqam* 'right before' (cf. *qam* 'before'), *xamūšeb* 'Thursday'.

Features (b), (c), (h), (i), (k), (l) and the forms of the lexical items *'áqqara, 'əl'uwwa* 'inside', *kəl* 'to, with', and *xamūšeb* 'Thursday" appear to be unique to JChalla at this point in the general research of *lishana deni* dialects.

CHAPTER THREE

PHONOLOGY

3.1. Consonants

The consonantal inventory of JChalla is

	bi-labial	labio-dental	alveo-lar	post-alveolar	pala-tal	velar	uvu-lar	pharyn-geal	glottal
plosive									
voiced	b ḅ		d ḍ			g	q		ʾ
voiceless	p p̣		t ṭ			k ḳ			
nasal	m ṃ		n ṇ						
trill			r ṛ						
fricative									
voiced	v ṿ	z ẓ	ž			ġ	ʿ		
voiceless		f	s ṣ	š		x	ḥ	h	
affricate									
voiced				j					
voiceless				č č̣					
approximant	w				y				
lateral			l ḷ						

- *f* is restricted to loanwords, e.g., *farq* 'difference', *feka* 'fruit', *kafíl* 'guarantor', *kāfər* 'infidel'. *flān, flāna* 'such and such' (ClAram פְּלָן) is either a borrowing from Arabic or Kurdish, or else the *f* of the Arabic cognate فُلَان and the Kurdish *filan* has influenced the native Aramaic form. *flānkas* 'so and so' is a loan from Kurdish (§ 4.2.10.b). *nāfeʾ* 'it is useful' < Arabic نفع is also heard as *nāpeʾ* (hypercorrection?).
- *v* is limited to Kurdish and ModH loanwords, e.g., from Kurdish: *veza* 'so, like this', *kavra* 'cliff'; from ModH: *qvʿ* 'determine', e.g., *wetun kviʿe* 'you have determined'; *ʿvr* 'cross over', e.g., *ʿvərri* 'I crossed over'.[1] The *v* of ModH shows up as *b* in JChalla in *vkḥ* 'argue': *mbokaḥlan* 'we argued', *mbokāḥe* 'arguing'.[2]

---

[1] Cf. the genuine NeoAram reflex *ʾwr*, e.g., *ʾürri* 'I entered'.
[2] See Sabar 1990:55 for examples of loanwords in which *v > b* in JZakho.

- *ġ* is attested in Arabic loanwords, e.g., *ġer* 'another', *ġrq* 'sink'. In native Aramaic words it is an allophone of *x* (§ 3.6.g).
- *p* and *t* are often strongly aspirated.

3.2. BGDKPT

a. The ClAram *bgdkpt* consonants have the following reflexes in JChalla:

ClAram	JChalla	
b	*b*	*bərqa* 'lightning'
ḇ[3]	*w*	*dehwa* 'gold'
g	*g*	*gəlda* 'skin'
g	*'/ø*	*zo'a* 'pair', *bənhe* 'morning'
d	*d*	*de'sa* 'sweat'
ḏ	*d*	*'ida* 'hand'
k	*k*	*kalba* 'dog'
ḵ	*x*	*nəxrāya* 'foreigner'
p	*p*	*pəmma, pumma* 'mouth'
p̄	*p*	*kəpna* 'hunger'
t	*t*	*tar'a* 'door'
ṯ	*s*	*besa* 'house'

b. A salient phonological feature of JChalla is the reflex of the interdentals: **ṯ > s* (*sele* 'he came'), **ḏ > d* (*qdāla* 'neck'). Cf. JZakho and JGzira *s* and *z*, JAmid *ṯ* and *d*, JDohok and JBetan *ṯ* and *ḏ*, JAradh *ṯ* and *d*.[4] *ṯ > t*, however, in all forms of the particles of existence, e.g., *'it* 'there is' (< *'iṯ*), *'ətwāli* 'I had', and *let* 'there is not' (< *leṯ*), *lətwāli* 'I didn't have'. The shift originated in the partial assimilation of *ṯ* to *l* (*ϑ > t/_l*) in forms such as *'ətli* 'I have' (< אית לי) and *letli* 'I don't have' (< לית לי). *l* is also responsible for the *t* (< *ṯ*) of *mətle* 'he died' (cf. *māyəs* 'he may die'). Surprisingly *ṯ > t* in the forms of the verb *ptx* 'open' (cf. JZakh *psx*, JBetan and JDohok *ptx*).

c. As in other NeoAram dialects, either the plosive or the fricative realization of the *bgdkpt* consonants has become lexicalized. Thus from the ClAram root **dgl* 'lie' one finds the plosive pronunciation preserved throughout, e.g., *dugla* 'lie', *mdaglən* 'I may lie'; from ClAram *rgš* 'wake

---

[3] The ClAram fricative *ḇ* (< *b*) and the approximant *w* merged in some older Aramaic dialects as can be seen from the graphic fluctuation of ב and ו in JPA and SA (and also MishH). Ben-Ḥayyim 2000:34 believes that *w > v* in these dialects, whereas Kutscher 1982:121 thought it was impossible to ascertain the direction of the merger. In *lishana deni* dialects *ḇ > w* (Sabar 2002a:24).

[4] See Kapeliuk 1997 on the reflexes of *ṯ* and *ḏ* in NeoAram.

up' one finds *g* > ', e.g., *mur'ǝšǝnnox* 'you woke me up'. In *'ǝl'uwwa* 'inside' (< ClAram גּוֹ) **g* > *g* > '. *b* has become lexicalized in two verbs borrowed from ModH, בְּקֵשׁ 'request' and סָבַל 'suffer', e.g., *mbokǝšli* 'I requested', *sabli* 'they may suffer'.

d. Reflexes of *bgdkpt* that originated in voicing or devoicing from contact with contiguous consonants have also become lexicalized, as in other NeoAram dialects, e.g., **b* > *p* in *pǝsra* 'meat' (< ClAram בִּסְרָא), *xpq* 'embrace' (< ClAram חבק), *gupta* 'cheese' (cf. Syr ܓܒܬܐ, ܓܒܬܐ; JBA גּוּבְנֵי, גְּבִינְתָא);[5] possibly *d* > *t* in *txr* 'remember' (< ClAram דכר).[6] The possessive-relative particle *d* when suffixed to a noun is devoiced to [t] before an unvoiced consonant, e.g., *nixǝd bābi* ['niːχɪd 'bʰaːbʰi] 'my late father' vs. *'idǝd ḥukum* ['ˀiːdʰɪt 'ḥukum] 'the hand of the government'. *d* of the indefinite pronoun *kud* 'each, every' is devoiced before unvoiced consonants in **kud + xa* > *kutxa* 'each one', **kud + 'arbeni* > *kút'arbeni* 'the four of them'. *d* is devoiced to *t* before unvoiced consonants in forms based on the Subjunctive of *hwy* (**d-hūwa* > *t-ūwa*) and the 3rd person forms of the Present Copula (**d-'ile* > *t-ile*; (§§ 4.1.8.m; 4.4.6.1.f).

3.3. Pharyngeals and Glottals

a. The ClAram pharyngeals *ḥ* and ' have reflexes of *x* and ' respectively, e.g., *xmāra* 'donkey' (ClAram חֲמָרָא), *xāsa* 'new' (ClAram חֲדַתָּא), *balo'ta* 'throat' (BTA בְּלוֹעָא), *'ǝrota* 'Friday' (Syriac ܥܪܘܒܬܐ). ClAram ' is preserved in the vicinity of *r* in the inflection of the root *ṣ'r* 'curse', *ṣa'āre* 'barley', and *'urṭūsa* 'fart', and in *t'y* 'search' in the vicinity of *ṭ*. Words with *ḥ* and ' are either loans originally from Arabic (e.g., *ḥaqq* 'price', *ḥāl* 'situation', *'āṣǝrta* 'evening', *'aṭarka* 'peddler') or from Hebrew (*'āwon* 'sin').[7] The JChalla nouns *ḥakoma* 'ruler' and *ḥukum, ḥukūma, ḥukumiya* 'government' are derived from Arabic حكم and not from ClAram *ḥkm*.

b. The voiceless fricative glottal *h* is sometimes replaced in word-initial position by a weak glottal stop ', e.g., *'atxa* 'so, such' alongside the more frequent *hatxa*.

---

[5] Talay 2008:58 n. 98. See also Sabar 1990:55 on *b* > *p* in loanwords (e.g., *potine* 'boots').

[6] Khan 1999:32. On the possibility of the root *txr* originating in backformation from a ClAram Gt, see Mutzafi 2008a:390 and also below § 4.4.1 n. 109.

[7] On pharyngealization in NeoAram, see Hoberman 1985; Mutzafi 2004:27–33.

c. The glottal stop ’ is often weakly pronounced ("creaky voice") and at times replaces in initial position the approximant *w*, e.g., *’ewa* 'he was' for *wewa*, at other times it is elided altogether (§ 4.4.6.4.a). In medial position it may replace *w*: *yā’eli* 'he may give me' (< *yāweli*). A medial glottal stop ’ is occasionally difficult to discern in rapid speech and at times elided, e.g., *’ar(’)a* 'land', *tar(’)a* 'door', *šme(’)le* 'he heard'. The glottal stop is preserved medially in roots borrowed from ModH, e.g., *da’gax* 'we may take care of'.

d. ’ shifts to the pharyngeal ʿ in a few Arabic loans, a phenomenon that is also attested elsewhere in NeoAram:[8] *ʿṃṛ* 'boss around', *maʿṃụ̄ṛ* 'officer-in-charge', *ʿanjil* 'Gospels', *qurʿān* 'Quran', *ʿaṣəl* '(good) origin', *ʿaṣlāye* 'of good origin', *ʿaṣli* 'genuine'. It happens in the Aramaic verb *šyʿ* 'plaster' (§ 4.4.27.5), which elsewhere in NeoAram is attested as *šyʾ* < שוע or שעע. It is also attested in the Hebrew hypocoristic *ʿĀbo* (אַבְרָהָם) and ModH *ʿazor*, *ʾəzór* 'area' (אֵזוֹר).

e. The ʿ of the ModH verb שִׁכְנֵעַ 'persuade' is realized surprisingly as *x* in *mšaxnəxle* 'he may persuade him'.

3.4. AFFRICATES

a. *j* and *ž* occur in loanwords, the former from Arabic, and the latter from Kurdish, e.g., *julle* 'clothes', *žang* 'rust', *-ži* 'also, even'. *ž* also occurs as an allophone of *š* in the preposition *reš* before a voiced consonant (§ 3.6.e)

b. *č* occurs in Kurdish and Turkish loanwords,[9] e.g., *ʿačāyəb* 'how strange!', *čamča* 'teaspoon', *čaydanka* 'teapot', and in the ModH based *pənčərāli* 'I caused a flat tire.' It is attested in a reflex of an old loan into Aramaic (< תִּשְׁרֵי) from Akkadian, *čeri* 'spring'. It is also heard in Present forms of the verb *y’y* 'know' (§ 4.4.9.c) in addition to the forms with *k*, e.g., *lá-čiʾan* 'I don't know' (also *lá-kiʾan*), *čiʾətte* 'you know him' (also *kiʾətte*[10]). An emphatic realization, *č̣*, is found in the native Aramaic words *č̣ym* 'close (eyes; < טמם)', *mṛč̣* 'crush' (< מרס), *č̣my* 'extinguish' (< סמי), *č̣o’a* 'smooth' (< שעע), and *ʾəč̣ʾa* 'nine' (< תִּשְׁעָה).

c. Shabbo sometimes realizes historical ṣ as the affricate *ṭs* in ModH loans, e.g., *kfəṭsle* 'he jumped'.

---

[8] See, e.g., Sabar 1990:56; Fassberg 2005.
[9] Sabar 1990:55.
[10] One also hears frequently fronted *k*: [kʸɪtte].

3.5. EMPHATICS

a. The emphatic (pharyngealized) pronounciation is found regularly in *ṣ* and *ṭ* that are direct reflexes of the corresponding ClAram emphatic consonants, e.g., *ṣlosa* 'prayer', *ṭina* 'mud'. Non-emphatic consonants in native Aramaic words sometimes become emphatic in certain words in JChalla as in other NeoAram dialects,[11] e.g., *ṛ* in *'uṛwa* 'big', *naxṛāya* 'foreigner', *ṛāba* 'much', *ṛapsa* 'big (f.)', *ṛomāna* 'high', *ṣa'āṛe*[12] 'barley', *šaṛūsa* 'lunch'; *ṃ* in *ṃāye* 'water'.[13] Emphaticization of ClAram *t* (as well as the contiguous *l*) is attested in the numbers based on 'three': *ṭḷāha* 'three' and *ṭḷāsi* 'thirty', but not in *taltaʾsar* 'thirteen'.[14] It does not occur in *tmanya* 'eight' but it is found in *ṭṃāneʾsar* 'eighteen' and *ṭṃāni* 'eighty'. Secondary emphatic consonants due to assimilation to a contiguous inherited Aramaic *ṭ* or *ṣ* are unmarked, e.g., *mṭele* [əmˤtˤelɛ], whereas unmotivated, spontaneous emphaticization is marked, e.g., *ṭḷāha* 'three'.[15] As elsewhere in Neo-Aram, emphaticization may be phonemic, e.g., *ṃly* 'be sufficient' vs. *mly* 'fill', *tora* 'ox' vs. *ṭoṛa* 'Torah' (attested in the corpus only in the compound *séfarṭoṛa* 'Torah scroll').

b. Emphatic consonants also show up in JChalla in loanwords[16] many of which do not have an emphatic consonant in the original language. Often the emphaticization spreads throughout the word. The following loanwords with emphatic consonants are listed according to the first emphatic consonant in the word:

ḅ: *ḅank* 'bank', *ḅaṛāne* 'rams', *ḅaṛāza* 'pig', *ḅāš* 'good',[17] *ḅạč'a* 'bastard'
č̣: *pyč̣* 'break'
ḍ: *ʾoḍa* 'room'
ḳ: *ḳappāra* 'expiation'
ḷ: *ḷappa* 'lump'
ṃ: *ṃāl* 'property', *ṃamzer* 'bastard', *'ạṃḅāsi* 'corporal'
ṇ: *quṇṣul* 'consul', *quṇṣulya* 'consulate'

---

[11] Sabar 2002:32–33; Mutzafi 2008a:19–20.
[12] The emphaticization is the result of assimilation to neighboring *ṣ* and *'*.
[13] See Fassberg 1997 for possibly emphatic forms of 'water' in JPA.
[14] Sabar 2002a:33.
[15] Following Mutzafi 2008a:20.
[16] This reflects the phenomenon of 'emphatic foreignization of borrowed forms'. See Campbell 2004:82. On emphaticization in loanwords in JZakho, see Sabar 1990:55–56.
[17] Shabbo sometimes pronounces *baškalnāye* 'resident of Bashkala' with an emphatic realization (*ḅaškalnāye*) under the influence of *ḅāš*.

p: *gopāla/gopalta* 'shepherd's stick', *palǝstināye* 'Palestinians', *palle* 'coals',
     panqánoṭ 'lira, paper money', *pássaporṭ* 'passport', *posṭa* 'mail', *qapṭán*
     'captain'

r: *barāxa* 'blessing', *doṛ* 'generation', *rabbi* 'My Lord!', *raḏyo* 'radio', *raṣṭe*
     'right', *reṃa* 'pus', *zyāṛa* 'visit to a shrine'

ṭ: *ṭārix* (also *ṭārix*) 'date of event', *ṭélgǝraf* 'telegraph', *ṭélgǝram* 'telegram',
     ṭraṃbel automobile', *payṭūna* 'carriage'

ʏ: *'Aʏrāham* 'Abraham'

ẓ: *bǝẓẓoṭe* 'torches', *ġaẓab* 'anger', *qoẓẓǝlqorṭ* 'hell, disgusting', *ẓoṛ* 'force'

3.6. ASSIMILATION

a. The verbal prefix *b* assimilates to a following nasal and shifts to *m*
(§ 4.4.11.c), e.g., *rešu mmakipíwāle* 'they would lower their heads', *mnapli*
'they will fall', *'āna mnablǝnnax* 'I will lead you away', *mmaxlǝt* 'will you
feed?', though not always, e.g., *bmāxǝl* 'he will feed'. The verbal prefix *b*
> *p* by assimilation to a contiguous unvoiced consonant, e.g., *pšāke* 'he
will complain'. The preposition *b* also assimilates to a following unvoiced
consonant and is realized as *p*.

b. The absence of *d/ḏ* in the preposition *qam* would appear to be the
result of assimilation to *m* in a biform of ClAram *qǒḏām* when bound by
pronominal suffixes *qudm-*,[18] as evidenced already in the LAram forms
of the preposition with geminated *m*, e.g., SA *qammi* 'before me', JBA
qamme 'before him' (cf. JChalla *qāme*). A similar case of assimilation to *m*
ocurs in *'amǝdnāye* > *'amǝnnāye* 'residents of Amidya' and *baġdadnesa*
> *baġdannesa* 'f. resident of Baghdad'. *d* assimilates to *š* in *kuššat* 'every
year' (< *kud šāta). *d* assimilates to *t* in the f.s. Participle *'wǝdta* >
'ütta 'done' and in the feminine adjective *naqidta* > *naqǝdta* > *naqǝtta*
'thin'.

c. *l* of the L-suffix pronouns (§§ 4.1.4; 4.4.23.1) assimilates to a preceding *n*, *r*, and *t* in Subjunctive- and Preterite-based inflected forms,
e.g.,

qaṭlǝnnox	< *qaṭlǝn + lox	'I (m.s.) may kill you (m.s.)'
mirǝnne	< *mirǝn + le	'he said to me (m.s.)'
miratti	< *mirat + li	'I said to you (f.s.)'

---

[18] Cf. PrAram *qudm > ClAram קוֹדָם/קְדָם/קֳדָם, and with pronominal suffixes, e.g.,
קֳדָמוֹהִי, קֳדָמַי.

ʾamrəttu	<	*ʾamrət + lu	'you (m.s.) may say to them'
kpənnu	<	*kpən + lu	'they starved'
dʾərrox	<	*dʾər + lox	'you (m.s.) returned'

l in *kull assimilates to the following possessive-relative particle *d* in the indefinite pronoun *kull d- > *kud* 'each, every (§ 4.1.12.f). On the partial assimilation of *ṯ to *l* in the particles of existence, see § 3.2.b.

d. *n* has assimilated to a following consonant in inherited Aramaic words, e.g., *ʾəzza < *ʿinzā* 'goat', *šāta < *šantā* 'year'. *n* assimilates to *l* in the Turkish loanword *osmanlı > *ʾoṣmoḷḷi* 'Ottoman'. *n* assimilates partially to *p* in *npəlle > *mpəlle* he fell' and in *npox > *mpox* 'blow!'

e. *š* in the preposition *reš* 'on, upon' (< *reša* 'head') assimilates in voicing (> *ž*) to a contiguous voiced consonant. Cf. *reš kāse* ['rɪʃ 'kʰa:sɛ] 'on his belly' vs. *reš dide* ['rɪʒ 'dʰi:dʰɛ] 'on him'.

f. The verbal prefix *k-* (§ 4.4.9) found on inflected forms of the Present and Past Habitual (e.g., *kemər* 'he says', *kesewa* 'he used to come') assimilates (> *g*) in voicing to a following consonant, e.g., *gezəl* 'he goes'; before *q* it assimilates entirely, e.g., *lá-qqarwən* 'I do not approach', *šúli qqādənne* 'I finish my work'. It is sometimes difficult to discern the prefix *k* before unvoiced consonants, e.g., *(k)taxret* 'Do you remember?'

g. *x* assimilates in voicing (> *ġ*) to the contiguous consonant in the verbs *xzy* 'see', *xdr* 'go around', and *xzd* 'harvest' in the G stem, e.g., *xzeli* ['ɣze:li] 'I saw', *xzi* [ɣzi] 'see (m.s.)!',[19] *xdor* [ɣdʰor] 'go around (c.s.)!', *wən xdira* [wɪn 'ɣdʰi:ra] 'I (m.s.) have gone around', *xzədle* ['ɣzɪrrɛ] 'he harvested'. Cf. *xāze* ['χa:zɛ] 'he may see'. *x* also assimilates in voicing in the adverb *ʾaxxa* 'here' in the expression *ʾáx-geb tán-geb* [ˈʔaɣgʰɪb 'tʰangʰɪb] 'when all's said and done', and in the neo-construct form *bax* 'woman' from *baxta* (e.g., *bax mədor* [bʰaɣ 'mɪdʰor] 'the wife of the mudir') and the neo-construct form *tax* from *tāxa* 'quarter of town' in *tax mallāye* (['tʰaɣ mal'la:yɛ] 'the Mullahs' Quarter'. *x* also assimilates in voicing in *wax* 'we are' and *ṣāx* 'healthy' when in sandhi before a vowel: *wáx-əsye* ['waɣˌɪsyɛ] 'we have come', *ṣáx-ile* ['sˤa:ɣˌi:lɛ] 'he is healthy'.

---

[19] This is not always true in the C stem 'show', however. Cf. Past Habitual 1 m.s. [maχ'zɪnwɒ] 'I used to show', Participle m.s. ['muχza] 'shown', pl. ['muχze], but Subjunctive 1 m.s. [maɣ'zɪnnax] 'I (m.s.) may show you (f.s.)', Gerund [maɣ'zo:yɛ] 'showing'.

h. *x* assimilates to a contiguous *q* in *rəqqa* 'distance' (< *rəxqa < PrAram *rḥq), though *reqa* with loss of gemination is also attested.

i. *r* assimilates to *t* in in the feminine adjective *qarirta > *qarərta > *qarətta* 'cold, cool'.

3.7. DISSIMILATION

m dissimilates to *n* before *b* in the C verb *nbl* 'lead away', e.g., *mābəl > *nābəl* 'he may lead away', *mabole > *nabole* 'leading away'.

3.8. VOWELS

a. JChalla appears to have a vocalic phonemic inventory of: *ā, a, e, ə, i, o, ö, u, ū, ü,* and *ǖ*. The following minimal pairs were found in the corpus:

ā vs. *a*	*bāle* 'his attention'	vs.	*bale* 'yes, indeed'	
ā vs. *e*	*dāna* 'time'	vs.	*dena* 'debt'	
ā vs. *ə*	*kāra* 'black'	vs.	*kəra* 'rent'	
ā vs. *i*	*māsa* 'village'	vs.	*misa* 'dead'	
ā vs. *o*	*yāma* 'sea'	vs.	*yoma* 'day'	
ā vs. *ū*	*gāre* 'roof'	vs.	*gūre* 'men'	
a vs. *ə*	*qaṭla* 'she may kill'	vs.	*qəṭla* 'killing'	
a vs. *i*	*xamša* 'five'	vs.	*xamši* 'fifty'	
a vs. *o*	*didax* 'your (f.s.)'	vs.	*didox* 'your (m.s.)'	
a vs. *u*	*dida* 'her'	vs.	*didu* 'their'	
e vs. *i*	*xze* 'see (f.s.)!'	vs.	*xzi* 'see (m.s.)!'	
e vs. *o*	*qema* 'she may arise'	vs.	*qoma* 'stature'	
e vs. *ū*	*qeṭa* 'summer'	vs.	*qūṭa* 'vagina'	
i vs. *ə*	*kis* 'moneybag'	vs.	*kəs* 'to, with'	
i vs. *o*	*misa* 'dead'	vs.	*mosa* 'death'	
i vs. *u*	*seli* 'I came'	vs.	*selu* 'they came'	
o vs. *ū*	*koša* 'she may descend'	vs.	*kūša* 'descended'	
o vs. *ö*	*zora* 'she may go around'	vs.	*zöra* 'small'	
ū vs. *ə*	*kūra* 'young goat'	vs.	*kəra* 'rent'	
ū vs. *ǖ*	*šūqa* 'market'	vs.	*šǖqa* 'left'	

Because of the limited size of the corpus, it is difficult to find exact minimal pairs of *e* vs. *ə* (cf., however, *kemər* 'he says' vs. *kəmra* 'she says'), *u* vs. *ū* (cf. *kur* 'blind' and *kūra* 'young goat'), and *u* vs. *ü*.

b. *a* is usually realized as [a], though one also hears [ae], e.g., *tar'a* 'door' ['tʰar'a]/ ['tʰær'a]. Final *a* may be rounded, e.g., the final *a* in *tāma* 'there' ['tʰa:mɒ], particularly following /w/, e.g., *ʾətwa* [ˈʔɪtwɒ]. Near an emphatic consonant *a* moves back to [ɑ], e.g., [bˤɑːʃ] 'good'. Stressed *e* is usually realized as [e], e.g., *b-é-dor* [ˈbʰedorˤ] 'in that generation', though sometimes it is more open and realized as [ɛ], e.g., *sele* [ˈselɛ]/[ˈsɛlɛ].

c. *ə* is normally realized as [ɪ], e.g., *mən* 'from, with' [mɪn], though it may be pronounced [ɣ] in the vicinity of an emphatic, labial, or velar, e.g., *qṭəlle* 'he killed' [ˈqṭɪllɛ]/[ˈqṭɣllɛ], *šqəlle* 'he took' [ˈʃqɪllɛ]/[ˈʃqɣllɛ], *ptəxle* 'he opened' [ˈptʰɪxlɛ]/[ˈptʰɣxlɛ]. It is realized as [i] before or after *y*, e.g., *zəmrəyāsa* 'songs' [zɪmriˈyaːsa], *yəmma* 'mother' [ˈyimma]. On occasion *ə* may be realized as [y], e.g., [ˈʔynwɛ] 'grapes'.

d. *ü* is is a reflex of **wi* and is mostly limited to verbs II-*w* (§ 4.4.27.4), e.g., *düqa* 'seized' ([ˈdʰy:qɑ]) alongside *dwiqa* [ˈdʰwi:qɑ], or *türa* 'broken' ([ˈtʰy:rɑ]), alongside *twira* [ˈtʰwi:rɑ]. *ü* is attested in closed and pretonic syllables in verbs II-*w*, e.g., *ʾüdle* 'he did' alongside *wədle*, *düqāla* 'she seized it', as well as in the II-*w* adjective *zürta* 'small' (m.s. *zöra*, c.pl. *zöre*) and in *Türkiya* 'Turkey'. Cf., however, the lack of fronting in *kúšleni* 'we descended' and the the the II-*w* adjective *ruxta* 'wide' (m.s. *rwixa*).

e. *ö* ([ø]) is poorly attested. It is heard in the nouns *lö'a* 'jaw' and **sapöxa* 'wrap sandwich', the adjective *zöra*, *zöre* 'small', and in the numbers *šö'a* 'seven', *šö'i* 'seventy', and *šö'amma* 'seven hundred'. Rarely *o* is fronted to *ö* in additional words, e.g., *ʾödax* 'we may do' as against the more common *ʾodax*.

3.9. GENERAL DISTRIBUTION OF VOWELS

a. *ā, i, e, o, ö, ū, ü* are generally long and *a, ə, u* are short. Long vowels usually shorten in open unstressed non-final syllables and become short in closed syllables and open unstressed final syllables.[20]

b. Long vowels occur in open syllables:

1. most frequently in stressed syllables, e.g., *kātəb* 'secretary', *qāzi* 'qadi', *ʾida* 'hand', *spisa* 'rotten', *qeṭa* 'summer', *reša* 'head', *dūša* 'honey', *gūre* 'men', *qora* 'grave', *tora* 'ox', *tūra* 'broken', *zöra* 'small';
2. *ā, i, e, o* may be found in pretonic syllables, e.g., *ʾāġāye* 'aghas', *qyāməta* 'resurrection', *čiroke* 'story', *jirāne* 'neighbors', *ḥewāne*

---

[20] See the detailed description of JBetan in Mutzafi 2008a:25.

'animals', *gopāḷa* 'shepherd's stick', *qotiya* 'small box', *šö'amma* 'seven hundred'; with the exception of the last example, all of the nouns are loanwords; *ā* is attested in this environment in the verbal system in inflected forms based on the Subjunctive, e.g., *kšāqəlwa* 'he used to take';

3. *i* is attested in a propretonic syllable: *kilomətre* 'kilometers';

4. *ā* and *ū* may occur in a posttonic syllable: *qṭəlwāle* 'he had killed him'; *dārétūle* 'you may put him';

5. in monosyllabic words: *gā* 'time',[21] *hā* 'here, so!', *mā* 'what?', *xzi* 'see (m.s.)!', *ke* 'c'mon', *go* 'in', *ko* 'that, since', *qū* 'get up! (c.s.)'

c. Long vowels may also occur in closed syllables:

1. in stressed syllables, e.g., *flānkas* 'so and so', *qapṭán* 'captain', *giska* 'young goat', *guník* 'gunny sack', *dehwa* 'gold' (§ 3.11.a), *desta* 'portion of food', *darwéž* 'dervish', *mamnún* 'grateful', *qorúš* 'piaster', *kolka* 'hovel', *qaraqól* 'garrison'; most of the examples are loanwords;[22]

2. in monosyllabic words, e.g., *bān* 'I shall go', *ḅāš* 'good', *ḥāl* 'situation', *'it* 'there is', *pis* 'filthy', *beb* 'together with', *heš* 'yet, still', *bron* 'son of', *šqol* "take (c.s.)!', *qūn* 'get up! (c.pl.)', *rūt* 'naked';

3. in final unstressed syllables, e.g., *jəwāb* 'answer', *wəždān* 'conscience', *qaddiš* 'memorial prayer', *tagbir* 'counsel, conspiracy', *tārix*, *ṭārix* 'date of event', *ṭrambel* 'automobile, bus', *'āwon* 'sin'; all the examples are loanwords with the exception of the E-suffix 1 c.pl. form *-axin* (*pátxaxin* 'we may open'; § 4.1.6.f);

4. in pretonic and even earlier syllables in loanwords: *qāymaqam* 'local governor', *pisyatūsa* 'filth', *nerwāya* 'resident of Nerwa', *hekkarnāya* 'resident of Hakkari', *hekkaratūsa* 'residents or region of Hakkari'.

d. The long vowels *i*, *e*, *o* are realized as short in

1. unstressed final open syllables, e.g. *hedi* 'slowly', *ṭlāsi* 'thirty', *kalbe* 'dogs', *denāne* 'debtors', *māṭo* 'why?', *raḍyo* 'radio'

e. Short vowels occur in open syllables:

1. in monosyllabic words, e.g., *sa* 'come! (c.s.)', *ta* 'to', *xa* 'one';

---

[21] In rapid speech the final *a* of *gā* often tends to sound short.
[22] Cf. the inherited Aramaic word *palgúϑ* in JBetan (Mutzafi 2008a:29) with JChalla *pálgus*.

2. *a, u, ü, ə* may be found in unstressed syllables (propretonic, pretonic, and posttonic), e.g., *ganāwūsa* 'thievery', *ḥakome* 'kings', *məsəlmāna* 'Muslim', *muselu* 'they brought', *čádəra* 'tent', *xāṭəreni* 'our sake', *guniya* 'bramble', *gurāne* 'men', *ḥukumiya* 'government', *qṭəllu* 'they killed', *ṭāpu* 'title deed', *düqāle* 'he seized her';

3. *a* and *ə* may be found in stressed syllables, e.g., *fišaka* 'bullet', *malək* 'ruler', *masale* 'matter', *kəra* 'rent', *mədor* 'mudir', *ʿādəta* 'custom'.

f. Short vowels occur in closed syllables:

1. in unstressed syllables, both non-final and final: *baxtūsa* 'wifehood', *darhāme* dirhams', *bəndaqiya* 'rifle', *kəndāla* 'steep slope', *kurtāke* 'garments', *qurdāya* 'Kurd'; *qaċax* 'smuggled goods', *treʾsar* 'twelve', *qāṭəl* 'he kills', *tābur* 'battalion', *təttun* 'tobacco';

2. in stressed syllables: *ṛapsa* 'big', *sahma* 'portion, lot', *pəsra* 'meat', *wəždān* 'conscience', *ḥušta* 'excuse', *qurʿān* 'Quran', *ʾüdle* 'he did'.

3.10. SHORTENING OF LONG VOWELS

a. Long vowels in an open syllable shorten when the syllable becomes closed:

ā > a	*nābəl*	'he may lead away'	>	*nabli* 'they may lead away'
	hādax	'this'	>	*hatxa* 'like this'
i > ə	*ʾitən*	'there is'	>	*ʾətle* 'he has'
	basima	'pleasant (m.s.)'	>	*basəmta* 'pleasant (f.s.)'
	grišāli	'I pulled her'	>	*grəšli* 'I pulled him'
e > ə[23]	*kemər*	'he says'	>	*kəmra* 'she says'
ū > u	*dūka*	'place'	>	*duksa* 'place'
ǖ > ü	*ʾüda*	'done'	>	*ʾüdla* 'she did'
o > u	*koma*	'black (m.s.)'	>	*kumta* 'black (f.s.)'
	mpoləṭli	'I took him out'	>	*mpulṭāli* 'I took her out'.

b. When the stress shifts in nouns, *ā > a* in open pretonic and propretonic syllables, e.g.,

bāba	'father'	>	*babawāsa*	'fathers'
gāre	'roof'	>	*garawāsa*	'roofs'
hudāya	'Jew'	>	*hudayeni*	'our Jews'
kāpa	'shoulder'	>	*kapāne*	'shoulders'

---

[23] But not in *mese* 'he brings' vs. *mesya* 'she brings' or *menəx* 'look around! (c.s.)' vs. *menxun* 'look around! (c.pl.)'. See also Mutzafi 2008a:82.

This applies also to the D Gerund, e.g., *mšadore* 'sending' (cf. *(m)šādər* 'he may send').

c. *ā* and *i* do not shorten, however, in loanwords:

'āġa	'agha'	>	*'āġāye*	'aghas'
			'āġātūsa	'masterdom'
pis	'filthy'	>	*pisyatūsa*	'filth'

d. *ā* remains in neo-construct forms:

bāba	'son'	>	*bāb-*	'father of'
brāta	'daughter'	>	*brāt-*	'daughter of'
qdāla	'neck'	>	*qdāl-*	'neck of'

e. *ū* shortens to *u* in open pretonic syllables, e.g.,

dūka	'place'	>	*dukāne*	'places'
ṭūra	'mountain'	>	*ṭurāne*	'mountains'

3.11. CONDITIONED VOWEL SHIFTS

a. *ə* > *e* before a syllable closing ' and *h*, e.g.,[24]

behna	'moment'
de'sa	'sweat'
dehna	'fat'
dehwa	'gold'
nehra	'river'
pehna	'kick'
se'ra	'goat hair'
šme'lu	'they heard'[25]
ṭe'na	'load'

b. *u* > *o* before syllable-closing ', e.g.,[26]

balo'ta	'throat'
ṣabo'ta	'finger'
zdo'sa	'fear'
mo'rəqle	'he chased him away

---

[24] Hobermann 1997:324–325; Mutzafi 2008a:27.

[25] In forms of the C Imperative, **mašmə' 'listen! (m.s.)'* > *mašme(')*, but also *mašmi(')* as a result of the partial merger of verbs III-' and III-*y* (§ 4.4.27.7).

[26] Hoberman 1997:324–325; Mutzafi 2008a:27.

mo'rənne	'he brought me in'
[H]*mo'šəmənnu*[H]	'they accused me'

3.12. RISING DIPHTHONGS

a. The attested rising diphthongs are:

we:	*wetun* 'you were', *pāwe* 'it will be'
wā:	*barwāra* 'slope', *'uṛwāne* 'leaders', *babawāsa* 'fathers'
wa:	*wa'dūsa* 'promise', *warāqe* 'documents'
wi:	*wiza* 'visa', *wida* 'done (m.s.)'
wə:	*ywəšlu* 'they dried up', *yāwən* 'I may give'
yā:	*yāwi* 'they may give', *toryāsa* 'cows'
ya:	*yarxa* 'month', *yamya* 'she may swear'
yə:	*yəmma* 'mother', *yamyən* 'I may swear'
ye:	*hudāye* 'Jews', *qurdāye* 'Kurds'

b. The rising diphthong *wə* frequently contracts to *ü* in closed syllables in forms of II-*w* verbs (< II-*b*; §§ 4.4.27.4; 4.4.28.1): *'üdle* 'he did' (< *wədle*), *düqle* (< *dwəqle*) 'he grasped', though one also hears the uncontracted forms *wədle* and *dwəqle*, as well as *kúšleni* 'we descended', *mākušli* 'he may bring me down'. In open syllables one hears both *wi* and the contracted form *ū*,[27] e.g., *wida*, *'üda* 'done' (< *'wida*), as well as *'wida*, and both *dwiqa* and *düqa* 'seized'.

3.13. FALLING DIPHTHONGS

ay, aw: The PrAram diphthongs *aw* and *ay* have contracted to *e* and *o* respectively, e.g., *qeṭa* 'summer', *sepa* 'sword', *mosa* 'death', *yoma* 'day'. In loanwords, however, the diphthongs are preserved, e.g., *dawla* 'state', *čayxāna* 'tea house', *mābayn* 'between'. The diphthong *aw* in *gaw-* 'in' is a reduction from *-aww* found in the ClAram determined form *gawwā* (cst. *go-*) or the ClAram form with pronominal suffix, e.g., *gawwe* 'in it'.

āy: is attested in the loanword: *čāy* 'tea'. *āy > ay* when this noun becomes part of the compounds (§ 4.2.10.b) *čaydanka* 'teapot', *čayxāna* 'tea house'. The diphthong *āy* contracts to *e* in the f.s. gentilic suffix *-āyətā > *-āytā > -esa*, e.g., *baġdannesa* 'resident of Baghdad', *maroknesa*

---

[27] Shabbo alternates both forms, even in the same sentence: *hatxa le 'üda hatxa le wida* 'Like this he has done, like that he has done.'

'Moroccan', *nerwesa* 'resident of Nerwa', *qurdesa* 'Kurd', *wānesa* 'resident of Wan'.

uy: *uy* appears in the C stem of *y'y* (< *yd'*) 'make known', e.g., *muyde(')lu* 'they made known'.

əw: See § 3.14

3.14. OTHER DIPHTHONGS THAT HAVE CONTRACTED IN JEWISH CHALLA

*ab > aḇ > aw > o: The ClAram diphthong *aḇ > aw* (§ 3.2.a n.3) that resulted from the contraction of *a* and spirantized *b* (> *ḇ* > *w*) has contracted further to *o*, e.g., *qora* 'grave' (< *qawrā* < *qaḇrā*), *gora* 'man' (< *gawrā* < *gaḇrā*). In the case of the plural *gūre* 'men', an additional shift of *o > u* is attested already in earlier Aramaic (BiblAram גֻּבְרַיָּא). The vowel *o* in *xošeba* 'Sunday' is a contraction of the diphthong *aw*, which arose from *xo + šeba < *xaw + šeba < *xa +b-šabbā < *ḥad b-šabbā* (§ 4.2.10.a).

*ib > iḇ > əw > u/ū: This contraction takes place before a consonant e.g., *dūša* 'honey' (cf. TO, JPA *diḇšā*; Syr ܕܒܫܐ; TO, BTA, Mand *duḇšā*); *hūle* 'he gave' (< **həwle < *həḇle < *yhible*); *kāsu* 'he may write' (< **kāsəw < *kāsib*), *ksūli* 'I wrote' (< **ksəwli < *ksibli*), *ksūta* 'written' (< **ksəwta < *ksibtā*). Before a vowel, the diphthong is retained, e.g., *ksiwa* 'written' (< **ksiḇa < *ksībā*), *hiwe* 'given' (Participle pl. **hiḇe <*yhibe*). The diphthong *əw* is attested, however before *y*, in **ṣwīya > *ṣiwya > ṣəwya* 'dyed', and the loanwords *qəwya* 'strong', *qəwyūsa* 'strength'.

*ap > ap > aw > o: *ṭloxe* 'lentils' (< **ṭlawxe < ṭlapḥe*; cf. TO, BTA טְלוֹחֵי; Syr ܛܠܘܦܚܐ).

3.15. CONTRACTION OF TRIPHTHONGS AND RELATED FORMS

a. *āya* often contracts to *ā*. This is attested frequently in

1. the 3 c.s. independent pronoun *'āya* 'he, she' > *'ā* (§ 4.1.1.e)
2. the m.s. gentilic suffix: *hudāya* 'Jew' > *hudá*, *qurdāya* 'Kurd' > *qurdá*
3. the Gerund of verbs III-*y*: *bəxzāya* 'seeing' > *bəxzá*; *bəjrāya* 'flowing' > *bəjrá*
4. *ṭappāya > ṭappá* 'hillside' (§ 5.7.5)

b. *oyo > o* in **'amoyo + d > 'amód* 'the paternal uncle of', **xaloyox > xalóx* 'your maternal uncle'

c. *āwa* > *ā* in the 1 c.pl. forms of the verb *yhw(l)* 'give' (§ 4.4.28.20) that are based on the Subjunctive, e.g., *yāwaxla* > *yāxla* 'we may give her', *byāwaxlu* > *byāxlu* 'we will give them'.

d. *-awya* > *ūwa*[28] in the 3 f.s. inflected forms of the verb *hwy* that are based on the Subjunctive: *hawya* > *hūwa* 'may she be', *khawya* > *kūwa* 'she is' and *phawya* > *pūwa* 'she will be'.

3.16. GLIDES

a. The glide *y* occurs when the plural ending *-e* is added to a loanword ending in a final vowel:

'āġaye	'agha' (s. 'āġā)
balāye	'trouble(s)' (§ 4.2.3.1.d)
kiloye	'kilos' (s. *kilo*)

b. The glide *y* (< *w*?) is attested in 'amoya ('amo + a) 'paternal uncle', and *xaloya* (*xālo* + a) 'maternal uncle' (§ 4.2.9.7).

c. The glide *w* appears to be attested in *qurdawūsa* (< *qurdā*? + *ūsa*) 'Kurds' (§ 4.2.9.3.d).

3.17. APHAERESIS

a. Aphaeresis of initial ' or *y* preceding a consonant is attested in verbs I-' (§§ 4.4.27.1; 4.4.28.8–9) and I-*y* (§§ 4.4.27.2; 4.4.28.20–21):

hūle	'he gave' < *yhəwle
mira	'said' < *'mira
mərre	'he said' < *'mərre
səqli	'I went up' < *ysəqli
sira	'bound' < *ysira[29]
sirilu	'they bound them' < *ysirilu
seta	'come (f.s.)' < *'seta
sela	'she came' < *'sela
tiwa	'seated' < *ytiwa

---

[28] It would appear that *awya > *oya > *uya (partial assimilation of *o* to *y*, which is attested in other *lishana deni* dialects; § 4.4.28.12) > *ūwa* (partial assimilation of *y* to *u*).

[29] *ysira* is attested once in Shabbo's speech.

tūle   'he sat' < **ytəwle*
xila   'eaten' < **ʾxila*
xəlle   'he ate' < **ʾxəlle*[30]
zəlle   'he went' < **ʾzəlle*

b. Aphaeresis does not occur, however, in forms of *ymy* 'swear' (§4.4.28.4), e.g., *ymeli* 'I swore', *ymi* 'swear (m.s.)!', or *ywš* 'dry up' (§ 4.4.28.2): *ywəšle* 'he dried up', *ywəšlu* 'they dried up'.

c. Nor does it occur in the Gerund of Verbs I-ʾ, where #ʾC > #ʾiC: *ʾisāya* 'coming', *ʾixāla* 'eating', *ʾizāla* 'going'.

c. ʾ appears to be optional before *w* in the verb *ʾwd* 'do' (§ 4.4.28.1), e.g., *ʾwida, wida* 'done (m.s.)', *ʾwāda, wāda* 'doing'.

d. Aphaeresis of ʾ (< ClAram ʾ and ʿ) and a following vowel is attested in the following nouns and adjective:

koma   'black' (ClAram אוּכָּם); f. *kumta*
tiqa   'old' (ClAram עַתִּיק; cf. *ʾatiqa* elsewhere in *lishana deni* dialects); f. *təqta*, pl. *tiqe*
dāna   'time' (ClAram עִדְנָא 'time'); pl. *dāne* and the conjunction *kud dān* 'whenever'

e. *m* is sometimes not audible (and perhaps absent entirely; § 4.4.3) before an initial labial in verbal forms, e.g., *(m)bāqərwa* 'he would ask', *(m)pəlle* 'he fell', *(m)pəllu* 'they fell'. *m* is also not heard occasionally before other consonants in the D stem, e.g., *(m)šadore* 'sending'.

f. The first syllable of the Past Copula (§ 4.4.6.4.c) may be elided when enclitic, leaving only *-wa*, e.g., **ʿÉraq-wāwa* > *ʿÉraq-wa* 'It was Iraq'.

3.18. SYNCOPE

a. Unstressed *ə* is syncopated in the plural forms[31] *kilometre* 'kilometers' (sg. *kilometər*), *metre* 'meters' (s. *metər*), *malkāni* 'chieftains' (s. *malək*), and in *maʿalmine* 'teachers' (s. *maʿalləm*).

---

[30] Shabbo also once says *ʾxəlli* 'I ate'.
[31] Cf. the syncope of *ə* or *e* in a singular base when the suffix *-āϑa* is added (Mutzafi 2008a:97).

It is unsyncopated in *'áqəli* 'my mind', *'áqəlu* 'their mind', *xāṭəreni* 'our sake' because of the syllabic nature of the resonants *l* and *r*. Unstressed *u* is sometimes syncopated in the nouns *kusisa / ksisa* 'hat', *xlūla / xulūla* 'wedding feast'.

b. ' (< ClAram ') has been syncopated in *zora* 'small' < *z'ora* (< ClAram וְעוֹרָא).[32]

c. *n* is syncopated before L-suffix object pronouns in the plural of the Imperative and in 2 pl. forms inflected on the basis of the Subjunctive (§ 4.1.6.j), e.g., *mándūle* 'throw it!', *máttūle* 'put it!', *'amrétūle-ži* 'you may also say to him', *'odétūleni* 'you may do to us', *dārétūle* 'you may put it', *kšaqlétūle* 'you take him', *godétūle* 'you do to him'.

d. With the exception of the 3 m.s. *'āzəl* 'he may go',[33] *l* is syncopated in the forms of the root *'zl* 'go' based on the Subjunctive (e.g., **'azlən* > *'āzən* 'I may go'; § 4.4.28.9) Some of the forms of the Future of *'zl* have undergone further syncope:

*bāzən	>	bān	'I shall go'
*bāzət	>	bāt	'you will go (m.s.)'
*bāzat	>	bāt	'you will go (f.s.)'
*bāzəl	>	bāl	'he will go'

e. *d* is syncopated in all attested forms of the G stem *y'y* (< ClAram ידע; § 4.4.28.19), e.g., *yā'e* 'he may know', *ki'e* 'he knows', *y'elox* 'you knew'. It is preserved, however, in the C stem 'inform', e.g., *mayd(')ənnu* 'I may inform them', *muyde'li* 'I informed'. *d* is syncopated in *kawənta* 'mule' (cf. the biform *kawdənta*).

f. *s* is syncopated in the preposition *kəsəl* (cf. § 3.19.f), e.g., *kəl muxtar* 'with the mukhtar'.

g. Medial *h* is sometimes elided, particularly in rapid speech, in the 2 c.s. independent pronoun *'āhat* 'you' > *'āt*.

---

[32] Sabar 2002a:156.

[33] Note also the syncope of *l* in the inflected forms of the verb *yhw(l)* (§ 4.4.28.20) based on the Subjunctive, e.g., *yāwən* 'I may give', *yāwət* 'you may give'. *l* is preserved only in the 3 m.s. *yāwəl* 'he may give'. The *l* in the verb, however, is not part of the ClAram root (יהב).

3.19. Apocope

a. Vowels may be apocopated on an noun that is annexed to another noun
(§ 4.2.2.b), e.g.,

'axona	'brother'	>	*'axon ma'alləm* 'the brother of the teacher'
baxtắsa	'women'	>	*baxtắs qurdâye* 'the women of the Kurds'
brona	'son'	>	*bron sâwox* 'your grandfather's son'

In the following two examples the final vowel or syllable is apocopated in
a noun that joins another noun in forming a compound:

palg(a)	'half'	>	*pálsâ'a* 'half an hour'
			pálpaṇqàṇoṭ 'half lira'

b. Vowels may be apocopated when preceding the independent genitive
pronoun *did-* (§ 4.1.3) or the reflexive pronoun *gyān-* (§ 4.1.9), e.g.,

bāba	'father'	>	*bāb dide* 'his father'
besa	'house'	>	*bes gyāne* 'his own house'
pāre	'money'	>	*pār gyāni* 'my own money'
xulamawắsa	'servants'	>	*xulamawắs dide* 'his servants'

c. Apocope takes place in the indefinite pronoun *kull + d > *kud* and in
the noun following it:

*kull + d dāna	>	*kud dān* 'every time'
*kull + d yoma	>	*kúd-yom* 'every day'
*kull + d šāta	>	*kuššat* 'every year'
*kull + d lele	>	*kúd-lel* 'every night'

The final syllable of *yoma* is apocopated in

*palgeh d-yomā	>	*palgədyo* 'noon'
*hā d-yomā	>	*'ədyo* 'today'

Note that *lele* is not apocopated in *'ádlele* 'tonight', unlike in *palgədlel*
'midnight'. Cf. the JBetan forms *'ədlel, palgədlel, palgədyom, 'ədyo.*

d. Other examples of apocope include *bə́š-rabbā > *bə́š-ṛab* 'more', *'axxa*
'here' (> *'ax-*) and *geba* 'side, direction' (> *geb*) in *'áx-geb tán-geb* (*ṭamāha-geb*) 'when all's said and done'. It occurs sporadically also in (*'əl-)tāma*
> (*'əl-)tam* 'there, to there'. The final vowel or syllable of the indefinite
pronoun *xeta* 'other' (§ 4.1.10.b) may be apocopated, e.g., *xá-l-e-xet* 'one
to that other', *xa le mšaboḥe 'e xe* 'one is praising that other'. In the
demonstrative pronoun *'anna* 'these, those', the final syllable is at times
apocopated before a word-initial consonant: *'anna pāre* > *'an pāre* 'that
money'. *d* of ClAram דֲח 'one' is apocopated (*xa*, in pause *xa'*).

e. Apocope occurs in the compounds that express the days of the week (§ 4.3.8): *tre* + **b-šabba* > *trūšeb* 'Monday', *ṭlāha* + **b-šabbā* > *ṭlāhūšeb* 'Tuesday', *'arba* + **b-šabba* > *'arbūšeb* 'Wednesday' *xamšā* + **b-šabba* > *xamūšeb* 'Thursday'. Vowels are apocopated in other compounds too (§ 4.2.10;), e.g., *b* + *'o* + *yomā* + *xeta* > *bomāxəd* 'day after tomorrow'.

f. *l* is apocopated in the preposition *kəsəl* (§ 3.18.f): *kəs spindarnāye* 'with the residents of Spindar'.[34]

g. *m* is apocopated in the G c.s. Imperative *qū* 'stand up!' *n* is apocopated in תִּשְׁרִין > *čeri* 'autumn'. *n* of the preposition *mən* is sometimes apocopated,[35] e.g., *m-pārox* 'from your money'.

3.20. GEMINATION

a. In general ClAram gemination has been lost and replaced by a lengthening of the preceding vowel (quantitative metathesis).[36] Were the plural of *dukkāna* 'shop' attested (**dukkāne?*), then gemination could be shown to be phonemic: cf. the plural of *dūka* 'place', *dukāne*.

b. The loss of gemination and resulting lengthening of preceding vowel is seen clearly in D verbs, where one finds *ā* in open stressed syllables, e.g., *(m)šādər* 'he may send' (cf. ClAram מְשַׁדַּר), *mdāgəl* 'he may lie' (ClAram מְדַגֵּל). The lack of lengthening of *a* > *ā* in the Gerund *mšadore* 'sending' (JBA מְשַׁדּוֹרֵי) may be attributed to the fact that the pattern is treated by speakers as belonging to the nominal system, where *ā* shortens to *a* before stressed syllables (§ 3.10.b).[37]

c. ClAram gemination is sometimes preserved in the nominal system, e.g., in certain reflexes of the **qvll* noun pattern (§ 4.2.6.2): *dəbba* 'bear', *gəlla* 'grass', *ləbba* 'heart', *pəmma, pumma* 'mouth', *xumma* 'heat',[38] *yəmma*

---

[34] This is the only example (in other *lishana deni* dialects it is more frequent) and it should be noted that the following word begins with *s*. Mutzafi (2008a:356) believes the *l* of *kəsəl* was elided by metanalysis: *kəšl-e* > *kəs-le*.

[35] Mutzafi (2008a:124) raises the possibility that *m-* is also a reduced form of **ʾəm* < **ʿam* 'with'.

[36] A trace of gemination can be seen in the Gerund of geminate verbs (§ 4.4.27.6). See also in JBetan (Mutzafi 2008a:47–48, 77–79). Quantitative metathesis (CvCC = Cv:C) is the rule in Ṭuroyo for all ClAram gemination. See Jastrow 1985:XXI.

[37] See Mutzafi 2008a:30.

[38] Syr ܚܘܡܐ and JBA חֻמָּא, but TO חוּמָא.

'mother'.[39] At other times the gemination in these patterns is simplified and one hears a long penultimate vowel, e.g., *gūba* 'loom', *gūda* 'wall', *dūka* 'place', *kāke* 'teeth', *ṛāba* 'much', *xāye* 'life'. Gemination is preserved in cases where the gemination is the result of an assimilated *n*: *'ǝzza* 'goat' (< **'izzā* < **'inzā'*) and *xǝṭṭe* 'wheat' (< **ḥiṭṭe* < **ḥinṭayyā'*). Cf., however, the simplification of ClAram gemination before the f. morpheme -*t* and compensatory lengthening in *šāta* 'year' (ClAram שַׁתָּא < PrAram **šantā'*). Fluctuation is found in the forms of the noun *skina/sǝkkina* 'knife'.[40] Gemination is not preserved in adjectives of the **qattīl* noun pattern, e.g., *basima* 'pleasing' (f.s. *basǝmta*),[41] *šamina* 'fat' (pl. *šamine*), *yarixa* 'long' (f.s. *yarǝxta*, pl. *yarixe*), or in nouns of the **qattāl* pattern, e.g., *ganāwa* 'thief', *sahāda* 'witness', *ṣawā'a* 'dyer', *šahāra* 'blind'. Gemination of an earlier period that stemmed from the assimilation of *t* in the noun *kāpa* 'shoulder' (< **kappa* < ClAram כַּתְפָּא < PrAram **katipā'*; pl. *kapāne*) has been simplified.

d. Gemination in loanwords is preserved, e.g., *čakke* 'weapons', *čappa* 'left', *ḥaqq* 'salary', *julle* 'clothes', *ḳappāra* 'expiation'. The gemination in the loanword *ma'allǝm* 'teacher' is lost in the plural form along with the following vowel *ǝ*: *ma'almine*.

e. Secondary gemination of *m* is attested in several ClAram nouns,[42] e.g., *'ǝmma* 'hundred', *dǝmma* 'blood', *šǝmma* 'name', *šǝmme* 'heavens', *šǝnne* 'years', *tǝmmal* 'yesterday'. Secondary gemination of *d* is also attested in *xǝdda* 'someone'.[43] The secondary gemination in these words seems to have been preceded by the retraction of stress at an early period of NeoAram.[44]

f. The gemination in *rǝqqa* 'distance' comes from the assimilation of *x* (< *ḥ*) to *q* (LEAram רוּחְקָא).[45]

---

[39] < אמא.

[40] Cf. ClAram סַכִּינָא (and BiblH סַכִּין) and MishH סְכִין.

[41] Cf. JZakho *bassima* with JBetan *basima*.

[42] For a discussion of the phenomenon see Hoberman 2007. The gemination in *pǝmma*, *pumma* 'mouth' goes back to PrAram. For the forms of this word in Aramaic dialects see Nöldeke 1910:177–178.

[43] Cf. ClAram חֲדָא 'one (f.)'. Gemination is also attested in this number in SA *'ådda* 'the one (m.)' and JPA חַתָא 'the one (m.)' (Fassberg 1985).

[44] The retraction of stress in these nouns is attested also in WNeoAram, e.g., *aḥḥad* 'one (m.)', *eḥda* 'one (f.)', *ešma* 'name', *edma* 'blood'. See Spitaler 1938:48–49, 63–65, 113; Arnold 1990:40,314,400.

[45] Quantitative metathesis is also attested in this form: *reqa* (§ 3.6.h). The assimilation of gutturals to contiguous consonants is surprising in NeoAram, though it is attested

g. The gemination in *xuṭṭa* 'stick, rod' results from the assimilation of *r* to *ṭ* (ClAram חוּטְרָא).

h. The inflected forms of the preposition *l-* 'to, for' and *b-* 'in' exhibit what might be secondary gemination that arose by analogy to the gemination of the inflected forms of the preposition *mən* 'from, with' (e.g., *mənni* 'from me' [ClAram מִנִּי], *mənnexun* 'from you'), e.g., *ʾalle* 'to him', *ʾəbbe* 'in him'.[46] It is also possible, however, that the gemination of *ʾall-* comes from the affixation of the L-suffix pronouns to the preposition *ʾəl* (< ClAram עַל).[47]

i. Non-ClAram gemination is found regularly in the affixing and assimilation of the L-suffix pronouns to final *n* and *r* on verbal bases and to the E-suffix pronouns ending in *n* and *t* on the Subjunctive, e.g.,

*kpən + lu	>	*kpənnu* 'they starved'
*dʾər + lox	>	*dʾərrox* 'you returned'
*ʾamrən + lox	>	*ʾamrənnox* 'I may say to you'
*ʾamrət + lu	>	*ʾamrəttu* 'you may say to them'.

l does not assimilate to final *t* of verbal bases, e.g.,

mətle	'he died'
skətle	'he croaked'

3.21. SYLLABLE STRUCTURE

Unlike in ClAram where only Cv, Cv̄, CvC, and Cv̄C syllables were allowed, JChalla, like other NeoAram dialects, evidences additional syllable types: CCv and CCv̄, which in ClAram have the shape CəCv, CəCv̄ (e.g., *ṣlosa* 'prayer' < ClAram *ṣəloṭā*), and CvCC, which occurs only in loanwords (e.g., *ḥaqq* 'right'; *žang* 'rust').

---

in this word also in other *lishana deni* dialects. Cf. SH (Ben-Ḥayyim 2000:39) and SA where gutturals regularly assimilated to contiguous consonants (Ben-Ḥayyim 1954:102; Macuch 1982:77).

[46] Hoberman 2007:147 is uncertain as to the mechanism involved in creating these forms.

[47] Mutzafi 2008a:123.

3.22. ANAPTYXIS

a. A synchronic cluster of three consonants is usually resolved by the insertion of an anaptyctic vowel between the second and third consonants, e.g., *[H]bma'šmi[H] > mmá'šəmi 'they will accuse', *mburbza > mbúrbəza 'scattered'; *mad'raxle > mad'əraxle 'we may return him'; *maqtlīli > maqtəlili 'they may have me killed'.

b. When the second consonant is a resonant, however, anaptyxis occurs between the first and second consonants. See, e.g., in verbal forms: *mašlmile > mašəlmile 'they may convert him to Islam'; *muxrwālu > muxərwālu 'they destroyed her'; *ma'rqile > ma'ərqile 'they may smuggle him out'; and in nouns: 'aqalta 'foot' (< *'aqlta),[48] tawərta 'cow' (< *tawrta). Perhaps anaptyxis is also the origin of ū in 'axūsa 'brotherhood' (< *'axəwsa < *'axwsā?) and *naṣwsā > naṣūsa 'fight' (< *naṣəwsa < *naṣwsā?; § 4.2.9.3.a). Even though the resonant is the first and not the second consonant in the cluster, anaptyxis occurs between the first and second consonants in kaləpsa 'bitch' (< *kalbtā). This occurs regularly when b- is prefixed to the Gerund, e.g., b + qṭāla > bəqṭāla 'in killing'.

c. Anaptyxis is attested in neo-construct forms (§ 4.2.2.b), e.g., 'əpər 'soil' (< *'əpr < 'əpra), 'əqər 'bottom' (< *'əqr < 'əqra), naqəl 'time' (< *naql < naqla), qəṭəl 'killing' (< *qəṭl < qəṭla), and xətən 'son-in-law' (< *xətn < xətna).

d. There is no anaptyctic vowel in the following words due to their syllabification:

Parsnāye 'Persians'	=	par-snáye.
'əltxé(t?) 'under'	=	'əl-txé(t?)
mundyālu 'they threw her down'	=	mun-dyālu
škaftyāsa 'caves'	=	škaft-yāsa
lá-gmzabnetun 'you don't sell'	=	lág-mzabnetun

e. Occasionally an anaptyctic vowel, sometimes preceded by a glottal stop, is added to an initial consonantal cluster, e.g.,

'əhmalle, ḥmalle	'he stood'
əmṭelan, mṭelan	'we arrived'
əmre(')la	'it hurt'
əmpalle, mpalle	'he fell'

---

[48] The expected anaptyctic vowel ə appears to have assimilated to the preceding a vowel.

əmxéwālu	'they had beaten'
əšqəllu, šqəllu	'they took'
əxzi, xzi	'look (m.s.)!'

3.23. Stress

Stress in JChalla is mainly penultimate and follows that described in detail by Mutzafi for JBetan.[49] It will be marked only when it deviates from the penultima. Exceptions to this pattern include the following categories:

a. in loanwords, where stress is sometimes according to the donor language, e.g., *čádəra* 'tent', *dúnume* 'dunams', *faqír* 'poor', *kafíl* 'guarantor' (also *káfil*), *máḥkama* 'court', *taḥqiqát* 'investigations'. Some loanwords have been assimilated to the regular JChalla stress pattern, e.g., *'arzúḥal* 'petition' (but also *'arzuḥál* § 4.2.1.h), *gazeṛa* '(evil) decree', *wakil* 'deputy';

b. in proper nouns, where stress is variable, e.g., the Hebrew name אַבְרָהָם is pronounced with three different stresses: *'Awṛáham* (general JChalla stress pattern as well as colloquial Hebrew stress pattern), *'Awṛahám* (formal Hebrew stress pattern), and *'Áwṛaham* (also colloquial Hebrew stress pattern);

c. Stress is prepenultimate on verbs that have the past marker *-wa* followed by an L-suffix, e.g., *'ə́twāle* 'he had', *gbéwāle* 'he used to want', *xaprí-wālu* 'they used to dig', *kaswə́nwālu* 'I used to write them';

d. Stress is prepenultimate on verbal forms with the final allomorphs *-a, -ən(a), -an(a),* and *-in* on inflected forms of the Subjunctive base and Imperative, e.g., *'ázəna* 'I (m.s.) may go', *yā'étuna* 'you (c.pl.) may know', *ḥmóləna* 'wait!', *qématən* 'you (f.s.) may arise', *šáqlaxin* 'we may take'. Stress is also prepenultimate on forms of the Preterite with the 1 c.pl. and 2 c.pl. L-suffixes, e.g., *zə́lleni* 'we went', *zə́llexun* 'you went'.

e. Stress is prepenultimate on certain adverbs and prepositions, e.g., *'áqqara* 'so much' (< *'ad + qadara; also *'aqqar); reduplicated forms with stress on the first syllable: *básbasər* 'right after', *bárbara* 'towards', *qámqāmu* 'right before them'.

---

[49] See Sabar 2002a:6–37 on stress in *lishana deni* dialects in general, Hoberman 1989: 216–217 on stress in JAmid, and Mutzafi 2008a:35–39 on stress in JBetan.

g. Enclitic particles and words (a hyphen is used to mark enclisis) do not take the stress:

1. the particle *-ž(i)* 'also, even', e.g., *'á-ži* 'he too', *'ətwa suráye-ži* 'there were Christians too'
2. LL-suffix pronouns, e.g., *lewən xə́zya-lle* 'I haven't see him', *wax ptáxa-lla* 'we are opening her'
3. forms of the Copula, e.g., *'āna hudáya-wən* 'I am a Jew', *má-yle* 'what is it?', *hátxa-la* 'that's the way it is', *mare təffáqe-lu* 'they are rifle owners'
4. verbs negated by the particles *la* and *ču*, e.g., *lá-ki'ən* 'I don't know', *lá- gbəttu* 'you don't want them', *lá-gpālxax* 'we don't work', *čú-məndi* 'nothing', *čú-gā* 'never'
5. nouns following attributive demonstrative pronouns (§ 4.1.7.h), e.g., *'é-waxt* 'at that time', *b-é-dor̯* 'in that generation'
6. nouns preceded by numbers, e.g., *xá-gā* 'once', *xá-yoma* 'one day', *tré- yome* 'two days', *šö'á-nāše* 'seven people' (§ 4.3.1.i). Numbers are not always enclitic, however.
7. the noun *geb* 'side' when enclitic to truncated forms of the adverbs *'axxa* 'here' and *tāma* 'there', e.g., *'áx-geb tán-geb* 'when all's said and done'

There may also be three and four element syntagms with one major stress, in which case two of the elements become enclitic, e.g., *l-é-'ida-ži* 'to that side too', *ḥál-u-masale* 'the upshot'.

h. Stress may be variable with the indefinite pronoun *flāna* (§ 4.1.12.d), e.g., *l-flāná-dūka* 'such and such a place' vs. *'əl-flána dūka*.

i. Stress on nouns in the vocative is variable, e.g., *qurdá* 'Kurd!', *má'alləm* 'teacher!'; and with a Kurdish vocative ending (§ 4.2.11.b): *'amo* 'Uncle!', *bābo* 'Father!', *māmo* 'Uncle!', *quró* 'boy!', *kəče* 'woman!'

3.24. PAUSE

Two pausal forms of numbers are attested, both of which take an excrescent glottal stop: *xa'* 'one' and *tre'* 'two' (§ 4.3.1).

CHAPTER FOUR

MORPHOLOGY AND MORPHOSYNTAX

4.1. PRONOUNS

4.1.1. *Independent Pronouns*

a. The inventory of independent pronouns in JChalla is

1 c.s.	*'āna*
2 c.s.	*'āhat*
3 c.s.	*'āya, 'ā*
1 c.pl.	*'axnan*
2 c.pl.	*'axtun*
3 c.pl.	*'āni*

b. It is noteworthy that there is only one form for masculine and feminine in all persons, both singular and plural. It would appear that the feminine forms of the 2nd person singular and 3rd person singular have replaced the 2nd person and 3rd person singular masculine forms. The epicene forms may be the result of the adstrata influence of Kurdish and Turkish.

c. *'āhat* (sometimes *'āt*; § 3.18.g) is used for both the masculine and feminine, unlike in other *lishana deni* dialects, where one finds 2 m.s. *'āhət* and 2 f.s. *'āhat*.

d. The 3rd person *'āya* is used for both masculine and feminine, unlike in other *lishana deni* dialects, where one finds m. *'āwa*, f. *'āya*. In the Jewish dialects of the Trans-Zab area, however, one also finds a 3 c.s. form, albeit different: *'o < *'áhu*.[1] *'āya* sometimes contracts to *'ā* (§ 3.15.a), particularly in rapid speech and before the postpositive particle *-ži* (*'á-ži* 'also he'). *'āya* also functions as a far demonstrative (§ 4.1.7.b).

---

[1] See Mutzafi 2004:10 and 2008b:417–418.

e. The 1 pl. *'axnan* is also attested in some *lishana deni* dialects (JAmid, JGzira, JZakho), but not in others (*'axni* in JDohok, and JNerwa texts). JBetan has both *'axnan* and *'axni*.

f. The independent pronouns function as subjects of clauses. In the following example the independent pronoun *'āna* appears to function as a direct object:[2]

> *mərri ^Hmmá'šəmi et-(h)a məštará^H. lá-^Hgmá'šəmi^H 'āna.*
> 'I said: "They will accuse the police. They aren't accusing me."'

In this example *'āna* parallels the Hebrew direct object marker *'et* (את), though it may be just be an awkwardly-formed sentence in which one might have expected *'āna* 'as for me', at the beginning of the clause.

4.1.2. *Pronominal Suffixes on Nouns*

a. The pronominal suffixes in JChalla are

1 c.s.	-i	*besi* ('my house')
2 m.s.	-ox	*besox*
2 f.s.	-ax	*besax*
3 m.s.	-e	*bese*
3 f.s.	-a	*besa*
1 c.pl.	-an, -eni	*besan, beseni*
2 c.pl.	-exun	*besexun*
3 c.pl.	-u	*besu*

b. Representative examples include

ləbbi	'my heart'
sāwi	'my grandfather'
pārox	'your (m.s.) money'
pāsox	'your (m.s.) face'
yəmmax	'your (f.s.) mother'
xaswāsax	'your (f.s.) sisters'
kusise	'his hat'
'ide	'his hand'
pumma	'her mouth'
'ena	'her eye'
lišaneni	'our language'
hudayeni	'our Jews'
rešan	'our heads'
besan	'our house'

---

[2] In additional passages where one finds occurrrences of *'āya* that might be interpreted as a direct object, it is preferable to explain it as a demonstrative (§ 4.1.7.b).

'əprexun	'your (pl.) soil'
məllətexun	'your (pl.) ethnic group'
qalunku	'their narghiles'
'idāsu	'their hands'

c. The 1 pl. suffixes *-an* and *-eni* are free variants in JChalla, as they are in many other NeoAram dialects, e.g.,

kullan, kulleni ki'ax
'All of us, all of us know.'[3]

d. The 2 pl. *-exun* is also attested in the JNerwa texts as against other *lishana deni* dialects, which have *-oxun* (JAmid, JAradh, JBetan, and JZakho). An *e*-type vowel is also attested, e.g., in Hertevin *-eḥon*, CAradh *-ɛxu* (L-set form), Bohtan *-exün*,[4] and in some Tiari dialects *-ɛxun*, *-ɛxu*.[5]

e. The JChalla 3 pl. *-u* differs from *-ohun* in JAmid and JZakho. One finds both *-u* and *-ohun* in JBetan, and *-ehun*, *-u*, and *-uh* in the JNerwa texts. See also *didu* (§ 4.1.3.a), *-lu* (§ 4.1.4) and *-llu* (§ 4.1.5).

4.1.3. Independent Genitive Pronoun

a. Possesion may also be expressed by the addition of the pronominal suffixes to the independent genitive pronoun *did-*:[6]

1 c.s.	*didi*
2 m.s.	*didox*
2 f.s.	*didax*
3 m.s.	*dide*
3 f.s.	*dida*
1 c.pl.	*deni*[7]

---

[3] Fluctuation is also attested in the L-suffix pronouns and LL-suffix pronouns (§§ 4.1.4–5). Cf. the marking of exclusiveness by the 1 pl. suffix *-enij* noted by Polotsky 1961:19–20 in CUrmi. See also Khan 2007:315.

[4] Fox 2002:160.

[5] Talay 2008:191.

[6] Epstein 1960:27 and Khan 1999:87 believe that *did* developed by assimilation from *di l-*. Others have proposed an origin of *d* + *id* 'of the hand' (e.g., Nöldeke 1868:83; Brockelmann 1908:316; Dalman 1905:118; Ben-Ḥayyim 1976:79 n. 4).

[7] In all the hours of recording only once did Shabbo say *didan* instead of *deni*. *didan* is the form found in dialects to the east of the Greater Zab River. The lone occurrence of *didan* in Shabbo's speech may be the result of analogy with the *did-* forms (*didi, didox, didax, dide, dida,* and *didu*) or dialectal interference from the language of his wife, who is from Sando (Mutzafi p.c.).

2 c.pl.   *dexun*[8]
3 c.pl.   *didu*

b. *did* + pronominal suffix may follow neo-construct forms (§ 4.2.2.b), nouns in annexation with suffixed -*əd* (§ 4.2.2.a), nouns ending in -*a*, -*e*, or ø, as well as prepositions (with or without suffixed -*əd*), e.g.,

1 s.   *ṭas didi* 'for me', *pássaporṭ didi* 'my passport', *xāye didi* 'my life';
2 m.s.   *sāwa didox* 'your grandfather', *'urxəd didox* 'your way', *bargūze didox* 'your suit'; *'āwon didox* 'your fault';
2 f.s.   *'āwon didax* 'your fault';
3 m.s.:   *bron dide* 'his son', *dabanja dide* 'his pistol', *din dide* 'his religion', *šəmməd dide* 'his name', *ṭanəštəd dide* 'his side', *reš dide* 'on him';
3 f.s.   *qəṭ'a dida* 'her piece', *balo'təd dida* 'her throat', *mənnəd dida* 'from her', *pummed dida* 'her mouth';
1 pl.   *hudāyəd deni* 'our Jews', *lišāna deni* 'our language (= Jewish NeoAram)', *məndid deni* 'something of ours';
2 pl.   *'əbbəd dexun* 'in you', *'āwon dexun* 'your fault', *pássaporṭ dexun* 'your passport';
3 pl.   *'idəd didu* 'their hands', *qatxe didu* 'their cups', *pār didu* 'their money', *xulamawás didu* 'their servants', *potine didu* 'their boots', *'əlləd didu* 'to them'

c. There is no apparent difference in meaning or usage among the following triplets:

bāb dide / *bābəd dide* / *bābe*
'his father'

'urxa dide / *'urxəd dide* / *'urxe*
'his path'

gor dida / *gora dida* / *gora*
'her husband'

d. *did* + pronominal suffix may also function without a head noun as in, e.g.,

didox 'áya-la.
'It is yours (m.s.).'

didax 'áya-la.
'It is yours (f.s.).'

---

[8] Once Shabbo uses the form *didexun: la didexun wax xiye* 'not yours (life) have we lived'. Like *didan*, this too is either analogy with the forms with *did-* or dialectal interference from his wife (Mutzafi p.c.).

'āya dídi-le.
'It is mine.'

dexun 'áya-la.
'It is yours (c.pl.).'

e. There is only one example in the corpus of a form without a pronominal suffix, *dəd*:

nāš d-éka-wət? kəmri dəd Wān.
'"Where are you from?" They say from Van.'

f. The 3 pl. *didu* contrasts with *dohun* in JZakho, JAmid, and JBetan, and *dēhun* (דיהון) in the JNerwa texts.

4.1.4. *L-Suffix Pronouns*

a. L-suffix pronouns are composed of the preposition *l-* and the pronominal suffixes affixed to nouns (§ 4.1.2.a.)

1 c.s.	*-li*
2 m.s.	*-lox*
2 f.s.	*-lax*
3 m.s.	*-le*
3 f.s.	*-la*
1 c.pl.	*-lan(a), -leni*
2 c.pl.	*-lexun*
3 c.pl.	*-lu*

b. L-suffix pronouns mark the agent on the Preterite (§ 4.4.13) or the object on the Imperative and Subjunctive based forms (§ 4.4.23.1). They may also be suffixed to the interrogative *mā*: *mā́-lox* 'What's with you?'

c. The 1 pl. suffixes *-lan(a)* and *-leni* fluctuate freely, e.g.,

zə́lleni mṭelan ᴴgvulᴴ.
'We went (and) we arrived at the border.'

kúšlana 'əltəx 'əltəx. kúšleni ḥel tāma.
'We went way down. We went down until there.'

d. *l* assimilates to a preceding *n*, *r*, or *t* in inflected forms of the Subjunctive and Preterite (§ 3.6.c)

4.1.5. *LL-Suffix Pronouns*

a. LL-suffix pronouns may have been formed historically by the affixation of the L-suffix pronouns to the preposition ʾ*əl* (< ClAram עַל):[9]

1 c.s.	*-lli*
2 m.s.	*-llox*
2 f.s.	*-llax*
3 m.s.	*-lle*
3 f.s.	*-lla*
1 c.pl.	*-llan(a), -lleni*
2 c.pl.	*-llexun*
3 c.pl.	*-llu*

b. LL-suffix pronouns serve as enclitic object suffixes to forms of the Perfect and Gerund (§ 4.4.23.2).

c. They also function as free-standing object suffixes (< preposition ʾ*əl*) following forms of the Perfect and Gerund (§ 4.4.23).

4.1.6. *E-Suffix Pronouns*

a. The forms of the E(nclitic)-suffix pronouns are

1 m.s.	*-ən(a), -an(a)*
1 f.s.	*-an(a)*
2 m.s.	*-ət(ən)*
2 f.s.	*-at(ən)*
3 m.s.	*-ø*
3 f.s.	*-a*
1 c.pl.	*-ax(in)*
2 c.pl.	*-étun(a)*
3 c.pl.	*-i*

b. E-suffix pronouns are affixed to forms based on the Subjunctive and the Copula, where they mark the agent (§§ 4.4.6–7), and to forms based on the Preterite, where they mark the object (§ 4.4.23.4).

c. The 1 f.s. form *-an* seems to have begun to encroach on the 1 m.s. *-ən* in inflected forms based on the Subjunctive and is heard occasionally in place of it, e.g.,

> *lá-gmzabnan*
> 'I (m.s.) shall not buy' (§ 5.2.7)

---

[9] Mutzafi 2008a:85. See also § 3.20.h.

In the following examples Shabbo alternates the *-ən* and *-an* forms when referring to a male in the 1ˢᵗ person:

> *baxlan pār didu… 'āna baxlən pār didu*
> 'I shall use up their money… I shall use up their money' (§ 5.3.16)

> *'āna gəbən pálpaṇqaṇoṭ mən pārox tad dārənna go pāri ta* ᴴ*šamran*ᴴ *pāri ta baṛāxa.*
> 'I want a half lira of your money in order to put it in with my money for a blessing (alms).' (§ 5.3.12)

d. There is one example in which Shabbo uses the 2 f.s. *-at* where the 2 m.s. *-ət* is expected: *yā'at* 'you should know' (§ 5.10.16). There is not enough evidence to conclude that the 2 f.s. suffix is also beginning to encroach on the 2 m.s. suffix.

e. E-suffix pronouns on the Subjunctive base are attested already in MidAram in TO, and in LAram in JBA, Syr, and Mand. They are clipped forms of the independent pronoun in postpositive position.

f. As in other *lishana deni* dialects, the 2 m.s. and 2 f.s. forms may take an additional final *-ən(a)*; this is also the case for the particles of existence *'it, 'itən, 'ítəna* 'there is' and *let, letən, létəna* 'there is not' (§ 4.8.1). Final *-əna* is also attested on the singular Imperative *ḥmóləna* 'wait!' The 1 m.s., 1 f.s., and 2 pl. forms may also take an additional *-a*. The most frequent 1 pl. suffix is *-ax*, which is known from other *lishana deni* dialects. The less frequent *-axin* stands in contrast to *-axni*, which is widespread: JAmid, JBetan, JDohok, JNerwa texts, and JZakho. *-in* in the longer JChalla 1 pl. ending *-axin* appears to be a metathesis of the *-ni* of *-axni* attested in the other dialects; despite the distance from the stress, the vowel *i* has not shortened as expected to *ə*.

Note the fluctuation of 1 pl. forms (*-ax* and *-axin*) in the same sentence:

> *'axnan kpalxax hənna kpálxaxin 'əbbəd* ᴴ*kuwaḥ ha-šem*ᴴ *la 'əbbəd* ᴴ*kuwaḥ*ᴴ *gyānan.*
> 'We work, um, we work by the power of God, not by our own power.'

g. The longer forms of the E-suffixes are attested mainly on G verbs and do not affect the position of word stress (§ 3.23.d).

h. E-suffixes precede L-suffixes on inflected forms based on the Subjunctive, e.g.,

> *qaṭlaxle*
> 'we may kill him'

yāwaxle
'we may give it'

i. The past marker *-wa* is infixed between E-suffixes and L-suffixes in the Past Habitual (§ 4.4.10), e.g.,

šalxáxwālu
'we used to take them off'

'axnan panjāre ᶻgəmráxwālaᶻ.
'We used to call it *panjare* (window).'

j. Final *-n* of the 2 pl. E-suffix *-etun(a)* is deleted before an L-suffix (§ 3.18.c), e.g.,

ki'étūle, naxón? ktaxrétūle.
'You (pl.) know him, correct? You (pl.) remember him.'

4.1.7. Demonstrative Pronouns

a. Compared with other *lishana deni* dialects, a limited inventory of demonstrative forms is attested in the corpus:

Near	Far
c.s. *'iya (yā)*	c.s. *'e*
c.pl. *'anna ('an)*	

b. The independent pronoun *'āya ('ā)* also serves as a far demonstrative 'that (one)'.[10] In the first three examples below, it is possible to understand *'āya* as the independent pronoun in extraposition; however, neither the intonation of the sentences nor the other examples support such an interpretation and instead point to a demonstrative use:

'āya qṭəllu Spindarnāye.
'The residents of Spindar killed that one.' (§ 5.6.8)

u-'āya mokušlu m-kawə́nta
'and that one they brought down off the mule' (§ 5.2.11)

lewət wida lə-'áya u-lə-'áya u-lə-'áya
'you haven't done (it) to that one and to that one and to that one'

'āya ṭarma šúqlu l-ta(ma).
'They left that corpse the(re).' (§ 5.2.14)

---

[10] Cf. JBetan far demonstrative f.s. *'āya* (Mutzafi 2008a:42–43).

c. The near demonstrative pronoun *'iya* has a clipped form *yā*[11] that occurs only in the expression *b-íya-'ida u-yā́-'ida* 'when it comes down to it' (lit., 'in this hand and this hand'). The pl. demonstrative also has a clipped form *'an* that occurs before consonants (§ 3.19.d):

> *'an bargūze / 'anna bargūze*
> 'these suits'

d. As is the case with the independent pronouns, the common form of the far demonstrative *'e* looks as if it is the feminine far demonstrative.[12]

e. The far singular pronoun *'o* is rare in Shabbo's speech and occurs in borrowed expressions from JZakho, e.g., *mən dogā* 'from that time', *'ó-yoma* 'that day'. Cf. the usual JChalla forms *mən d-é-doṛ* 'from that generation', *'é-yoma* 'that day'.

f. There is once occurrence in the corpus of a far demonstrative (m.s.) *'ayāha* 'that one over there'.[13]

g. The demonstrative *'ad* is attested in the words *'ədyo* 'today' and *'ádlele* 'tonight' (cf. *'é-lele* 'that night'), and *'áqqar(a)* (< *ad + qadara) 'so much'.[14]

h. Demonstratives occur attributively before the noun modified, e.g.,

'iya gora	'this man'
'e gora	'that man'
'anna 'uṛwānəd didu	'those leaders of theirs'

Often the following noun is enclitic to the demonstrative (§ 3.23.g)

i. Demonstratives may function independently, e.g.,

> *'iya 'ādə́ta-la.*
> 'This is a custom.' (§ 5.6.6)

> *'anna lu wide 'askar go Túrkiya.*
> 'Those have done military service in Turkey.' (§ 5.6.12)

---

[11] So too in JArbel. See Khan 1999:85.

[12] Elsehwere in *lishana deni* dialects *'e* marks the f.s. as against the m.s. *'o*.

[13] When asked if there is a far demonstrative 'those', Shabbo, after hearing his cousin Ahiya and his brother Ḥayyo use JZakho *'anāha*, also says *'anāha*, but he never uses it in the many hours of recorded speech.

[14] See Jastrow 1990:101–102 on the reflexes of *'ad* in NeoAram, where he notes that *'ad-* is best preserved in Hertevin. It occurs on a limited scale in Ṭuroyo but in most NENA dialects only in one or two fossilized words.

j. The far demonstrative *'e* + 'woman' is attested as a euphemism for the 1st person independent pronoun in *'é-baxta pṣarxa* 'I shall shout' (§ 5.8.6). This usage is attested in JPA and JBA.[15]

4.1.8. *Possessive-Relative Particle* d

The ClAram relative pronoun (דִּי/דְּ) has allomorphs in JChalla: *-əd, -d, d-, 'əd-*.

a. One reflex occurs as the suffix *-əd* (before unvoiced consonants [-ɪt]; § 3.2.d)[16] on nouns in annexation (§ 4.2.2.a), e.g., *'āǧāyəd Čalla* 'the aghas of Challa', *qəṭləd 'aṭarka* 'the killing of the peddlar', *nixəd 'amoyi* 'my late paternal uncle', *yəmməd bābox* 'your father's mother'. The vowel *i* of *məndi* 'thing' is preserved before *-d* in *məndid deni* 'something of ours' (§ 5.4.1; see also below *'ānid* § 4.1.8.g).

b. *-əd* is also suffixed to nouns and prepositions bound by the independent genitive pronoun *did-* (§ 4.1.3), e.g.,

šāləd dide	'his belt'
ṭarməd dide	'his corpse'
'əbbəd dide	'in him'
'əlləd didu	'to them'
mənned dide	'from him'

c. *-əd* may be suffixed to a noun that serves as the head of a relative clause,[17] e.g.,

yoməd pləṭlan
'the day we went out'

yarxəd kese
'the month he comes'

denānəd muselu
'the debtors whom they brought'

kud duksəd gəbe
'whatever place they want'

---

[15] See, e.g., Dalman 1905:108; Sokoloff 1990:120 and 2002:128, 259.

[16] Khan 2007:322. See Khan 1999:169 on the possibility of the vowel *ə* of *-əd* originating in the LEAram ending *-ā* on sg. nouns (< ClAram def. article), *-e* on pl. nouns (ClAram cst. pl.), or, most likely, the 3 m.s. proleptic suffix *-e* in a syntagm of the type בֵּיתֵהּ דְּמַלְכָּא 'the king's palace' < 'his palace of the king'.

[17] Goldenberg 1993:631 and 1995.

nāšəd gbe ^{H}*'emét*^{H}
'people who want truth'

'áxxa-ži let xa dūkəd xapči šətyəd gyāni maštən 'əlla.
'There isn't here even a place (where) I can (stretch out and) moisten a bit of my own yarn.' (§ 5.6.3)

'é-məšəlmānəd nixəd bābi muqṭəlle
'that Muslim whom my father had killed' (§ 5.6.19)

d. -*əd* may be suffixed to a noun in annexation to a cardinal number (§ 4.3.5), e.g.,

yarxəd 'arba
'fourth month'

e. -*d* is suffixed to *kull-* 'all' yielding the indefinite pronoun *kud-* 'each, every' (§§ 4.1.12.f; § 4.3.1.h).

f. -*d* is suffixed to the interrogative *mā* yielding *mād* 'whatever', e.g.,

mād gbənwa muselu.
'Whatever I would want, they brought.'

mād 'amraxlu la ^{Z}*gəmrilan*^{Z} *la.*
'Whatever we say to them, they don't say no to us.'

g. -*d* may be suffixed to independent and demonstrative pronouns, e.g.,

'ānid lu máxye-lle 'āya. ^{H}*ken*^{H}*, 'ānid əmxéwālu 'əlle.*
'Those who have beaten him, that one. Yes, those who had beaten him.' (§ 5.2.16)

'annəd qāmi
'those that (are) on me'

h. -*d* may be suffixed to the preposition *ta* forming the conjunction 'in order to':

tad dārənna
'in order to put her'

i. -*d* is prefixed to the negative particle *la* and forms the preposition 'without' (§ 4.5) and the conjunction 'lest' (§ 4.6), e.g.,

dla pāre   'without money'
dla šarwāla 'without trousers'
dlá-'árəqla 'lest he flee'

j. *d-* may be prefixed to a demonstrative pronoun or adverb following a preposition (§ 4.5):

mən d-axxa	'from here'
mən d-iya	'from this'
xor d-axxa	'like here'

k. *d-* may be prefixed to a noun following an early or recent loan ending in *-a*:

ʾāġa d-Čalla	'an agha of Challa'
ʾāġa d-láxma-ewa	'he was the Agha of bread'
^H*taḥaná*^H *d-basra*	'the next station' (cf. *kud* ^H*taḥanəd*^H *gezaxwa* 'every station which we went to' (§ 5.10.1)
wal ^H*polátika*^H *d-hudāye ṛába-la.*	'Indeed, the craftiness of the Jews is great.' (§ 5.6.5)
^H*históriya*^H *d-kullu kiʾənna.*	'I know the history of everyone.' (§ 5.6.11)

d- also is prefixed to a noun following a ModH loan that ends in *-e*:

^H*kafé d-bokər*^H   'the morning coffee' (§ 5.4.6)

l. *d* may occur twice in succession: first suffixed to a noun and then prefixed to a relative clause, demonstrative pronoun, or adverb:[18]

xalwəd d-iwət xíla-lle mən xədyawāsəd yəmmox
'the milk which you have drunk[19] from your mother's breasts'

ʾaxnan lewax nāšəd d-axxa.
'We are not (like) the people here.'

m. When prefixed to the Subjunctive of the verb *hwy* and to the 3rd forms of the Present Copula,[20] *d > t* (§ 3.2.d):

māṭo t-ūwa?
'How will it be?'

mā t-ūwa
'what should be'

ʾanna t-ilu ʾuṛwānəd hənna...
'those who are the leaders of, um...'

---

[18] It is also found suffixed to a noun and as part of the independent genitive pronoun *did*. See above § 4.1.8.b.

[19] Lit., 'eaten'.

[20] As in JBetan (Mutzafi 2008a:42).

ʾe hudāya t-ile nəxrāya l-tāma
'that Jew who is a foreigner there'

n. Sometimes *d* has the allomorph *ʾəd-*,[21] e.g.,

ʿāwon didox ʾəd-kúlla hudāye mən kullu dukāne
'your guilt (and) of all the Jews from everywhere' (§ 5.8.19)

ʿāwon didax u-ʾəd-górax b-qdāléxun
'you and your husband are responsible' (§ 5.9.13)

ʾatta ʾəd-gyāni pšalxənnu
'now I will take them off of myself' (§ 5.2.8)

ʾegā ʾāni ʿādətəd dídu-la ʾəd-ʾáġa.
'Now it is a custom of theirs with the Agha.' (§ 5.4.6)

4.1.9. *Reflexive Pronoun*

gyāna 'soul' serves as the reflexive pronoun: *gyāni* 'myself', *gyānox* 'yourself (m.s.)', *gyānax* 'yourself (f.s.)', etc. It may occur as the second element in an annexation construction, e.g.,

dūkəd gyāne
'his own place'

ḥaqqəd gyānan
'our due'

ʾāna ᴴmbakšənᴴ pār gyāni.
'I request my money.' (§ 5.2.2)

ᴴdowarᴴ gyānu zəlle kəl qāymaqam, ᴴdowarᴴ gyānan msulmālan.[22]
'Their mail went to the local governor, our mail we delivered.' (§ 5.7.1)

4.1.10. *Reciprocal Pronouns*

a. The form *ʾə́ġdād* 'each other, one another' may occur with the prefixed prepositions *m-* and *l-* as well as the suffix *-e*: *ʾə́ġdād(e), l-ə́ġdād(e), m-ə́ġdād(e)*:

ʾāni kiʾewa b-əġdād.
'They knew (of the matter from) each other.' (§ 5.8.13)

tūlu barqul ʾə́ġdāde.
'They sat opposite each other.' (§ 5.3.3)

---

[21] See also in JBetan (Mutzafi 2008a:41).
[22] Note that Shabbo treats ᴴdowarᴴ as both m. (*zəlle*) and f. (*msulmālan*).

lu tiwe ʾāni barqul ə́ǧdād.
'They had sat opposite each other.' (§ 5.3.10)

rə́qqe-lu m-ə́ǧdād(e).
'They are far from each other.'

b. Reciprocity may also be expressed by the construction *xa l-e-xeta/xet/ xe* 'one to the (lit., 'that') other':

xa ᴴgʿazriᴴ l-e-xét, xa mraḥmi l-e-xéta.
'One helps the other, one pities the other.'

ṣrəxlu xá-l-e-xet
'they shouted to each other' (§ 5.2.10)

xa lu mšaboḥe ʾəl-xé
'one is praising the other' (§ 5.3.10)

4.1.11. *Interrogative Pronouns*

mā   'what?'
        má-lox. 'What's with you?'
        má-le. 'What's with him?
        mā wáxt-ile. 'What time is it?'
        mā ʾódəna. 'What should I do?'

mani   'who?'
        lá-kiʾən mani xéta-ži
        'I don't know (on) whom else either' (§ 5.5.1)

        mani lu qṭíle-lle ʿaṭarka?
        'Who have killed him, the peddler?' (§ 5.5.1)

ʾeni   'which?'[23]
        mar ʾeni ᴴmədináᴴ bəšṭor.
        'Say which state (is) better!'

        mən ᴴTúrkiyaᴴ ʾeni dūka?
        'From which place (in) Turkey?'

The interrogative *mā* is also used to express exclamation:

mā qársa-la l-tāma go ṭūra!
'How cold it is there on the mountain!' (§ 5.2.11)

ʾiya mā qurdáya-le! hatxa narm u-ḥāle garməd dide.
'What (sort of) a Kurd this is! His bones are so soft and the like!' (§ 5.3.6)

---

[23] Cf. *ʾemi* (JZakho and JDohok), *ʾema* (JBetan). It also functions as an adjective in *ʾéni-əšti kiloye, šoʾi kiloye* 'some sixty kilos, seventy kilos' (§ 5.3.15).

4.1.12. *Indefinite Pronouns*

A number of words function as indefinite pronouns:

a. *xa* 'a, a certain':[24]

xa nəqwa	'a female'
xa šwāna	'a shepherd'
xa yalunka	'a child'

b. *xanči* 'some, a few':

xanči qṭililu. xanči drelu go ᴴbet soharᴴ. xanči 'riqālu mən ᴴpaḥadᴴ. xanči pəšlu.
'Some they killed. Some they put in prison. Some fled out of fright. Some remained.' (§ 5.1.8)

c. *xədda*[25] 'someone':

xədda qāṭəllexun
'someone may kill you (pl.)'

'ən xədda ᴴpṣə'leᴴ
'if someone got injured'

d. *flān(a)* 'such and such, a certain'. *flān* is used with humans, e.g.,

flān brāta	'such and such a daughter'
flān muxtar	'such and such a mukhtar'
flān nāša	'such and such a person'
flān bər flān kəslox 'āya?	'Is so and so with you?'

flāna is used with non-humans, e.g.,

flāna dūka	'such and such a place' (also *flāná-dūka*; § 3.23.h)
flāna māsa	'such and such a village'
flāna šāta	'such and such a year'

e. *flānkas* 'so and so, a certain person':

flānkas ké-le?
'Where is so and so?'

f. *kud* (< *kull + d-; § 3.6.c) 'each, every':

kud duksa	'each place'
kúd-dūka-u-dūka	'each and every place'

---

[24] For a detailed analysis of the use of *xa* as an indefinite pronoun in NENA, see Khan 2008:288–293.

[25] See §§ 3.20.e; 4.3.1.d.

kud kma yarxe	'every few months'
kúd-lel	'every night'
kud mḥokéle-ži	'whoever also spoke'
kud šuftiya	'each watermelon'
kúd-yom	'every day'
kuššat	'every year' (§ 3.6.b)

g. *kutxa* (< *kud* + *xa*; § 3.2.d) 'each one':

> *kútxa-le dūkəd gyāne.*
> 'Each one is (in) his own place.' (§ 5.11.6)

> *kutxa xa 'ənglízi-la l-kāpəd dide.*
> 'Each one (has) an English (rifle) on his shoulder.' (§ 5.11.9)

> *kutxa səkkinəd dide l-axxa.*
> 'Each one's knife is here.' (§ 5.4.10)

h. *kút-xa-u-xa* 'each and every one'

i. *kud* + numbers (above 'one') + pronominal suffix:

kútreni	'the two of us'
kútrexun	'the two of you'
kutru	'the two of them'
kútlāhun	'the three of them'
kút'arbeni	'the four of us'

j. *kull-* 'all'

kullan, kulléni	'all of us'
kúllexun	'all of you'
kullu lu zile	'all of them have gone'
kulle lašše	'all of his body'
kulle gəldəd 'ide	'all of the skin of his hand'
kulle mənni šqə́llexun	'You have taken all of it from me.'
kulle məndi	'all sorts of things'
kulla 'ar'a	'all of the land'
kulla 'Iraq	'all of Iraq'
kullu xāṣu	'all of their backs'

k. *məndi* 'thing':

> *mesewa məndi.*
> 'They would bring something.'

> *mərru məndid deni šqəllu.*
> 'They said they took something of ours.'

l. *xá-məndi* 'something':

> *mərru xá-məndi.*
> 'They said something.'

m. *čú-məndi* 'nothing':

> *čú-məndi xet let.*
> 'There is nothing else.'
>
> *lewe bāda čú-məndi.*
> 'He isn't doing anything.'
>
> *lá-ki'etun čú-məndi.*
> 'You (pl.) don't know anything.'

n. *čú-xa* 'no one':

> *čú-xa xet lə́twāle.*
> 'He didn't have anyone else.'
>
> *čú-xa lewe míra-lli.*
> 'No one has told me.'
>
> *čú-xa lewe pliṭa.*
> 'No one has come out.'

o. *kma* 'some':

> *kma qorūše*
> 'some piasters'

4.2. NOUNS AND ADJECTIVES

4.2.1. *Inflection of Nouns*

a. The inflected endings on inherited Aramaic nouns in JChalla are

	singular	plural
m.	*-a*	*-e*
f.	*-ta, -sa*	*-āsa*

b. As in other *lishana deni* dialects and elsewhere in NENA, inherited Aramaic masculine nouns end in *-a* (< *ā'*, the old determined suffix), e.g.,

> *dəmma* 'blood'
> *gəlda* 'skin'
> *qāša* 'priest'
> *pəsra* 'flesh'

sahāda	'witness'
ṣiwa	'wood'
talġa	'snow'

c. Some inherited Aramaic nouns that end in -*a* are feminine, e.g.,

ʾaqla	'foot'
ʾarʾa	'land'
ʾena	'eye, well'
ʾərba	'sheep'
ʾida	'hand'
ʾurxa	'path'
kāsa	'belly'

d. Some feminine nouns ending in -*a* in JChalla are of ultimate Arabic origin, where they were feminine with *tā' marbūṭa*, e.g.,

bəndaqiya	'rifle'
daqiqa	'minute'
ḥukūma	'government'
máḥkama	'court'
qaḥba	'whore'
səjjāda	'prayer rug'

e. Most inherited Aramaic feminine nouns end in either -*ta* or -*sa* (< ClAram -*tā*, *ṯā*),[26] e.g.,

ʾəlisa	'fat tail'
basəmta	'pleasing'
kaləpsa	'bitch'
səpsa	'lip'
ṣaboʾta	'finger'

f. The following Arabic words entered JChalla through Kurdish, where they ended in -*t*. The Aramaic suffix -*a* has been added to them:

ʿādəta	'custom'
darbəta	'blow from God'
məlləta	'ethnic group'
qudrəta	'(Divine) omnipotence'
qyāməta	'resurrection'

ʾəmməta 'nation' and *məlkəta* 'property' may have also entered through Kurdish (or Turkish).

---

[26] See Khan 2007:323–324 for a discussion of conditioning factors in NENA in the choice of the feminine suffix (-*ta* or -*ṭa*) and subsequent deviations.

g. Some loanwords ending in -ø are also feminine, though not all of them are so in the donor languages: *ḥukum* (Ar m.) 'government',[27] *kāwód* (H m.) 'honor', *madām* (T, K f.) 'Madam', *maṭár* (Ar m.) 'airport', *ṭaffaq* 'rifle (K f.)', *xānəm* (T, K f.) 'Madam', *žang* (K f.) 'rust'.

h. Many loanwords in JChalla do not receive the ending -*a*, e.g.,

'arzūḥal	'petition' (also *'arzuḥál*)
'askar	'army, soldier'
'āwon	'guilt, sin'
'ənyān	'matter'[28]
doktor	'doctor'
ḥākəm	'judge'
ḥarb	'war'
māḷ	'property
pássaporṭ	'passport'
sartuk	'cream'

Others loanwords, however, do, which indicates that they were borrowed into Aramaic at an early period and have over time become Aramaized,[29] e.g.,

'aqida	'(military) leader'
baṛāza	'pig'
dašta	'field'[30]
kavra	'cliff'
máfəra	'opportunity'
naqla	'time'
nəzima	'low'
pehna	'kick'
qatxa	'cup'[31]
ṛeṃa	'pus'
šarwāla	'trousers'

Some loanwords appear both with and without -*a*:[32]

---

[27] Perhaps under the influence of the feminine synonyms (also loanwords) *ḥukūma*, *ḥukumiya*.

[28] The noun is attested in LAram. On the one hand, the absence of the ending -*a* in Shabbo's speech suggests it may be a recent borrowing (from ModHeb); the penultimate stress, on the other hand, suggests it is not.

[29] Note also the following ModH nouns in Shabbo's speech, which he has Aramaized with either singular or plural suffixes: *dapé* (דַּף) 'pages'; *pastela* (פַּסְטֶל < Judeo-Spanish) 'pie'; *ṣrife* (צְרִיף), pl. 'cabins'.

[30] Already in JBA. An older borrowing from Iranian is attested in QAram דחשת.

[31] Already in Syriac.

[32] Cf. also the indefinite pronoun *flān(a)* 'such and such' (§ 4.1.12.d).

harâm, harāma	'forbidden'[33]
həzur, hə́zura	'estimation'
kef, kefa	'joy'
sayyid, sayyida	'descendant of Muhammad'
wāli, walya[34]	'vali'
waxt, waxta	'time'
xanjar, xanjāra	'dagger'

Shabbo seems to use the addition of the suffix -*a* to distiguish between *qačax* 'smuggled goods' and *qačāxa* 'smuggler'.

i. There are additional singular nouns that end in a vowel other than *a* or ø.[35] One finds in the inherited Aramaic vocabulary:

e: *'ərxe* 'mill', *dugle* 'lie(s)', *gāre* 'roof',[36] *lele*
i: *čeri* 'autumn',[37] *məndi* 'thing'

Loanwords include

e: *čappe* 'left', *dunye* 'world', *masale* 'matter', *məzgafte* 'mosque', *panjāre* 'window', *raṣṭe* 'right'
i: *gərāni* 'famine', *kursi* chair', *nāwí* 'prophet', *tangāwi* 'distress', *tūsi* 'type of thorn'
o: *raḍyo* 'radio'
u: *ṭāpu* 'title deed'

4.2.2. Annexation of Nouns

The genitive relationship is expressed in JChalla by the annexation of one noun to another:

a. The most frequent method of annexation is the suffixing of the possessive-relative particle *d* (§ 4.1.8.a) to the first of two nouns, be it of original Aramaic stock or a loanword, e.g.,

'idəd ḥukum	'the hand of the government'
'urxəd ṭḷā́ha-yome-ži	'also a path of three days'
baxxatəd[38] *'ilāha*	'for the mercy of God!'
denəd hudāye	'the debt (owed) to the Jews'
marəd dukkāna	'the shopkeeper'

---

[33] Cf. the antonym *ḥalāla* 'kosher, lawful'.
[34] See s.v. in the glossary for a possible origin of the form *walyá-bak*.
[35] See Mutzafi 2008a:90.
[36] On the development in NENA of this originally Akkadian noun, see Mutzafi 2008a:91.
[37] An early loan into Aramaic from Akkadian.
[38] Cf. *baxxat 'ilāha* (Sabar 2002a:110).

ṭalāqəd báxtox-ži	'also the divorce of your wife'
yoməd din	'the Day of Judgment'

b. Less common are neo-construct syntagms in which the final *-a* or *-e* of the first noun is apocopated (§ 3.19.a),[39] e.g.,

'əpər hudāye	'the soil of the Jews'
'əqər dunye	'the bottom of the world'
dum ḥoq	'the tail of the law'
lel šapsa	'Saturday night'
naqəl 'arba	'the fourth time'
palgus māsa	'center of the village'
naqoṣ 'əṣra	'minus ten'
tol babexun	'revenge for your father'
xāy yəmmox	'By the life of your mother!'
xətən walyā̂-bak	'the son-in-law of the Vali Bey'[40]
yom 'ərota	'Friday'

This construction also occurs with loanwords that do not take a final vowel in NENA, e.g., *māḷ hudāye deni* 'the property of our Jews'. In the case of *baxta* 'woman, wife', the final syllable is apocopated yielding *bax*,[41] e.g., *bax 'axone* 'his sister-in-law', *bax mədor* 'the mudir's wife'.

There are no differences in usage between nouns annexed by *-əd* and by neo-construct forms. Cf. *lel šapsa* 'Saturday night' and *yoməd šapsa* 'the Sabbath' (also *yoma šapsa* § 4.2.2.e).

c. A third type of annexation is what appears to be the direct reflex of ClAramaic construct forms. It is attested with the nouns *brona* 'son', *brāta* 'daughter', and *māra* 'owner', where one hears in construct the forms *bər*,[42] *brāt*, and *mare*:[43] *bər Nəfto* 'son of Naphtali', *xmāra bər xmāra* 'what an ass!'; *brāt ma'alləm Mədo* 'the daughter of the teacher Mido', *brāt qaḥba* 'daughter of a whore'; *mare gora* 'married woman' (< 'owner of a husband'), *mare 'aṣəl* 'possessing a good nature'. A fourth noun, *besa* 'family, household, house' differentiates between *be* 'family',[44] which

---

[39] Sabar 2002a:38–39; Mutzafi 2008a:33,92. Another example may be *'omər* (< *ʾumra* < *ʿumra* 'monastery') in the syntactically difficult and awkward *'ítəna tāma 'omər Biya u-hənna l-tāma* 'there is over there the monastery of Biya and, um, there.'

[40] See s.v. in the glossary.

[41] See § 3.6.g for the phonetic realization of this form.

[42] A neo-construct form *bron* is also attested, but never annexed to a personal name, e.g., *bron 'āǧa* 'son of the agha'.

[43] A neo-construct form *mar* is also attested, e.g., *mar dukkāna* 'shopkeeper'. Cf. also the annexed form with *-əd*: *márəd dukkāna*.

[44] בי 'house' can be found as an absolute form in EgAram, JPA, and Syr (Leander

serves as a construct form in JBA (in addition to בית), and *bes* 'house': *be ʾAsmāre* 'Asmare's family', *be brāt xmāsi* 'the family of my mother-in-law's daughter', *bes muxtar* 'house of the mukhtar'. The preposition *reš* 'on, upon' may also be a direct reflex of the ClAram construct state.[45]

d. The Kurdish genitive particle *-e* is attested in the originally Arabic expression *ʾawlād-e rasúl* 'descendant of the Messenger (i.e., Muhammad)'.[46]

e. There is no morphological marker of annexation between two apposed nouns in *qəṭʾa gāla* 'an item of kilim rug' or *yoma šapsa* 'the Sabbath day'. The same may or may not be true for *ʾida čappe* 'left hand (= to the left)' and *ʾida ṛaṣṭe* 'right hand (= to the right)' (§ 4.2.4.b. n. 57).

f. Annexation by the independent genitive particle *did* is attested in other *lishana deni* dialects[47] but is rare in JChalla (§ 4.1.3.e).

4.2.3. *Nominal Plural Forms*

4.2.3.1. *Plural Forms Ending in* -e

a. The most frequent plural suffix is *-e* (< LEAram *-e*). It occurs on both inherited Aramaic nouns and loanwords. It replaces the ending *-a* on masculine and feminine singular nouns, e.g.,

ʾərbe	'sheep' (s. *ʾerba*)
baxte	'women, wives' (s. *baxta*)
daqiqe	'minutes' (s. *daqiqa*)
dawāre	'riding animal' (s. *dawāra*)
ganāwe	'thieves' (s. *ganāwa*)
garme	'bones' (s. *garma*)
guniye	'bramble' (s. *guniya*)
kalbe	'dogs' (s. *kalba*)
kepe	'stones' (s. *kepa*)
kutwe	'thorns' (s. *kutwa*)
lašše	'corpses' (s. *lašša*)
lišāne	'tongues' (s. *lišāna*)
malʾāxe	'angels' (s. *malʾax*)

1928:23–24), and possibly even in OA (בי טב KAI 216:16 unless the orthography reflects the assimilation of the final *taw* to the word-initial *ṭet*).

[45] Mutzafi 2008a:92.

[46] The *-i* vowel in *tuxmi xalwa la pāyəš go xədyawās didu* 'no trace of milk remains in their breasts' may be another example of the Kurdish *izafet*.

[47] In JBetan it is also rare (Mutzafi 2008a:92).

naxire	'noses' (s. *naxira*)
qəṭ'e	'pieces' (s. *qəṭ'a*)
reše	'heads' (s. *reša*)
sahāde	'witnesses'(s. *sahāda*)
ṣiwe	'trees' (s. *ṣiwa*)
skine, səkkina	'knives' (s. *skina, səkkina*)
sūse	'horses' (s. *sūsa*)
šafqe	'hats (with a brim)' (s. *šafqa*)
tene	'figs' (s. *tena*)

b. -*e* may be suffixed to nouns whose singular form ends in ø, e.g.,

dināre	'dinar' (s. *dinar*)
qorúše	'piasters' (s. *qorúš*)
ṭraṃbele	'automobiles' (s. *ṭraṃbel*)

c. -*e* may replace the ending -*ta* on feminine nouns, e.g.,

kawdəne	'mules' (s. *kawdənta*)
ṭarrāše	'bushes' (s. *ṭarrašta*)

d. -*e* may be added following the glide *y* to loanwords whose singular ends in a vowel:

'āġāye	'aghas' (s. *'āġa*)
kiloye	'kilos' (s. *kilo*)
mallāye	'mullahs' (s. *malla*)

balāye functions as both a singular and plural "trouble(s)", as in JBetan,[48] and appears to have been based on a singular *bala* (attested elsewhere in NENA),[49] to which the glide *y* was added when -*e* was suffixed.

4.2.3.2. *Plural Forms Ending in* -āne

a. The plural suffix -*āne* (< LEAram -*āne*) most frequently replaces -*a* found on bisyllabic singular nouns:[50]

'ar'āne	'lands' (s. *'ar'a*)
dukāne	'places' (s. *dūka*, also *duksa*)
govāne	'stalls' (s. *gova*)
gudāne	'walls' (s. *gūda*)
kapāne	'shoulders' (s. *kāpa*)
misāne	'dead' (s. *misa*)

---

[48] Mutzafi 2008a:336.
[49] Sabar 2008a:110.
[50] The suffix -*ān* on the Kurdish loanword *mamāni* 'my uncles' is the Kurdish plural morpheme.

    qanāne   'horns' (*qāna < *qanna < *qarna)
    qaṣrāne 'mansions' (s. *qaṣra*)
    tarʾāne   'doors' (s. *tarʾa*)
    ṭurāne   'mountains' (s. *ṭūra*)

b. -*āne* is attested on a noun whose singular ends in a geminated consonant

    ḥaqqāne 'rights' (s. *ḥaqq*)

as well as on a loanword that ends in -*i*:

    ṣofyāne 'sufis' (s. *ṣofi*)

c. The bases of two plural forms that take the suffix -*āne* differ slightly from the bases of the corresponding singular forms:

    gurāne   'men' (s. *gora*, also pl. *gūre*)
    malkāne 'chieftains' (s. *malək*)[51]

4.2.3.3. *Plural Forms Ending in* -āhe

The suffix -*āhe* (< LEAram -*āhe*) replaces the singular suffix -*a* on two nouns:[52]

    ʾəmmāhe 'hundreds' (s. *ʾəmma* 'hundred'; § 4.3.3)
    dəmmāhe 'guilt of bloodshed' (s. *dəmma* 'blood, blood money')

4.2.3.4. *Plural Forms Ending in* -āsa

The feminine plural suffix -*āsa* (< LEAram -*āṯā*) replaces the singular suffix -*a*[53] attested on masculine and feminine nouns, e.g.,

    ʾaqlāsa 'feet' (s. *ʾaqla*, also *ʾaqalta*)
    ʾidāsa   'hands' (s. *ʾida*)
    baxtāsa 'wives' (s. *baxta*)
    dəbbāsa 'bears' (s. *dəbba*)
    qorāsa 'graves' (s. *qora*)
    yomāsa 'days' (s. *yoma*, also pl. *yome*)

---

[51] On the syncope of *ə*, see § 3.18.a.

[52] The plural marker -*āh* is not atttested on either noun in older Aramaic. The suffix is found on additional nouns in other *lishana deni* dialects, e.g., JBetan (Mutzafi 2008a:96) *ʾalpāhe* 'thousands' (cf. JChalla *ʾalpe*), *šəmmāhe* (~ *šemmāne*) 'names', *dargāhe* 'gates'. A plural *šəmmāhe* 'heavens' is found in the 17th and 18th century manuscripts of the Song of Songs (6:5) (Sabar 1991:62).

[53] In JBetan (Mutzafi 2008a:96–98) -*āsa* may also be added to feminine nouns ending in -*ta* or -*ϑa*. In JChalla the *t* of *baxta* is part of the root and the plural *ʾaqlāsa* may be based on either or *ʾaqla* or *ʾaqalta*.

y is the final root consonant in the following feminine nouns:

kəsyāsa	'hens' (s. *ksesa*)
šaqyāsa	'(water) channel' (s. *šaqisa*)

w may be the final root consonant in the following nouns:

naṣwāsa	'fights' (s. *naṣūsa*; § 3.22.b)
xaswāsa	'sisters' (s. *xāsa*)
qaṭwāsa	'cats' (s. unattested, but cf. JBetan *qaṭūϑa*).

4.2.3.5. *Plural Forms Ending in -yāsa*

The feminine plural suffix *-yāsa* is found on the following feminine singular nouns:

knəšyāsa	'synagogues' (s. *knəšta*)
maxəlyāsa	'fine sieves' (s. *maxəlta*)
nasyāsa	'ears' (s. *nāsa*)
ṣuryāsa	'cheeks' (s. *ṣurta*)
škaftyāsa	'caves' (s. *škafta*; § 3.22.d)
ṭanəšyāsa	'sides' (s. *ṭanəšta*)
toryāsa	'cows' (s. *tawərta*)

The singular form of the following plurals is not attested in the corpus:

čanyāsa	'satchels'
kuləkyāsa	'ulcers'
nunyāsa	'fish'
zəmrəyāsa	'songs'

4.2.3.6. *Plural Forms Ending in -awāsa*

The plural suffix *-awāsa* is attested on several nouns, most of which take the suffix *-a* in the singular:

'amawāsa	'paternal uncles' (s. *'amoya*)
'axawāsa	'brothers' (s. *'axona*)
'edawāsa	'holidays' (s. *'eda*)
babawāsa	'fathers' (s. *bāba*)
garawāsa	'roofs' (s. *gāre*)
marawāsa	'masters' (s. *māra*)
nehrawāsa	'rivers' (s. *nehra*)
xəzmawāsa	'in-laws' (s. *xəzma*)
xulamawāsa	'servants' (s. *xulāma*, also pl. *xulāme*)

y of *xədyawāsa* 'breasts' is part of the root.

4.2.3.7. *Plural Forms with Reduplicated Consonant*

A few nouns form a plural by reduplicating the final consonant and inserting *ā*:[54]

ʾalāle	'sides' (s. *ʾāla*)
ʾəzlāle	'yarn' (s. *ʾəzla*)
gəllāle	'grasses, plants, herbs' (s. *gəlla*)
jebābe	'pockets' (s. *jeba*)

4.2.3.8. *Plural Forms Ending in -ine*

There is only one noun attested with the plural ending *-ine*:[55]

maʿalmine   'teachers' (s. *maʿalləm*; § 3.18.a)

4.2.3.9. *Multiple Plural Forms*

a. Some singular nouns take more than one plural form:

ʾaqla	'foot', pl. *ʾaqle* and *ʾaqlāsa* (< *ʾaqalta?*)
ʾarʾa	'land', pl. *ʾarʾāsa* and *ʾarāne*
gora	'man', pl. *gūre* and *gurāne*
yoma	'day', pl. *yome* and *yomāsa*

b. Different plural forms distinguish between the two meanings of the s. *ʾena* 'eye, well': pl. *ʾene* 'eyes', *ʾenāsa* 'wells'.

4.2.3.10. *Irregular Plural Forms*

a. The plural forms of some nouns are not derived directly from the singular base:

ʾaxona	'brother'; pl. *ʾaxawāsa*
ʿаširat	'tribe'; pl. *ʾaširatte*
besa	'house'; pl. *bāte*
brāta	'daughter'; pl. *bnāsa*
brona	'son, boy'; pl. *bnone*
gora	'man, husband'; pl. *gūre, gurāne*
šāta	'year'; pl. *šənne*
šex	'sheikh'; pl. *šexāye*
šūla	'work, affair'; pl. *šuʾāle*

---

[54] See Nöldeke 1868:143–145; Sabar 2002a:44.
[55] This ending is typical in religious titles in JBetan (Mutzafi 2008a:103).

b. In the following example a suppletive paradigm is formed from the singular, which has the Kurdish/Arabic gentilic suffix -*i*, and the plural, which has the Aramaic plural gentilic suffix -*āye*:

> *ḥajji* 'hajji, pilgrim'; pl. *ḥajjāye* (§ 4.2.9.1. n. 74)

4.2.3.11. *Pluralia Tantum*

The following *pluralia tantum* are attested:

'ahāli	'population, people'
'əxre	'excrement'
čakke	'weapons'
ganmoke	'maize'
māye	'water'
pāre	'money'[56]
prāge	'millet'
šəmme	'sky'
təhome	'abyss'
xarbé	'ruins'
xruwiye	'sorghum'

4.2.4. *Inflection of Adjectives*

a. Adjectives of Aramaic origin, including participles, are inflected for gender and number, e.g.,

m. *tiqa*	'old' (§ 3.17.d), f. *təqta*, pl. *tiqe*
m. *qida*	'burnt', f. *qədta*, pl. *qide*
m. *yarixa*	'long', f. *yarəxta*, pl. *yarixe*
m. *zöra*	'small' (§ 3.18.b), f. *zurta* (§ 3.10), pl. *zöre*

b. Several adjectives of non-Aramaic origin have one invariable form in the singular:[57]

'āni	'poor' (*lu piše 'āni* 'they became poor')
'aṣli	'genuine' (*səjjāde 'aṣli* 'genuine rugs'; cf. Aramaized *'aṣlāye* 'of good origin')
ḅāš	'good' (*ḅáš-ila* 'it is good')

---

[56] A singular form *pāra* 'coin' is not attested in the corpus unlike JBetan (Mutzafi 2008a:368) and elsewhere (Sabar 2002a:253).

[57] Nöldeke 1868:125–126. One might add to the list presented below *čappe* 'left' and *raste* 'right' in the expressions *'ida čappe* 'to the left (= left hand)', *'ida raste* 'to the right (= right hand)', though elsewhere in NENA both words appear as the second noun in an annexation construction, e.g., JBetan *'iðəd čappe* (Mutzafi 2008a:331). See § 4.2.2.e.

faqír   'poor' (*peši faqír* 'they become poor')[58]
gərūwer   'round-shaped' (*tre gərūwer* 'two round-shaped [objects]')
həšyar   'careful' (*həšyar wetun* 'you [pl.] are careful')
məšša   'many' (*ṭarke məšša-lu* 'there are many sticks')
muḥtāj   'in need' (*lewu muḥtāj* 'they are not in need')[59]
narm   'gentle' in *narm u-ḥāle* 'soft and the like' (*hatxa nāše ḅāš. hatxa narm u-ḥāle. hatxa nāše ḅāš* 'Such good people. So soft and the like. Such good people.')
ṣāx   'healthy' (*'íwaxən ṣāx* 'we are healthy')
xurṭ   'aggressive' (*xúrṭ-ilu* 'they are aggresive')

Though the following adjectives are attested only in a masculine singular context, elsewhere in NENA they are invariable:

naxwaš   'ill'
pis   'filthy, dirty'
rūt   'naked'
xwaš   'good'

c. The loanword *tāza* 'new, precious' has both masculine singular and plural forms,[60] but not a feminine form:

dūka tāza   'new place'
mən ^Hyahalóm^H-ži bə́š-tāza-la   'she is more precious than a diamond'
bāte tāze   'new houses'

d. There is one attested inherited Aramaic adjective that is invariable, *xeta*[61] 'other':

pelafta xeta   'the other shoe'
xá-nāša xeta   'a certain other person'
nāše xeta   'other people'
'anna xeta   'those others'

4.2.5. *General Remarks on Noun and Adjective Patterns*

The morphology of the nominal system[62] has allowed non-ClAram phonotactics that have led to nominal patterns not found in ClAram, e.g., patterns with final consonantal clusters, e.g., CaCC *hatk* 'disgrace', *ḥarb*

---

[58] Also attested with a Hebrew plural suffix: *lá-gpēšax faqirím* 'we are not becoming poor'. See Sabar 2002a:264: pl. פקירין/ם *faqīrīn/m, faqīre*.
[59] Shabbo glossed this as *lewu sniqe*.
[60] See Nöldeke 1868:126,135.
[61] This is a reflex of an older feminine singular form. Cf. Syr ܐܚܪܬܐ.
[62] For discussions of nominal morphology in *lishana deni* dialects see Sabar 2002a:38–47; Mutzafi 2008a.

'war'; CəCCaCC *kərmanj* 'Kurd, peasant'; CaCCaCoCC *pássaporṭ* 'passport'. Many patterns contain only loanwords, e.g., CiCCa and CeCCa, whereas inherited Aramaic nouns and Aramaized loanwords take the form CəCCa. The inventory of patterns is rich as a result of the mixing of foreign and inherited nouns, and in many cases loanwords have assimilated into Aramaic patterns and as such are indistinguishable from inherited Aramaic vocabulary, e.g., in the CāCa pattern, the loanwords *gāla* 'kilim' and *tāxa* 'quarter of village' are no different in form from the inherited Aramaic *qāla* 'voice' and *qāša* 'priest'. The most frequently attested patterns in the speech of Shabbo are CvCa and CvCCa.

Nouns and adjectives are presented below according to their synchronic patterns. When a singular form happens to be unattested in the corpus (and its plural form is attested) and, based on other *lishana deni* dialects, the singular form seems certain, the singular noun is listed with an asterisk. When one cannot be certain about the singular, however, the word is not included below, e.g., *dədwe* 'flies', which has attested singular forms in NENA of *dɩdwa* or *dɩdūṭa* (Sabar 2002a:138); similarly, *bāqe* 'mosquitoes', which shows up in NENA dialects as *bāqa* (Sabar 2002a:104) and *baqta* (Mutzafi 2008a:337).

4.2.6. Noun and Adjective Patterns

4.2.6.1. Monosyllabic[63]

CV

	Ca	*xa* 'one'
	Cā	*gā* 'time'

CCV

	CCe	*tre* 'two'

CVC

	CaC	*bak* 'bey'
		xam 'care'
	CāC	*bāš* 'good'
		čāy 'tea'
		gār 'time'
		ḥāl 'situation'
		māl 'property'
		ṣāx 'healthy'
	CeC	*'el* 'family'
		kef 'joy' (also *kefa*)

---

[63] With the exception of *xa* 'one' and *tre* 'two', all monosyllabic nouns are loanwords.

		šex 'sheikh'
		ter 'sufficient'
	CiC	*din* 'religion, judgment'
		kis 'money bag' (cf. *kəsta*)
		pis 'filthy'
	CoC	*doṛ* 'generation'
		ẓoṛ 'force'
	CuC	*kur* 'blind'
	CūC	*ḥūt* 'large fish'
		rūt 'naked'
CCVC		
	CCāC	*flān* 'such and such' (also *flāna*)
		jwāb 'answer' (also *jə́wāb*)
CVCC		
	CaCC	*baḥs* 'report'
		baṇk 'bank'
		dard 'pain'
		farq 'difference'
		hatk 'disgrace'
		ḥaqq 'right'
		ḥarb 'war'
		narm 'soft'
		waxt 'time' (also *waxta*)
		žang 'rust'
	CəCC	*jəns* 'type'
	CuCC	*xuṛṭ* 'aggresive'

4.2.6.2. *Bisyllabic*

CVCV

CaCa	*bala* 'misfortune'
	šawa 'week'
CāCa	*ʾāġa* 'agha'
	ʾāla 'side'
	ʿāra 'shame'
	bāba 'father'
	bāla 'attention'
	dāda 'justice'
	dāna 'time'
	gāla 'kilim'
	*kāka 'tooth'
	kāpa 'shoulder'
	kāsa 'belly'
	māsa 'village'
	nāsa 'ear'
	nāša 'person'

	pāša 'pasha'
	qāla 'voice'
	*qāna 'horn'
	qāša 'priest'
	sāʿa 'hour'
	sāwa 'grandfather'
	tāxa 'quarter of town'
	tāza 'fresh'
	xāsa 'new'
	xāṣa back'
	yāla 'child'
CāCe	*gāre* 'roof'
CāCi	*kāni* 'spring'
	qāzi 'qadi'
	nāwí 'prophet'
	wāli 'vali' (also *walya*)
CāCu	*ṭāpu* 'title deed'
CeCa	*ʾeda* 'holiday'
	ʾena 'eye, spring'
	ʾera 'penis'
	ʿeba 'disgrace'
	besa 'house'
	dena 'debt'
	feka 'fruit'
	geba 'side'
	gera 'threshing'
	jeba 'pocket'
	jeza 'penalty' (also *jezá*)
	kefa 'joy' (also *kef*)
	kepa 'stone'
	qeṭa 'summer'
	ṛeṃa 'pus'
	reqa 'distance' (also *rəqqa*)
	reša 'head'
	sepa 'sword'
	tena 'fig'
	ṭera 'fowl'
CeCe	*lele* 'night'
CeCi	*čeri* 'autumn'
CəCa	*kəra* 'rent'
CiCa	*ʾida* 'hand'
	lira 'lira'
	misa 'dead'
	nixa 'deceased'
	piča 'small quantity'
	qida 'burnt'

tiqa 'old'
ṣiwa 'wood'
ṭima 'price'
ṭina 'mud'
wiza 'visa'

CiCi *hivi, hiwi* 'hope'
CiCo *kilo* 'kilo'
CoCa *'oḍa* 'room'
čo'a 'smooth'
gora 'man'
gova 'stall'
*goza 'walnut'
koma 'black'
mosa 'death'
moxa 'brain'
poxa 'wind'
qoma 'stature'
qora 'grave'
ṣopa 'stove'
tola 'revenge'
tora 'ox'
xora 'friend'
yoma 'day'
zo'a 'pair'

CöCa *lö'a* 'jaw'
šö'a 'seven'
zöra 'small'

CoCi *ṣofi* 'sufi'
CöCi *šö'i* 'seventy'
CuCa *qura* 'boy'
CūCa *čūka* 'bird'
dūka 'place' (also *duksa*)
dūma 'tail'
dūra 'durra'
dūša 'honey'
gūba 'loom'
gūda 'wall'
nūra 'fire'
qūṭa 'vagina'
sūsa 'horse'
šūla 'work'
šūqa 'market'
ṭūra 'mountain'
tūsa 'mulberry tree'

CūCi *tūsi* 'type of thorn'

CCVCV

    CCāCa   *flāna* 'such and such' (also *flān*)
                   gdāda 'thread'
                   qdāla 'neck'
                   šwāna 'shepherd'
                   xmāra 'ass, donkey'
                   *xwāra 'white'
                   zyāṛa 'visit to a shrine'
    CCāCi   *ṭmāni* 'eighty'
                   ṭlāsi 'thirty'
    CCeCa   *ṣfera* 'whistle'
    CCiCa   *'jiza* 'tired, weary'
                   nqiṣa 'lacking'
                   pṭixa 'wide'
                   qdila 'key'
                   rwixa 'wide'
                   skina 'knife' (also *səkkina*)
                   sniqa 'needy'
                   spiqa 'empty'
                   spisa 'rotten'
                   *sqila 'beautiful'
                   *swi'a 'satiated'
                   xlima 'thick'
    CCoCa   *brona*
                   ṭrosa 'truth'
    CCūCa   *xlūla* 'wedding feast' (also *xulūla*)

CVCCV

    CaCCa   *abla* 'older sister'
                   'alla 'God'
                   'alpa 'thousand'
                   'amra 'wool'
                   'aqla 'foot' (also *'aqalta*)
                   'ar'a 'earth'
                   'arba 'four'
                   'abba 'inner pocket of garment'
                   bamba 'bomb'
                   *baqqa 'frog'
                   baxta 'woman'
                   čamča 'spoon'
                   dahba 'animal'
                   darga 'gate'
                   dawla 'state'
                   daxla 'crop'
                   falda 'strip of meat placed in cholent'
                   garma 'bone'
                   ḥafla 'party'

kalba 'dog'
kar'a 'butter'
kavra 'cliff'
ḷappa 'lump'
lašša 'body, corpse'
laxma 'bread'
malla 'mullah'
naqda 'bride price'
naqla 'time'
palga 'half'
paq'a 'crack'
*paḷḷa 'live coal'
qahwa 'coffee'
qaḥba 'whore'
qalya 'fried and heavily salted meat'
qaṣra 'mansion'
qatxa 'cup'
qaṭra 'boulder'
ṣadra 'chest'
šafqa 'hat (with a brim)'
šalla 'pants'
*šaqfa 'piece'
šaqqa 'half, section'
šar'a 'religious law'
talga 'snow'
talma 'water-jug'
tar'a 'door'
ṭarka 'stick'
ṭarma 'corpse'
walya 'vali' (also *wāli*)
waxta 'time' (also *waxt*)
xabra 'thing, word'
xalwa 'milk'
xamša 'five'
yarxa 'month'
zanqa 'chin'

CaCCe   *čappe* 'left'
         ṛaṣṭe 'right'
CaCCi   *'arbi* 'forty'
         'aṣli 'genuine'
         ḥajji 'pilgrim'
         xamši 'fifty'
         xanči 'some, a few'
CeCCa   *kelka* 'stone wall'
         *teška 'whelp'

CəCCa[64]   ʾəčʾa 'nine'
            ʾəmma 'hundred'
            ʾəpra 'earth, soil'
            ʾəqra 'bottom'
            ʾərba 'sheep'
            ʾəspa 'loan'
            ʾəṣra 'ten'
            ʾəšta 'six'
            ʾəzla 'yarn'
            ʾəzza 'goat'
            bəčʾa 'bastard'
            bərqa 'lightning'
            *bəṣla 'onion'
            bəxya 'crying'
            bəzza 'wretched person'
            čəpka 'drop'
            dəbba 'bear'
            dəmma 'blood'
            dənga 'punch'
            dəpna 'side'
            dəqna 'beard'
            gəlda 'skin'
            gəlla 'grass'
            gəšṛa 'bridge'
            gəxka 'laughter'
            gəzra 'pile of chopped wood'
            kəpna 'hunger'
            kərma 'worm'
            kərya 'short'
            ləbba 'heart'
            məšxa 'liquid butter'
            nəqwa 'female'
            *nəžda 'gang'
            pəmma 'mouth' (also pumma)
            pəsra 'meat'
            qəbla 'qiblah'
            qəṭʾa 'piece'
            qəṭla 'killing'
            qəṭma 'ashes'
            rəqqa 'distance' (also reqa)
            ṛəzza 'rice'
            səswa 'winter'

---

[64] See also nouns in which ə > e before ʾ and h (§ 3.11.a): inherited Aramaic words include dehna 'fat', dehwa 'gold', nehra 'river', seʾra 'goat hair', and ṭeʾna 'load'; loanwords include behna 'moment' and pehna 'kick'.

ṣəḥya 'thirsty'
šəmma 'name'
šəmša 'sun'
šərma 'buttocks'
šərṭa 'policeman'
šətya 'warp'
šəxda 'good tidings'
šəxta 'dirt'
təqla 'weight'
*xəlya 'sweet'
xətna 'bridegroom'
xəṭṭa 'a grain of wheat'
xəška 'darkness'
xəzma 'in-law'
yəmma 'mother'
zəbla 'garbage'

CiCCa	giska 'young goat'
	xiṭka 'bar indicating military rank on a uniform'
CəCCa	qəwya 'strong'
	ṣəwya 'dyed'
CəCCe	ʾərxe 'mill'
	bənhe 'morning
CəCCi	ʾəsri 'twenty'
	ʾəšti 'sixty'
	məndi 'thing'
CoCCa	kolka 'hovel'
	poṣta 'post'
CoCCi	ʾordi 'army'
CuCCa	ʾurxa 'road'
	ʾurwa 'big'
	ʾušya 'cluster (of grapes)'
	julla 'article of clothing'
	kutka 'knee'
	kutwa 'thorn'
	pumma 'mouth' (also pəmma)
	qurwa 'vicinity'
	ṣudra 'shirt'
	ṣurta 'face'
	tuxma 'type, kind'
	xulma 'dream'
	xumma 'heat'
	xurga 'step-son'
	xuṭba 'Muslim Friday sermon'
	xuṭṭa 'stick'
	xuwwa 'snake'

	CuCCe	*dugle* 'lie(s)' *dunye* 'world'
	CuCCi	*kursi* 'chair'
CCVCCV		
	CCaCCa	*tmanya* 'eight'
CVCVC		
	CaCaC	*bahar* 'spring season' *falaq* 'bastinado' *jalab* 'herd' *qačax* 'smuggled goods' *ṭaraf* 'side'
	CaCāC	*'alắy* 'military regiment' **'aqār* 'immovable property' *garắč* 'garage' *ḥarắm* 'forbidden' (also *ḥarāma*) *madắm* 'Madam'
	CaCəC	*'aṣəl* '(good) origin' *maləḳ* 'chieftain' *qaṭəl* 'killing'
	CaCiC	*faqír* 'poor' *kafil* 'guarantor' (also *kafíl*) *wakil* 'agent'
	CāCaC	*šākar* 'sugar'
	CāCāC	*ḥāxắm* 'rabbi'
	CāCəC	*čāwəš* 'sergeant' *ḥākəm* 'judge' *kāfər* 'heretic' *kātəb* 'secretary' *lāzəm* 'necessary' *xānəm* 'Madam' *xāṭər* 'sake'
	CāCiC	*tārix* 'date of event' (also *ṭārix*)
	CāCuC	*nāmus* 'proper behavior' *qānun* 'law' *qāṣud* 'messenger' *ṣābun* 'soap' *tābur* 'battalion'
	CeCaC	**ḥewan* 'animal' *jemaʿ* 'mosque'
	CeCəC	*'eġəl* 'the Golden Calf' *metər* 'meter'
	CeCiC	*nečir* 'hunting'
	CəCāC	*'ənād* 'mutual resistance' *jəwāb* 'answer' (also *jwāb*)
	CəCəC	*'əmər* 'order'
	CəCuC	*ḥəzur* 'estimation' (also *ḥə́zura*)

	CiCaC	*dinar* 'dinar'
	CiCāC	**jirān* 'neighbor'
	CoCaC	*šoḥad* 'bribe'
	CoCoC	*domóz* 'pig'
	CoCūC	*qorúš* 'piaster, small coin'
	CuCiC	*guník* 'gunny sack'
	CuCuC	*ḥudud* 'border'
		ḥukum 'government'
		quṣur 'defect'
	CūCaC	*ṛūbar* 'stream'
CVCCVC		
	CaCCaC	*ʾawwal* 'first'
		ʿaskar 'army'
		baḥḥar 'sea'
		baxxat 'mercy'
		*darham 'dirham'
		kallax 'corpse'
		naxwaš 'ill'
		xanjar 'dagger' (also *xanjāra*)
	CaCCāC	*qapṭán* 'captain'
	CaCCeC	*darwéž* 'dervish'
	CaCCəC	*sayyəd* 'descendant of Muḥammad'
		(also *sayyəda, sayyədka*)
	CaCCiC	*ʿanjil* 'Gospels'
		qaddiš 'memorial prayer'
		tagbir 'counsel'
	CaCCuC	*mažbur* 'forced'
		sartuk 'cream'
	CaCCūC	*maʿmúṛ* 'officer-in-charge'
	CəCCaC	*təmmal* 'yesterday'
	CəCCaC	*həšyar* 'careful'
		təffaq 'rifle'
	CəCCāC	*ʾəštár* 'document'
		wəždān 'conscience'
	CəCCəC	*dəžmən* 'enemy'
	CəCCuC	*təttun* 'tobacco'
	CoCCoC	*doktor* 'doctor'
	CuCCaC	*muxtar* 'mukhtar'
	CuCCāC	*muḥtāj* 'in need'
		qurʿān 'Quran'
	CuCCəC	*gumrək* 'customs'
	CuCCuC	*qunṣul* 'consul'
CVCCVCC		
	CəCCaCC	*kərmanj* 'Kurd, peasant'
CCVCCVC		
	CCaCCeC	*ṭṛambel* 'automobile'

4.2.6.3. *Bisyllabic with Feminine Ending*

CVCV

	CāCa	*pāsa* 'face'
		šāta 'year'
		xāsa 'sister'
	CeCa	*xeta* 'other'

CCVCV

	CCāCa	*brāta* 'daughter'
		xmāsa 'mother-in-law'
	CCiCa	*ksisa* 'hat' (also *kusisa*)
	CCeCa	*ksesa* 'hen'
	CCoCa	*ṣlosa* 'prayer'

CVCCV

	CaCCa	*'amta* 'maternal aunt'
		dašta 'field'[65]
		ṛapsa 'big, large'
		karta 'load'
		masta 'yoghurt'[66]
		qarsa 'cold'
		šapsa Sabbath'
		xalta 'maternal aunt'
		xasta 'new'
	CəCCa[67]	*kəsta* 'small bag'
		nəxta 'deceased'
		qədta 'burnt'
		səksa 'peg'
		šənsa 'sleep'
		səpsa 'lip, edge'
		təksa 'waistband'
		təqta 'old'
	CeCCa[68]	*desta* 'portion of food'
	CuCCa	*duksa* 'place' (also *dūka*)
		gupta 'cheese'
		kumta 'black'
		ruxta 'wide'
	CüCCa	*zürta* 'small'

CCVCCV

	CCaCCa	*škafta* 'cave'
		swa'ta 'satiety'
		žwanta 'expecting'

---

[65] *t* of the original Kurdish word has been reinterpreted as the feminine marker.
[66] Ibid.
[67] Also *de'sa* 'sweat' in which *ə* > *e* before ' and h (§ 3.11.a).
[68] See above n. 64.

CCəCCa[69]   *knəšta* 'synagogue'
              jmətta 'frozen'
              sməxta 'pregnant'
              sqəlta 'beautiful'

4.2.6.4. *Trisyllabic*

CVCVCV

CaCaCe	*masale* 'matter'	
CaCāCa	**baṛāna* 'ram'	
	baṛāxa 'blessing'	
	baṛāza 'pig'	
	dabāḥa 'ritual slaughterer'	
	dawāra 'riding animal'	
	ganāwa 'thief'	
	hayāma 'period of time'	
	ḥalāla 'kosher'	
	ḥarāma 'forbidden' (also *ḥarăm*)	
	našāma 'soul'	
	nawāga 'grandson'	
	qačāxa 'smuggler'	
	qalāma 'pen'	
	rakāwa 'rider'	
	sahāda 'witness'	
	ṣawā'a 'dyer'	
	šahāra 'blind'	
	*ṭabāqa 'story, floor'	
	warāqa 'paper'	
CaCāCe	*ṭalāqe* 'divorce'	
CaCāCi	*rašādi* 'gold lira'	
CaCeCa	*gazeṛa* '(evil) decree'	
	ṭarefa 'non-kosher meat'	
CaCiCa	*'amita* 'civilian police'	
	'aqida '(military) leader'	
	'aziza 'beloved'	
	basima 'pleasing'	
	gamiya 'ship'	
	daqiqa 'minute'	
	naxira 'nose'	
	šamina 'fat'	
	*qarira 'cold'	
	qaṭi'a 'stick'	
	xazina 'treasure, safe'	
	yarixa 'long'	

---

[69] Also *mre'ta* 'hurting', *zde'sa* 'fear' (ə > e /_ '; § 3.11.a).

	zaviya 'field'
CaCoCa	**ḥakoma* 'ruler'
	*kapora 'faithless, cruel'
	naqoṣa 'minus, less'
	qaṭola 'killer'
	ṭahora 'clean, pure'
CaCöCa	**sapöxa* 'wrap sandwich'
CaCoCe	*qadome* 'tomorrow'
CaCūCa	**bahūra* 'bright'
	*garūsa 'large'
	qalūla 'quick, fast'
CāCəCa	*čádəra* 'tent'
CeCiCa	*setira* 'long three-shot rifle'
CəCāCa	*jəgāra* 'cigarette'
	məzāda 'auction'
CəCiCa	*nəzima* 'low, inferior'
	šərika '(business) partner'
CəCuCa	*ḥəzura* 'estimation' (also *ḥəzur*)
CiCaCa	*fišaka* 'bullet'
CiCāCa	*ʼilāha* 'God'
	ʼilāna 'tree'
	ʼixāla 'food'
	lišāna 'tongue'
CiCiCa	*riviya* 'fox'
CiCoCe	*čiroke* 'story'
CoCāCa	*gopāḷa* 'shepherd's stick' (also *gopaḷta*)
	kolāna 'alley'
CoCiCa	*qotiya* 'small box'
CuCāCa	*xulāma* 'servant'
CuCiCa	*guniya* 'bramble'
CuCūCa	*ḥukūma* 'government'
	xulūla 'wedding feast' (also *xlūla*)
CūCəCa	*tūkəla* 'piece of clothing'

CCVCVCCV

CCaCəCCa	*sparəgla* 'quince'

CVCCVCV

CaCCaCa	*kaččala* 'bald'
CaCCāCa	*barwāra* 'shortcut route'
	kappāṛa 'expiation'
	*šaqqāma 'slap on face'
	šarwāla 'trousers'
	ṭayyāra 'airplane'
	xanjāra 'dagger' (also *xanjar*)
CaCCāCe	*panjāre* 'window'
CaCCiCa	*sayyəda* 'sayyid, descendant of Muḥammad' (also *sayyəd, sayyədka*)

	CaCCūCa	*pappūka* 'pitiful'
		payṭūna 'carriage'
	CəCCāCa	*'ərbāla* 'coarse sieve'
		*bəzmāra '(metal) nail'
		dərmāna 'medicine'
		kəndāla 'steep slope'
		səjjāda 'prayer rug'
		təjjāra 'merchant'
		xəyyāra 'cucumber'
	CəCCāCi	*'əmbāši* 'corporal'
	CəCCeCa	*səmbela* 'mustache'
	CəCCiCa	*səkkina* (also *skina*)
	CəCCoCa	*šəryoxa* 'shoe-string'
		šəxxoṛa 'coal'
	CəCCūCa	*bənjūka* 'bead to avert the evil eye'
	CoCCiCe	*qolčiye* 'custom-house guards'
	CuCCāCa	*dukkāna* 'shop'
	CuCCiCa	*šuftiya* 'watermelon'
CVCVCCV		
	CaCaCCa	*dabanja* 'pistol'
		kalamča 'handcuff'
	CaCuCCa	*'aqubra* 'mouse'
CVCCVCCV		
	CaCCaCCi	*'affandi* 'effendi'
	CaCCəCCa	*jandərma* 'gendarme'
	CuCCuCCa	*qunṣulya* 'consulate'
CVCVCVC		
	CaCaCoC	*qaraqól* 'garrison'
	CaCaCiC	*'araqin* 'arrack'
	CaCiCaC	*'aširat* 'tribe, clan'
	CeCaCoC	*télafon* 'telephone' (also *télefon*)
	CeCeCoC	*télefon* 'telephone' (also *télafon*)
CVCCVCVC		
	CaCCaCoC	*paṇqáṇoṭ* 'lira, paper money'
	CaCCeCəC	*'abresəm* 'silk'
	CeCCəCaC	*ṭélgəraf* 'telegraph'
		ṭélgəram 'telegram'
CVCVCCVC		
	CeCəCCaC	*gehənnam* 'hell'
CVCCVCVCC		
	CaCCaCoCC	*páṣṣapoṛṭ* 'passport'

4.2.6.5. *Trisyllabic with Feminine Ending*

CVCVCV

	CaCiCa	*maxisa* 'blow'
		šaqisa '(water) channel'
	CāCəCa	*ʿādəta* 'custom'
	CəCiCa	*ʾəlisa* 'fat tail'
	CəCoCa	*ʾərota* 'Friday'
	CuCiCa	*kusisa* 'hat' (also *ksisa*)

CCVCVCV

| | CCāCəCa | *qyāməta* 'resurrection' |

CVCVCCV

	CaCaCCa[70]	*ḥalalta* 'kosher'
		ḥaramta 'forbiddden'
		nawagta 'granddaughter'
		*ṣaʿarta 'grain of barley'
		šaharta 'blind'
	CaCəCCa[71]	*ʾarməlsa* 'widow'
		basəmta 'pleasing'
		kawənta 'mule' (also *kawdənta*)
		maxəlta 'fine sieve'
		naqətta 'thin'
		qarətta 'cold'
		rakəxta 'soft'
		šaxənta 'warm'
		ṭanəšta 'side'
		yarəxta 'long'
	CaCuCCa[72]	*xanuqta* 'throat'
		yatumta 'orphan'
	CāCəCCa	*ʿāṣərta* 'evening'
	CeCaCCa	*pelafta* 'shoe'
	CəCCəCa	*ʾəmməta* 'nation'
		məlkəta 'property'
		məlləta 'ethnic group'
	CuCCəCa	*qudrəta* '(Divine) omnipotence'

CVCCVCCV

| | CaCCaCCa | *ṭarrašta* 'thicket' |
| | CaCCəCCa | *kawdənta* 'mule' (also *kawənta*) |

---

[70] *ʾaqalta* 'foot' < **ʾaqlta* (§ 3.22.b).
[71] *kaləpsa* 'bitch' < **kalbta* and *tawərta* 'cow' < **tawrta* (§ 3.22.b).
[72] **baluʾta* > *baloʾta* 'throat' and **ṣabuʾta* > *ṣaboʾta* 'finger' (§ 3.11.b).

4.2.6.6. *Quadrisyllabic*

CVCVCVCV

	CaCaCāCi	*jamadāni* 'keffiya'
	CaCaCiCa	*'amaliya* '(medical) operation'
		balamina 'iron pole for making holes to insert dynamite' (pl. *balamine*)
	CaCaCūCa	*maḥafūza* 'guarding' (also *muḥáfəza*)
	CuCāCəCa	*muḥáfəza* 'guarding' (also *maḥafūza*)
	CuCuCiCa	*ḥukumiya* 'government'

CVCCVCVCV

	CəCCaCiCa	*bəndaqiya* 'rifle'

CVCVCCVCV

	CaCaCCiCa	*qarantina* 'quarantine'

CVCVCVCVC

	CiCoCeCəC	*kilometər* 'kilometer'

CVCCVCVCVC

	CaCCiCeCəR	*sántimetər* 'centimeter'

4.2.6.7. *Quadrisyllabic with Feminine Ending*

CVCCVCVCV

	CaCCaCiCa	*ḥambaqisa* 'dense smoke'

4.2.7. *Diachronic Overview of Patterns*

Some of the JChalla nouns that are inherited from older Aramaic are presented below according to reconstructed original Aramaic patterns in order to show, on the one hand, the JChalla forms that are linear descendants of older Aramaic patterns,[73] and on the other, how far other forms have diverged and cannot be derived from the reconstructed general Aramaic patterns. The latter group of forms are the result of internal developments such as analogy or sound change, which took place during the Proto-NENA period or even earlier. In some cases the reconstructed form may be reconstructed differently. When it is difficult to reconstruct the original vowel of the noun because of the different realizations in the various Aramaic dialects, *v* is used to designate the uncertain vowel.

---

[73] These are not reconstructed Proto-Semitic patterns. Were these Proto-Semitic reconstructions, *'əpra* and *xətna*, e.g., would be assigned to *qatal and not to *qatl.

*qal	ʾida, dəmma, xa
*qalt	šāta
*qilat	ʾəmma, šənsa
*q(v)l	bər, šəmma
*q(v)lat	brāta
*qāl	qāla, sāwa
*qīl	ṣiwa, ṭina
*qīlat	kəsta
*qūl	nūra, šūqa, ṭūra
*qall	ʾuṛwa, geba, *kāka, qāša
*qallat	qarsa, ṛapsa
*qill	gəlla, ləbba, yəmma
*qillat	səksa, təksa
*qull	dūka, gūba, gūda, moxa, xumma
*qullat	duksa
*qvll	bəzza, dəbba
*qatl (including II-w/y)	ʾalpa, ʾamra, ʾaqla, ʾarʾa, ʾeda, ʾena, ʾəpra, besa, darga, garma, gora, kalba, kāpa, karʾa, kāsa, kepa, kəpna, laxma, loʾa, mosa, palga, poxa, *qāna, qoma, qora, sepa, talga, talma, tarʾa, tora, xalwa, xāṣa, xətna, xora, yoma, yarxa
*qitl	ʾəčʾa, ʾərba, ʾəspa, ʾəšta, ʾəzla, ʾəzza, gəlda, gəšṛa, məšxa, pəsra, qəṭma, reša, šəmša, šətya, təqla, xəška, xulma
*qutl	ʾurxa, dugle, nāsa, qurwa, ṛəqqa, reqa, šərma, šəxda, xuṭṭa
*qvtl	ʾərxe, ʾəṣra, dəpna, dūša, gəzra, qəṭla, səswa, šawa, šöʾa
*qatlat	ʾaqalta, kaləpsa, tawərta
*qatilat	knəšta
*qatāl	qdāla
*qatīl (including II-w/y and III-y)	kərya, misa, naxira, nixa, qida, rwixa, sniqa, šəmya, xəzya, xlima
*qatīlat	ʾəlisa, nəxta, qədta, ruxta, sməxta, xzeta
*qitāl	xmāra
*qutāl	nāša, zöra
*qutālat	zürta
*qvtāl	gdāda
*qātvl	*kapora, qaṭola
*qattāl	ganāwa, rakāwa, sahāda, ṣawāʾa, šahāra
*qattalat	šapsa
*qittal	xuwwa
*qittāl	ʾəqra, dāna, lišāna, *xwāra

*qattīl	basima, *qarira, šamina, skina,
	səkkina, tiqa, yarixa
*qattīlat	basəmta, naqətta, qarətta, rakəxta,
	šaxənta, yarəxta
*qattūl	*bahūra
*quttāl	koma
*quttālat	kumta
*qalqal	lele

The best-attested inherited Aramaic pattern is *qatl followed by *qitl.
Analogical developments and sound changes have severed many nouns
from their original patterns. See, e.g., the JChalla nouns that in older Aramaic belonged to *qal and *qittāl, and which show different synchronic
realizations, all of which are far removed from the Proto-Aramaic and
even Classical Aramaic patterns. Original gemination is generally lost,
e.g., in the *qattāl and *qattīl patterns, though in *qvll nouns the gemination is sometimes preserved (*qill: gəlla, ləbba, yəmma), yet other times
replaced by compensatory lengthening (*qull: dūka, gūba, gūda, but not
so with xumma). The process of compensatory lengthening (§ 3.20.c) is
alive in JChalla as attested by the pair of forms rəqqa, reqa. Secondary
gemination is attested in some JChalla nouns (§ 3.20.e).

4.2.8. Prefixes

a. The classical Aram prefix mv- is no longer productive and is attested
only on inherited Aramaic words, e.g., momāsa 'oath', and on loanwords
such as

ma'qūle	'nobles'
máfəra	'escape, opportunity'
máḥkama	'court'
mamnún	'grateful'
marḥāma	'mercy'
məṣwá	'religious duty'
məšpāḥa	'family'

b. The Kurdish proclitic preposition be- 'without' is attested with non-
native words:

be-'áṣəl	'bad origin'
be-čára	'helpless'
be-dáda	'without justice'
be-dín	'religionless'
be-dárd	'painlessly'

be-hívi   'hopeless'
be-nā́mus   'improper behavior'

4.2.9. Suffixes

4.2.9.1. -āya, -esa, -āye

a. The reflexes of the ClAram gentilic suffixes are productive in JChalla (m.s. *-āya*, f.s. *-esa*, pl. *-āye*). They are found on the inherited Aramaic adjectives

> *qamāya*   'previous'
> *šulxāya*   'naked' (pl. *šulxāye*)
> *xəpyāya*   'barefoot'

b. The suffix-*āye* also appears on two adverbs of Aramaic origin:

> *qamāye*   'at first'
> *xarāye*   'finally'

c. The suffixes occur on the inherited Aramaic nouns:

> *hudāya, hudesa, hudāye*   'Jew(s)'
> *nexṛāya*   'foreigner'
> *surāya, suresa, surāye*   'Christian(s)'

d. The pl. suffix is found on the following loanwords,[74] whose singular forms are not attested in the corpus:

> *ʿarabāye*   'Arabs'
> *qaṛacāye*   'gypsies, highway robbers'

e. The feminine singular form is attested on the adjective *drangesa* 'late' (m.s. **drangāya*).

f. The gentilic suffixes are well attested on place names:

> *barzanāya*   'resident of Barzan'
> *goranāye*   'residents of Gorani'
> *karāye*   'residents of Kara'
> *muṣlāya*   'resident of Mosul'

---

[74] Mutzafi 2008a:96 notes in JBetan a group of nouns denoting titles that take this plural suffix (*mallāye, ʾāġāye, pāšāye, kohanāye, lewāye*). In § 4.2.3.1.d it has been suggested analyzing two of these nouns in JChalla, *ʾāġāye* and *mallāye* as the singular base (*ʾāġa, malla*) + glide *y* + plural *-e*, though it is also possible to include them in a subgroup of titles or professions, as does Mutzafi, in which case JChalla also exhibits *ḥajjāye* (§ 4.2.3.10.b), *qaṛačāye*, and *šexāye* (§ 4.2.3.10.a).

nerwāya, nerwesa, nerwāye	'resident(s) of Nerwa'
paləstināye	'Palestinians'
pənčāya, pənčāye	'resident(s) of Pinianish'
qurdāya, qurdesa, qurdāye	'Kurd(s)'
rekanāya, rekanāye	'resident(s) of Rekan'
ṭəyarāye	'residents of Tiari'
türkāya, türkāye	'Turk(s)'
wānesa	'resident of Van'

4.2.9.2. -nāya, -nesa, -nāye

There is also a series of gentilic suffixes beginning with *n-*:[75] m.s. -*nāya*, f.s. -*nesa*, pl. -*nāye*. Attested forms include:

ʾanglisnāya, ʾənglisnāya	'Englishman'[76]
ʾaṭrušnesa	'resident of Atrush'
ʾuramarnāya	'resident of Uramar'
ʿamənnāye (§ 3.6.b)	'residents of Amidya'
ʿeraqnāya, ʿeraqnāye	'Iraqi(s)'
baġdannesa (§ 3.6.b)	'resident of Baghdad'
baškalnāye[77]	'residents of Bashkala'
čalnāya	'resident of Challa'
hekkarnāya	'resident of Hakkari'
kurdināya, kurdināye	'Kurdistani Jew(s)'
maroknāya, maroknesa, maroknāye	'Moroccan(s)'
parsnāye	'Persians'
spindarnāya, spindarnāye	'resident(s) of Spindar'
ṭəyarnāya	'resident of Tiari'
zaxonāya	'resident of Zakho'
zebarnāya, zebarnāye	'resident(s) of Zebar'

4.2.9.3. -ūsa, -atūsa

a. The ClAram abstract suffix -*ūṯā* > -*ūsa* is productive. It occurs widely on inherited Aramaic words as well as loanwords, and almost all of them express abstract concepts:

---

[75] The insertion of *n* in gentilics of locations is attested already in Syriac. The increased usage attested in JChalla (and elsewhere in NENA) may lie in the metanalysis of certain place names (e.g., Barzan, Rekan, Wan) that end in *n* (*barza* + *nāya*, *reka* + *nāye*, *wā* + *nesa*). The metanalysis may have been motivated in part by the existence of the inherited Aramaic suffixes -*ān*, -*āna*, -*āne*.

[76] Cf. the adjective *ʾanglizi* 'English'.

[77] Also realized as *ḅaškalnāye*. See § 3.5.b n. 17. The Jews from Bashkala referred to their city as *Bašqalán* (§ 5.1.7 n. 11).

ʿurṭūsa	'fart'
bahwarūsa	'faith'
bārawanūsa	'separation'
baxtūsa	'wifehood'
farqūsa	'distinction'
fasādūsa	'corruption'
ganawūsa	'thievery'
gorūsa	'manliness'
hawūsa	'favor'
ḥaramūsa	'prohibition'
nəxpūsa	'embarrassment'
qəwyūsa	'strength'
šaṛūsa	'lunch'
šidanūsa	'craziness'
waʿdūsa	'promise'
wājəbūsa	'obligation'
xədyūsa	'joy'
xorūsa	'friendship'
xurṭūsa	'force'
yārūsa	'camaraderie'

In the case of ʾaxūsa 'brotherhood' and naṣūsa 'fight' (pl. naṣwāsa), it is possible that the vowel -ū of what appears to be the abstract -ūsa suffix might actually be a reflex of w and an anaptyctic vowel (*ʾaxwsā > *ʾaxəwsa > ʾaxūsa; *naṣwsā > *naṣəwsa > naṣūsa; § 3.22.b).

b. -ūsa is attested sometimes on loanwords suffixed to -at (< the Kurdish abstract ending -ati):[78]

ʾāġātūsa	'masterdom'
jirānatūsa	'neighborliness'
pisyatūsa	'filthiness'

c. -atūsa is also attested on place names and expresses either the gentilic plural or the region including its inhabitants:[79]

hekkaratūsa	'residents/region of Hakkari'
karatūsa	'residents/region of Kara'
pənčatūsa	'residents/region of Pinianish'

d. In qurdawūsa 'Kurds' the suffix -ūsa seems to have been added with a glide to qurdā 'Kurd' (§§ 3.15.a; 3.16.c)

---

[78] MacKenzie 1981, 1:217; Blau & Barak 1999:110.

[79] There are traces of the use of this suffix to express plurality also in Qaraqosh. Khan (2002:180–181) cites xalyuṭa 'syrup of cooked dates', xwaruṭa 'dairy products', and yaltuṭa 'group of youths' as referring to tangible entities. For a recent treatment of the development from abstract > collective > plural, see Hasselbach 2007:130–131.

4.2.9.4. -ona, -one

The ClAram diminutive suffix -ōnā (< *-ānā) is attested only on the kinship terms

> 'axona   'brother' (pl. 'axawāsa)
> brona   'son' (pl. brone)

4.2.9.5. -unka, -unke

The diminutive -ūn[80] (< -on < *ān) is attested with the Kurdish diminutive suffix -k (§ 4.2.9.8) and the Aramaic ending -a on the noun yalunka 'child', and with the Aramaic ending -e on the plural yalunke.[81]

4.2.9.6. -āna, -anta, -āne

a. The suffix -āna is productive in JChalla and is attested suffixed to

1. verbs:

> mraḥmāna   'merciful' (mrāḥəm 'he may have mercy')

2. nouns and adjectives:

> 'əryāna   'rain' (Syr ܐܪܝܢ)
> *'uṛwāna   'leader' (pl. 'uṛwāne; 'uṛwa 'big')
> de'sāna   'sweaty' (de'sa 'sweat')
> denāna   'debtor' (dena 'debt')
> *milāna   'blue' (pl. milāne; Syr ܡܝܠܐ)
> ṛomāna   'high' (f. ṛomanta; pl. ṛomāne; ClAram רְמָא)
> šəxtāna   'dirty' (šəxta)
> šidāna   'crazy' (ClArm שֵׁדָא)
> *zad'əwāna   'fearful' (pl. zad'əwāne; *zado/u'a?)
> zodāna   'additional' (pl. zodāne; Ar زَوْد)

3. It occurs as part of the nouns məšəlmāna 'Muslim' (f. məšəlmanta; pl. məšəlmāne) and xəmyāna 'father-in-law'.

---

[80] Nöldeke 1868:107.
[81] For examples of additional nouns with the diminutive suffixes -unka, -unke in JBetan, see Mutzafi 2008a:109.

b. -ān is also found on inherited Aramaic nouns and on loanwords, e.g.,

'ərwāna	'kindness'
qorbāna	'sacrifice'
ramazán	'Ramadan'
yuqdāna	'conflagration'

4.2.9.7. -oya

A suffix -oya is found on the kinship terms

'amoya	'paternal uncle' (cf. 'amta 'paternal aunt')
xaloya	'maternal uncle' (cf. xalta 'maternal aunt')

The forms may have arisen from the vocative forms amo (Kurdish) and 'ammu / xālu (Iraqi Arabic) with the addition of a glide (w > y) and the suffix a.[82]

4.2.9.8. -k

The Kurdish suffixal element -k, which sometimes expresses the dimimutive and other times is a free variant,[83] is found on the following nouns:

1. with the singular ending -a:[84]

'aṭarka	'peddler'
qalunka	'narghile'
sayyədka	'sayyid, descendant of Muhammad' (also sayyəd, sayyəda)

and possibly also on xiṭka 'bar indicating military rank on a uniform', though the etymology of the noun is uncertain. See also yalunka 'child' (§ 4.2.9.5).

2. with the plural ending -e:

govke	'stalls'
pəšūke	'gnats'
qaṛačke	'gypsies'
qoruške	'piasters, small coins'

See also yalunke 'children' (§ 4.2.9.5).

---

[82] Rizgar 1993:22 and Woodhead & Beene 2003, 2:149, 324. Maclean 1895:231 lists both nouns under the agent noun pattern qātōl. On the glide see § 3.16.b.

[83] MacKenzie 1981, 1:217; Rizgar 1996:274; Blau & Barak 1999:110–111.

[84] Garbell 1965:48.

3. on hypocoristics followed by the vowels -o, -a, and -u (§ 4.2.9.11):

> 'Awṛahamko
> 'Azizko, 'Azizku
> Maḥmudko
> Mərko
> Mošāka, Moška
> Najəmko
> Noka
> Šambiko

4.2.9.9. -əski

This suffix, derived from the ClAram adverbial ending -ā'iṯ with the Kurdish suffix -ki,[85] is attested in the corpus once marking a language (see also § 4.2.9.10.c):

> qurdəski 'Kurdish (language)'

4.2.9.10. -i

a. The Kurdish suffix -i, which is used to form abstract nouns from adjectives,[86] is attested on the following loanwords:

> gərāni   'famine'
> kotakki   'hardship'
> tangāwi   'distress'

b. The Kurdish/Arabic suffix -i, which is used to form adjectives from nouns,[87] is attested on the following loanwords:

> 'anglizi 'English'[88]
> 'aṣli   '(good) origin'

c. The suffix -i marks languages (see also § 4.2.9.9):

> qurdi   'Kurdish (language)'
> türki   'Turkish (language)'

---

[85] See Mutzafi 2008a:110 for additional languages marked by the suffix.
[86] MacKenzie 1981, 1:217.
[87] MacKenzie 1981, 1:218.
[88] As in təffaq 'anglizi 'an English rifle'. Cf. the noun 'Englishman' with the Aramaic gentilic suffix: 'anglisnāya, 'ənglisnāya.

4.2.9.11. -li

The Turkish suffix -*li* indicating possession of a quality is attested on the loanword

ʾoṣmoḷḷi   'Ottoman' (§ 3.6.d)

4.2.10. Compound Nouns

a. Compounds formed with inherited Aramaic elements are

ʾarbamma < ʾarba + ʾəmma	'four hundred'
ʾarbaʾsar < ʾarba + *ʿəsar	'fourteen'
ʾarbūšeb < ʾarba + *b-šabba	'Wednesday'
ʾəčča'sar < ʾəčʿa + *ʿəsar	'nineteen'
ʾəšta'sar < ʾəšta + *ʿəsar	'sixteen'
baxbāba[89] < bax + bāba	'stepmother'
bomāxəd < b-ʾo + yōmā + xetā	'day after tomorrow'
gob'ena < go + be + ʿena?	'forehead'
palgədlel < *palgeh + d + lele	'midnight'
palgədyo < *palgeh + d + yomā	'noon'
pálpaṇqàṇoṭ < palg(a) + paṇqáṇoṭ	'half lira'
pálsāʿa < palg(a) + sāʿa	'half an hour'
šöʾamma < šöʿa + ʾəmma	'seven hundred'
tremma < tre + ʾəmma	'two hundred'
trūšeb < tre +*b-šabba	'Monday'
ṭlāhūšeb < ṭlāha + *b-šabba	'Tuesday'
xamšamma < xamša + ʾəmma	'five hundred'
xamūšeb < xamša + *b-šabba	'Thursday'
xošeba < *ḥaḏ + b-šabba	'Sunday' (§ 3.14)

b. Loans that are compounds in the donor languages include

ʾarzuḥál	'petition (also ʾarzūḥal)'
čaydanka	'teapot'
čayxāna	'tea house'
flānkas	'so and so'
gehənnam	'hell'
genʿedən	'Garden of Eden'
jəzdān	'purse'
marʿaz	'cloth made of fine goat-wool'
pəzaġāya (?)	'village noble'
qáymaqam	'local governor'
qólordi	'army corps'
séfarṭora	'Torah scroll'
səfərṭās	'lunch box'

---

[89] Realized as [ˌbʰɑɣˈbʰaːbʰa].

4.2.11. *Proper Names and Hyporcoristics*

a. The following are some of the proper names attested in the corpus.
Many of them contain the suffix -*o*, which is both a Kurdish and general
Semitic hypocoristic suffix.[90] A few names also contain the Kurdish
hypocoristic -*k* (§ 4.2.9.8).

> ʾAḥmado (Ar أَحْمَد)
> ʾĀko (H יַעֲקֹב)[91]
> ʾAwrāham, less frequently ʾAyrāham, ʾAwṛáw (H אַבְרָהָם)[92]
> ʾAwṛahamko (H אַבְרָהָם)
> ʾAzizko, ʾAzizku (K < Ar عَزِيز)
> ʾIsāxar (H יִשָּׂשׂכָר)
> ʿĀbo (H אַבְרָהָם) (§ 3.3.d)
> ʿAmmo (H עַמְרָם)
> Baṣāle (H בְּצַלְאֵל)
> Bənyāme (H בִּנְיָמִן)
> Faṭmāye (Ar فَاطِمَة)
> Fray (H אֶפְרַיִם)
> Hārun (H אַהֲרֹן)
> Hoče (H יְהוֹשֻׁעַ)[93]
> Home (H אַבְרָהָם)
> Ḥamo (K < Ar مُحَمَّد)
> Ḥayyo (H חַיִּים)
> Magaddi (H גְּדַלְיָהוּ)
> Maḥmudko (K < Ar مَحْمُود)
> Māno (H מְנַחֵם)
> Maṣlo (H מַצְלִיחַ)
> Mədo (H מָרְדְּכַי)
> Məxo, Məxwa (H מִיכָאֵל)
> Məṣṭo (K < Ar مُصْطَفَى)
> Miʾər, Mərko (H מֵאִיר)
> Mošāka, Moška (H מֹשֶׁה)
> Murdax (H מָרְדְּכַי)
> Najəmko (K < Ar نَجْم)
> Nəfto (H נַפְתָּלִי)
> Noka (H נוֹחַ)
> Nuwaḥ (H נוֹחַ)
> Pəto (H פִּנְחָס)

---

[90] On hypocoristics in general in Semitic languages, see Lidzbarksi 1898. On hypocoristics in Jewish NeoAram dialects see Sabar 1974, and on Christian NeoAram dialects
see Krotkoff 1982:115–116 and Odisho 1997.

[91] Cf. ʾĀqo (Sabar 1974:46).

[92] Cf. ʾAyrāham, ʾAyro, ʾAyyi (Sabar 1974:50). See also § 3.23.b.

[93] Cf. ʾŌče (Sabar 1974:46).

Qāle (H יְחֶקֵאל)[94]
Rašo (K < Ar رَشيد)
Sise (K Sisıne, H שׁוֹשַׁנָּה)
Šaʿya (H יְשַׁעְיָהוּ)
Šabbo (H שַׁבְּתָאי)
Šambi, Šambiko (K Šambo, H שַׁבְּתָאי)
Šəlo (H שְׁלֹמֹה)
Šino (H שֵׁם טוֹב)
Yosef (H יוֹסֵף)
Zāwo (H זְבֻלוּן, זְבוּלֻן)

b. Note also the following nouns, all attested also in Kurdish, which end
with the Kurdish vocative endings -o (masculine) and -e (feminine):

ʾamo	'Uncle!'
bābo	'Father!' (= 'By God!')
kəče	'Woman!'
māmo	'Uncle!'
quró	'Boy!'[95]

4.3. Numerals

4.3.1. *Cardinal Numbers 1–10*

xa, xaʾ	'one'
tre, treʾ, tərte	'two'
ṭlāha	'three'
ʾarba	'four'
xamša	'five'
ʾəšta	'six'
šöʾa	'seven'
tmanya	'eight'
ʾəčʾa	'nine'
ʾəṣra	'ten'

a. *xa* may function adverbially (§ 4.7.4) before a numeral with the meaning 'about, approximately,' e.g.,

xa ʾəṣra ʾalpe
'about ten thousand'

---

[94] Cf. Ḥasqo (Sabar 1974:50).
[95] The ultimate stress is unexpected on this Kurdish loanword (MacKenzie 1981,
1:156). See § 3.23.i.

bābəd xa ʾəṣra treʾsar yalúnke-le.
'He is the father of about ten, twelve children.'

b. On the multiplicative use of *xa*, see below § 4.3.7.

c. A pausal form *xaʾ* occurs with the meaning 'only one' (as in JBetan[96]):

ʾe dexun pášwāle xaʾ.
'That one of yours (house) remained the only one (still standing).'

d. 'One' has an originally feminine form, *xədda*, which functions as the indefinite pronoun 'someone' (§§ 3.20.e; 4.1.12.c)

e. The form *treʾ* occurs in pause, and like *xaʾ*, seems to have the meaning 'only two':

waḷḷa ʾe ᴴhavérᴴ u-nixəd bābi, treʾ, qəmlu zəllu.
'By God, that friend and my late father, only the two (of them), up (and) went.' (§ 5.6.17)

ʾá-ži kemər: hal treʾ!
'He also says: "Give (me) only two!"' (§ 5.10.4)

f. The old ClAram f. form *tərte* is attested only in pause in the recitation of the *haggada*:

karb xaʾ; ġazab tərte; ʾeqo ṭlāha[97]
'anger—one; rage—two; trouble—three'

ṭpārəd jəgra xaʾ; karb tərte; ġazab ṭlāha[98]
'burning of his wrath—one; rage—two; and trouble—three'

g. Cf. *šöʾa* 'seven' and *šawa* 'week,' both of which are reflexes of ClAram שבעא.

h. Indefinite pronouns may be formed from *kud* + number (+ pronominal suffix) (§ 4.1.12.g-i).

i. A cardinal number may form a clitic compound with a following noun, in which case the ultimate syllable of the cardinal number receives the stress,[99] e.g., *xamšá-yāle* 'five children,' *šöʾá-brone* 'seven sons.' Often,

---

[96] Mutzafi 2008a:114.
[97] Cf. כַּרְבָּא—כָא, וּגֵזֶב—תְּרֵי, וְאִיקוֹ טְלָאהָא (Avidani 1959:38) and גְדָאב כָא. וְגֻרָא תְּרֵי. וְאִיקוֹ טְלָאהָא, וְאַקָא טְלָהָא (Alfiye 1986:47).
[98] Cf. טְפָארֵית גֻּרֵי תְּרֵי. גְדָאב כָא. וְסַהְמָא טְלָאהָא (Avidani 1959:39) and גְּגֵר סַמְתֵּה—כָא, כַּרְבָּא—תְּרֵי, מַב—טְלָהָא (Alfiye 1986:47).
[99] See, e.g., Meehan & Alon 1979:177 n. 15; Mutzafi 2008a:114.

however, the number is not clitic, e.g., *tmanya baṛāne* 'eight rams'. Both accentual patterns are also attested for cardinal numbers above ten, e.g., *xamša'sár-metre* 'fifteen meters', *tmane'sar yome* 'eighteen days'.

4.3.2. Cardinal Numbers 11–20

xade'sar	'eleven'
tre'sar	'twelve'
tǝlta'sar	'thirteen'
'arba'sar	'fourteen'
xamša'sar	'fifteen'
'ǝšta'sar	'sixteen'
šwa'sar	'seventeen'
tmane'sar	'eighteen'
'ǝčča'sar	'nineteen'

4.3.3. Cardinal Numbers—Tens and Hundreds

'ǝsri	'twenty'
ṭlāsi	'thirty'
'arbi	'forty'
xamši	'fifty'
'ǝšti	'sixty'
šö'i	'seventy'
ṭmāni	'eighty'
'ǝmma	'hundred'
'ǝmmāhe	'hundreds'
tremma u-xamši	'two hundred and fifty'
'arbamma	'four hundred'
xamšamma	'five hundred'
šö'amma	'seven hundred'

The plural of *'ǝmma* 'one hundred' (e.g., *'ǝmma dūkāne* 'a hundred places') is *'ǝmmāhe* (§ 4.2.3.3):

kma 'ǝmmāhe šǝnne?
'How many hundreds of years?' (§ 5.13.4)

Above 'one hundred' the noun *'ǝmma* compounds with the numbers from 2–9 (§ 4.2.10) and takes the form *-mma*,[100] e.g.,

---

[100] See Steiner 1995 for evidence of the shortened form מה as attested in Hebrew *derashot* based on popular dialects of Late Aramaic.

tremma[101] *u-xamši kilo*
'two hundred and fifty kilos'

'an xamšamma bāte
'these five hundred houses' (§ 5.1.2)

There is an exception:

kalba bər šö'ammāhe kalbe!
'Son of seven hundred bitches!'

4.3.4. *Cardinal Numbers—Thousands and Above*

'alpa, 'alpe	'thousand, thousands'
'əsri u-tmanya 'alpe	'twenty-eight thousand'
məlyone	'millions'
'əšta məlyone	'six million'

4.3.5. *Ordinal Numbers*

The ordinals consist of a noun annexed to a cardinal number. The counted noun may be either a neo-construct form (e.g., *yom, naqəl*) or a form with the possessive-relative *-əd* (e.g., *yarxəd*):

yom 'awwal[102]	'the first day'	*náqəl-ži 'awwal*	'also the first time'
yom tre	'the second day'	*naqəl tré-ži*	'also the second time'
yom ṭlāha	'the third day'	*naqəl ṭlāha*	'the third time'
yom 'arba	'the fourth day'	*naqəl 'arba*	'the fourth' time'
yom xamša	'the fifth day'		
yom 'əšta	'the sixth day'		
yom šö'a	'seventh day'	*naqəl šö'a*	'seventh time'
yarxəd tre	'the second month'		
yarxəd 'arba	'the fourth month'		
yarxəd 'əšta	'the sixth month'		
yarxəd tmanya	'the eighth month'		
yarxəd xade'sar	'the eleventh month'		

---

[101] Rabbi Hashiloni reads תְּרֵי אִמָּא דַרבְּיֵי in the *haggada* (Avidani 1959:38) as *tre 'əmmāya darbiye* but later on in the same paragraph he reads תְּרֵי אִמָּא וְכַמְשִׁי דַרבְּיֵי (Avidani 1959:39) as *tre 'əmma u-xamši darbiye*. Cf. in the Zakho *haggada* (Alfiye 1986:47–49): תְּרַתְּאֱמָה וַחֲמִשֵׁי זַרְבְּתִיסָא and תַּרְתְּאֱמָה זַרְבְּתִיסָא.

[102] Also in the JNerwa texts (Sabar 1984:248). Cf. JBetan *qamāya* 'first' (Mutzafi 2008a:117). Forms of *'awwal* penetrated Aramaic already in the Middle Ages as attested in Palestinian Aramaic corpora (Samaritan Aramaic, Targum Pseudo-Jonathan, Targum Psalms, and Targum Job). See Weiss 1979:99.

4.3.6. *Fractions*

a. Attested fractions are

palga 'half'
rubaʿ 'quarter'

b. One finds *pal* (§ 3.19.a) and *palgəd* in the following compounds
(§ 4.2.10):

pálsāʿa	'half an hour'
pálpaṇqàṇoṭ	'half lira'
palgədlel	'midnight'
palgədyo	'noon'

c. The fossilized form *palge* (< *palgeh* 'half of him') follows a noun, e.g.,

sāʿa u-palge	'an hour and a half'
tre u-palge	'two and a half'
šắta-u-palge	'a year and a half'

4.3.7. *Multiplicatives*

xá-u-tre	'double'[103]
xá-u-ʾarba	'fourfold'
xá-u-šöʾa	'sevenfold'[104]

4.3.8. *Days of the Week*

xošeba	'Sunday'
trūšeb	'Monday'
ṭlāhūšeb	'Tuesday'
ʾarbūšeb	'Wednesday'
xamūšeb	'Thursday'
ʾərota	'Friday'
šapsa	'Saturday'

Note also *lel xošeba* 'Saturday evening'.

---

[103] 'Double' and 'fourfold' occur in Rabbi Shiloni's recitation of the *haggada*: *hawūsa xa b-tre xa ʾarba* (טוֹבָה כְּפוּלָה וּמְכֻפֶּלֶת). Cf. in the written *haggadot*: הַוֵּיסָא דְּאִפְתָא וּמוּדְאַפְתָּא (Avidani 1959:43) and הַוּוֹסָא דְּאִפְתָא וּמוּדְאַפְתָא (Alfiye 1986:53).

[104] Cf. the multiplicative use of *xa* + cardinal number in BiblAram (חַד שִׁבְעָה Dan 3:19).

4.3.9. *Other Expressions of Time*

šāta (pl. *šənne*)	'year'
šawa (pl. *šawe*)	'week'
yarxa (pl. *yarxe*)	'month'
sāʿa (pl. *sāʿe*)	'hour'
sāʿa tre	'two o'clock'
sāʿa ṭḷāha	'three o'clock'
sāʿa xamša	'five o'clock'
sāʿa ʾəč̣ʾa	'nine o'clock'
sāʿa ʾəṣra	'ten o'clock'
ʾəsri u-ʾarba sāʿe	'twenty-four hours'
rúbaʿ-sāʿa	'quarter of an hour'
pálsāʿa	'half an hour'
daqiqa (pl. *daqiqe*)	'minute'
tre'sar naqoṣ ʾəṣra, rubaʿ	11:50, 11:45 a.m./p.m.

4.4. VERBS

4.4.1. *Stems*

a. There are three productive stems (*binyanim*) in JChalla: G (*pəʿal*), D (*paʿʿel*), and C (< *ʾafʿel*), as well as a quadriliteral stem Q. The older Aramaic relationship between G and D (factitive), and G and C (causative) is still preserved in many verbs, e.g., G *qālu* 'it may be clean' vs. D *mqālu* 'he may clean', and G *qāṭəl* 'he may kill' and C *maqṭəl* 'he may have killed'. This inventory of stems is found in other *lishana deni* dialects[105] as well as in other Neo-Aramaic dialects.[106] It contrasts with several Trans-Zab dialects, where there is a binary opposition between two stems, one based on ClAram G, and the other an amalgamation of ClAram D and C.[107]

b. In JChalla there are a few verbs that may be reflexes of older t-stem forms in Aramaic:

---

[105] JAmid (Hoberman 1090:196–197), JBetan (Mutzafi 2008a:44–45), JDohok, JNerwa texts (Sabar 1984:241–242), JZakho (Sabar 2002a:48).
[106] See, e.g., Maclean 1895:90–105.
[107] See, e.g., Fox 1997:23; Khan 1999:89. The reflexes of the ClAram stems is a bit more complicated in JKoyS (Mutzafi 2004:75–77).

1. G *d'p* 'fold' (ܐܬܛܐܦ)[108]
2. G *txr* 'remember' (אתדכר)[109]
3. Q *šthr* 'go blind' (אשתהר)[110]
4. G *zd'* 'fear' (ܐܬܛܐܙܝ)[111]

c. Cf. the NeoAram dialects of Ṭuroyo and Mlaḥso, which preserve ClAram t-stems (Gt, Dt, and Ct [rare]), and NeoMand, which preserves the Gt and traces of the Dt.[112]

d. The *t* of the G verb *tfq* 'occur, happen' is a reflex of the geminated *t* of the Ar VIII stem form *'ittafaqa* (√وفق).

4.4.2. G Stem

	Subjunctive	Preterite
grš 'pull'		
1 m.s.	*gáršən(a)* 'I may pull'	*grešli* 'I pulled (him)'
1 f.s.	*gáršan(a)*	*grešli*
2 m.s.	*gáršət(ən)*	*grešlox*
2 f.s.	*gáršat(ən)*	*grešlax*
3 m.s.	*gāreš*	*grešle*
3 f.s.	*garša*	*grešla*
1 c.pl.	*gáršax(in)*	*gŕəšlan(a)*, *gŕəšleni*
2 c.pl.	*garšétun(a)*	*gŕəšlexun*
3 c.pl.	*garši*	*grešlu*

Infrequently also 1 m.s. *garšan* (§ 4.1.6.c).

Preterite with f. base (*griša*): *grišáli* 'I pulled her', *grišálox*, *grišálax*, *grišále*, *grišála*, *grišálan(a)*, *grišáleni*, *grišálexun*, *grišálu*

Preterite with pl. base (*griši*): *grišíli* 'I pulled them', *grišílox*, *grišílax*, *grišíle*, *grišíla*, *grišílan(a)*, *grišíleni*, *grišílexun*, *grišílu*

For the inflection of the Preterite with incorporated objects in the 1st and 2nd persons, see § 4.4.23.4.

---

[108] Mutzafi 2008a:343.
[109] Nöldeke 1968:194–195; Sabar 2002a:48; Mutzafi 2008a:390. Mutzafi points out, however, that it is possible that *t* is the result of partial assimilation to the contiguous *x* in G forms like **dxar* 'he remembered' > *txar* (see above § 3.2.d).
[110] Mutzafi 2008:387.
[111] Nöldeke 1868:195.
[112] Jastrow 1997:360.

Participle m.s. *griša*, f.s. *grəšta*, c.pl. *griše*
Imperative c.s. *groš*,[113] c.pl. *grošun*
Gerund *grāša*

4.4.3. *D and C Stems*

	D Stem *plṭ* 'take out'	C Stem *plx* 'employ'
Subjunctive		
1.m.s.	*mpalṭən* 'I may take out'	*mápləxən* 'I employ'
1 f.s.	*mpalṭan*	*mápləxan*
2 m.s.	*mpalṭət*	*mápləxət*
2 f.s.	*mpalṭat*	*mápləxat*
3 m.s.	*mpāləṭ*	*mapləx*
3 f.s.	*mpalṭa*	*mápləxa*
1 c.pl.	*mpalṭax*	*mápləxax*
2 c.pl.	*mpalṭetun*	*mapləxetun*
3 c.pl.	*mpalṭi*	*mápləxi*

Infrequently also 1 m.s. *mpalṭan* and *mápləxan* (§ 4.1.6.c).

Preterite		
1.s.	*mpoləṭli* 'I took out'	*mupləxli* 'I employed'
2 m.s.	*mpoləṭlox*	*mupləxlox*
2 f.s.	*mpoləṭlax*	*mupləxlax*
3 m.s.	*mpoləṭle*	*mupləxle*
3 f.s.	*mpoləṭla*	*mupləxla*
1 c.pl.	*mpoləṭlan, mpolə́ṭleni*	*mupləxlan, muplə́xleni*
2 c.pl.	*mpolə́ṭlexun*	*muplə́xlexun*
3 c.pl.	*mpoləṭlu*	*mupləxlu*

D Preterite with f. base (*mpulṭa*): *mpulṭāli* 'I took her out', *mpulṭālox*, *mpulṭālax*, *mpulṭāle*, *mpulṭāla*, *mpulṭālan*, *mpulṭā́leni*, *mpulṭálexun*, *mpulṭālu*

with pl. base (*mpulṭi*): *mpulṭili* 'I took them out', *mpulṭilox*, *mpulṭilax*, *mpulṭile*, *mpulṭila*, *mpulṭilan*, *mpulṭíleni*, *mpulṭílexun*, *mpulṭilu*

C Preterite with f. base: *mupləxāli* 'I employed her', *mupləxālox*, *mupləxālax*, *mupləxālan*, *mupləxáleni*, *mupləxálexun*, *mupləxālu*

---

[113] See also § 4.4.15.

with pl. base: *mupləxili* 'I employed them', *mupləxilox, mupləxilax, mup-ləxilan, mupləxíleni, mupləxílexun, mupləxilu*

Participle		
m.s.	*mpulṭa*	*múpləxa*
f.s.	*mpolaṭṭa*	*muplaxta*
c.pl.	*mpulṭe*	*múpləxe*

Imperative		
c.s.	*mpāləṭ*	*maplэx*
c.pl.	*mpalṭun*	*mápləxun*

Gerund	*mpaloṭe*	*maploxe*

The longer forms of the E-suffix pronouns (§ 4.1.6.a,f) are infrequent on D and C verbs, e.g., 1 m.s. *menxəna* 'I may look'.

The prefix *m-* in forms of the Subjunctive and Preterite of the D verbs is not always audible and often is clearly absent from Shabbo's speech. It would appear that *m-* has begun to disappear from the stem. This is well-attested, e.g., in the many attestations of *šdr* 'send', e.g., *(m)šodərre* 'he sent him', *(m)šadər* 'he may send', *(m)šādər* 'send!', *(m)šadore* 'sending'.

4.4.4. Q Stem

The attested Q verbs in Shabbo's speech,[114] many of which are loanwords, are *'rgn* 'organize', *ṣbn* 'irritate', *brbz* 'scatter, disperse', *bzbz* 'squander', *dmbk* 'pummel', *drmn* 'medicate', *gndr* 'roll down', *grgš* 'drag', *ġrgr* 'be hoarse', *ḥlḥl* 'peremeate', *hymn* 'believe', *krkm* 'make yellow', *lxlx* 'dirty', *nxnx* 'mumble threats', *pčkn* 'finish', *pnčr* 'cause a flat tire', *prns* 'manage', *prpr* 'writhe', *prpṭ* 'agonize', *pršq* 'stretch', *prtx* 'make change', *ptpt* 'shred', *qrpč* 'snatch', *ṣfṣf* 'utterly disregard', *šḥrr* 'free, release', *šthr* 'become blind' (§ 4.4.1.b), *tlfn* 'telephone', *wlwl* 'wail', *xṛxṛ* 'have pity'.

Subjunctive	3 m.s. *mbarbəz* 'he may scatter'
Preterite	3 m.s. *mburbəzle*
Imperative	m.s. *mbarzbəz*
Participle	*mbúrbəza, mburbazta, mbúrbəze*
Gerund	*mbarboze*

---

[114] On Q verbs in NeoAram, see Murad 1963; Sabar 1982.

There are examples of a longer E-suffix form on the Q verb *hymn*, e.g., *mhémnəna* 'I may believe'.

The prefix *m-* is often not audible or lacking, as in the D stem (§ 4.4.4), e.g.,

> *(m)walwole*   'wailing' (§ 5.7.9)
> *(m)dambəkle*   'he pummels him' (§ 5.6.4)

4.4.5. *Inventory of Verbal Forms*

The inventory of verbal forms in JChalla is that known from other *lishana deni* dialects and consists of the Copula, Subjunctive, Preterite, Imperative, Gerund, and the Participle.[115] These inflectional bases combine with affixes and the Copula to form the different tenses and moods. Affixes include

> *k/g-*   expressing the indicative present (§ 4.4.9)
> *b/p-*   expressing the future (§ 4.4.11)
> *-wa/-wā-*   expressing the past or remote past (§§ 4.4.8,10,12)
> *-wa*   expressing repetition or reversion back to a place (§ 4.4.26)

4.4.6. *Copula*

4.4.6.1. *Present Copula*

> 1 m.s.   *(')íwən(a), wən*
> 1 f.s.   *(')íwan(a), wan*
> 2 m.s.   *(')íwət(ən), wət*
> 2 f.s.   *(')íwat(ən), wat*
> 3 m.s.   *(')ile, -yle, le*
> 3 f.s.   *(')ila, -yla, la*
> 1 c.pl.   *(')íwax(in), wax*
> 2 c.pl.   *(')iwétun(a), wetun*
> 3 c.pl.   *(')ilu, -ylu, lu*

---

[115] Capital letters (e.g., Preterite) marks the morphological form; small-case letters (e.g., preterite) indicate the function of the form. Cf. the terminology used by Hetzron 1969 and adopted by Hoberman 1989 and Fox 1997: Preterite = P(reterite), Subjunctive = J(ussive), Imperative = O(rder), and Verbal Noun = C(continuous); Mutzafi 2003 and 2008a: Preterite = P, Subjunctive = S, Imperative = O, Gerund = I(Infinitive); Tsereteli 1978 and Krotkoff 1982: Subjunctive = 1ˢᵗ conjugation and the Preterite = 2ⁿᵈ conjugation; Nöldeke 1868: Subjunctive = 1. Partic.; Preterite = 2. Partic.

a. The Perfect is composed of the shorter forms of the Present Copula and the Participle (§ 4.4.16.a); the actual and continuous present (§ 4.4.19) is expressed by the shorter forms of the Present Copula and the Gerund.

b. After a word-final vowel one usually finds the shorter forms of the Present Copula, e.g.,

> *máni-le?*
> 'Who is it?'

> *rešexun šaxína-le*
> 'You (pl.) are hot(-headed)'

> *ʿāṣə́rta-la.*
> 'It is evening.'

> *mare təffáqe-lu.*
> 'They are rifle owners.'

c. Occasionally, however, one hears longer forms of the Present Copula after a word-final vowel, and it is attested with or without a slight initial glottal stop ('creaky voice'; § 3.3.c), e.g.,

> *xa ʾárʾa-ʾila qam tar didu.*
> 'There is a (plot of) land outside their door.' (§ 5.8.7)

> *ʾéka-ʾile*
> 'where it is' (§ 5.1.12; cf. *ʾéka-le*)

Note both

> *Qóto-ʾile l-flāná- dūka.*   and   *Qóto-le go gūba.*
> 'It is Qoto in such and such a place.'   'Qoto is at the loom.'

d. The shorter forms of the Present Copula may also be found after a word-final consonant. Cf. the longer and shorter forms in the following sequence of sentences:

> *walḷa Qárani naxwaš ʾile. náxwaš-le.*
> 'By God, Qarani is ill. He is ill. Yes.' (§ 5.4.6).

e. Unlike several NeoAram dialects, the final *a* vowel of a noun does not normally coalesce with the initial *i* of the Copula to produce an *e*-vowel,[116] e.g.,

---

[116] Krotkoff 1982:36; Jastrow 1988:28; Hoberman 1989:33; Fox 1997:40; Mutzafi 2008a: 51.

Rašíd 'áǧa-'ile
'Rashi is an agha' (§ 5.5.5.)

bas 'āni ṛába-ilu
'but they are many' (§ 5.4.2)

a does coalesce with *i*, however, in *ké-le* 'Where is he?' (cf. *'éka-'ile*)

The 3rd person allomorphs *-yle, -yla, -ylu* may occur after *mā* 'what' and *kma* 'how much':

má-yle, má-yla
'What is it?'

Cf. the following three allomorphs:

kmá-'ile / kmá-yle / kmá-la
'How much is it?'

f. The relative *d-* > *t-* before forms of the Present Copula (§§ 3.2.d; 4.1.8.m).

g. The Present Copula is enclitic to the new prominent information in the clause,[117] which is usually the predicate:

'āna Hekkarná-wən.
'I am a resident of Hakkari.' (§ 5.2.3)

jebi mə́lya-le.
'My pocket is full.' (§ 5.3.13)

tar'eni b-léle-ži ptíxa-le.
'And our door is open at night.' (§ 5.2.16)

'ár'a-ži xapči jmə́tta-la.
'Also the earth is a bit frozen.' (§ 5.2.12)

ṛápsa-la 'e-məzgáfte.
'That mosque is large.' (§ 5.1.7)

'iya 'ādə́ta-la.
'This is a custom.' (§ 5.6.6)

qatxe didu zóre-lu.
'Their glasses are small.' (§ 5.10.11)

In the following examples, the Copula is enclitic or postpositive to the subject, which is the prominent new information, e.g.,

---

[117] Khan 2002:396.

Qóto-le go gūba.
'Qoto is at the loom.' (§ 5.4.3)

kəsyāsa lu gāwa.
'Hens are on it.' (§ 5.10.4)

kullu xāṣu le l-gūda.
'All of them, their back is to the wall.' (§ 5.11.3)

marawāse lu 'əltəx 'əl-'ár'a. 'áya-le go ᴴrəkevetᴴ.
'The owners are below, on the ground. He is in the train.' (§ 5.10.1)

4.4.6.2. Negated Present Copula

1 m.s.	*léwən(a), láwən(a)*[118]
1 f.s.	*léwan(a)*
2 m.s.	*léwət(ən)*
2 f.s.	*léwat(ən)*
3 m.s.	*lewe, lāwe*
3 f.s.	*lewa*
1 c.pl.	*léwax(in)*
2 c.pl.	*létun(a)*
3 c.pl.	*lewu*

a. The negated Present Copula is usually preposed to the predicate, e.g.,

waḷḷa lewe qṭila.
'By God, he has not been killed.' (§ 5.7.9)

'Eli! 'āhat lewət mən gūre 'ida gdāre l-kəstox
'Eli! You are not (one) of (those) men (who) puts (his) hand in his money-bag' (§ 5.6.21)

sartuk lewe məšxa
'*sartuk* (cream) is not *məšxa* (cooking oil)' (§ 5.8.2)

though it may follow it to stress the prominent new information, e.g.,

áġa-ži xmāra lewe.
'And the Agha is not an *ass*.' (§ 5.4.6)

ki('ət) 'āna xorexun xmāra léwəna.
'You kn(ow that) I, like you, am not an *ass*.' (§ 5.3.16)

čú-məndi lewe.
'It is *nothing*.' (§ 5.6.6)

---

[118] *lāwən* and *láwəna* are significantly less frequent than *lewən, léwəna*.

4.4.6.3. Deictic Present Copula

a. Infrequently one finds present copular forms *wəlle* (3 m.s.), *wəlla* (3 f.s.), and *wəllu* (3 c.pl.), which are attested also in in JAmid and JBetan,[119] and appear to have a deictic nuance emphasizing the here and now, e.g.,

> *wəlle Ben-Guryón dexun, ʿaqida dexun, wəlle l-axxa.*
> 'Right here is your Ben-Gurion, your (military) leader, he is right here.'

> *tene wəllu qam tarʾeni.*
> 'Figs are right here in front of our door.'

b. There are rare attestations of what appear to be present deictic copular forms *wele*, *wela*, etc., as in JZakho, JAmid, and JBetan:[120]

> *walḥāṣəl malšən deni máni-le? máni-le? wele kəsleni.*
> 'In short, our slanderer, who is he? Who is he? He is right here with us.'

> *ʾən wela, wela tangāwi ʾəllexun, ʾaxtun kesetun kəsleni. ʾən wela hənna kəslexun wela ᴴb-sedərᴴ, ʾaxtun lá-kiʾètūlan*
> 'If you are right now, right now in distress, you come to us. If there is, right now, um, with you, (if) it is now okay, you don't know us.'

4.4.6.4. Past Copula

1 m.s.	*wənwa, (ʾ)ənwa*
1 f.s.	*wanwa, (ʾ)anwa*
2 m.s.	*wətwa, (ʾ)ətwa*
2 f.s.	*watwa, (ʾ)atwa*
3 m.s.	*wewa, (ʾ)ewa*
3 f.s.	*wāwa, (ʾ)āwa*
1 c.pl.	*waxwa, (ʾ)axwa*
2 c.pl.	unattested
3 c.pl.	*wewa, (ʾ)ewa*

a. The initial *w* of the Past Copula is sometimes replaced by an initial glottal stop (*wewa* > *ʾewa*) after word-final vowels (§ 3.3.c) or elided completely, e.g.,

> *múfti-ʾewa. qázi-ʾewa. kullu šuʾāle ʾewa.*
> 'He was the mufti. He was the judge. He was all things.' (§ 5.1.10)

---

[119] Hoberman 1989:33; Mutzafi 2008a:52,57–58 (perhaps from *u* 'and' + *ʾəlla* 'behold' p. 393). It is clearly distinguished in pronunciation from the interjection *walḷa* 'By God.' See also the adverbial *wal* (§ 4.7.4).

[120] Polotsky 1967:111; Meehan & Alon 1979:179 n. 22; Hoberman 1989:33,173–176; Mutzafi 2008a:393; Cohen 2008.

ya'ni 'āġa d-láxma-ewa.
'That is, he was the "agha of bread".' (§ 5.5.5)

b. Initial *w* usually occurs after word-final consonants, e.g.,

wakil qāymaqam wewa.
'He was the deputy of the local governor.' (§ 5.9.1)

ṭlāha jandərme mənnan wewa.
'Three policemen were with us.' (§ 5.13.2)

though it can also be heard after vowels, e.g.,

pa 'ega 'eka wewa 'iya?
'So then where was this?'

qóme-ži kərya wewa, la yarixa.
'His height was short, not tall.' (§ 5.8.12)

c. The Past Copula is infrequently clipped and reduced to enclitic *-wa* (§ 3.17.f), e.g.,

'Éraq-wa ...
'It was Iraq ...' (§ 5.2.6)

gə́zra-wa l-tāma.
'There was a pile of chopped word there.' (§ 5.13.11)

la, 'āna ^{H}mazkír^H-wa.
'No, I was the secretary.'

d. The 2 pl. form of the Past Copula is unattested in the corpus. Cf. JAmid 2 m.s. *witwa* vs. 2 c.pl. *wɨtwa*;[121] JBetan 2 m.s. *wətwa* vs. 2 c.pl. *wə́tūwa*;[122] CAradh 2 m.s. *witwa* vs. 2 c.pl. *wútu:wa*.[123]

e. Like the Present Copula, the Past Copula may occur before or after the predicate, depending on what information is given prominence, e.g.,

Qoto wewa šəmməd dide
'His name was Qoto' (§ 5.4.3)

bāb didu 'é-Piro wewa.
'Their father was that Piro.' (§ 1.1.3)

'axnan wewax b-^{H}ṣad^H.
'We were at the side.' (§ 5.3.10)

---

[121] Hoberman 1989:198.
[122] Mutzafi 2008a:52.
[123] Krotkoff 1982:37–38.

f. So rarely does Shabbo use the past copular forms *wele, weli*, etc.,[124] that, as in the case of JAmid and JBetan, it is likely that they are the result of JZakho influence.[125]

4.4.7. Subjunctive

a. The Subjunctive base developed from the older Aramaic active participle (G *qāṭəl* < *qāṭil*, D *mqāṭəl* < *mqaṭṭil*, C *maqṭəl* < *maqṭil*), to which have been added E-suffix pronouns (§ 4.1.6), which mark the agent. See, e.g., G *ptx* 'open':

1 m.s.	*pátxən(a)*	'I may open'
1 f.s.	*pátxan(a)*	
2 m.s.	*pátxət(ən)*	
2 f.s.	*pátxat(ən)*	
3 m.s.	*pātəx*	
3 f.s.	*patxa*	
1 c.pl.	*pátxax(in)*	
2 c.pl.	*patxétun(a)*	
3 c.pl.	*patxi*	

1 m.s. *pátxan(a)* is infrequent. (§ 4.1.6.c).

b. The Subjunctive expresses modality, e.g.,

mā ʾamrənnox?
'What can I tell you?' (§ 5.6.2)

ʾatta mắ-odi b-Qoṭo? mā lá-odi b-Qoṭo?
'What on earth should they do with Qoto?'

c. The Subjunctive may be preceded by *mən* or *məl*, e.g.,

mən hāwe
'Let it be!'

mən ṭāləq
'Let him divorce!'

məl ʾāzəl
'Let him go!'

mắd-gbe ʾāmər mən ʾāmər!
'Whatever he wants to say, let him say (it)!'

---

[124] E.g., *Čalla wela* 'it was Čalla', *zöre welu* 'they were small.' When Shabbo does use it, it comes after the predicate as in JZakho (Polotsky 1967:111).
[125] Hoberman 1989:177–178; Mutzafi 2008a:393.

d. The negative is expressed by *m(ən)-lá*:

'āni m-lá-ḥarmi!
'They shouldn't become impure!'

e. The origin of *mən* and *məl* is unclear.[126] Cf. the syntagm *mən d-* + Subjunctive (ClAram מֶן ד- 'as soon as, after') as in JZakho *mın yā'e* 'as soon as he knows.'[127] Optional subjunctive particles in other NeoAram dialects include JZakho and JBetan *šud/t* (< שבוק ד[128]); Maha Khtaya D-Baz *hal* (< √yhwl);[129] Telkepe *šud/šwoq d-*,[130] Qaraqosh *(šə)d-*;[131] Ṭuroyo *ṭro-* (<√ṭry 'allow, leave');[132] JKoyS *mar* (< √'mr imperative),[133] *ba*, and *dabi*; JArbel *mar, da,* and *ba*; JSuleim *mar* and *ba*;[134] Mlaḥso *mlo* (< √ml'?);[135] *khûsh* (< √ḥwš) is also attested in several dialects.[136]

f. The Subjunctive may occur in the protasis of conditional clauses, e.g.,

[H]be'emét[H] 'ən ba'yat, la', xamša'sar yomāsa xet 'āhat la pūwat 'axxa. 'ən la ba'yat-ži 'áwon dīdax u-'əd-gorax b-qdalexun.
'Really, if you want (me to arrange the transfer, then) no, you won't be here in another fifteen days (because I can arrange your transfer). If you don't want (me to arrange it), then you and your husband are responsible.' (§ 5.9.13)

g. The Subjunctive serves in asyndetic constructions where in ClAram an infinitive might have been expected, e.g.,

gəbən 'āzən
'I want to go'

u-'āhat lá-mṣət māḷeni 'axlətte.
'And you cannot filch our possessions.' (§ 5.2.3)

wax 'əsye xāzax dəmmox. kmá-le?
'We have come to see (about) your blood money. How much is it?' (§ 5.5.6)

---

[126] The syntagm *mən* (preposition) + active participle is a salient feature of LWAram (JPA, CPA, and SA) where it functions as a predicative accusative of state (*ḥāl*). See Kutscher 1976:51–58.

[127] Sabar 2002a:220. On מֶן ד- and other subordinators in the historical development of Aramaic syntax, see Pat-El 2008.

[128] Sabar 2002a:275; Mutzafi 2008a:387. Also *dı* (Sabar 1976:XL).

[129] Mutzafi 2000:315.

[130] Mutzafi 2008a:387.

[131] Khan 2002:305.

[132] Jastrow 1985:157.

[133] Mutzafi 2004:110, 231. Khan 1999:252 believes *mar* is of Kurdish origin.

[134] Khan 2004:287.

[135] Jastrow 1994:51,183.

[136] Maclean 1901:96.

4.4.8. *Past Subjunctive (Subjunctive + wa)*

The Subjunctive + *wa* represents a contrary-to-fact condition:[137]

čú-məndi lewu 'anna pāre. 'atta hāwéwāli xa 'əmma tremma paṇqáṇoṭe yāwə́nwālox. 'āna [H]*sameaḥ*[H] *wənwa hādax.*
'This money isn't (worth) anything. Now were I to have about a hundred, two hundred liras, I would give (them) to you. I would have been happy (if it were) like this.' (§ 5.3.12)

'ən (hwe)wále məšəlmāna, 'ida dārewa, dārewa skina go kāse. čāyə́qwāle mātúwāle hənna 'afəllu xamšamma šənne hāwewa go [H]*bet sohar.*[H]
'Had he been born a Muslim, he would have inserted (his) hand (and) stuck a knife in his stomach. He would have ripped him open, he would have knocked him down, um, even if he had to be in jail five hundred years.'

4.4.9. *Present (g/k + Subjunctive)*

a. The Subjunctive base with prefixed *g-/k-*[138] expresses the present tense (general present[139]). In the case of the verbs *'mr* 'say', *'wd* 'do', *'sy* 'come', and *'xl* 'eat', the vowel of the Present differs from the vowel found in the Subjunctive (§ 4.4.9.i).

b. Before voiced consonants one finds *g-* (§ 3.6.f), e.g.,

gbāxən   'I cry'
gdāre   'he puts in'
gzaqri   'they weave'

c. Before unvoiced consonants one finds *k-*, e.g.,

kpeši   'they remain'
kšāme'   'he hears'
ktaxrətta?   'Do you remember it?'

k is sometimes fronted to *k*[y] (§ 3.4.b) and other times *k* > *č* /_*i* in *či'ətte* 'you know him' and *lá-či'an* 'I don't know' (§§ 5.6.13; 5.13.3).

---

[137] Hoberman 1989:68.

[138] See Heinrichs 2002:243–257 on the prefixing of *k-/g-* in NeoAram, their distribution in different dialects, and the origin of the particles (the syntagm -קָא‎ [< קָאֵים‎] + participle as exemplified by JBA and Mandaic, where it marks the continuous aspect). See also Khan 2002:299; Rubin 2005:129–136; Mutzafi 2008b:420–421; Breuer 1997.

[139] The continuous (actual) present is expressed by the Copula + *b* + Gerund (§ 4.4.19.b).

d. The prefix assimilates to a following *q* (§ 3.6f), e.g.,

lá-qqarwən 'I do not approach'
šūli qqāḍənne 'I finish my work'

e. The prefix is sometimes difficult to hear before an unvoiced consonant (§ 3.6f).

f. In the case of the verbs I-ʾ *'mr* 'say', *'sy* 'come', and *'xl* 'eat', as well as the I-h verb *hwy* 'be', *k-* is heard because historically the prefix was contiguous to an unvoiced consonant:

*k'āmər > kemər[140]
*k'āse > kese
*k'āxəl > kexəl
*khāwe > kāwe

This is not the case, however, with the verb *'zl* 'go':

*k'āzəl > gezəl

Cf. the verb *'wd* 'do' < ClAram עבד, in which *k-* has assimilated to a following originally voiced consonant (ʿ):

*k'āwəd > gewəd

g. *g-/k-* is sometimes absent after the first verb in a series, e.g.,

kesən besa u-menxən kullu.
'I come home and look at all of them.' (§ 5.11.6)

ᴴma šeᴴ-gmesétun 'ida dāretun go jebābu.
'What you bring (is because) you put (your) hand into their pockets.'

Cf. the following passage where *g-/k-* occurs with each verb in the sequence:

tāma 'axnan gzar'ax gmar'ax gmaštax kxazdax ṣiwe gmesax mən tāma.
'There we sew, we take to pasture, we irrigate, we harvest, (and) we bring wood from there.'

h. *g-/k-* is obligatory after all negatives, even in a series, lest the verbal forms be understood as modal, e.g.,

lá-gzonetun lá-gmzabnetun[141] *lá-gzaqretun lá-kəmḥaketun lá-kxadretun.*
'You don't buy, you don't sell, you don't weave, you don't talk, you don't go around.' (§ 5.11.6)

---

[140] *gemər* is also attested in JChalla. It is, however, the result of JZakho influence.
[141] On the syllabification of this verb preceded by the negative, see § 3.22.d.

la gzāde' mənni u-lá-gnāxəp mənni.
'He doesn't fear me and he isn't embarrassed by me.'

i. As in other *lishana deni* dialects, there is a clear distinction in the thematic vowel between I-' forms (including ClAram ' > NENA ') expressing the present tense and those expressing modality. The former have an initial *e*-vowel, whose origin is unclear, whereas the latter have an *a*-vowel:

kemər 'he says'	vs.	*'āmər* 'he may say'
gezəl 'he goes'	vs.	*'āzəl* 'he may go'
kese 'he comes'	vs.	*'āse* 'he may come'
gewəd 'he does'	vs.	*'āwəd* 'he may do'
kexəl 'he eats'	vs.	*'āxəl* 'he may eat'

j. The Present of *b'y* 'want', *gəbən, gəbət*, etc. (§ 4.4.28.10) is not formed from the Subjunctive base (*bā'e*) but rather from the old passive participle *b'e*.[142]

4.4.10. *Past Habitual (g/k + Subjunctive + wa)*

The past habitual is expressed by the prefixing of *g-/k-* and the suffixing of the past tense marker *-wa* to the Subjunctive base, e.g.,

waḷḷa mən tāma mən Ṣṭambul kud ᴴtaḥanə́dᴴ gezaxwa, mesewa mən̄di gəmzabniwa.
By God, from there, from Istanbul, (at) every station which we went to, they would bring something (and) would sell.' (§ 5.10.1)

dəbbāsa 'ətwa. kesewa u-maxərwiwa dukāne... 'ar'āsa.
'There were bears. They would come and destroy places... the fields.' (§ 5.6.16)

ᴴ'azᴴ kəsleni gyatwiwa. kudlel kesewa ᴴ'orḥímᴴ zamriwa ḥil palgədlel.
'So they would sit with us. Every night guests would come. They would sing till midnight.' (§ 5.8.17)

'āna ki'ənwa xa šắta-u-palge xa məndi.
'I knew (it was) something (like) a year and a half.' (§ 5.1.13)

4.4.11. *Future (b/p + Subjunctive)*

a. The future is expressed by the prefixing of *b-* (before vowels and voiced consonants) to the Subjunctive base, e.g.,

---

[142] Mutzafi 2008a:80.

bāzən	'I shall go'
bāsən	'I shall come'
bodi	'they will do'
bdaʾrən	'I shall return'
byāwət	'you will give'

b. *b-* is devoiced to *p-* before unvoiced consonants, e.g.,

pšāke	'he will complain'
pqaṭʾən	'I shall cut'
ppešan	'I shall become'

In the case of *pāwe* 'he will be', *b* > *p* /_*h*: *bhāwe > * *phāwe* > *pāwe*.[143]

c. *b* > *m* before a nasal (§ 3.6.a), e.g.,

ʾāya mmājəblox
'he will answer you'

la māra: mmaxlət ṭarefa l-yalunke?
'She is saying: "Will you feed the children non-kosher meat?"
(§ 5.10.8)

xá-gdāda garšət mənne ʾalpa rqāʾe mnapli mənnəd dide.
'(If) you pull one thread from it, a thousand patches will fall from it.'
(§ 5.3.11)

though not always:[144]

ʾá-ži mhomənna ko bmāxəl l-yalunke.
'Also she believed that he will feed the children.' (§ 5.10.5)

d. *b-/p-* is prefixed also in the other *lishana deni* dialects of JAmid,[145] JZakho,[146] JAradh,[147] and JBetan,[148] though in JDohok, JAradh and in the older texts of JNerwa one finds the free standing בד/בת (*bəd/bət*),[149] which is also attested elsewhere in NENA.[150]

---

[143] Mutzafi 2008a:24.
[144] An example in the Past Prospective is *bnāšə́twāle* 'you would have forgotten it'. Cf. with assimilated *b* in the Past Prospective *mmakipíwāle* 'they would bend (their head)'.
[145] Hoberman 1989:30.
[146] Sabar 2002a:104.
[147] See the sample text published in Mutzafi 2002:485.
[148] Mutzafi 2008a:54.
[149] Sabar 1984:242.
[150] See, e.g., Maclean 1895:82, Krotkoff 1982:33, Fox 1997:32; Talay 2008:307–309.

4.4.12. *Past Prospective* (b/p + *Subjunctive* + wa)

The past prospective[151] is expressed by the prefix *b-/p-* on forms of the Subjunctive base with the past tense marker suffix *-wa*; it is attested in the apodosis of hypothetical conditional sentences:

> *pāša, 'ən hāwéwāli bamrənwa 'əlle.*
> 'Pasha, if I had (the money), I would have told him.'

It also functions similarly to the Past Habitual, e.g.,

> *bāziwa b-xurṭūsa go besa pšaqliwa mād gbewa.*
> 'They would go by force into the house (and) they would take whatever they wanted.' (§ 5.1.12)

> *m-axxa byātūwa qalunka mayráxwāle l-tāma.*
> 'One would sit here (and) would extend the narghile (all the way) over there.' (§ 5.11.3)

> *basər hādax 'egā bāsewa rešu mmakipíwāle.*
> 'Afterwards then they would come (and) they would bend their head.'

> *bāsewa dax kpánwālu, (b)'oriwa.*
> 'They would come, as soon as they had gotten hungry they would enter.' (§ 5.4.2)

4.4.13. *Preterite*

a. The Preterite is formed from the base of the older Aramaic passive participles (G *qṭəl-* < קְטִיל; D *mqoṭəl-* < מְקַטַּל, C *muqṭəl-* < מְקַטַּל) to which are attached E-suffix pronouns (§ 4.1.6), which function as the object, followed by L-suffix pronouns (§ 4.1.4), which function as the agent.[152]

b. It occurs with both transitive and intransitive verbs, e.g., *qṭilili* 'I killed them', *šqilāli* 'I took her', *kpənnu* 'they were hungry', *kəple* 'he bent over', *mṭeli* 'I arrived'.

---

[151] Hoberman uses the term 'conditional' (1989:68 "fulfilled consequence of a condition in the past time"); Mutzafi, on the other hand, prefers 'past prospective' (2008a:61).

[152] Original *qṭīl li* 'is killed by me' > 'he is killed by me' > *qṭəlli* 'I killed (him)'. On the formation of the Preterite in NeoAram, see Hopkins 1989a.

c. The Preterite is the most commonly used form in narrating past events, e.g.,

> *pār gyāni šqilili. bargúze-ži lu qāmi zəllan besa. zəllan besa šlixili. hiwili ṭas dide. zəllu 'án-bargúze. zəlli l-tāma xá-gā xet. mərri...*
> 'I took my money. And we went home (with) the woolen suit on me. We went home, (then) I took them off. I gave them to him. That woolen suit went (to the Agha). I went there another time (and) I said...' (§ 5.2.9)

> *walla šqilālu təffaq. hedi ^Hkané^H dəryālu hənna ^Hkané^H dəryālu go nāsəd dide. ṭiq! walla zəlle. baxta qəmla har hatxa wədla.*
> 'By God, they took the rifle. Slowly they stuck the barrel, um, they stuck the barrel in his ear. Bang! By God, he died. The wife got up (and) did just like this.' (§ 5.6.18)

> *bāb dide skətle zəlle. nixəd bábi-ži nəxle. xá-yoma zəlli 'əlləd pareni l-tāma.*
> 'His father croaked (and) died. Also my late father passed away. One day I went there for our money.' (§ 5.2.1)

d. For the passive Preterite, see § 4.4.20.e.

4.4.14. *Plupreterite (Preterite + Infixed* wa)

a. The Plupreterite is formed from the infixing of the the past tense marker -*wā* between the Preterite base and an L-suffix pronoun.

b. It expresses background information in the past, e.g.,

> *hudāyəd pə́šwālu-ži kə́tt-u-māt 'riqālu.*
> 'And the Jews who had remained fled bit by bit.' (§ 5.1.11)

> *bāb didu 'é-Piro wewa. 'āya séwāle m-go Pənčāye. mən Blejan séwāle.*
> 'Their father was that Piro. He had come from (the area of) Pinianish. He had come from Blejan.' (§ 5.1.3)

c. It may be used to express the distant past, e.g.,

> *...'ako zə́lwālu go ^Hgalút^H. mani 'ā séwāle l-axxa? Nawoxadnesər, ^Hnaxón^H?*
> '...when they went into exile. Who (was) it (who) had come here? Nawo-chadnezer, correct?' (§ 5.1.1)

> *flāná-yoma séwāle l-axxa.*
> 'One day he had come here.'

4.4.15. *Imperative*

a. The Imperative in JChalla is a reflex of the older Aramaic imperative. In the G stem the thematic *o*-vowel (< *u) of transitive verbs has replaced entirely the thematic *a*-vowel of older intransitive verbs and of verbs III-guttural and *r*,[153] with the exception of the Imperative forms of *'mr* 'say': s. *mar*, pl. *marun*. There are two forms, a singular and a plural, e.g., c.s. *ptox* 'open!', c.pl. *ptoxun*. *o* > *u* in the Imperative when there is an object suffix, e.g., *ptuxle* 'open it!' In verbs III-*y* there are three forms: m.s. *xzi* 'say!', f.s. *xze*, c.pl. *xzūn*. A lengthened form of the singular Imperative is attested in Shabbo's speech only with the verb *ḥml* 'wait': *ḥmóləna*.[154]

b. The suffix *-un* on the plural form is attested already in LAram in Syr, Mand, and JPA.

c. The imperative is negated with the particle *la* + Subjunctive (as in ClAram), e.g.,

> *lá-mḥākət!*
> 'Don't talk!'

or, unlike in ClAram, by *la* + Imperative:

> *lá-šti!*
> 'Don't drink!'

These two methods of expressing the negative imperative are attested elsewhere in NeoAram, though in some dialects, e.g., CUrmi, JZakho, and JBetan, *la* + Subjunctive denotes a continued or general action, whereas *la* + Imperative denotes a single action.[155]

---

[153] Nöldeke 1868:225–226, but cf. *a* in Ṭuroyo (Jastrow 191985:62) and Mlaḥso (Jastrow 1994:50). Cf. the thematic *o* vowel of the plural Imperative in JChalla *ptoxun* and JZakho (Sabar 2002a:261) *psoxun* with the *u* vowel in JBetan (Mutzafi 2008a:64) *pϑūxun* and JAmid (Hoberman 1989:196) *ptuxun*.

[154] The shorter form *ḥmol* also occurs. The suffix *-ən* is also attested in the JNerwa texts: שקולן (*šqōlın*). See Sabar 1976:XXXVII and 1984:241.

[155] Maclean 1895:147 relates to CUrmia, and Hoberman 1989:70–71 reports that Polotsky finds the same distinction in JZakho. For JBetan see Mutzafi 2008a:84. In JArbel (Khan 1999:282) *la* + Subjunctive is imperfective as against *la* + Imperative, whch is aspectually neutral. Both Hoberman 1989:71 and Fox 1997:33 n. 9 do not feel they have enough evidence to show whether this is true for JAmid and Jilu respectively. Khan 2004:322 indicates that both syntagms may express contingent and permanent prohibitions in JSuleim. Cf. Mlaḥso, where the Imperative is negated by *lo* + Imperative as opposed to Ṭuroyo, where one finds *la* + Subjunctive (Jastrow 1994:51).

d. The reflexive (2nd person L-suffix) or so-called 'ethical dative'[156] is sometimes suffixed to the forms of the Imperative, as elsewhere in Neo-Aram,[157] e.g.,

hal, hallox	'give (m.s.)!'
se, selax	'go (f.s.)!'
soq, soqlox	'ascend (m.s.)!'
šmo', šmo'lox	'hear (m.s.)!'
šqol, šqullox	'take (m.s.)!'

e. The 'narrative' imperative[158] occurs in narrative descriptions:[159]

šqǝlle xa ṣiwa 'ǝllǝd dide u-xṭǝrre hatxa. krox! tāma Tŭrkiya-la. godi šar'a ᴴnaxón.ᴴ
'He took a stick to him and beat him like this. He smashed (him) [Lit., 'Smash!'] There it is Turkey. They enforce religious law properly.'

mǝtwāli l-'ar'a 'egā krox! ᴴbli raḥma(nūt), türkit türkitᴴ. króx-u-króx-u-króx-u-króx-u-króx-u!
'I laid her down on the ground (and) so then I smashed her [Lit., 'Smash!'] Without mer(cy)—Turkish, Turkish (style?). I smashed her over and over and over again. [Lit., 'Smash and smash and smash and smash and smash and!'] (§ 5.8.11)

mǝndelu qāman. mǝndelu. mxi u-mxi u-mxi u-mxi u-mxi u-mxi! ḥel wǝlle desta, ᴴpastelaᴴ reš ᴴpas 'adamáᴴ.
'They threw him down in front of us. They threw him down. They beat him over and over and over again. [Lit., 'Strike and strike and strike and strike and strike and strike!'] Until he is right now a portion of food, mincemeat, on the face of the earth.' (§ 5.2.12)

4.4.16. *Perfect (Present Copula + Participle)*

a. The Perfect is composed of the shorter form of the Present Copula (§ 4.4.6.1) and the Participle (§ 4.4.18), e.g.,

---

[156] For the vast literature on the function of the ethical dative in Semitic languages, particularly in the different periods of Hebrew, see most recently Halevy 2004 and the bibliography there. In discussing the situation in CUrmi, Polotsky 1979:206, 211 cites only verbs of motion with the L-suffixes, which he desribes as a reflexive use.

[157] E.g., JZakho ('i:)sálo:xun 'come'! (Avinery 1988:216), JAmid *'ăhit lä=dᴴqlᴴx káwod* 'Don't insist on your honor' (Hoberman 1989:70). In Qaraq (Khan 2002:350–351) the second person L-suffix expresses greater immediacy; it is the norm for the imperative *'ϑy* and attested occasionally on other verbs.

[158] For a treatment of the narrative imperative in Arabic and other languages as well as bibliography, see Henkin 1994.

[159] See Mutzafi 2004:112.

1 m.s.	*wən ptixa* 'I have opened'
1 f.s.	*wan ptəxta*
2 m.s.	*wət ptixa*
2 f.s.	*wat ptəxta*
3 m.s.	*le ptixa*
3 f.s.	*la ptəxta*
1 c.pl.	*wax ptixe*
2 c.pl.	*wetun ptixe*
3 c.pl.	*lu ptixe*

b. There is, however, an occasional example of the longer form of the Present Copula in the Perfect construction:

kullu ^{H}rošé^H hənna ^{H}švatím^H 'ilu 'əsye kəsleni.
'All the heads of, um, tribes have come to us.' (§ 5.11.3)

bamri ^{H}šotrím^H-ilu qṭíle-llu.
'They will say policemen have killed them.'

c. For the negation of the Present Copula, see § 4.4.6.2.

d. The Perfect construction usually expresses a dynamic present perfect event,[160] e.g.,

'iya nāša ^{H}k-nər'é^H mən gen'edən le 'əsya.
'This person apparently has come from the Garden of Eden.' (§ 5.3.6)

le xdira go d-an ^{H}ṣrife^H kullu.
'He has gone around in all of those huts.' (§ 5.3.4)

'ena la dreta 'əlli.
'She has put her eye on me.' (§ 5.8.1)

'iya 'idəd hudāye la mṭeta 'əbbəd dide.
'This (is the) hand of the Jews (that) has reached him.' (§ 5.4.7)

xa julla la mtúta-lli tam qam ^{H}ḥalón.^{H}
'She has put a piece of cloth there for me in front of the window.' (§ 5.8.6)

^{H}ba-'érex^H bə́z-zodāna m-alpa šənne lu tiwe 'əbbəd Čalla
'more than about a thousand years they have been settled in Challa' (§ 1.1.1)

---

[160] Hoberman 1989:86–90; Mutzafi 2008a:56–59. For a detailed investigation of the uses of the Perfect in CUrmi, see Kapeliuk 2008.

e. Not infrequently, however, the Perfect expresses preteriteness,[161] noticeably the remote past, e.g.,

be sāwi xa ^{H}tkufá^H l-Kára-ewa. xarāye m-Kāra lu zile l-Šiwa. lu piše l- Šiwa. xarāye m-Šiwa xá-gā xet lu d'íre-wa l-Čalla. basər hənna... lu zile mən Kāra l-Šiwa. m-Šiwa xá-gā xet lu d'íre-wa l-Čalla.
'The family of my grandfather was in Kara for a period. Later they have gone from Kara to Shiwa. They have remained in Shiwa. Later once again they have returned back to Challa from Shiwa. After, um... they went from Kara to Shiwa. From Shiwa once again they have returned back to Challa.'
(§ 5.6.7)

kem(ər:) ḥál-u-masaləd bronox hatxa 'āwa. flán-brāta lewa próqta-lle. le dwŭqa-lla. hāda(x) le ltixa 'əbba. hāda(x) le krixa 'əbba. le wida 'əlla ^{H}ḥolá^H. le múndye-lla l-tāma. (b-)xurtūsa gəba—, gbāwa 'āya dāməx mənnəd dida. tar'a la ḥləqta 'əlləd dide. mā le ^{H}mbukša^H mənna? lewa ^{H}mšuḥrərarta^H 'əlle. tar'a lewa ptəxta-lle. b- ^{H}kowaḥ^H tar'a le ptíxa-lle u-hátxa-la. hátxa la breta. ke(mər): lewe nqiša 'əlləd dida.
'He sa(ys): "The upshot of the story of your son was like this. A certain girl hasn't left him alone. He has grabbed her (in order to get the key out of her pocket so that he could open the locked door). For this reason he (went up and) has strugged with her. Like th(is) he has beaten her. He has made her ill. He has thrown her down there. (By) force she want(ed)—, wanted him to sleep with her. She has locked the door on him. What has he asked of her? She hasn't let him go. She hasn't opened the door. By force he has opened the door and that's the way it is. That's the way it happened." He said: "He hasn't touched her."' (§ 5.8.19)

walla grešla, lá-ki'ən xá-šāta, šáta-u-palge. 'iya kalba bər kalba le 'wida ṛazza, 'ar'āsa. ṛazza le 'úda reqa mən ^{H}kfar.^{H}
'By God, it dragged on, I don't know, a year, a year and a half. This son of a bitch has grown rice, (in) fields. He has grown rice far from the village...'
(§ 5.6.15)

f. The Perfect construction may also express a stative/passive present perfect.[162] In most of the cases the Present Copula precedes the Participle,[163] e.g.,

'eka le qtila?
'Where has he been killed?'

---

[161] As in Jilu. See Fox 1997:86–87. To highlight the use of the form, it is translated, however, as a perfect.

[162] Hoberman 1989:84–89; Hopkins 2002:288–298; Mutzafi 2004:105–109; Mutzafi 2008a:56–57.

[163] Cf. in JBetan, where the Copula may be preposed or postposed (Mutzafi 2008a:56–57). The normal position of the Copula in the non-perfect constructions is postpositive.

ʾən le qṭila, ^Hgufát^H dide. ʾən ʾile ^Hḥay^H, (m)palṭile.
'If he has been killed, (let's see) his corpse. If he is alive, let them bring him out.' (§ 5.13.6)

xa dūka har kāsox ʾila mreʾta, hudá.
'Somehow your stomach still hurts, Jew.' (§ 5.11.7)

waḷḷa har tāma le qwira. lewu músye-lle.[164]
'By God, he is buried right there. They haven't brought him.' (§ 5.6.10)

žang la mrupeta
'rust has come loose' (§ 5.7.2)

sa ʾida dre go jebābi. ʾāna wən sira. šqol mād gəbət.
'Come (and) put (your) hand in my pockets! I am tied up. Take whatever you want!'

ʾāna wən piša šəxtāna.
'I have become dirty.'

...ʾaqlāsi síre-lu? lewu ysire ʾaqlāsi.
'...are my feet tied up? My feet aren't tied up.' (§ 5.8.20)

g. Sometimes the Copula is omitted in the Perfect construction after a preceding Perfect construction, e.g.,

ʾāya le ʾəsya, le ^Hmúrgəša^H. ʾəsya le wira go ^Htiras mul ḥalón.^H
'He has come (and) he has noticed. (He has) come (and) he has entered the corn(field) opposite the window.' (§ 5.8.7)

ʾāna kiʾən ʾAwṛāham le ʾəsya mulšəna ṭasexun.
'I know Abraham has come (and has) informed on (me) to you.' (§ 5.8.16)

This is not the case, however, in, e.g.,

ṭlāha jandərme mənnan wewa. ḥmile... lu ḥmile tam manox(e).
'Three policemen were with us. (They have) stopped. They have stopped there (and are) looking around.' (§ 5.13.2)

^Hʾasúr^H-la ^Hli^H baqrənne čuku yəmya ʾəlle.
'It is forbidden for me to ask him because he (has) sworn to him.'

ḥil yoma gənya
'until the sun (has) set'

---

[164] Cf. the immediately following *la, lu qwíre-lle l-tāma* 'No, they have buried him there.'

4.4.17. *Pluperfect (Past Copula + Participle)*

The Pluperfect is composed of the Past Copula + Participle and is relatively infrequent in the corpus. It is attested expressing the stative/passive
past perfect. The Past Copula may precede or follow the Participle:

> *waxwa skine*
> 'we had lived'

> *lá-wǝnwa gwira. la waḷḷa lá-wǝnwa gwira.*
> 'I hadn't married. No, by God, I hadn't married.' (§ 5.8.4)

> *hudāye pə́lye-wa. kutxa 'ə́twāle hudāyǝd gyāne.*
> 'The Jews had been divided up. Each one (agha) had his own Jew(s).'
> (§ 5.6.1)

> *kusise u-gopaḷte tǝlye-wa b-xá-sǝksa l-tāma*
> 'His hat and his shepherd's stick had been hung on a peg there.' (§ 5.13.5)

4.4.18. *Participle*

a. The Participle is a reflex of the determined forms of the older Aramaic
passive participles.

> G   m.s. *qṭila* 'killed', f.s. *qṭǝlta*, pl. *qṭile*
> D   m.s. *mšudra* 'sent', f.s. *mšodarta*, pl. *mšudre*
> C   m.s. *múqṭǝla* 'put to death', f.s. *muqṭalta*, pl. *múqṭǝle*

b. The Passive Participle in D and C in older Aramaic dialects has the
thematic vowel *a*, e.g., BiblAram מְקַטַּל, מְקַטֵּל. The *u*-vowel marking the
passive is attested (alongside with forms with an *a*-vowel) in the Yemenite
traditions of Biblical Aramaic, Targum Onqelos, and JBA.[165]

c. Word order usually distinguishes between the use of the Participle as
an adjective and its use as part of the Perfect construction. In the case of
the former the Copula is mostly found after the predicate whereas in the
latter the copula precedes the Participle.

> Cf.   *tar'a ptíxa-le.*   vs.   *tar'a la ḥlǝ́qta-lle.*
>   'The door is open.' (§ 5.8.5)   'She has locked the door.' (§ 5.8.8)

Note also the distinction in word order and meaning in the following
contiguous sentences:

> *'axnan wax mbuqre. 'axtun hudāye gzire wetun*
> 'We have inquired. You are circumcised Jews' (§ 5.8.10)

---

[165] Morag 1988:151,161.

4.4.19. *Gerund*

a. The forms of the Gerund are reflexes of older Aramaic infinitive forms.[166]

b. The Gerund is used to express the continuous and actual present in the construction Present Copula[167] + *b* + Gerund, e.g.,

> *go ləbbi wən bimāra*
> 'in my heart I am saying' (§ 5.3.3)

> *wən bəxzāya nūra le bizāla m-pāsox.*
> 'I am seeing fire going (forth) from your face.' (§ 5.3.13)

> *xmāra hənna le bəgráša-lla.*
> 'A donkey, um, is pulling her.'

> *lewən bəxzáya-lle.*
> 'I don't see him.' (§ 5.8.12)

Usually one finds the shorter form of the Present Copula, though the longer form is also attested, e.g.,

> *'ile bəṭlāba baxxatəd 'ilāha*
> 'and he is requesting the mercy of God'

> *mədore ṛāba 'ilu bisáya.*
> 'Many mudirs are coming.'

> *'ilu ᴴbəšlātaᴴ l-axxa.*
> 'They are in control here.'

The distance between the Present Copula and *b* + Gerund in the following sentence shows that syntactically the construction expressing continuous action is still relatively free:

> *wax reš gāre l-xulūla kulleni kapaneni lu b-əġdad bərqáda.*
> 'We are on the roof at the wedding feast, all of us, our shoulders are together, dancing.' (§ 5.2.5)

c. Unlike the *lishana deni* dialects of the JNerwa texts,[168] JZakho,[169] JAmid,[170] and JBetan,[171] there are no examples of *pyš* + *b-* + Verbal Noun

---

[166] Fassberg 2008.
[167] The Present copula is omitted in *'axnan-… la, l-tāma, tāma go ᴴrəkevetᴴ yom (wax) b-izāla ta Ṣtambul* 'We-… no, there, there in the train the day we (are) going to Istanbul'. (§ 5.10.4).
[168] Sabar 1976:XL, Sabar 1983:242.
[169] Polotsky 1967:109; Sabar 2002a:48.
[170] Hoberman 1989:81–82.
[171] Mutzafi 2008a:64.

(expressing the past inchoative, e.g., JBetan *dəmme pəšle bəṛϑāxa* 'his blood began to boil' Mutzafi 2008a:64).

d. On the Gerund following the verbs *'sy* 'go' and *ytw* 'sit' see § 4.4.21.

e. The prefixed *b-* is usually not audible before labials (*b*, *p*, and *m*),[172] e.g.,

lewe mḥakoye mənni ᴴyafé məsudárᴴ.
'He is not speaking with me nicely (or on a) regular (basis).' (§ 5.8.15)

báxte-ži la manoxe 'əbbe.
'Also his wife is looking at him.' (§ 5.10.8)

lu plāṭa m-ᴴbet sefərᴴ lewu mṣāya...
'they are graduating from school, (but) they are not able...'

lewa práqa-lli.
'She isn't leaving me (alone).' (§ 5.8.9)

On occasion, however, *b-* is clearly audible, e.g.,

tūla bəbxāya[173] *(m)walwole.*
'She began crying (and) wailing.' (§ 5.7.9)

le bəmyāsa.
'He is dying.'

xədda sele bəmzabone čāy.
'Someone came selling tea.' (§ 5.10.11)

'it xa məndi kəslox. 'áqqara bə'wāra bəplāṭa bə'wāra bəplāṭa. xa məndi 'it.
'There is something (funny) about you. So much entering, leaving, entering, leaving. There is something (funny about it).' (§ 5.9.9)

f. The Gerund is attested as a verbal noun infrequently in the corpus:

mərri: la, la, mxalope let l-axxa.
'I said: "No, no, there is no exchanging here."' (§ 5.2.8)

g. The Gerund may function adverbially, e.g.,

manoxe xāze julləd mani bəš tāza-l(e).
'Looking around, he sees whose garment is nicer.' (§ 5.2.5)

manoxe le māra
'Looking (at Abraham) he is saying' (§ 5.10.7)

---

[172] As, e.g., in the standardized literary dialect of Urmi (Nöldeke 1868:225, Polotsky 1991:270) and in Jilu (Fox 1997:32). Mutzafi 2008a:63 describes *b-* as facultative with G infinitives and absent before D and C infinitives.

[173] In the oral texts from JAmid published by Hoberman *b-bxaya* seems to be attested to the exclusion of *bxāya* (Hoberman 1989:215).

sūn maṣoḥe!
'Go check (it out)!'

'ána-ži qəmli manox(e).
'Also I got up to look.' (§ 5.2.16)

4.4.20. *Passive Voice*

a. The expression of the passive is uncommon in JChalla.[174]

b. The passive voice may be expressed by an inflected form of *'sy* 'come' + Gerund:[175]

'an ^Hnyarót^H selu mgalgole kəsəl ^Hrašám 'agudót^H.
'Those papers were transferred to the registrar of companies.'

kullu bāse ksāwa go ^Hmixtáv^H.
'All of them will be written in a letter.'

'áqqara lire 'é-gora—, byāwən ham 'āya nāša... 'āse l-qəṭla.
'So many liras that man—, I will also give (in order that) that person... should be killed.' (§ 5.6.19)

'ən māḷeni 'āse l-'ixāla
'if our possessions should get filched' (§ 5.2.3)

c. The passive voice is also expressed by *mṭy* 'arrive' + Gerund:

'atta ^Hgam^H mṭelu 'əlləd hənna qəṭla.
'Also now they were, um, killed.' (§ 5.1.12)

qəṭla replaces the expected Gerund *qṭāla* in the idioms *sele/mṭele l-qəṭla* 'he was killed'.[176]

d. The expression of the passive voice by the Preterite base + E-suffix is attested only once in the corpus:[177]

hiwa xanči ^Hxəm'a^H
'a bit of butter was given' (§ 5.8.2)

e. There are no examples of an inflected form of *pyš* + Participle.[178]

---

[174] As in JBetan (Mutzafi 2008a:67–69).
[175] Hoberman 1989:90–91.
[176] Mutzafi 2008a:69.
[177] See also JBetan (Mutzafi 2008a:67–69).
[178] See Krotkoff 1982:39. This use is also unattested in JBetan (Mutzafi 2008a:68).

4.4.21. *Inchoative Aspect*

In the corpus inchoateness in the past is expressed by *ytw* + *b* + Gerund:[179]

> *walḥāṣəl tūlu bəštá.*
> 'In short, they began drinking.' (§ 5.10.11)

> *tūla bəbxāya (m)walwole.*
> 'She began, crying (and) wailing.' (§ 5.7.9)

> *waḷḷa tūlu mbakoḥe 'āni mābayn gyānu.*
> 'By God, they began arguing among themselves.'

> *tūle ᴴmtakoneᴴ pəlafte.*
> 'He began fixing his shoe.'

> *'ā le tiwa ᴴmtakoneᴴ pəlafte.*
> 'He has begun fixing his shoe.'

4.4.22. *Negation of Verbs*

Verbal forms are negated by *la*, which is often proclitic to the verb, e.g., *lá-gbən* 'I don't want to', *lá-ktaxrət* 'you don't remember', but at times is free standing, e.g., *la qbílwāle* 'he hadn't received', *la šqəlle* 'he didn't take'. For the negation of the Imperative, see § 4.4.15.c. For the forms of the negated Present Copula, see § 4.4.6.2.

4.4.23. *Object Markers*

The forms of the L-suffix pronouns, LL-suffix pronouns, and E-suffix pronouns are presented in §§ 4.1.4–6.

4.4.23.1. *Objects Marked by L-Suffix Pronouns*

a. L-suffixes mark the object on forms derived from the Subjunctive base (§ 4.4.7–10) and on the Imperative (§ 4.4.15), e.g.,

> *byāmaxlox.*
> 'We will swear to you (m.s.).'

> *kulleni gbe qaṭlilan mandelan 'əbbəd ṃāye!*
> 'They want to kill all of us (and) throw us into the water!'

---

[179] Cf. *pyš* + *b* + Gerund in JBetan (Mutzafi 2008:64), and *pyš/tḥl/hrš* + *b* + Gerund in JAmid (Hoberman 1989:79).

nåbᵊlle!
'Take him away!'

ptuxle!
'Open it!'

šqulla!
'Take her!'

qbulla!
'Accept it!'

mqálūle!
'Clean him!'

b. The *l* of the suffix assimilates to a preceding *n*, *r*, and *t* (§ 3.6.c). *n* of the plural forms of the Imperative and of the 2nd person plural on forms derived from the Subjunctive are syncopated when L-suffixes are added (§§ 3.18.c; 4.1.6.j).

4.4.23.2. *Objects Marked by LL-Suffix Pronouns*

LL-suffixes mark objects of the Perfect (§ 4.4.16) and of the Gerund (§ 4.4.19), e.g.,

čú-xa lewe xíla-lle.
'No one has eaten it.'

tarʾa la ḥlᵊqta-lle.
'She has locked the door.' (§ 5.8.8)

lewᵊn míra-llu-ži.
'I haven't even told them.' (§ 5.8.15)

ʾāni lu zwíne-llu.
'They have bought them.'

ᴴtürkitᴴ le måra-lli.
'He is speaking Turkish to me.'

ṭamå wetun mačṃóye-lle?
'Why are you extinguishing it?' (§ 5.4.10)

qᵊbla lewa bᵊdwåqa-lla.
'It is not facing (lit., 'grasping') the qibla.' (§ 5.3.5)

4.4.23.3. *Objects Marked by Independent Forms of LL-Suffix Pronouns*

a. LL-suffixes marking objects of the Perfect and Gerund may be free standing (§ 4.1.5.a), e.g.,

'āni lu qṭile 'əlle.
'They have killed him.' (§ 5.5.6)

'iya ᴴsevəlᴴ 'axnan wax ᴴsbileᴴ 'əlle.
'We have suffered this burden.'

Cf. the following two contiguous sentences in which one finds in the first an enclitic LL- pronoun, but in the second a free standing form:

lewan xzéta-lle. 'āhat lewat xzeta 'əlle?
'I (f.s.) haven't seen him.' 'You (f.s.) haven't seen him?'

b. Independent LL-suffixes are used to mark the object following forms of the Preterite:[180]

kāsan əmre(')la 'əllan mən gəxka.
'Our stomach hurt us from laughter.' (§ 5.3.6)

hatxa 'üdle 'əlle.
'Like this they did to him.'

mxele 'əlle.
'He hit him.'

mxelu 'əllu.
'They hit them.'

One also finds objects marked by *'əlləd did-*:

u-ᴴm'oyəmluᴴ 'əlləd didu
'and they threatened him'

c. The object of an Imperative may be marked by a free standing LL-suffix instead of the L-suffix (§ 4.4.23.1):

hatxa 'odun 'əlle!
'Like this do (c.pl.) to him!' (§ 5.4.7)

mxalṣun 'əlli!
'Save (c.pl.) me!' (§ 5.6.5)

d. Forms based on the Subjunctive may not take two L-suffixes; instead one finds an L-suffix and a free standing LL-pronoun, e.g.,

mad'ərətte (< mad'əret + le) 'əlleni.
'You (m.s.) should return him to us.'

---

[180] They are an alternative to the use of E-suffix pronouns (§ 4.4.23.4).

4.4.23.4. *Objects Marked by E-Suffix Pronouns*

a. E-suffix pronouns function as object affixes in forms of the Preterite. They are added to the base of the Preterite in all persons and are followed by L-suffix pronouns (which mark the subject). In the following paradigm the subject is expressed by the 3 m.s. L-suffix pronoun -*le*:

Object
1 m.s.   *nšiqənne* (< nšiq + ən + le) 'he kissed me'
1 f.s.   *nšiqanne* (< nšiq + an + la) 'he kissed me'
2 m.s.   *nšiqətte* (< nšiq + ət + le) 'he kissed you'
2 f.s.   *nšiqatte* (< nšiq + at + le) 'he kissed you'
3 m.s.   *nšəqle* (< nšiq + ø + le) 'he kissed him'
3 f.s.   *nšiqāle* (< nšiq + a + le) 'he kissed her'
1 c.pl.   *nšiqaxle* (< nšiq + ax + le) 'he kissed us'
2 c.pl.   *nšiqétūle* (< nšiq + etun + le) 'he kised you'
3 c.pl.   *nšiqile* (< nšiq + i + le) 'he kissed them'

b. The E-suffix pronouns may function as indirect objects, e.g., *widənna* ᴴ*ʾaruḥā́*ᴴ 'She made me a meal' (§ 5.9.8), *məsennax julle* 'You brought me clothes' (§ 5.9.11).

c. One cannot tell from the restricted corpus if there is a difference in III-y verbs between *xzele* 'he saw him' and **xzele(?)* 'he saw them'.

d. The affixing of E-suffix pronouns of all persons obtains also in the JNerwa texts,[181] JAmid,[182] and JAradh.[183] In JZakho[184] and JBetan[185] Preterite forms containing the E-suffixes of the 1ˢᵗ and 2ⁿᵈ persons are replaced by the synthetic structure *qam*[186] + Subjunctive + E-suffix pronoun + L-suffix pronoun,[187] e.g., *qam xāpəqli* 'he embraced me' (JChalla *xpiqənne*), *qam ʾamrənnox* 'I told you' (JChalla *mirətti*). In JAmid and JAradh *qam* + Subjunctive may alternate with the E-suffix pronouns in all

---

[181] Sabar 1976:xl.
[182] Sabar 2002a:49.
[183] Mutzafi 2002:481–482.
[184] Hoberman 1989:36,40; Sabar 2002a:49.
[185] Mutzafi 2008a:86.
[186] Its origin has been explained in several ways: (1) *qdām* (adverb); (2) *qədam/qaddem* (G/D verb); (3) the Participle *qāʾim*. For a discussion of the possibilities see Pennacchietti 1997 (who suggests an original grammaticalized form of the Participle *qāʾim*) and Rubin 2005:33–34 (who prefers an original G verb).
[187] In the 3rd person in JZakho and JBetan (Mutzafi 2008a:86) the Preterite base + L-suffix form (e.g., *murpyāle* 'he released her') may interchange with *qam* + Subjunctive base + E-suffix pronoun + L-suffix pronoun (*qammarpela*).

persons. The structure *qam* + Subjunctive is so rarely attested in JChalla (*'e-'arməlsa qam gāwərra* 'he married that widow'; § 5.1.3) that it is clearly the result of JZakho influence.

e. The object E-affixes may be replaced by the independent LL-suffixes (§ 4.4.23.3), e.g., "he spoke to me' may be expressed by both *mirənne* and *mərre 'əlli*.

4.4.23.5. Dummy Objects

Dummy 3 f.s. object affixes[188] are attested on the verbs *'rq* 'flee' (§ 4.4.28.7), *qḍy* 'spend time',[189] and *xdy* 'rejoice'. Representative examples are 1 c.s. *'riqāli* 'I fled', 2 m.s. *'riqālox* 'you fled', 3 m.s. *xədyāle 'əlli* 'he rejoiced over me', 3 c.pl. *qəḍyālu* 'they passed the time' (§ 5.6.6), *xədyālu 'əlleni* 'they rejoiced over us'. It would appear that there are also examples with a dummy 3 f.s. object on the verbs *rpy* 'C loosen, release, attack', *mxy* G 'strike, hit', and *plṭ* D 'take out':

> *kalbe mrupyālu l-'Awrāham gəbe qaṭlile. b-íya-'ida u-yá-'ida 'anna nāše mrupyālu 'əlləd 'Awrāham.*
> 'The dogs let Abraham have it, they wish to kill him. When all's said and done, those people let Abraham have it.' (§ 5.7.10)

> *tar'a ptəxli gyāni. məxyāla 'əlli xá-gā xeta basri.*
> 'I opened the door myself. She hit me once again from behind.' (§ 5.8.13)

Though one may see in the following three examples a 3 f.s. dummy object on the verbs D *plṭ* 'take out' and Q *prtx* 'make change', it appears more likely that the noun *paṇqáṇoṭe*, despite its plural suffix, is treated as a feminine singular:

> *xamši paṇqáṇoṭe xá-yoma mpulṭāle.*
> 'One day he took out fifty liras.' (§ 5.10.2)

> *mpulṭāle xamši paṇqáṇoṭe*
> 'he took out fifty liras' (§ 5.10.6)

> *'egā 'āhat byāli xamši paṇqáṇoṭe? pa da-ḥmól. mpartəxənna.*
> 'So now you'll give me fifty liras? (Abraham says:) "So just wait. I will get change for it."' (§ 5.10.2)

---

[188] On the phenomenon of the dummy morpheme in other dialects, see, e.g., Garbell 1965:76; Hoberman 1989:215,221; Israeli 1998:117–118; Mutzafi 2004:103.

[189] But not when it is transitive ('finish something'), e.g., *šūli qqāḍənne* 'I finish my work'.

4.4.24. Qym + *Verb*

a. A frequent narrative construction in JChalla is a Subjunctive form of *qym* followed by another Subjunctive governing an object, e.g.,

qemən mpalṭənne
'I (m.s.) up (and) take him out'

qémana xapqannox
'I (f.s.) up (and) hug you (m.s.)'

qemət gālətti
'you (m.s.) up (and) reveal to me'

qema doqāli xapqāli
'she up (and) grabs me (and) hugs me'

qemi doqile
'they up (and) grab him'

b. Significantly less common are constructions with the Preterite or the Imperative, e.g.,

qəmle mšudraxle
'he up (and) sent us'

qəmlu zəllu
'they up (and) went'

de qū misi!
'so up (and) bring (it)!'

c. The origin of the construction *qym* + verb would appear to lie in the ingressive use of *qym* as an auxiliary verb, which is well attested in NeoAram as well as in general Semitic.[190] In JChalla it is used to mark ingressive action, be it in narrating past, present or future action. Cf. the ingressive auxiliary use of *qym* in JBetan, which is restricted to the Preterite.[191]

---

[190] See Dobbs-Allsopp 1995. According to Pennacchietti (1997:478), in dialects of Ashita and Upper Tiari, the syntagm expresses the imminent future whereas in dialects of the Mosul area it expresses a past event immediately following a preterite. Mutzafi (2007:353), however, considers the manuscript that Pennacchietti bases his description on to be "a concoction of various Christian NENA dialectal words and forms and is replete with fictitious and hyper-corrected forms, although quite a few other words and forms indeed reflect Ṭyare."

[191] Mutzafi 2008a:376.

d. JChalla *qym* + Subjunctive frequently occurs following a verbal form
marking the past:

zǝlle mjāmǝ' denānǝd gyāne. qemi qaṭlile.
'He went to gather together his debtors. They up (and) kill him. (§ 5.6.9)

walla 'iya 'axoni Mǝdo mpǝlle b-'idǝd didu. qemi doqile.
'By God, this brother of mine, Mido, fell into their hands. They up (and)
seize him.' (§ 5.13.1)

walḥāṣǝl walla Qoto zǝllu muselu. qemi qorile.
'In short, by God, they went (and) brought Qoto. They up (and) bury him.'
(§ 5.4.11)

*mǎtwāle b-gyāne l-tāma go mǝzgafte. qemi dārele balāye 'ǝbbǝd reš hudāye
ta šāqǝl mǝnnu pāre.*
'He had died by himself there in the mosque. They up (and) put trouble on
the Jews in order to take money from them.' (§ 5.5.8)

4.4.25. *Sequences of Verbal Forms*

a. A story that took place in the past may be told with alternating
verbal forms. The Preterite is the most common, though, as can be seen
below, one also finds the Perfect, *qym* + Subjunctive, Present, Future,
and Gerund (in the continuous present syntagm), each one expressing
a different tense or aspectual nuance. See, e.g.,

*mǝn 'áx-geb 'itǝn tāma škaftyāsa 'uṛwe 'uṛwe. qemi nablile xá-yomǝd 'ǝryā-
na… walḥāṣǝl nobǝllu l-tāma. nobǝllu l-tāma. lu zile xa 'ǝsrí-nāše mare
xanjāra. kutxa sǝkkinǝd dide l-axxa. u-zǝllu ḥil zǝllu l-tāma. 'ǝryána-le
bisāya. tlǝllu. zǝllu škafta. bodi nūra. zǝllu. 'üdlu nūra. kǝmri ta Qoto: 'āhat
mesǝt ṣiwe! Qoto musele ṣiwe. mǝttūle. drele reš-, 'üdle nūra. 'āni nūra
mučṃelu. xá-gā xet kemǝr: ṭamá wetun mačṃóye-lle? kǝmri: ma'lǝqle!
'āni-, 'iya, 'iya mā kǝmrila, 'āya gǝbe kāyǝp d-āni ḥmǝllu 'ǝbbǝd ᴴsǝkkiním.
kenᴴ. walḥāṣǝl xá-gā xet mo'lǝqle nūra. 'āni mučṃelu nūra. naqǝl ṭlāha
mo'lǝqle. mučṃelu. walla m-é-'ida kǝple. kemǝr: de-mpóx 'ǝbbǝd palle ta
pāyǝš ḥǝnna ta lā'ǝq. walla kǝple reš dide. mundelu qam xanjāra. qemi
qaṭlile. šoqile l-tāma u-selu. 'āṣǝrta.*
On this side (of Bet Kare) there are very big caves there. They *up* (and)
lead him one rainy day… In short, they *led* him there. They *led* him there.
About twenty people (each one) with a dagger *have gone*. Each one's knife
is here (at the side). And they *went* and by the time they got there rain
is falling. They *got wet*. They *went* (to) a cave. They *will make* a fire. They
went. They *made* a fire. They *say* to Qoto: "You should bring wood!" Qoto
brought wood. He *put it down*. He *placed* it on—, he *made* a fire. They
extinguished the fire. Once again he (lights the fire, they extinguished it
and he) *says*: "Why *are you extinguishing* it?" They *say*: "Light it"! They—,
this, what do they call it?—he *has to bend* down (to light the fire) so that

they *could attack* him with knives. Yes. In short, once again he *lit* the
fire. They *extinguished* the fire. A third time he *lit* it. They *extinguished*
it. By God, he *bent* over (the fire) from that side. (One) *says* (to Qoto):
"Now blow on the coals so that (the fire) will become, um, will catch." By
God, he *bent* over it (the fire). They *attacked* him with a dagger. They *up*
(and) *kill* him. They *leave* him there and *came*. (It is) evening. (§ 5.4.9–
11)

f. The fluctuation of tenses in narrative, particularly of participial and
preterite forms, is known from earlier Aramaic.[192]

4.4.26. *Repetitive—Reversive Postverbal Particle*

There are a few examples of a clipped form of the repetitive-reversive
postverbal Kurdish particle -*wa* (< *hawa*):[193]

> *ʾən gebat dáʾrat-wa ʾəl-Čalla—*
> 'If you (f.s.) want to return back to Challa—' (§ 5.9.12)

> *xarāye m-Šiwa xá-gā xet lu dʾíre-wa l-Čalla… m-Šiwa xá-gā xet lu dʾíre-wa
> l-Čalla.*
> 'Later once again they have returned back to Challa from Shiwa… 'From
> Shiwa once again they have returned back to Challa.' (§ 5.6.7)

> *ʾáqqara bə'wāra bəplāṭa bə'wāra bəplāṭa… ᴴbe'emétᴴ séli-wa.*
> 'So much entering, leaving, entering, leaving… Really, I had come (and
> gone and come and gone).' (§ 5.9.9–10)

> *ʾāya séle-wa dáre-wa quṭməd jigáre go ʾene*
> 'He came back to put ashes in his eyes again' (§ 5.6.12)

4.4.27. *Verb Classes*

The different verb classes are presented below according to the following
order: I-ʾ, I-*y*, II-ʾ, II-*w*, II-*y*, II-geminate, III-ʾ, III-*w*, III-*y*. They are
followed by doubly weak and irregular verbs: I-ʾ and II-*w*, I-*y* and II-
w, I-*y* and III-*w*, I-*y* and III-*y*, II-*w* and III-ʾ, II-*w* and III-*y*, ʾ*sy*, ʾ*zl*, *b'y*,
hwy, *hymn*, *mnx*, *mṣy*, *nbl*, *npl*, *xyy*, *y'y*, *yhw(l)*, *ytw*. When the verb is

---

[192] Cf., e.g., the following selection in JPA from Ms. Vatican 30 of *Genesis Rabba*
(Kutscher 1967:62): אזלין ואזון בני תלתה יומין, ועל ארגינטי ומזגא קודמיהון ועלין וסחון ואתון
לגביה... 'they *go* and they *heated up* the bath for three days, and 'RGYNṬY (a demon)
entered (the bathhouse) and *mixed* it (the water of the bath) before them and they *enter*
and *bathed* and *came* to him (Emperor Diocletian). See also the situation in BiblAram
(Rosenthal 1995:59–60).
[193] On the uses of this particle in NENA, see, e.g., Mutzafi 2004:85–86.

infrequent in the corpus, only attested forms (including those with object affixes) are cited.

4.4.27.1. Verbs I-ʾ

Attested original I-ʾ roots include ʾmr (< אמר) 'say' and ʾxl (< אכל) 'eat'.

G ʾmr 'say'				
	Subjunctive	Present	Future	Preterite
1 m.s.	ʾámrən(a)	kámrən(a)	bámrən(a)	mərri
1 f.s.	ʾámran(a)	kámran(a)	bámran(a)	mərri
2 m.s.	ʾámrət(ən)	kámrət(ən)	bámrət(ən)	mərrox
2 f.s.	ʾámrat(ən)	kámrat(ən)	bámrat(ən)	mərrax
3 m.s.	ʾāmər	kemər	bāmər	mərre
3 f.s.	ʾamrat	kəmra	bamra	mərra
1 c.pl.	ʾámrax(in)	kámrax(in)	bámrax(in)	mərran, mə́rreni
2 c.pl.	ʾamrétun(a)	kəmrétun(a)	bamrétun(a)	mə́rrexun
3 c.pl.	ʾamri	kəmri	bamri	mərru

The prefix g- on forms of the Present, e.g., gemər, gəmri, is significantly less frequent than k-, and thus is most likely the result of JZakho interference.

Imperative	c.s. mar, c.pl. marun
Participle	m.s. mira, f.s. mərta, c.pl. mire
Gerund	ʾimāra

G ʾxl 'eat'				
	Subjunctive	Present	Future	Preterite
1 m.s.	ʾáxlən(a)	káxlən(a)	báxlən(a)	xəlli[194]
1 f.s.	ʾáxlan(a)	káxlan(a)	báxlan(a)	xəlli
2 m.s.	ʾáxlət(ən)	káxlət(ən)	báxlət(ən)	xəllox
2 f.s.	ʾáxlat(ən)	káxlat(ən)	báxlat(ən)	xəllax
3 m.s.	ʾāxəl	kexəl	bāxəl	xəlle
3 f.s.	ʾaxlat	kəxla	baxla	xəlla
1 c.pl.	ʾáxlax(in)	káxlax(in)	báxlax(in)	xəllan, xə́lleni
2 c.pl.	ʾaxlétun(a)	kəxlétun(a)	baxlétun(a)	xə́llexun
3 c.pl.	ʾaxli	kəxli	baxli	xəllu

Imperative	c.s. xol, c.pl. xolun
Participle	m.s. xila, f.s. xəlta, c.pl. xile
Gerund	ʾixāla

---

[194] ʾxəlli is also attested once. See § 3.17.a.

C *'xl* 'feed'

> Subjunctive 2 m.s. *maxlət*, 3 c.pl. *maxli*
> Present 2 m.s. *gmaxlət*
> Future 2 m.s. *mmaxlət*, 3 m.s. *bmāxəl*

Note the loan from ModH (הֶאֱשִׁים):

> 3 c.pl. *mo'šəmənnu* 'they accused me'

' in *'wd* 'do, make' and *'wr* 'enter' (§ 4.4.28.1) is a reflex of original ʿ, as is '
in *'lq* G '(search and) find', C 'kindle, light', e.g., *k'alqax* 'we earn', *mo'əlqāla*
'she lit it'. See also *'rq* 'run, flee' (§ 4.4.28.7), *'sy* 'come' (§ 4.4.28.8) and *'zl*
'go' (§ 4.4.28.9).

4.4.27.2. *Verbs I-y*

An original I-*y* root is *yrq* 'become green' (< ירק). Inflected similarly is
yrx 'be long' (< ארך):

> G Present 3 m.s. *gyārəq* 'he becomes green'
> Preterite 3 m.s. *yrəxle* 'he has become long'
>
> C Subjunctive 2 m.s. *mayrəxətta* 'you may lengthen her', 3 m.s. *mayrəx* 'he may lengthen', *mayrəxla* 'he may lengthen her'; 3 c.pl. *mayrəxilu* 'they may lengthen them'

Two additional verbs have gone over to I-*y*: *ysq* 'ascend' (< סלק) and *ysr*
'bind' (< אסר):

> G Subjunctive 3 m.s. *yāsəq* 'he may ascend', 1 c.pl. *yasqax* 'we may ascend', 3 c.pl. *yasrilox* 'they may bind you'
> Present 1 m.s. *gyasrənnexun* 'I bind you (pl.)', 1 c.pl. *gyasraxlu* 'we bind them', 3 c.pl. *gyasrile* 'they bind him'
> Future 3 c.pl. *byasríleni* 'they will bind us'
> Preterite 1 c.s. *səqli*, 'I ascended', 3 m.s. *səqle* 'he ascended', 3 c.pl. *sirilu* 'they bound them'
> Participle m.s. *sira* 'bound', *ysira*, c.pl. *sire*

There is only one example of a C form:

> Preterite 3 m.s. *musqaxle* 'he brought us up'

Note also the loan from ModHeb (יִשֵּׁר):

> D Future 3 c.pl. *(m)myašrilu* 'they will straighten them'

See also verbs I-*y* and II-*w* (§ 4.4.28.2), *y'y* 'know' (§ 4.4.28.19), *yhw(l)*
'give' (§ 4.4.28.20), and *ytw* 'sit' (§ 4.4.28.21).

4.4.27.3. *Verbs II-ʾ*

II-ʾ verbs are reflexes of different verbal roots:

a. ClAram II-*g*: *rʾš* C 'wake up' (< רגש)
b. ClAram II-*w*: *dʾš* 'tread on' (< דוש? or conflation of Aram דוש + Ar
   دعس?)
c. ClAram II-ʿ: *dʾp* 'fold' (< ܐܬܟܠܚ; § 4.4.1.b), *dʾr* 'return' (< ܪܚܕ), *ṭʾn*
   C 'load' (< טען)

G *dʾr* 'return (intr.)'		
	Subjunctive	Preterite
1 m.s.	*dáʾrən(a)*	*dʾərri*
1 f.s.	*dáʾran(a)*	*dʾərri*
2 m.s.	*dáʾrət(ən)*	*dʾərrox*
2 f.s.	*dáʾrat(ən)*	*dʾərrax*
3 m.s.	*dāʾer*	*dʾərre*
3 f.s.	*daʾra*	*dʾərra*
1 c.pl.	*dáʾrax(in)*	*dʾərran, dʾə́rreni*
2 c.pl.	*daʾrétun(a)*	*dʾə́rrexun*
3 c.pl.	*daʾri*	*dʾərru*

Imperative	c.s. *dʾor*, c.pl. *dʾorun*
Participle	m.s. *dʾira*, f.s. *dʾərta*, c.pl. *dʾire*
Gerund	*dʾāra*

C 'return (tr.)'

Subjunctive	1 m.s. *madʾərənna* 'I may return her', 2 m.s. *madʾərətte* 'you may return him', 1 c.pl. *madʾəraxle* 'we may return him'
Preterite	3 c.pl. *mudʾərənnu* 'they returned me'

See also *bʾy* 'want' (§ 4.4.28.10) and *yʾy* 'know' (§ 4.4.28.19).

4.4.27.4. *Verbs II-w*

This verb class is made up of reflexes of

a. ClAram II-*b*: *dwq* 'hold' (< דבק), *gwr* 'marry (intr.)' (< גבר), *jwj*
   'move' (< שבש), *kwš* 'descend' (< כבש), *lwš* 'wear' (< לבש), *nwḥ* 'bark'
   (< נבח), *qwr* 'bury' (< קבר), *šwq* 'leave' (< שבק), *twr* break (< תבר),
   zwn 'buy' (< זבן)

b. ClAram II-*w*: *xwr* 'be white' (< חור)
c. loanwords: *zwr* 'go around'

G *dwq* 'hold, grasp'		
	Subjunctive	Preterite
1 m.s.	*dóqən(a)*	*düqli*
1 f.s.	*dóqan(a)*	*düqli*
2 m.s.	*dóqət(ən)*	*düqlox*
2 f.s.	*dóqat(ən)*	*düqlax*
3 m.s.	*dāwəq*	*düqle*
3 f.s.	*doqa*	*düqla*
1 c.pl.	*dóqax(in)*	*düqlan, dúqleni*
2 c.pl.	*doqétun(a)*	*dúqlexun*
3 c.pl.	*doqi*	*düqlu*

Imperative   c.s. *doq*, c.pl. *doqun*
Participle: m.s. *dwiqa, düqa*, f.s. *dwəqta, düqta*; c.pl. *dwiqe, düqe*
Gerund   *dwāqa*

C	Subjunctive	3 m.s. *mādüqlu* 'he may have them seized', *mākušli* 'he may bring me down', *manwəxle* 'he may make him bark', 3 c.pl. *magwərila* 'they may marry her off', *makšilu*[195] 'they may bring them down'
	Past Habitual	3 m.s. *māzúrwāle* 'he would turn him around', 3 c.pl. *mazüríwāle* 'they would turn him around'
	Preterite	3 c.pl. *mugwərālu* 'they married her off', *mokušlu* 'they brought down'
	Plupreterite:	1 s. *mugəráwāli* 'I had her married off'
	Participle	c.pl. *múgwəre* 'married off'

On the contraction of *wi* > *ū/ü*, see § 3.12.b.

See also the doubly weak verbs I-ʾ and II-*w* (§ 4.4.28.1), I-*y* and II-*w* (§ 4.4.28.2), II-*w* and III-ʾ (§ 4.4.28.5), II-*w* and III-*y* (§ 4.4.28.6).

4.4.27.5. *Verbs II-y*

This class consists of the following verbs:

a. ClAram II-*w*: *mys* 'die' (< מות; § 3.1.b), *nyx* 'rest' (< נוח), *pyš* 'remain' (< פוש), *pyx* 'become cool' (< פוח), *qym* 'stand up' (< קום), *rym* C 'lift' (< רום)

---

[195] For expected *makušklu* or *makwəšilu*.

b. ClAram geminate: *čym* 'close' (< טמם), *kyp* 'bend' (< כפף), *pyd* 'pass by' (<פגג), *syl* 'fuck' (< סלל), *tym* 'finish' (< תמם), *xyk* 'scratch' (< חכך), *xyp* 'wash' (< חפף)

c. ClAram I-*y*: *lyp* 'learn' (< ילף), *qyd* 'burn' (< יקד)

d. loanwords: *čyq* 'tear out', *čyr* 'move around', *dyʿ* 'be lost', *ḥyl* 'desecrate' (see also § 4.4.27.6), *ḥyš* 'insert', *jyb* 'answer', *pyč* 'crush', *ṣyḥ* 'check', *zyd* 'increase'

G *pyš* 'remain'	Subjunctive	Preterite
1 m.s.	*péšən(a)*	*pəšli*
1 f.s.	*péšan(a)*	*pəšli*
2 m.s.	*péšət(ən)*	*pəšlox*
2 f.s.	*péšat(ən)*	*pəšlax*
3.m.s.	*pāyəš*	*pəšle*
3 f.s.	*peša*	*pəšla*
1 c.pl.	*péšax(in)*	*pəšlan, péšleni*
2 c.pl.	*pešétun(a)*	*péšlexun*
3 c.pl.	*peši*	*pəšlu*

Imperative c.s. *poš*, c.pl. *pošun*
Participle m.s. *piša*, f.s. *pəšta*, c.pl. *piše*
Gerund *pyāša*

The imperative forms of *qym* 'arise' are c.s. *qū* and c.pl. *qūn*.[196]

Of interest is the root *šyʿ* 'plaster', which elsewhere shows up in NeoAram as *šyʾ* (< שוע or שעע; § 3.3.d):

G Preterite 3 m.s. *šəʿle* 'he plastered it'
   Imperative c.pl. *šúʿūle* 'plaster it'

In the D stem one finds only the verb *hyr* 'dare':

Subjunctive 3 m.s. *mhāyər*, 1 c.pl. *mherax*, 3 c.pl. *mheri*

In the C stem, original II-geminate and II-w/y verbs, which have collapsed together into one inflection in G, show different inflections, even in the same verb:

---

[196] Cf. in other NeoAram dialects *qū(lox)*, *qūmun*, *qūn*, *qū(lōxun)*. See, e.g., Krotkoff 1982:29; Sabar 2002a:278. For a survey of literature on the origin of *qu*, pl. *qumun*, and the imperative suffix *-mun*, see Polotsky 1961:27–29.

Subjunctive	1 m.s. *mākipən* 'I may bend (tr.)', *malpənnox* 'I may teach you', *majbənne* 'I may answer him', *malpənne* 'I may teach him', m.s. *marṃət* 'you may lift up', *majbətti* 'you may answer me', 3 m.s. *māṛəm* 'he may lift up', 1 c.pl. *ᴴmaxinaxluᴴ* 'we may prepare them', 2 c.pl. *maqimetun* 'you may set up', 3 c.pl. *madiʿilu* 'they may miss them', *majbili* 'they may answer me', *malpile* 'they may teach me'
Present	3 m.s. *gmākəple* 'he bends him (tr.)'
PastHabitual	3 c.pl., *mapidiwa* 'they were making (it) pass by'
Future	3 m.s. *mmājəblox* 'he will answer you'
Past Prospective	3 c.pl. *mmakipíwāle* 'they were bending it'
Preterite	1 s. *ᴴmoḥəlliᴴ* 'I desecrated', *mujbāli* 'I answered her', 3 m.s. *mokəple* 'he bent it', 1 c.pl. *mojəblan* 'we answered him', 3 c.pl. *mokəplu* 'they bent it'
Imperative	c.s. *māṛəm* 'lift up!', *mājəb* 'answer!'
Gerund	*maṣoḥe* 'checking', *maṛome* 'lifting up', *ᴴmaxoneᴴ* 'preparing'

4.4.27.6. *Geminate Verbs*

The attested geminate verbs are *tll* 'get wet' (< תלל) and *xll* 'wash (tr.)' (< חלל):[197]

G	Preterite	3 m.pl. *tləllu* 'they got wet'
D	Preterite	3 m.s. *mxuləlle* 'he washed it'
Gerund	*mxassóse-lla* 'renewing her'	

See also *xyy* 'live' (§ 4.4.28.18). H חלל 'desecrate' shows up as as a II-*y* root *ḥyl* (§ 4.4.27.5), but also as a geminate root in the Participle in the Perfect construction: *wən mḥúlla-lla* 'I have desecrated it'.

4.4.27.7. *Verbs III-ʾ*

a. There are three sources of III-ʾ verbs:

1. ClAram III-ʿ: *blʾ* 'swallow' (< בלע), *grʾ* 'shave' (< גרע), *šmʾ* G 'hear' and C 'listen' (< שמע), *mrʾ* 'be in pain' (< מרע), *pqʾ* 'cut' (< פקע), *qtʾ* (< קטע), *zdʾ* 'fear' (< זוע; § 4.4.1.b), *zrʾ* 'sow' (< זרע)
2. ClAram III-*g*: *plʾ* 'divide' (< פלג)
3. loanword (III-ʿ): *nf* 'be useful'

See also the C stem of *yʾy* 'know' (§ 4.4.28.19).

---

[197] Cf. JBetan (Mutzafi 2008a:77–79).

b. ' is often difficult to hear or elided. When questionable it appears in parentheses.

c. *ə* > *e*/_ ' (§ 3.11.a), e.g., *gšāmə' > gšāme' 'hears', *šmə'li > šme'li 'he heard'.

Attested forms include

G	Subjunctive	2 m.s. *zad'ət* 'you may fear', *qaṭ'ətta* 'you may cut her', 3 m.s. *šāme'* 'he should hear', 3 f.s. *zadya* 'she may fear', *marya* 'she may hurt', 1 pl. *qaṭ'axlu* 'we may cut them'
	Present	2 m.s. *gzad'ət* 'you fear', 3 m.s. *gšāme'* 'he hears', *gnāfe'* 'it is useful', 1 c.pl. *gzad'ax* 'we may fear'
	Future	1 m.s. *bzad'ən* 'I shall fear', *pqaṭ'ənne* 'I shall cut him', 2 m.s. *pšām(')ət* 'you will listen', 3 f.s. *pqaṭya* 'she will cut',
	Preterite	1 m.s. *qəṭyāli* 'I cut her', 3 m.s. *šme'le* 'he heard', *qṭe'le* 'he cut', 3 f.s. *əmre(')la* 'it hurt', 1 c.pl. *šme'lan* 'we heard'
	Imperative	c.s. *šmo'*, m.s. *šmo'lox*, c.pl. *šmo'un*
	Participle	m.s. *šəmya* 'heard', *zərya* 'sown', f.s. *mre'ta* 'hurt', c.pl. *šəmye, qəṭye*
D	Subjunctive	3 m.pl. *mpāle(')lu* 'they distributed'
	Participle	f.s. *mpole(')ta* 'distributed', c.pl. *mpulye*
C	Subjunctive	2 m.s. *mašm(')ət*
	Imperative	c.s. *mašmi(')/ mašme(')*, c.pl. *mašm(')un*
	Gerund	*mašmoye*

The partial merger of verbs III-' with verbs III-*y* is evident, e.g., in the final vowel *i* before ' in the Imperative *mašmi(')* (cf. III-*y maxzi* 'show!') alongside *mašme(')*, and in those forms where *y* has replaced historical ', e.g., *zadya* 'she may fear' (< *zad'a), *šemya* 'heard' (< *smi'a).

See also verbs II-*w* and III-' (§ 4.4.28.5) and *y'y* 'know' (§ 4.4.28.19).

4.4.27.8. *Verbs III-w*

This class is a reflex of ClAram verbs III-*b*: *gnw* 'steal' (< גנב), *ksw* 'write' (< כתב), *rkw* 'ride' (< רכב), *xlw* 'milk' (< חלב), *xrw* 'be destroyed' (< חרב), *xšw* 'think' (< חשב). On the contraction of the diphthongs leading to the *ū*-vowel in several of the forms, see § 3.14.

G *ksw* 'write'		
	Subjunctive	Preterite
1 m.s.	*káswən(a)*	*ksūli*
1 f.s.	*káswan(a)*	*ksūli*
2 m.s.	*káswət(ən)*	*ksūlox*
2 f.s.	*káswat(ən)*	*ksūlax*
3 m.s.	*kāsu*	*ksūle*
3 f.s.	*kaswa*	*ksūla*
1 c.pl.	*káswax(in)*	*ksūlan, ksúleni*
2 c.pl.	*kaswétun(a)*	*ksúlexun*
3 c.pl.	*kaswi*	*ksūlu*

Imperative   s. *ksū*, pl. *ksūn*
Participle   m.s. *ksiwa*, f.s. *ksūta*, pl. *ksiwe*
Gerund   *ksāwa*

D   Subjunctive   2 m.s. *mqalwətta* 'you may clean her', 3 c.pl. *mqalwilu* 'they may clean them'
    Imperative   c.s. *mqālu* 'clean!'

C   Subjunctive   3 m.s. *maxrūla* 'he may destroy her', *maxrúlexun* 'he may destroy you (pl.)'
    Past Habitual 3 c.pl. *maxərwíwa* 'they used to destroy'
    Preterite   3 m.s. *muxərwále* 'he destroyed her', 3 c.pl. *muxərwálu* 'they destroyed her'
    Participle   m.s. *múxərwa* 'destroyed', c.pl. *múxərwe*

See also *ytw* 'sit' (§ 4.4.28.21).

4.4.27.9. *Verbs III-y*

This is the largest of the weak classes and includes

1. ClAram III-y: *bry* 'happen' (< ברי), *čmy* 'be extinguished' (< סמי),
   dry 'put in' (< דרי), *gly* 'reveal' (< גלי), *gny* 'set (sun)' (< גני), *ksy* 'cover'
   (< כסי), *msy* 'wash' (< מסי), *mṭy* 'arrive' (< מטי), *mly* 'fill' and *mly*
   'be sufficient', (< מלי), *mxy* 'strike' (< מחי), *ndy* 'throw down/away'
   (< נדי), *nṣy* 'fight' (< נצי), *nšy* 'forget' (< נשי), *qry* 'call, read' (< קרי),
   rpy 'release, loosen' (< רפי), *sny* 'hate' (< סני), *sxy* 'bathe' (<סחי), *ṣly*
   'pray' (< צלי), *šny* 'move' (< שני), *šry* 'untie' (< שרי), *šty* 'drink' (< שתי),
   tly 'hang' (< תלי), *ṭ'y* 'search' (< טעי), *ṭpy* 'stick, kindle' (< טפי), *ṭry*
   'drive' (< טרי), *ṭšy* 'hide' (< טשי), *xdy* 'rejoice' (< חדי), *xzy* 'see' (< חזי)
   zky 'deserve' (< זכי)

2. loanwords: *d'y* 'pray', *dġy* 'be branded', *jry* 'flow', *kry* 'be short', *lzy* 'hurry', *mḥy* 'erase', *qdy* 'spend time, finish', *šky* 'lodge a complaint', *zxy* 'deserve'

G *xzy*[198] 'see'		
	Subjunctive	Preterite
1 m.s.	*xázən(a)*	*xzeli*
1 f.s.	*xáyzan(a)*	*xzeli*
2 m.s.	*xázət(ən)*	*xzelox*
2 f.s.	*xázyat(ən)*	*xzelax*
3 m.s.	*xāze*	*xzele*
3 f.s.	*xazya*	*xzela*
1 c.pl.	*xázax(in)*	*xzelan, xzéleni*
2 c.pl.	*xāzétun(a)*	*xzélexun*
3 c.pl.	*xāze*	*xzelu*

Imperative m.s. *xzi*, f.s. *xze*, c.pl. *xzūn*[199]
Participle m.s. *xəzya*, f.s. *xzeta*,[200] c.pl. *xəzye*
Gerund *xzāya*

C Subjunctive 1 m.s. *maxzənnax* 'I may show you'
Past Habitual 1 m.s. *maxzənwa* 'I would show'
Imperative m.s. *maxzi* 'show!'

Other verbs:

D Subjunctive 1 c.pl. *mrāpaxlox* 'we may release you'
Preterite 1 c.s. *mrupyāli* 'I released her', 3 f.s. *mropənna* 'she released me', 3 c.pl. *mrupyālu* 'they released her'[201]
Participle f.s. *mrupeta* 'released'; c.pl. *mrupye*
Imperative m.s. *mrápilu* 'release them!'

C Subjunctive 1 m.s. *mandənne* 'I may throw him', 2 m.s. *mandət* 'you may throw', 3 m.s. *mazkela* 'may he grant her merit', 3 c.pl. *mandelu* 'they may throw them'
Past Habitual 3 c.pl. *mandéwālu* 'they used to throw'

---

[198] On the realization of /x/ as [ɣ] in this root, see § 3.6.g.
[199] Mutzafi 2002:480–481 presents the plural of verbs III-*y* ending in -*V̄wun* as a common feature of *lishana deni* dialects. I do not hear it, however, in the speech of Shabbo. It is found in JChalla only in the imperative of *'sy* 'come': *sāwun*.
[200] Cf. the f.s. with *i* in other *lishana deni* dialects, e.g., *xzisa* (JZakho), *xziϑa* (JBetan). Polotsky 1961:15–16 suggests that the feminine Participle in some NENA dialects was formed on the analogy of the Preterite. Mutzafi (p.c.) suggests that analogy to verbs III-' (e.g., *gre'ta* 'shaven') may be responsible.
[201] See § 4.4.23.5.

	Preterite	1 c.s. *mundeli, məndeli* 'I threw', 3 m.s. *mundele,* *məndele* 'he threw', 3 f.s. *mundela* 'she threw', 1 c.pl. *mundyālan* 'we threw her', 3 c.pl. *mundelu, məndelu* 'they threw him', *mundyālu* 'they threw her'

Preterite 1 c.s. *mundeli, məndeli* 'I threw', 3 m.s. *mundele, məndele* 'he threw', 3 f.s. *mundela* 'she threw', 1 c.pl. *mundyālan* 'we threw her', 3 c.pl. *mundelu, məndelu* 'they threw him', *mundyālu* 'they threw her'

Imperative m.s. *mandi*, 'throw!' *mándila* 'throw her!', c.pl. *mándūle* 'throw him!'

Participle c.pl. *múndye*

Gerund *mandoye* 'throwing'

See also verbs I-*y* and III-*y* (§ 4.4.28.4), II-*w* and III-*y* (§ 4.4.28.6), *ʾsy* 'come' (§ 4.4.28.8), *bʾy* 'want' (§ 4.4.28.10), and *mṣy* 'be able' (§ 4.4.28.15).

4.4.28. Doubly Weak and Irregular Verbs

4.4.28.1. Verbs I-ʾ and II-w

Two verbs are attested: *ʾwd* 'do, make' (< עבד) and *ʾwr* 'enter' (< עבר).

G 'do, make'	Subjunctive	Preterite
1 m.s.	*ʾódən(a)*	*ʾüdli, wədli*[202]
1 f.s.	*ʾódan(a)*	*ʾüdli, wədli*
2 m.s.	*ʾódət(ən)*	*ʾüdlox, wədlox*
2 f.s.	*ʾódat(ən)*	*ʾüdlax, wədlax*
3 m.s.	*ʾāwəd*	*ʾüdle, wədle*
3 f.s.	*ʾoda*	*ʾüdla, wədla*
1 c.pl.	*ʾódax(in)*	*ʾüdlan, ʾúdleni, wədlan, wə́dleni*
2 c.pl.	*ʾodétun(a)*	*ʾúdlexun, wə́dlexun*
3 c.pl.	*ʾodi*	*ʾüdlu, wədlu*

Imperative c.s. *ʾod*, c.pl. *ʾodun*

Participle m.s. *ʾwida, wida, ʾúda* (§ 3.12.b), f.s. *ʾütta* (§ 3.6.b), c.pl. *ʾwide, wide, ʾüde*

Gerund[203] *ʾwāda, wāda;* following the preposition *b-*: *bāda*

C Subjunctive 2 m.s. *maʾrətte* 'you may bring him in'

Preterite 3 m.s. *moʾərre* 'he brought him in', *moʾrənne* 'he brought me in', 3 c.pl. *moʾrənnu* 'they brought me in'

---

[202] *ʾüdli* < *ʾwədli. Cf. JZakh *ʾuzli* (Sabar 2002a:91), JAmid *ʾüdli,ʾwədli* (Hoberman 1989:214), JBetan *wədli* (Mutzafi 2008a:76).

[203] Cf. JZakh *wāza* (Polotsky 1967:105), JAmid *ʾwada* (Hoberman 1989:214), JBetan *wāða* (Mutzafi 2008a:76).

4.4.28.2. *Verbs I-y and II-w*

One verb is attested: *ywš* 'dry up' (< יבש)

> G   Preterite   3 m.s. *ywəšle* 'he dried up', 3 c.pl. *ywəšlu* 'they dried up'

4.4.28.3. *Verbs I-y and III-w*

See *ytw* 'sit' (§ 4.4.28.21).

4.4.28.4. *Verbs I-y and III-y*

Attested verbs are *ymy* 'swear' (< ימי) and *ypy* (< אפי).

> G   Subjunctive   3 m.s. and c.pl. *yāme* 'he may swear'
> Present   1 m.s. *gyāmən* 'I swear', 3 m.s. *gyāme* 'he swears',
>   *gyāpe* 'he bakes'
> Future   1 m.s. *byāmən* 'I shall swear', 1 f.s. *byamyannox* 'I
>   shall swear to you', 2 m.s. *byamət* 'you will swear', 2
>   f.s *byamyatti* 'you will swear to me', 1 c.pl. *byamaxlox*
>   'we shall swear to you'
> Preterite   1 c.s. *ymeli* 'I swore,' 2 m.s. *ymelox* 'you swore', 3 m.s.
>   *ymele* 'he swore'
> Imperative   m.s. *ymi* 'swear!'
> Gerund   following the preposition *b-*: *bipá* 'baking'
> Participle   m.s. *yəmya* 'sworn', c.pl. *yəmye*
>
> C   Present   1 m.s. *gmaymənnox* 'I adjure you'
> Participle   3 m.s. *múyəmya* 'adjured'

See also *y'y* (§ 4.4.28.19).

4.4.28.5. *Verbs II-w and III-*ʾ

Two verbs are attested: *ṣw'* 'paint, dye' (< צבע) and *ṭw'* 'fall asleep' (< טבע):

> G   Past Habitual   3 m.s. *ṣāwé'wāle* 'he used to dye'
> Pluperfect   1 c.s. *ṭwe'wāli* 'I had fallen asleep'
> Participle   m.s. *ṣəwya* 'dyed' (§ 3.14)

4.4.28.6. *Verbs II-w and III-y*

Attested verbs are *ṛwy* 'grow' (< רבי), and *ṭwy* 'roast' (< טוי):

G   Present   3 m.s. *gṛāwe* 'he grows'
     Preterite   2 m.s. *ṛwelox* 'you grew'
     Participle   m.s. *ṛəwya* 'grown'
D   Past Habitual 3 c.pl. *mṭāwéwālu* 'they would roast'
C   Preterite   1 c.pl. *muṛwelan* 'we raised'

See also *hwy* 'be, be born' (§ 4.4.28.12)

4.4.28.7. 'rq (< ערק)

The verb *'rq* is inflected regularly when it means 'run', e.g.,

G   Preterite   1 s. *'rəqli* 'I ran'
     Gerund   *'rāqa*

When it means 'flee', however, it takes a 3 f.s. dummy object, e.g.,

G   Subjunctive   1 m.s. *'arqənna* 'I shall flee', 3 m.s. *'ārəqla*
     Preterite   1 s. *'riqāli* 'I fled', 2 m.s. *'riqālox*, 3 c.pl. *'riqālu*
     Perfect   2 m.s. *wət 'ríqala* 'you have fled'
     Imperative   c.pl. *'rúqūla*
C   Subjunctive   2 m.s. *ma'ərqətte* 'you may chase him away', 3 c.pl.
                    ma'ərqile 'they may smuggle him out'
     Preterite   3 m.s. *mo'ərqle* 'he chased him away', 3 f.s. *mo'ərqāle*
                    'he smuggled her out', 3 c.pl. *mo'ərqilu* 'they chased
                    them away'
     Perfect   3 c.pl. *lu mó'ərqi-lle* 'they have smuggled him out'

4.4.28.8. 'sy (< אתי)

G 'come'				
	Subjunctive	Present	Future	Preterite
1 m.s.	*'ásən(a)*	*késən(a)*	*bấsən(a)*	*seli*
1 f.s.	*'āsyan*	*kəsyan*	*basyan*	*seli*
2 m.s.	*'ásət(ən)*	*késət(ən)*	*bấsət(ən)*	*selox*
2 f.s.	*'ásyat(ən)*	*kásyat(ən)*	*básyat(ən)*	*selax*
3 m.s.	*'āse*	*kese*	*bāse*	*sele*
3 f.s.	*'asya*	*kəsya*	*basya*	*sela*
1 c.pl.	*'ásax(in)*	*késax(in)*	*bấsax(in)*	*selan, séleni*
2 c.pl.	*'āsétun(a)*	*kesétun(a)*	*bāsétun(a)*	*sélexun*
3 c.pl.	*'āse*	*kese*	*bāse*	*selu*

Imperative[204]	c.s. *sa*, c.pl. *sāwun*
Participle	m.s. *ʾəsya*, f.s. *seta*,[205] c.pl. *ʾəsye*
Gerund	*ʾisāya*

Attested forms of C 'bring'[206] include

Subjunctive	2 m.s. *mesət* 'you may bring', *mesətte* 'you may bring him', 2 f.s. *mesyattu* 'you may bring them', 3 m.s. *mese* 'he may bring', *meselu* 'he may bring them', 2 c.pl. *mesétūla* 'you may bring her'
Present	3 m.s. *gmese* 'he brings'
Past Habitual	3 c.pl. *mesewa* 'they used to bring'
Preterite	1 c.s. *museli* 'I brought', *məseli*, 3 m.s. *musele* 'he brought', *məsele*, 3 f.s. *musela* 'she brought', 3 c.pl. *muselu* 'they brought', *məselu*
Imperative	m.s. *misi* 'bring!', *mísili* 'bring me!', f.s. *méselu* 'bring them!'; c.pl. *mŭsūle* 'bring him!'
Participle	m.s. *musya* 'brought', c. pl. *musye*
Gerund	*masoye* 'bringing'

4.4.28.9. ʾzl (< אזל)

G 'go'				
	Subjunctive	Present	Future	Preterite
1 m.s.	*ʾắzən(a)*	*gézən(a)*	*bāzən(a)*	*zəlli*
1 f.s.	*ʾắzan(a)*	*gézan(a)*	*bắzan(a)*	*zəlli*
2 m.s.	*ʾắzət(ən)*	*gézət(ən)*	*bắzət(ən)*	*zəllox*
2 f.s.	*ʾắzat(ən)*	*gézat(ən)*	*bắzat(ən)*	*zəllax*
3 m.s.	*ʾāzəl*	*gezəl*	*bāzəl*	*zəlle*
3 f.s.	*ʾāza*	*geza*	*bāza*	*zəlla*
1 c.pl.	*ʾắzax(in)*	*gézax(in)*	*bắzax(in)*	*zəllan, zə́lleni*
2 c.pl.	*ʾāzétun(a)*	*gezétun(a)*	*bāzétun(a)*	*zə́llexun*
3 c.pl.	*ʾāzi*	*gezi*	*bāzi*	*zəllu*

The following syncopated forms (§ 3.18.d.) of the Future are attested:

1 m.s.	*bān*
1 f.s.	*bān*
2 m.s.	*bāt*
2 f.s.	*bāt*
2 m.s.	*bāl*

---

[204] Cf. the different forms of the Imperative of 'come' in the *lishana deni* dialects of JAradh, JBetan, JDohok, and JZakho as listed in Mutzafi 2002:481. See also JAmid *ϑa*, pl. *ϑuwun* (Hoberman 1989:214).

[205] On the aphaeresis of initial ʾ see § 3.17.a.

[206] See Mutzafi 2008a:82 nn. 76–77 on vowel assimilations in the forms of this verb.

Imperative[207]   m.s. *si*, f.s. *se*, *selax*, c.pl. *sūn*
Participle   m.s. *zila*, f.s. *zǝlta*, c.pl. *zile*
Gerund   *'izāla*

4.4.28.10. b'y *(< בעי)*

Attested forms of G 'want, desire' include

Subjunctive	1 s. *bā'ǝn* 'I may want', 2 f.s. *ba'yat* 'you may want', 3 m.s. *bā'e* 'he may want', 2 c.pl. *bā'etun* 'you may want', 3 c.pl. *bā'e* 'they may want'
Present	1 s. *gǝbǝn* 'I want', *gbǝnne* 'I want him', *gbǝnnax* 'I want you', *gbǝnnu* 'I want them', 1 f.s. *gbannox* 'I want you', 2 m.s. *gǝbǝt* 'you want', *gbǝttan* 'you want us', 2 f.s. *gǝbat* 'you want', *gbatte* 'you want him', 3 m.s. *gǝbe* 'he wants', 3 f.s. *gbālox* 'she wants you', 1 c.pl. *gǝbax* 'we want', 2 c.pl. *gǝbetun* 'you want', 3 c.pl. *gǝbe* 'they want'
Past Habitual	3 m.s. and c. pl. *gbewa* 'he/they used to want', 3 f.s. *gbāwa* 'she used to want'
Preterite	1 c.s. *b'eli* 'I wanted', 1 c.pl. *b'elan* 'we wanted', 3 c.pl. *b'elu* 'they wanted'
Participle	c.pl. *be'ye* 'wanted'

The vowel *ǝ* of *gǝb-* is elided in the Present following a sandhi vowel, e.g., following the negative *la*, e.g., *lá-gbǝn* 'I don't want', *lá-gbe* 'he doesn't want'. On the difference between the base of the Subjunctive and the Present, see § 4.4.9.j.

4.4.28.11. hnnl *(< hǝnna)*

The filler *hǝnna* (§ 4.9.a) may be inflected verbally. Examples include

Subjunctive	3 c.pl. *mhannǝlili* 'they may do, um, to me'
Future	3 c.pl. *phannǝlilu* 'they will do, um, to them
Preterite:	3 m.s. *hǝnnǝlle* 'he did, um',[208] *hǝnnǝlle*, 3 c.pl. *hǝnnǝllu*, *hǝnnallu* 'they did, um'
Plupreterite	3 m.s. *hǝnnǝlwāle* 'he had done, um'

4.4.28.12. hwy *(< הוי)*

Attested forms of G 'be, be born' include

---

[207] The forms of the Imperative are derived from the root *sgy* < *śg'*. See Mutzafi 2005:105–106 and 2008a:379.

[208] Cf. *hnılle* (Sabar 2002a:151).

	Subjunctive	Present	Future	Preterite
1 m.s.	*hāwən*	*kāwən*	*páwən(a)*	*hweli* 'I was born'
2 m.s.	*hāwət*	*kāwət*	*pāwət*	
3 m.s.	*hāwe*	*kāwe*	*pāwe*	
3 f.s.	*hūwa*	*kūwa*	*pūwa*	
1 c.pl.	*hāwax*	*kāwax*	*pāwax*	
2 c.pl.	*hāwetun*	*kāwetun*	*pāwetun*	
3 c.pl.	*hāwe*	*kāwe*	*pāwe*	

The forms of the 1 f.s. and 2 f.s. are unattested in the corpus. The 3 f.s. forms with *ū* (*hūwa, kūwa, pūwa*; § 3.15.d) are unattested in other *lishana deni* dialects. Cf. 3 f.s. *hōya (höya), kōya* in JZakh, JAmid, and JBetan.[209] See § 4.4.9.f for the prefix *k-* on forms of the Present, § 4.4.11.b for the prefix *p-* on forms of the Future, and § 3.2.d and § 4.1.8.l for the relative *d- > t-* before forms of the Subjunctive.

There appears to be a fossilized form *welāle* (< *hwewāle*) in

wélāle šö'á-brone.
'Seven sons were born to him.' (§ 5.1.3)

4.4.28.13. hymn (< הימן < C אמן)

Attested forms of Q 'believe, trust' include

Subjunctive	1 m.s. *mhemnən* 'I may believe', *mhémnəna*, 2 m.s. *mhemnət* 'you may believe', 3 m.s. *mhemən* 'he may believe', *mhemənne* 'he may believe him', 3 f.s. *mhemnat* 'she may believe'
Present	1 m.s. *lá-gmhèmnəna* 'I don't believe', 3 f.s. *lá-gmhemna* 'she doesn't believe'
Preterite	3 m.s. *mhomənne* 'he believed', 3 f.s. *mhomənna* 'she believed'
Participle	c.pl. *mhumne* 'believed'

4.4.28.14. mnx (< נוח?; < עיני?)

Attested forms of C 'look at' include

Subjunctive	1 m.s. *ménxən(a)* 'I may look at', 3 c.pl. *menxi* 'they may look at'
Present	1 m.s. *gmenəx* 'I look at', 3 c.pl. *gmenxi* 'they look at'

---

[209] Polotsky 1967:107; Avineri 1998:226, Sabar 2002a:149, Hoberman 1989:32; Mutzafi 2008a:178,194.

Preterite	1 c.s. *monəxli* 'I looked at', 3 m.s. *monəxle* 'he looked at', 3 f.s. *monəxla* 'she looked at'
Imperative	c.s. *menəx* 'look at!', c.pl. *menxun*
Gerund	*manoxe*

4.4.28.15. mṣy 'be able' (< מצי)

The Subjunctive/Present of the verb is based on the ClAram passive participle *mṣe* rather than on the ClAram active participle *māṣe*.[210] The verb is more often than not attested with a negative:

G	Subj / Pres	1 m.s. *lá-mṣən* 'I am not able', *lá-mṣəna*, 2 m.s. *lá-mṣət* 'you are not able', 3 m.s. *lá-mṣe* 'he is not able'
	Past Habitual	1 m.s. *mṣənwa* 'I was able', *lá-mṣənwa* 'I wasn't able', 1 pl. *lá-mṣaxwa* 'we weren't able'
	Preterite	3 m.s. *əmṣele* 'he was able'
	Gerund	*lewu mṣāya* 'they are not able'

4.4.28.16. nbl (< יבל)

Attested forms of C 'lead away' include

Subjunctive	1 m.s. *nablən* 'I may lead away', 3 m.s. *nābəl* 'he may lead away', 3 f.s. *nabla* 'she may lead away', 3 c.pl. *nabli* 'they may lead away', *nablile* 'they may lead him away'
Preterite	3 m.s. *nobəlle* 'he led away', 3 c.pl. *nobəllu* 'they led away'
Imperative	c.s. *nābəl* 'lead away!', *nä́bəlle* 'lead him away!'
Gerund	*nabole* 'leading away'

On the shift *m* > *n* /_ *b* see § 3.7.

4.4.28.17. npl (< נפל)

Attested forms of G 'fall' and C 'fell' include

G	Subjunctive	3 m.s. *nāpəl* 'he may fall', 3 f.s. *napla* 'she may fall', 3 c.pl. *napli* 'they may fall'
	Future	3 c.pl. *mnapli* 'they will fall'
	Preterite	1 c.s. *(m)pəlli* 'I fell', 3 m.s. *(m)pəlle* 'he fell', 1 c.pl. *(m)pä́lleni* 'we fell', 3 c.pl. *(m)pəllu* 'they fell'
C	Subjunctive	*mampəl* 'it may fell'
	Gerund	*mampole* 'causing to fall'

---

[210] Mutzafi 2008a:83. There is one attestation, however, of *māṣe*: *'ako mən tāma 'āya*

$n > m$ /_p (§ 3.6.d). m appears to be optional before p in the G Preterite (§ 3.17.e).

4.4.28.18. xyy (*חיי*<)

Attested forms of G 'live' include

Subjunctive	3 m.s. *xāye* 'he may live', 2 m.pl. *xāyetun* 'you may live', 3 c.pl. *xāye* 'they may live'
Future	3 m.s. *pxāye* 'he will live'
Past Habitual	1 c.pl. *xāyaxwa* 'we were living'
Participle	m.s. *xiya* 'lived', pl. *xiye*
Imperative	m.s. *xi* 'live!'

4.4.28.19. yʾy (< *ידע*)

Attested forms of G 'know' include

Subjunctive	1 m.s. *yāʾən* 'I may know', 2 m.s. *yāʾət* you may know', *yāʾətte* 'you may know it', 3 m.s. *yāʾe* 'he may know', 2 c.pl. *yāʾetun* 'you may know'
Present	1 m.s. *kiʾən* 'I know', *kiʾənne* 'I know him', *kiʾənna* 'I know her', *kiʾənnu* 'I know them', 1 f.s. *lá-čiʾan* 'I don't know' (§ 4.4.9.c), 2 m.s. *kiʾət* 'you know', *kiʾətte* 'you know him', *čiʾətte* 'you know him' (§ 4.4.9.c), *kiʾəttu* 'you know them', 3 m.s. *kiʾe* 'he knows, 3 f.s. *kiʾa* 'she knows', *kiʾāli* 'she knows me', 1 c.pl. *kiʾax* 'we know', *kiʾaxlu* 'we know them', 2 c.pl. *kiʾetun* 'you know', 3 c.pl. *kiʾe* 'they know', *kiʾele* they know him'
Future	3 m.s. *byāʾət* 'you will know'
Past Habitual	1 s. *kiʾənwa* 'I used to know', 3 c.pl. *kiʾewa* 'they used to know'
Preterite	1 c.s. *yʾeli* 'I knew', *yeʾyāli* 'I knew her', 2 m.s. *yʾelox* 'you knew', 3 pl. *yʾelu* 'they knew'

A reflex of the original *d* of the root *ידע* does not appear in any of the attested forms of the G stem (§ 3.18.e), unlike in other *lishana deni* dialects.[211] *d* is preserved, however, in the C stem.

Attested forms of C 'inform' include

---

māṣe ᴴ*šālətᴴ* 'When from there he is able to control' (§ 5.11.7). Sabar reports a similar form also in 2002a:223.

[211] See, e.g., in JBetan (Mutzafi 2008a:81). The absence of a reflex of *d* in the Preterite seems unique to JChalla. Cf. JAmid *ydeʾli* (Hoberman 1989:224), JBetan *ðeʾle* (Muzafi 2008a:81), JNerwa texts *yḏeʾli* (Sabar 1984:277), JZakho *zeʾli* (Avinery 1988:232).

Subjunctive   1 c.s. *mayd(')ənnu* 'I may inform them'
Past Habitual   1 c.pl. *mayd(')axwala* 'we used to inform her'
Preterite   1 c.s. *muyde(')li* 'I informed', 3 m.s.*muyde(')le* 'he
                 informed', 1 c.pl. *muyde(')lan* 'we informed', 3 c.pl.
                 muyde(')lu 'they informed'

4.4.28.20. yhw(l) (< ל + יהב)

Attested forms of G 'give' include

Subjunctive: 1 m.s. *yāwən* 'I may give', 2 m.s. *yāwətta* 'you may give
                 her', *yāwətti* 'you may give me', *yāwəttu* 'you may give
                 them', 3 m.s. *yā'eli* 'he may give me, 1 c.pl. *yāxle* 'we
                 may give him', *yāxla* 'we may give her', 2 c.pl. *yāwetun*
                 'you may give', 3 c.pl. *yāwile* 'they may give him',
                 yāwilu 'they may give them'
Present   3 m.s. *gyāwəl* 'he gives', 2 c.pl. *gyāwetun*' you will give'
Future   1 m.s. *byāwən* 'I shall give', *byāwənnox* 'I shall give
                 you', *byāwənnu* 'I shall give them' 1 f.s. *byāwannox*
                 'I shall give you', 2 m.s. *byāwət* 'you will give', 3 m.s.
                 byāwəl 'he will give', *byāwélexun* 'he will give you', 1
                 c.pl. *byāxlox* 'we will give you', *byāxlu* 'we will give
                 them', 2 c.pl. *byāwétūle* 'you will give him'
Past Habitual   1 m.s. *yāwə́nwālox* 'I used to give you', 3 m.s.
                 gyāwəlwa 'he used to give'
Past Prospective 3 c.pl. *byāwíwāle* 'they would give him'
Preterite   1 c.s. *hūli* 'I gave, *hiwili* 'I gave them', 3 m.s. *hūle*[212] 'he
                 gave', 3 f.s. *hūla* 'she gave', 2 c.pl. *húlexon*, 3 c.pl. *hūlu*
                 'they gave', *hiwaxlu* 'they gave us'
Imperative   c.s. *hal* 'give!', m.s. *hallox* 'give!', *hallu* 'give them', c.pl.
                 halun 'give!', *hálūle* 'give him'
Participle   m.s. *hiwa* 'given', f.s. *hūta*, c.pl. *hiwe*

Note that *āwa* contracts to *ā* (§ 3.15.c) in the 1 c.pl. forms based on the
Subjunctive, and that intervocalic *w* > ' (§ 3.3.c) in *yā'eli* 'he may give me'.

See Mutzafi 2008a:81 on the underlying morphology of this verb. On *əw*
> *ū* in several of the forms, see § 3.14.

4.4.28.21. ytw (< יתב)

Attested forms of G 'sit' include

---

[212] Cf. *hulle* in JZakho (Polotsky 1967:107) vs. *hūle* in JAmid (Hoberman 1989:224)
and JBetan (Mutzafi 2008a:81).

Subjunctive	1 m.s. *yátwən* 'I may sit', *yátwəna*, 2 f.s. *yatwat* 'you may sit', 3 c.pl. *yatwi* 'they may sit'
Present	1 m.s. *gyatwən* 'I sit', 2 m.s. *gyatwət* 'you sit', 3 f.s. *gyatwa* 'she sits'
Past Habitual	3 m.s. *gyātúwa* 'he used to sit', 3 c.pl. *gyatwiwa* 'they used to sit'
Future	1 m.s. *byatwən* 'I sit', 2 m.s. *byatwət* 'you will sit'
Preterite	1 c.s. *tūli* 'I sat', 3 f.s. *tūla* 'she sat', 3 c.pl. *tūlu* 'they sat'
Imperative	c.s. *tū* 'sit!'
Participle	m.s. *tiwa* 'seated', c.pl. *tiwe*

Attested forms of C 'place, put' include

Preterite	1 c.s. *mətwāli* 'I placed her', 3 m.s. *mətwāle* 'he placed her', *məttūle* 'he placed', *mətwile* 'he placed them', 3 f.s. *məttūla* 'she placed'
Imperative	c.s. *mattu* 'put!', *máttūle* 'put him!'
Participle	m.s. *mətwa*
Gerund	*mattowe*

t is geminated before vowels.[213]

4.4.29. *Modern Hebrew Verbs*

a. Many Modern Hebrew verbs entered Shabbo's Aramaic speech after his arrival in Israel in 1951. When the root exists in both older Aramaic and in Modern Hebrew, the influence of the latter may be evidenced by (1) phonology, e.g., the pronunciation of ModH [k] instead of historical [q], ModH [h] instead of NeoAram [x], or [ʿ] where NeoAram [ʔ] is expected; (2) semantics, e.g., a ModH meaning for a root instead of the ClAram meaning of the same root, or ModH neologism or slang. Verbs are fully assimilated to the inflectional patterns of NeoAram, e.g., *ʿazrənwālox* 'I was helping you', *badkax* 'we may examine', *lu pgiʿe* 'they have injured', *maxone* 'preparing', *mən mašmədle* 'he should destroy it!', *mʿuṣbənne* 'he irritated him', *mnahalaxlu* 'we manage them', *mšaboḥe* 'praising', *mtakniwa* 'they were fixing', *mulšənne* 'he informed against me', *murgəšli* 'I felt', *muskəmli* 'I agreed', *nasʿax* 'let's travel', *qemi mafʿəlilu* 'they up (and) activate them', *wetun kviʿe* 'you have determined', *wetun mšurte* 'you have served', *zxeli* 'I merited'.

b. Loan verbs from ModHeb generally show up in JChalla in the same stem as in Hebrew. Dt and Qt ModH verbs, however, appear in the

---

[213] Mutzafi 2008a:83.

corresponding stem without *t*: הִתְגַּלְגֵּל 'roll around', הִתְוַכֵּחַ 'argue', הִסְתַּדֵּר 'manage, get along', הִתְעַלֵּל 'torment', and הִתְעַסֵּק 'deal with' > D and Q: *m‘āsək* 'he deals with', *m‘āləl* 'he torments', *mbokəhlan* 'we argued', *mbakohe* 'arguing', *mgalgole* 'rolling around', *(m)sadretun* 'you may get along'. The ModHeb C verb הֶעֱנִיש 'punish' is inflected in D: *(m)‘anšile* 'they punish him' and the ModHeb D verb חִלֵּל is inflected in C as II-*y* *moḥəlli* 'I desecrated' but also in D as geminate *wən mḥúlla-lla* 'I have desecrated it'.

c. The following verbal roots are from ModH: *’rgn* Q 'organize' (אִרְגֵּן), *’rz* G 'pack' (אָרַז), *’ym* D 'threaten' (אִיֵּם), *’šm* C 'accuse' (הֶאֱשִׁים), *‘bd* (עָבַד), *‘ll* D 'torment' (הִתְעַלֵּל), *nš* D 'punish, fine' (הֶעֱנִיש), *‘sk* D 'deal with' (הִתְעַסֵּק), *ṣbn* Q 'irritate' (עִצְבֵּן), *‘vr* G 'pass by, cross over', C 'bring over' (עָבַר; e.g., ModH *‘vərri* 'I passed by' vs. NeoAram G *’ürri* 'I entered'; ModH *mu‘vərre* 'he brought over' vs. NeoAram C *mo’rənne* 'he brought me in'), *‘wf* C 'cause to fly = throw out' (הֵעִיף), *‘zr* G 'help' (עָזַר), *bdk* G 'examine, investigate' (בָּדַק), *bkḥ* D 'argue' (הִתְוַכֵּחַ; § 3.1), *bkš* D 'request' (בִּקֵּש), *btl* D 'cancel' (בִּטֵּל), *d’g* G 'worry' (דָּאַג), *drx* G 'cock a gun' and C 'instruct' (הִדְרִיךְ; דָּרַךְ), *dḥy* G 'postpone' (דָּחָה), *f‘l* C 'activitate' (הִפְעִיל), *fsd* C 'lose' (הִפְסִיד), *gdr* D 'fence in' (גִּדֵּר), *glgl* Q 'roll around' (הִתְגַּלְגֵּל), *gyr* D 'convert' (גִּיֵּר), *gys* D 'draft' (גִּיֵּס), *hkr* G 'investigate' (חָקַר), *ḥlḥl* Q 'permeate' (חִלְחֵל), *ḥlk* D 'divide' (חִלֵּק), *ḥlt* C 'decide' (הֶחְלִיט), *ḥsl* D 'finish off, eliminate' (חִסֵּל), *ḥyv* D 'obligate' (חִיֵּב), *ḥzk* C 'hold' (הֶחֱזִיק), *k’v* G 'hurt' (כָּאַב), *kfts* G 'jump' (קָפַץ), *kv‘* G 'determine' (קָבַע), *lxlx* Q 'dirty' (לִכְלֵךְ), *mšx* C 'continue' (הִמְשִׁיךְ), *ng‘* C 'deserve' (הִגִּיעַ), *ngš* C 'present (trans.)' (הִגִּיש), *nhl* D 'manage' (נִהֵל), *ns‘* G 'travel' (נָסַע), *pg‘* G 'injure' (פָּגַע), *pnčr* 'cause a flat tire' (פִּנְצֵ'ר < 'puncture'), *pzr* D 'distribute' (פִּזֵּר), *r‘d* C 'tremble' (רָעַד), *r‘l* C 'poison' (הִרְעִיל), *rgš* C 'feel' (הִרְגִּיש), *rvḥ* C 'earn' (הִרְוִיחַ), *sbl* G 'suffer, bear' (סָבַל), *sdr* D 'arrange' (סִדֵּר), D manage, get along' (הִסְתַּדֵּר), *skm* C 'agree' (הִסְכִּים), *slḥ* G 'forgive' (סָלַח), *smḥ* D 'make happy' (שִׂמַּח), *smx* C 'authorize' (הִסְמִיךְ), *spk* C 'manage' (הִסְפִּיק; NeoAram cognate 'be empty'), *spr* D 'tell' (סִפֵּר), *skr* C 'rent out' (הִשְׂכִּיר), *sfsf* Q 'disregard utterly' (צִפְצֵף), *ṣlm* D 'photograph' (צִלֵּם), *šbḥ* D 'praise' (שִׁבַּח), *šdd* G 'rob' (שָׁדַד), *šft* G 'judge' (שָׁפַט), *šḥrr* Q 'free, release' (שִׁחְרֵר), *škn* D 'settle' (שִׁכֵּן), *šlm* D 'pay' (שִׁלֵּם), *šmd* C 'destroy' (הִשְׁמִיד), *šrt* D 'serve' (שֵׁרֵת), *štf* D 'let participate' (שִׁתֵּף), *šxnx* Q 'persuade' (שִׁכְנֵעַ; § 3.3.e), *tḥl* C 'begin' (הִתְחִיל), *tkn* D 'fix, repair' (תִּקֵּן; ClAram *tqn* 'set'), *tkf* C 'attack' (הִתְקִיף; ClAram 'strengthen'), *tmx* G 'support' (תָּמַךְ), *txnn* Q 'plan' (תִּכְנֵן), *xbd* D 'honor' (כִּבֵּד), *xrḥ* C 'force' (הִכְרִיחַ), *xtf* G 'seize' (חָטַף), *xyn* C 'prepare' (הֵכִין), *yšr* D 'straighten' (יִשֵּׁר), *zbr* C 'explain' (colloquial הִזְבִּיר < הִסְבִּיר), *zgr* C 'hand over' (colloquial הִזְגִּיר < הִסְגִּיר), *zxy* G 'merit' (זָכָה).

4.5. Prepositions

Some of the prepositions below have allomorphs with the possessive-relative particle *d* suffixed: *b-/ʾəbbəd, l-/ʾəl-/ʾəlləd, mābayn/mābaynəd, mən/mənnəd*. Several prepositions, with and without suffixed *-d*, are followd by the independent genitive pronoun *did-* with pronominal suffixes: *ʾəbbəd did-, ʾəlled did-, bárakus did-, barqul did-, basər did-, básbasər did-, dəpən did-, kəsəl did-, mənnəd did-*. Four prepositions exhibit reduplication:[214] *básbasər, kəsəkəsəl, qamqam, rešreš*. Prepositions may be followed by *d* (the possessive-relative particle) that is proclitic to a demonstrative (pronoun or adverb; § 4.1.8.j), e.g., *mən d-axxa* 'from here' (but also *m-axxa* and *mən ʾaxxa*), *xe d-iya ᴴdegelᴴ* 'under this flag', *xor d-axxa* 'like here', *xor d-iya* 'like this', *xor d-anna ʿarabāye* 'like those Arabs' (§ 5.1.9).

ʾəbbəd	see *b-*
ʾəl-, ʾəlləd	see *l-*
ʾəltxé(t?)	'under'
	This compound preposition is attested only once in *ʾit xa ʾena ʾəltxé(t?) ṭappá* 'there is a spring at the bottom of the hillside' (§ 5.7.5). One cannot be certain if *t* is pronounced or not before the noun *ṭappá*. Cf. *txe* and *txeṭ* in the JNerwa texts.[215]
b-, ʾəbb-, ʾəbbəd	'in, at, on'
	Before unvoiced consonants, *b-* is devoiced to *p* (§ 3.6.a) *b-* is more common preceding a noun than its allomorph *ʾəbbed*, e.g., *b-dor* 'in a generation', *b-xáṣe* 'on his back' vs. *ʾəbbəd ʾida* 'in her hand', *ʾəbbəd dugle* 'in lies'. Cf. *balāye lu dərye-lla b-reš qdāl Hoče u-Miʾər* 'they have blamed Hoče and Meir' (§ 5.5.3) vs. *qemi dārela balāye ʾəbbəd reš hudāye* 'they up (and) blame the Jews' (§ 5.5.8). The form *bəd*, known from other *lishana deni* dialects,[216] is unattested in JChalla. Pronominal suffixes may be attached to the base *ʾəbb-* (§ 3.20.h), e.g., *ʾəbbi, ʾəbbox, ʾəbbax, ʾəbbe, ʾəbba*, or to the independent genitive pronoun following *ʾəbbəd*, e.g., *ʾəbbəd dide, ʾəbbəd didu*.
badal, m-badal	'in place of'
	badal kullu 'in place of all of them', *m-badal ḥaqqox* 'in place of your salary'

---

[214] See also the adverb *gárgāra* 'from time to time' (§ 4.7.2). Cf. *báϑ-baϑər, mánne-mən, qám-qam, réša-reš,* and *xéϑa-xeϑ* in JBetan (Mutzafi 2008a:121, 125). See also Maclean 1895:175–176.

[215] Sabar 1984:343.

[216] E.g., JBetan (Mutzafi 2008a:121).

bárakus   'in front of, opposite'
                       barakuseni, bárakus dide
barqul   'in front of, opposite'
                       barqulexun, barqul dida, barqul 'eni 'before my eyes'
basər   'after, behind'
                       basre, basər dide, basər mənnexun, basər bes didu 'after
                       their house', *basər xa tar'a* 'after one door'
básbasər   'right after'
                       básbasre, básbasru, básbasər dide, básbasər didu
dəpən, l-dəpən   'next to'
                       dəpnexun, l-dəpni, l-dəpnox, l-dəpən dide
dax, daxwās-   'like'
                       dax occurs before nouns, e.g., *dax nāše* 'like people',
                       and *daxwās* when bound by pronominal suffixes,
                       e.g., *daxwāsa, daxwāseni*. It is also attested before a
                       filler: *daxwás hənna* [H]*hayót mtorafím*[H] 'like, um, crazy
                       animals'
dla   'without'
                       dla pāre 'without money', *dla šarwāla* 'without trousers'
go, gaw-   'in, within'
                       go is attested before nouns, *gaw-* when bound by
                       pronominal suffixes and the independent genitive
                       pronoun, e.g., *gawexun, gaw dide, gaw dida, go besa* 'at
                       home', *go 'idás didu* 'in their hands'
ḥil, ḥel   'until, as far as'
                       ḥil 'atta 'until now', *ḥil tāma mṭelu ḥil Məṣṣər* 'they
                       reached until there, as far as Egypt', *ḥel yom basra* 'until
                       the next day'
kəsəl, kəl, kəs   'to, with, chez'
                       *kəslexun, kəslu, kəsəl dide, kəsəl didu, mən kəsəl, kəsəl
                       Rašíd 'āġa* 'with Rashid Agha'. The syncopated form
                       kəl (§ 3.18.f) occurs only before nouns, e.g., *kəl muxtar*
                       'with the mukhtar', *kəl xmāse* 'with his mother-in-law';
                       an apocoated form *kəs*[217] (§ 3.19.f) occurs once: *kəs
                       spindarnāye* 'with the residents of Spindar'
kəsəkəsəl   'right with'
                       kəsəkəsleni 'right with us'
l, 'əl, 'əlləd   'to, at, for'
                       l- usually occurs after vowels, e.g., *'ako zəlli l-Čalla*
                       'when I went to Challa', *zəllu l-tāma* 'they went there'. It
                       is less frequent after consonants, e.g., *tam l-é-'al* 'from
                       there on'. It may mark an object, e.g., *ṣrəxle l-xet* 'he
                       called to the other', and it is the basis of the L-suffix

---

[217] *kəs* is attested in *lishana deni* dialects, e.g., JZakho (Sabar 2002:187), JBetan (Mutzafi
2008a:357), and the JNerwa texts (Sabar 1984:285).

pronouns (§§ 4.1.4; 4.4.23.1). There are allomorphs *ʾəl* and *ʾəlləd*, which follow both vowels and consonants, e.g., *sāwun ʾəlle* 'Come to him!', *xá-yoma zəlli ʾəlləd pareni l-tāma* 'One day I went there for our money.' Like *l-* in ClAram and in NeoAram, the preposition *ʾəl* also functions as an object marker: *go reš ṭura xá-gā xa'-bərqa le məxya ʾəlləd kepa* 'On the top of the mountain suddenly there was lightning that had struck a rock', *ṣrəxli ʾəlləd Ṣabri* 'I called out to Sabri', *ʾāna-ži ṭrəpli ʾəlləd dida* 'I also attacked her'. It is also the basis of the LL-suffix pronouns (§§ 4.1.5; 4.4.23.2). Pronominal suffixes may be attached to *ʾəll-* or to *ʾəlled did-*, e. g., *ʾəlli, ʾəllox, ʾəlle, ʾəlla, ʾəllan, ʾəlleni, ʾə́llexun, ʾəllu, ʾəlləd dida, ʾəlləd didu*.

mābayn, mābaynəd	'between, among'

mābayneni, mābaynəd didu, mābayn kepe 'among the stones', *mābayn nāše* 'among the people', *mābayn gyānu* 'among themselves', *mābayn d-anna baxtāsa* 'among those women'

mən, m-, mənnəd	'from, with'

mən, as well as a clipped form *m-* (§ 3.19.g), occurs before nouns, adverbs, the independent genitive particle *did-*, and other prepositions, e.g., *mən ʾaqle* 'with his feet', *mən Moṣəl* 'from Mosul', *mən tāma* 'from there', *mən didu,* 'with them', *m-qam gyāni* 'from on me', *m-ʾarʾa'* 'from the ground', *m-ʿEraq* 'from Iraq', *m-eka* 'from where'? *n* is geminated when bound by pronominal suffixes, e.g., *mənni, mənnox, mənne, mənna, mənneni, mənnexun, mənnu*.

m-badal	see *badal*
m-qam	'due to'

m-qam qaṛačke 'due to highway robbers'

qabəl mən	'before' (spatial)

qabəl mənni

qam	'before, in front of, on (clothes)'

qāmi, qāme, qam didu, qam qalʾa 'before the fortress', *qam tar didu* 'outside their door', *xa zoʾa bargūze le qāmi* 'a (lit., 'pair') woolen suit is on me'

*qamqam	'right before, right in front of'

qámqāman, qámqāmu

qurwa	'near'

qurwəd tāma 'near there', *qurwəd ḥanukka* 'near Hanukka'

reš	'on, at, upon'

rešeni, reš dide, reš didu. reš kāse 'on his belly', *reš ṭura* 'on the mountain'. The *š* of *reš* is voiced *ž* before voiced consonants (§ 3.6.e).

rešreš	'right above'
	rešreš dide 'right above him'
ta, ṭas, ti	'to, for'

ta occurs before nouns, e.g., *kəmra ta bāba* 'She says to
her father', *bāzət ta Čalla* 'you will go to Challa'. *ṭas* is
bound by pronominal suffixes and by *did-*: *ṭāsi, ṭāsox,
ṭāsax, ṭāse, ṭāsa, ṭāsan, ṭaseni, ṭasexun, ṭāsu, ṭas didi,
ṭas didox, ṭas didax, ṭas dide, ṭas dida, ṭas didan, ṭas
dexun, ṭas didu.* Infrequently JZakho *ṭāl-* is heard in
Shabbo's speech, primarily when he is speaking with
a JZakho speaker. *ti* is attested regularly before *gyān-*
and is the result of assimilation of the *a* vowel to the
following *y*.[218]

xe, xes-, xa-	'under'

xe occurs before nouns, e.g., *xe d-iya* ^H*degel*^H 'under
this flag'. *xes-* occurs when bound by pronominal
suffixes, e.g., *xese, xesu.* The allomorph *xa-* is found
only before *reš* 'head': *xa-réšəd dide* 'under his head';
m-xa-réšəd dide 'from under his head'

xor	'like'
	xore, xorexun, xor didu

dla, ḥil/ḥēl, and *qabəl mən* also function as conjunctions (§ 4.6).

4.6. CONJUNCTIONS

'afəllu	'even'

'an xeta 'afəllu mbárbəzi 'Even those others will scatter'
(§ 5.3.11); *'afəllu xá-*^H*ša'al*^H *'ar'a lə́twālu* 'they didn't
have even one inch of land' (§ 5.1.4)

'ako	'when'

'ako dena xləsle ^A*xalaṣ*^A 'When the debt is finished, it's
over' (§ 5.2.2); *'ako zəlli l-besa mšadrənnu 'əllox* 'When I
have gone home I will send them to you.' (§ 5.2.7)

'egā	'so then, now then'

'egā kí'ət-ži mā wáxt-ile? 'So then you know what time
it is?' (§ 5.2.11); *'egā lu bənšāqa 'ə́ǧdāde* 'so now they are
kissing each other' (§ 5.3.10)

'əlla[219]	'except, but rather'

la, la Rekanāya 'əlla Barzaná 'no, not a resident
of Rekan, but rather of Barzan' (§ 5.5.5); *dla b-doṛ
dide, 'əlla b-dóṛ bábe-'āwa* 'not in his generation,

---

	but rather it was in the generation of his father' (§ 5.1.10)
'ən	'if, either'
	'ən wət góra-ži, nåbəlli 'if you are a man, lead me away' (§ 5.8.8); ya'ni hudāye 'ən kpənnu, gezi reš dena tiqa 'That is to say, if Jews are hungry, they go for an old debt (to collect it)' (§ 5.2.2);
'ən la	'if not'
	'ən čfəlle... lu píče-lle. 'ən lá-čfəlle... 'if he is startled... they have crushed him. If he is not startled...' (§ 5.6.6); qaṭláxlexun 'ən lá-hatxa 'We'll kill you if (it is) not like this' (§ 5.8.21); bale, balé 'however' bale 'āhat mən ᴷawlåd-e rasûlᴷ-'iwət 'however, you are from the descendants of the Messenger' (§ 5.3.12); la skətle, bale pəšle pálgəd-nāša 'he didn't croak, but he became half a person' (§ 5.6.5)
čukun, čuku, čunku	'because'
	'āna lebi yatwəna čukun lə́tleni 'I am not able to sit (with you) because we don't have (enough honor)'; ᴴ'asúrᴴ-la ᴴliᴴ baqrənne čuku yəmya 'əlle 'It is forbidden for me to ask him because he (has) sworn to him'; čunku 'iya zaxút (m-)'əlohím lewa 'because this right is not (from) God'
dla	'lest'
	dlá-'ārəqla 'lest he flee'
ḥil, ḥel	'until'
	u-ḥil 'axnan wax pliṭe m-tāma 'and until we had left there' (§ 5.1.1); ḥel xləṣle 'until he finished' (§ 5.5.7)
ka-	'when, since'
	ka-'égā čāy šətyáleni 'since then we drank the tea' (§ 5.10.13)
ko	'because, that, since'
	pəšlu ko 'āna dá'rən-wa 'they remained since I would return back' (§ 5.11.5); mərri ma-yla ᴴsəbaᴴ ko 'āna bāsən tlā 'I said: "What's the reason that I am going to hang?"'; lá-'amrən ko 'āna gnaxpən mənnox 'I don't say because I am embarrassed by you.'
kud dān	'whenever'
	kud dān 'ilāha mšodərre xá-mal'ax 'whenever God sent an angel'
lākən	'but, however'
	zəlli kəsəl dide. lākən basər tré-yome ṭlāhá'-yome mṭeli l-besa 'I went to him, but after two days, three days, I came home.'
mādám	'since, as'
	mādám gəbət, sa! 'Since you want (to), come!'; mādám hādax gora 'iwət 'Since like this you are a man'

qabəl mən	'before'
	qabəl mən 'axnan 'āsaxwa 'before we used to come'
ta, tad	'in order to'
	'āna gəbən pálpaṇqànoṭ mən pārox tad dārənna go pāri ta ᴴšamranᴴ pāri ta baṛāxa 'I want a half lira of your money in order to put it in with my money for a blessing (alms)' (§ 5.3.12); ᴴ*(m)'anšileᴴ ta šaqli mənne pāre* 'they punish him in order to take his money away from him'
ta-lá	'lest'
	ta-lá-'āmər 'lest he say' ; *ta-lá-'āse balāye b-rešeni* 'lest disaster befall us' (§ 5.3.2)
u-	'and'
	u is usually proclitic, e.g., *'əsri u-šö'á-ma'almine* 'twenty-seven teachers', though not always, e.g., *ṣíwe-u ṣíwe-u ṣiwe* 'sticks and sticks and sticks', *xa šö'á-yāle-u xa tmanyá-yāle-u xa 'əṣrá-yāle-u xa xamšá-yāle* 'One (had) seven children and one (had) eight children and one (had) ten children and one (had) five children.' (§ 5.1.4)
-ž(i)	'also, and, even'[220]

dla, ḥil/ḥel, and *qabəl mən* also function as prepositions (§ 4.5).

4.7. ADVERBS

4.7.1. *Interrogative Adverbs*

'eka	'where?'
	m-eka 'from where?', *'éka-'ile* 'Where is he?', *'éka-le, ké-le*
'imal	'when?'
	ta 'imal 'until when?'
ke-	see *'eka*
kma	'how many?'
	b-kma 'for how much?'
māṭo	'how?'
qay	'why?'
	qay wetun qṭile xədda? 'Why, have you killed someone?' (§ 5.2.17)
ṭamá́[221]	'why?'

---

[220] For a detailed description of the functions of this adverb, see Khan 1999:371–378. See now also Cohen 2008b.

[221] Shabbo also says *ṭāma* under the influence of ModH לְמָה׳.

4.7.2. *Temporal Adverbs*

ʾádlele	'tonight'
ʾatta	'now'
	ʾatta-u-l-é-ʾāl 'from now on', m-atta 'from now'
ʾədyo	'today'
ᶻʾogāᶻ	'at that time'
ʿāṣərta	'(in the) evening'
basər hādax	'afterwards'
bənhe	'(in the) morning'
bomāxəd	'day after tomorrow'
čú-gā	'never'
čú-gār	'never'
gárgāra[222]	'from time to time'
dax	'as soon as'
	dax mundyālu l-ʾarʾa 'as soon as they threw it on the ground' (§ 5.3.8)
ham	'also'
har	'always, still, in any case'
hayāma	'(for a) period of time'
haya	'quickly, early'
kúd-lel	'every night'
kúd-yom	'every day'
kuššat	'every year'
lele	'(at) night'
lel basra	'the night after'
māṭod	'as soon as'
m-zūna	'long ago'
palgədlel	'(at) midnight'
palsāʿa	'(for) half an hour'
palgədyo	'(at) noon'
qabəl hādax	'beforehand'
qadome	'tomorrow'
qam hādax	'beforehand'
qamāye	'at first'
šawəd basra	'the week after'
təmmal	'yesterday'
xá-gā	'once'
xá-gā xet(a)	'once again'
xá-behna	'in a moment, suddenly'
xarāye	'later, finally'
yom basra	'the day after'

---

[222] For a similar reduplication see *bárbara* below and also § 4.5.

4.7.3. Locative Adverbs

ʾaxxa	'here'
	l-axxa, 'here, to here', mən-áxxa, m-axxa 'from here', mən d-axxa 'from here', mən d-axxa u-l-é-ʾal 'from here on'
ʾəltəx[223]	'below, beneath'
	ʾəltəx ʾəltəx 'way below'
ʾəlʿuwwa	'inside'
čappe	ʾida čappe 'to the left (= 'left hand')'
l-ʾələl	'above'
l-é-ʾāl	'beyond, further (lit., 'in that direction')'
m-rə́qqa	'from afar'
qam tarʾa	'outside' (lit., 'before the door')
raṣṭe	ʾida raṣṭe 'to the right (= 'right hand')'
tāma, tam, ʾəl-táma, ʾəl-tám	'there, to there'
	tam l-é-ʾāl 'from there on', mənne u-l-é-ʾāl 'from there on', m(ən)-tāma 'from there'

4.7.4. Adverbs of Manner

ʾaqqar, ʾáqqara	'so much, to such an extent'
ʾáškara[224]	'openly, publicly'
ʾəlla	'certainly'
	pummox patḥatte ʾəlla, kemər, ʾāna qaṭlənnox ' "Should you open your mouth," he says, "I'll certainly kill you." ' (§ 5.5.9)[225]
baláš	'for free'
balki, balkit	'perhaps'
bárbara[226]	'together'
bas, bassa	'enough'
	bassa bassa 'more than enough'
ḅāš	'well, very'
	Qárani pəšle naxwaš ḅāš 'Qarani became very ill'
b-əspa	'on loan'
b-dugle	'falsely'
be-dárd	'painlessly'
bəš	'more'
	bə́š-rab 'more', bəšṭor 'better', bə́z-zodāna 'more'
b-salāmat	'safely'
b-xurṭūsa	'forcefully'
b-ẓoṛ	'forcefully'

---

[223] Cf. the preposition ʾəltxé(t?) 'under' (§ 4.5).

[224] The stress on this word in lishana deni dialects usually falls on the penultima. Shabbo appears to have been influenced by the ModH stress on the prepenultima (אָשְׁכָּרָה).

[225] Cf. as a conjunction (§ 4.6).

[226] See gárgāra above.

ča	'c'mon!'
	before an imperative: *ča méselu xanči ṃāye* 'C'mon (and) bring them some water!'
ču	'no, not, any'
	čú-gā 'never', *čú-gār* 'never', *čú-xa* 'no one, anyone', *čú-məndi* 'nothing'
de, da	'so, now, well then'
	The particles occur frequently before imperatives, e.g., *de ksūn* 'So write!', *da-ḥmól* 'So wait!', *de qū misi* 'Now up (and) bring (it)!', *da qū mísili* 'Now up (and) bring (it) to me!', but not exclusively, e.g., *de xilālox* 'Now you've had it!', *de-bázi* 'so now they will go!'
dərəst	'correct, straight, straightaway'
dumāyik	'at the end'
hā	'so, then'
	It occurs before an imperative: *hā šqol ḥaqqox* 'Here take your due!' (§ 5.10.2)
hādax	'thus, so'
har hatxa	'just like this'
hatxa, 'atxa	'so, such, like this'
he	'yes'
hedi	'slowly'
hedi hedi	'very slowly'
heš	'yet, still'
ke	'c'mon!'
	ke occurs before an Imperative: *ke sa* 'c'mon!'
kə́tt-u-māt	'bit by bit'
la, lā, la'	'no'
	lā and *la'* are infrequent and emphatic.
pa	'so, then'
ṛāba	'much, very'
raḥat	'calmly, relaxed'
təne, b-təne	'alone, only'
veza	'so, in such a way, like this'
wal	'indeed, surely'
	wal ᴴpolátikaᴴ d-hudāye ṛába-la 'Indeed the craftiness of the Jews is great.' (§ 5.6.5)
walḥāṣəl	'in short'
xa	'about, approximately' (before a numeral)
	xa 'əṣra 'alpe 'about ten thousand', *xa 'əṣra tre'sar yalunke* 'about ten, twelve children'
xá-b-xa	'one by one'
xapči	'a bit, slightly'
	'ár'a-ži xapči jmə́tta-la 'also the earth is a bit frozen' (§ 5.2.12), *zəlla xapči ᴴlə'átᴴ* 'it departed a bit slowly'
ya'ni	'that is to say'

4.8. Particles of Existence and Ability

4.8.1. *Particles of Existence*

a. The predicators of existence are

'it / 'itən(a)	'there is'
'ətwa	'there was'
let / létən(a)	'there is not'
lətwa	'there was not'

b. Though deriving from ClAram *'it̠* and *let̠*, which according to the phonological rules of JChalla should have developed into *'is* and *les*, the *t* of *'it* and its congeners originated in the contact with the *l* of *'ətle, lətle*, etc. (§ 3.2.b). Cf. in other *lishana deni* dialects: JZakho *'īs, 'iswa, lēs, laswa* vs. *'ıtli, latli*; JAmid *'iϑ, 'itli, iϑwalan, lítle, liϑwāle*; JDohok *'iϑ, leϑ /lat, 'əϑwa, ləϑwa, 'əϑli / 'ətli, ləϑli/ latli*; JBetan *'iϑ/'iϑən(a), liϑ/liϑən(a), 'əϑwa, lə́ϑwāle, 'ətli, lətli*.

c. There is also an example of *lat* before the Copula: *lat 'iwən qṭila* 'I have not killed'.

d. The particles of existence with L-pronominal suffixes yield a meaning 'to have' (< *'it̠* + *l-* 'There is to…') and 'not to have' (< *let̠* + *l-* 'There is not to…'):

	Present	Past
1 c.s.	*'ətli* 'I have'	*'ə́twāli* 'I had'
2 m.s.	*'ətlox*	*'ə́twālox*
2 f.s.	*'ətlax*	*'ə́twālax*
3 m.s.	*'ətle*	*'ə́twāle*
3 f.s.	*'ətla*	*'ə́twāla*
1 c.pl.	*'ətlan, 'ə́tleni*	*'ə́twālan, 'ə́twāleni*
2 c.pl.	*'ə́tlexun*	*'ə́twālexun*
3 c.pl.	*'ətlu*	*'ə́twālu*

	Present Negative	Past Negative
1 c.s.	*lətli* 'I don't have'	*lə́twāli* 'I didn't have'
2 m.s.	*lətlox*	*lə́twālox*
2 f.s.	*lətlax*	*lə́twālax*
3 m.s.	*lətle*	*lə́twāle*
3 f.s.	*lətla*	*lə́twāla*
1 c.pl.	*lətlan, lə́tleni*	*lə́twālan, lə́twāleni*
2 c.pl.	*lə́tlexun*	*lə́twālexun*
3 c.pl.	*lətlu*	*lə́twālu*

4.8.2. Particles of Ability

Ability may be expressed[227] by the affixing of the preposition b- and pronominal suffixes to the particles of existence:

'iṯ + b- 'there is in'   >   'be able'
leṯ + b- 'there isn't in'   >   'be unable'

	Positive Ability	Negative Ability
1 c.s.	'ibi	lebi
2 m.s.	'ibox	lebox
2 f.s.	'ibax	lebax
3 m.s.	'ibe 'he is able'	lebe 'he is unable'
3 f.s.	'iba 'she is able'	leba 'she is unable'
1 c.pl.	'iban, 'íbeni	leban, lébeni
2 c.pl.	'íbexun	lébexun
3 c.pl.	'ibu	lebu

Representative examples include: 'ibi 'āzən 'I can go', lebe 'āmər 'he can't say', 'ən 'ibi 'āna yāwənne, byāwənne. 'ən lebi yāwənne… 'If I can give it, I will give it. If I can't give it …', lebi wən 'əsya 'I wasn't able to come'.

Depending on the context, these forms also show the literal meaning, e.g., 'ibe 'there is in him', lebe 'there isn't in him', e.g., 'ibe ^Hb-gil^H 'əšta šənne 'He is six years old'. (§ 5.8.3).

One finds in the past:

Čalla 'ə́twāba hudāye
'Challa contained (lit., 'there was in her') Jews.' (§ 5.1.1)

nixəd bābi 'akčən xá-'idəd dide lə́twābe
'My late father, (even if he were fighting with only) one hand, one couldn't best him.' (§ 5.6.4)

4.9. FILLERS

There are several different fillers[228] in Shabbo's speech:
   a. hənna 'um'.[229] This filler is ubiquitous:

---

[227] See also the use of mṣy 'be able' (§ 4.4.28.15).
[228] See Fox 1997:69 for examples of fillers in Jilu.
[229] Other translations found in the literature are 'whatchamacallit', 'thingamajig', 'that thing', 'what do you call it'?

'āni hƏnna ^Hfallahím^H wewa.
'They were, um, fellahin.' (§ 5.1.6)

'Ətwa qāymaqam 'ƏllƏd hƏnna... la, la, l-Baškala.
'There was a local governor at, um… no, no, at Bashkala.' (§ 5.1.7)

kemƏr hƏnna: 'āhat lá-mhakyat!
'He says, um: "Don't you talk!"' (§ 5.10.5)

Mašiah hƏnna sāwƏd bābox wewa.
'Mashiach, um, was your father's grandfather.' (§ 5.1.9)

hƏnna is sometimes attested with the copula, e.g., *hƏnna-le*. The possessive-relative particle *d* may be suffixed to it, e.g., *hƏnnƏd*. Infrequently it
takes the pl. form *hƏnne*, e.g.,

ksūli l-tāma má-^H(h)a-toxnìt^H lu wide hƏnne kurdināye taseni.
'I wrote there what the plan (was that) they have made, um, the Kurds for
us.' (§ 5.12.2)

Shabbo also once attaches a 2 pl. pronominal suffix to the filler:

'axnan hƏnnexun 'axwa—, 'iyya mā kƏmrila ^H'avadím^H dexun 'axwa
'We, um, we were—, what do you call it?—"we were your slaves".'

It also forms the basis of the verb *hnnl* 'do, um' (§ 4.4.28.12).

b. *'iya mā kƏmrila* 'what do they call it?—' (lit.,'this, what they call it').
This expression too is common:

'iya mā kƏmrila 'Eli mƏndele xabre.
'What do they call it?—Eli said things.' (§ 5.6.19)

'iya mā kƏmrila 'axoni Háyyo-ži zƏlle mƏnne 'anna kutru.
'What do they call it?—my brother Hayyo also went with him, those two.'

c. *ki'Ət* 'you know'. It is less frequent than the previous two fillers:

xá-yoma pƏšlu veza, ki'Ət?
'One day they became like this, you know?' (§ 5.11.3)

yomƏd ^Khašr u-našr^K ki'Ət, yomƏd din
'hašr u-našr, you know, the Day of Judgment' (§ 5.13.15)

d. *y'elox* 'you know' (lit.,' you knew'). This too is less frequent than the
first two fillers:

'idƏd hukum lá-gmātewa l-Čalla, y'elox, ráqqa-ewa mƏnnƏd didu
'the (long) arm of the government did not reach Challa, you know, it was
a distance from them' (§ 5.1.9)

e. *ḥāle* 'and the like' (lit., 'its condition') is attested infrequently:[230]

> *hatxa narm u-ḥāle garməd dide.*
> 'His bones are so soft and the like.'[231] (§ 5.3.6)

> *hatxa narm u-ḥāle. hatxa narm u-ḫāš.*
> 'So soft and the like. So soft and good.'

f. Shabbo sometimes uses more than one filler in a sentence, e.g.,

> *ʾə́twāle xa hənna ʾiya mā kəmrila* [H]*ḥagorá*[H] *ʾənglizi(t).*
> 'He had an, um, what do they call it?—an English belt.'

> *walḥāṣəl hənna ʾiya mā kəmrila Šambi qṭəllu.*
> 'In short, um, what do they call it?—they killed Shambi.' (§ 5.6.14)

g. The adverbs (§ 4.7) *walḥāṣəl* 'in short', *yaʿni* 'that is to say', [H]*az*[H] 'then' and the exclamation *walla* 'by God!' (§ 4.10) are so frequent in Shabbo's speech that they approach the status of fillers; with the exception of *yaʿni*, they occur only at the beginning of a clause.

4.10. EXCLAMATIONS AND EXPRESSIONS

Many of the following are borrowings from other languages, in several cases from Arabic through Kurdish:

> [A]*ʾahlan wa-sahlan*[A]
> 'Welcome!'

> *ʾalḥámdəlullà*
> 'Praise God!'

> [A]*ʾalla karím*[A]
> 'God is generous!'

> *ʾāxər*
> 'Well!'

> *ʾáx-geb tán-geb*
> 'when all's said and done' (lit. 'here side, there side')

> *ʾáx-geb tán-geb ṭamáha-geb*
> 'when all's said and done' (lit. 'here side, there side, way over there side')

> *ʾāya sāyəlla yəmmeni*
> 'He should fuck our mother!'

---

[230] Mutzafi reports (p.c.) that this usage is attested in several NeoAram dialects.
[231] See s.v. *garma* in the glossary for the meaning of this expression.

'ilāha mānəxle
'May God rest his soul'

'ilāha mazkela
'May God grant her merit!'

'ilāha lá-māzədlu
'May God not increase them!'

'ilāha mayrəx xāye dide u-dexun
'May God lengthen his days and yours!'

'išalla
'God willing'

ᵀ'ačāyəbᵀ
'How strange!'

ᴬ'ala bāb 'allaᴬ
'At God's mercy!'

ᴬ'ala 'eniᴬ (and its calque in JChalla: *go 'eni!*)
'At your service!'

ᴷbāba ṣtaǵfərəlláᴷ
'I ask God's forgiveness!'

bābo
'Father! My God!'

ᴴḅārux-xábbaᴴ
'Welcome!'

baxxatəd 'ilāha
'For the mercy of God!'

baxxatox u-baxxatəd 'ilāha
'For your mercy and the mercy of God!'

baxxatəd didu qur'ān didu u-Maḥammad didu
'For their mercy, their Quran, and their Muhammad!'

b-íya-'ida u-yá-'ida
'when it comes down to it, at any rate' (lit. 'in this hand and this hand')

ᴴb-séfər-ṭoṛaᴴ
'(I swear) by the scroll of the Pentateuch!'

b-xudreši
'(I swear) by my head!' (= 'Take my word for it!')

b-xudrešexun
'(I swear) by your head!'

b-xudreš 'axawāsox u-qur'ān dexun 'əbbəd Maḥammad dexun
'(I swear) by your brothers and your Quran and by your Muhammad!'

^Kčāwəm^K
'(I swear by) my eye!'

haḷḷa haḷḷa
'How fortunate!'

hay
'Hey!'

^Thoš géldənəz^T
'Welcome!'

kalba bər kalba, kalba bron kalba
'Son of a bitch!'

kalba bər šö'ammāhe kalbe
'Son of seven hundred bitches!'

kalbe yāl kalbe
'Sons of bitches!'

kaləpsa brāt kalba
'What a bitch!'

mād hāwe hāwe
'Whatever will be will be!'

mād zəlla zəlla
'Let bygones be bygones!'

(m)xabine
'What a loss!'

qaḥba brāt qaḥba
'Daughter of a whore!'

qəṭma go reše
'May he mourn!'[232]

^Tqozzəlqorṭ^T
'Hell!, Disgusting!'

reš səjjādəd Maḥammad
'(I swear) by the prayer rug of Muhammad!'

si qlo'!
'Go to hell!'

ta xāṭər 'ilāha
'For the sake of God!'

waḷḷa
'By God!'

---

[232] Lit., '(May) ash be upon his head!'

xmāra bər xmāra
'What an ass!'

xwazí ’āsewa
'Would that he would go!'

^A*yā ṛaḅḅi*^A
'Oh my Lord!'

CHAPTER FIVE

TEXTS AND TRANSLATION

The following texts are transcriptions of recorded conversations with Shabbo Amrani. His cousin Ahiya Hashiloni was present at all the tapings and occasionally added remarks that are noted in square brackets with the letters [A.H.].[1] Also present at one recording were Yosef (Joseph) Hashiloni [Y.H.],[2] and Shmuel (Samuel) Barzani [S.B.][3] from Kara. Three dots (...) mark a break in the narrative, diversions in Hebrew, or indistinct and incomprehensible speech. The em-dash indicates cases of anacoluthon, incomplete speech, or significant pause. Parentheses are used for restored vowels and syllables that Shabbo has clipped ad hoc in rapid speech, or uncertain phonemes. His speech is quite free, his sentences often badly formed, and he jumps around incessantly in relating a story. As will be apparent, it is at times quite difficult to follow the logical development of what he has to say.

I have preserved the many fillers and breaks in speech in order to transmit as accurately as possible the difficult staccato style of Shabbo's speech. Explanatory words in parentheses are added without which the text would often be incomprehensible.

---

[1] He was born in Challa. He speaks primarily JZakho. See § 1.5.

[2] Cousin of Shabbo and younger brother of Ahiya Hashiloni. He was born in Jerusalem and speaks JZakho.

[3] Cousin of Shabbo. He was born in Kara and speaks Jewish Kara.

5.1. The History of Jews in Challa

1 ^{H}v-^{H}'axnan tam 'axwa mād 'āna wən šəmya—, ^{H}ba-ʿérex^H bə́z-zodāna m-'alpa šənne lu tiwe b-Čalla. [A.H.: mā?] bə́z-zodāna m-'alpa šənne. yaʿni mən ^{H}yṣi'át^H d-axxa, ^{H}yṣi'át^H—, 'ako zə́lwālu go ^{H}galút^H. mani 'ā séwāle l-axxa? Nawoxadnesər, ^{H}naxón^H? mən d-é-doṛ u-ḥil 'axnan wax pliṭe m-tāma, Čalla 'ə́twāba hudāye.

2 xá-doṛ xamšamma bāte 'ewa. 'an xamšamma bāte, 'əsri u-šö'á-maʿalmine 'ətwa gaw dida. xamša knəšyāsa-ži 'ətwa, ḥil qam qal'a. qam qal'a. (k)tax-rətta? ḥil l-é-'ida-ži bāte 'ewa. bāte 'an—, 'e kəndāla. [A.H.: bātəd hudāye.] 'e kəndāla mṭéwāle l-Najəmko. ^{H}haré^{H4} yalunke zöre l-tāma qoríwālu. ktaxrət? yalunke zöre. 'e xeta. [A.H.: he, he, he.] 'e xeta—. ^{H}bet kavarót^H 'ətwa l-é-'āl kəndāl Kərika. [A.H.: he.]

3 ^{H}'az lə'át lə'át^H sele xa—, xa məšəlmāna. Piro ^{Z}gəmríwāle^Z. Piro. 'ā pəšle—, taxrət ^{Z}gəmriwāle^Z Piro Sbakyát? taxrət, ^{H}naxón^H? [A.H.: la', la', lá-ki'ən.] lá-ktaxrət. [A.H.: lá-ki'ən.] ta pəzaġāye—, ^{Z}gəmríwālu^{Z5} Piro Sbakyát. bāb didu 'é-Piro wewa. 'ā séwāle m-go Pənčāye. mən Blejan séwāle. šqəlle xa baxta ^{H}almaná^H mən Bet Kāre. Bet Kāre (k)taxrətta? mən tāma šqəlle xá-baxta ^{H}almaná^H. 'ə́twāla xa xurga… [Y.H.: mar ʿagunsa; A.H.: 'armə́lsa] he. 'ə́twāla xa xurga. 'e-'armə́lsa ^{Z}qam gāwərra^Z. wélāle šö'á-brone. 'e kalba bər kalba!

4 'anna, 'anna šö'á-bron(e), əxzi mād 'ətwa! 'anna šö'á-brone lə́twālu čú-məndi. ^{H}bə-xlál bə-xlál^H čú-məndi ču—, 'afəllu xá-^{H}šaʿal^H 'ar'a lə́twālu. séwālu l-tāma ^{H}b-tor^H hənna 'iya mā k(əmri)—mahájər. ^{H}palít^H. he. séwālu l-tāma. de má-'odax? 'án-šö'a-brone kutxa mpəlle basər dide. 'ilāha la māzədlu! (m)pəllu basər dide. xa šö'á-yāle-u xa tmanyá-yāle-u xa

---

^{4} Neo-Aramaic har 'e is less likely here since it is followed by yalunke zöre and not yalunka zöra.

^{5} Error for gəmríwāle.

5.1. THE HISTORY OF JEWS IN CHALLA

And we were there, as far as I have heard—, more than about a thousand **1**
years they (Jews) have been settled in Challa. [A.H.: What?] More than a
thousand years. That is to say, since the exodus from here, the exodus—,
when they had gone into exile. Who (was) it (who) had come here?
Nawochadnezer,[6] correct? From that generation and until we had left
there, there were Jews in Challa.

A generation (ago) there were five hundred houses, these five hundred **2**
houses. There were twenty-seven teachers in it (Challa). There were
also five synagoguges (situated) over towards the fortress. Towards the
fortress. Do you remember it? Also there were houses over towards that
side. The houses, those—, that steep slope. [A.H.: The houses of the Jews.]
That steep slope reached Najimko.[7] As you know, they used to bury the
little children there. Do you remember? Little children. And the other.
[A.H.: Yes, yes, yes.] The other—. There was a cemetery on that side of
the steep slope of Kerika. [A.H.: Yes.]

Then very slowly came a—, a Muslim. They called him Piro. Piro. **3**
He became—, you remember they used to call him Piro Sbakyat? You
remember, correct? [A.H.: No, no, I don't know.] You don't remember. [A.H.: I don't know.] To the village nobles—, they called him Piro
Sbakyat. Their father was that Piro. He had come from (the area of) Pinianish. He had come from Blejan. He married a widow from Bet Kare.
Bet Kare, you remember it? He married a widow ('almana) from there.
She had a stepson… [Y.H.: Say 'agunsa (deserted wife)! A.H.: Widow
('arməlsa).] Yes. She had a stepson. He married that widow. He had seven
sons. That son of a bitch!

Those seven sons, look what there was! Those seven sons didn't have **4**
anything. Nothing at all, nothing at (all)—, they didn't even have an inch
of land. They had come there as, um, what do they call it?—a refugee.
palit. Yes. They had come there. So what should we do? Each of those
seven sons followed him. May God not increase them! They followed
him. One (had) seven children and one (had) eight children and one

---

[6] = Nebuchadnezzar.
[7] The former business partner of Rabbi Jacob Hashiloni, Ahiya Hashiloni's father.

ˀəṣṛá-yāle-u xa xamšá-yāle. šöˀá-nāše u-ˀe xéta-ži har mənnu ˀanna
tmanyá-brone. walḥāṣəl de de de de de de zədlu. zədlu ˀánna-nāše. má-odi?
mā lá-odi?[8] lətlu čú-məndi.

5 ˀé-waxt, b-é-doṛ kulla ^Hareṯ^H hənna Čalla mpole(ˀ)ta ˀāwa. ^Hhelək ˀaxí
tof^H ˀəd-hudáye-ewa. xa ^Hhelək katán^H ˀit xa məzgafte l-tāma. xa məzgafte
ˀit. xa ^Hhelək^H məzgafte ˀāwa. [A.H.: ˀeka?] g(o)-Čálla. g(o)-Čalla. [A.H.:
Čalla? ˀeka go Čalla? məzgafte ˀeka ^Zwela^Z?...] məzgafte. he, he, he. go-Čá-
[A.H.:^Zˀāwa^Z? məzgafte ṛapsa did kiˀənna?] ˀé-məzgafte. ˀé-məzgafte. [A.H.:
ˀāya? basər ˀen be malla?] he. basər ˀen be malla. l-é-ˀāl-le Tax Mallāye l-
tāma.[A.H.: ˀāya ^Zwela^Z?] ˀāya ^Zwela^Z.[9]

6 walḥāṣəl tāma ˀətwa suráye-ži. ˀətwa surāye. ^Haz^H ˀán-surāye-ži ham ˀāni
hənna ^Hfallahím^{H10} wewa. godiwa hənna ^Hmˁabdiwa ˀadamót^H hudāye
u-^Hmˁabdiwa ˀadamót^H gyánu-ži... ˀanna má-odi? mā lá-odi? mašmiˀ!
^Hmtuxnənnu^H ti gyānu šaqli ˀəpər hudāye. (b-)xurṭūsa. šaqli ˀəpər hudāye.
[A.H.: mā?] šaqli ˀəpər hudāye.

7 hudāye ^Hmuzmənilu^H l-é-məzgafte. ṛápsa-la ˀe-məzgáfte... walḥāṣəl
^Hmuzmənilu^H l-tam xa yom ˀərota u-^Hmˀoyəmlu^H ˀəlləd didu. kəmri: ˀarˀa—,
ˀanna—, kulla ˀarˀa gəbe dārétūla b-šəmmeni. godax ^Hhozé^H-ži. ^Zˀogā^Z
ˀətwa b-é-doṛ—, ḥukum ˀoṣmoḷḷi ˀāwa. ˀətwa qāymaqam ˀəlləd hənna... la,
la, l-Baškala. l-Baškala. Baškala. Baškalan[11] ˀurxəd ṭḷá-yome m-Jólamerg[12]
l-é-ˀāl-ila.

---

[8] Positive-negative formulae are an areal feature (Hopkins p.c.) and are common
in NeoAram, e.g., JNaɣada ma odan ma l-odan 'What on earth can I do?' (Hopkins
1989b:258,274), JZakho ˀēka bāzax, ˀēka la gēzax? 'Where shall we go, where shall we
not go?' (Sabar 2005:216), JBetan mā ˀoðax mā la ˀoðax 'What [on earth] should we do
and what should we not do?' (Mutzafi 2008a:252–253), JChalla ^Hhkirənnu^H má-ˀətwa má-
lətwa 'They investigated me (as to) what there was, what there wasn't.' Cf. the use of a
different positive-negative formula that serves as an introduction to stories, e.g., in Jilu
(Fox 1997:96 iwa liwa 'Once upon a time' [= 'There was, there wasn't']) and Bohtan (Fox
2007:73 ˀətwa lətwa).
[9] In imitation of the preceding JZakho form spoken by Ahiya.
[10] Ar > ModH.
[11] The Jews of Bashkala referred to the place as Başqalán.
[12] Cf. JBetan Julamerg (Mutzafi 2008a:226).

(had) ten children and one (had) five children. Seven sons[13] and (with) that other one (Piro) still with them (that makes) eight grownups.[14] Those eight sons. In short, so, so, so, so, so, so, they increased. Those people increased. What on earth should they do?[15] They don't have anything.

At that time, in that generation, all the land, um, Challa, was divided. 5 The best part was of the Jews. (In) a small section there is a mosque. There is a mosque. (In) a section there was a mosque. [A.H.: Where?] I(n) Challa. I(n) Challa. [A.H.: Challa? Where in Challa? Where was the mosque?...] The mosque. Yes, yes, yes. In Cha(lla). [A.H.: That one? The large mosque that I know?] That mosque. That mosque. [A.H.: That one? Behind the spring of the mullah's family?] Yes. Behind the spring of the mullah's family. On that side is the 'Mullahs' Quarter'. [A.H.: It was (there)?] It was (there).

In short, there were Christians there too. There were Christians. So 6 those Christians too also they, um, were fellahin. They used to do, um, they would work the fields of the Jews and they would also work their own fields... What on earth should they do? Listen! They planned for themselves that they should take the soil of the Jews. (By) force. They should take the soil of the Jews [A.H.: What?] They should take the soil of the Jews.

They invited the Jews to that mosque. That mosque is large... In short, 7 they invited them there one Friday and they threatened them. They say: "The land—, those—, you should put all the land in our name. We even make a contract." At that time, in that generation—, it was Ottoman rule. There was a local governor at, um... no, no, at Bashkala. At Bashkala. Bashkala. From Bashkala it (is) a three day journey from Jolamerk, it is on the other side.

---

[13] Lit., 'people'.
[14] Lit., 'sons'.
[15] Lit., 'What should they do? What shouldn't they do?'

8 *walḥāsəl mắ-odax? mā lá-od(ax)? šqəllu mənnu. xanči qṭililu. xanči drelu*
go ^Hbet sohar^H. xanči 'riqālu mən ^Hpahad^H. xanči pəšlu. nixəd sāwox
u-xa xeta, 'e-xéta lá-ki'ən šəmme mắ-yle, qemi mšadrilu 'əl-Baškala q(am)
qāymaqam mən d-an hənna ^Hetekím 'et ḥozím mzuyafím u-d-rama'út^H
ko 'anna lu šqíle-lla hənna ^Hkowaḥ^H mən didu. mād 'ə́twālu-ži go besa
'áya-ži šqəllu. 'áya-ži zəlle. kud mḥokéle-ži qemi qaṭlile. u-'āni hənnə́llu-
ži ^Hmuspəklu^H 'arqila, 'riqālu.

9 *walḥāṣəl tāma qəmlu mšodərru l-nixəd sāwox xa xéta-ži mənne. lá-ktaxrən*
šəmme mắ-yle. ^Htiré^H. [A.H.: ^Zsāwoyəd^Z bābi. ^Zsāwoyəd^Z bābi. ^Zsāwoyəd^Z
bābi.] sāwox. Mašiaḥ hənna sāwəd bābox wewa. [A.H.: la, Mašiaḥ ^Zsāwó-
yi^Z-le.] ^Zsāwoyox wele^Z. qəmlu mšudrilu l-Baškala qam qāymaqam. ^H'az^H
'é-waxt b-é-doṛ 'idəd ḥukum lá-gmāṭewa^16 l-Čálla, y'elox, rə́qqa-ewa mən-
nəd didu. u-kurdináye-ži kalbe bəš́ṭor lu mənnu. be-dín-ilu xor d-anna
'arabāye.

10 *walḥāsəl walḷa šodərru be 'āġa l-Jólamerg. 'itən tāma xa ^Zgəmrile^Z Ḥusní-*
'affandi. ^H'az^H 'āya xətən Walyắ-bak^17 wewa, 'e Ḥusní-'affandi. 'āya xətən
Walyắ-ba(k) l-tắma-ži hənna 'ewa. múfti-'ewa. qázi-'ewa. kullu šu'āle
'ewa. šodərru l-tāma. u-bāb díde-ži darwéž-'affandi ^Zgəmríwāle^Z. 'anna
hudāye mən tāma la da'ri. [A.H.: Walyắ-bak 'āga did Čalla ^Zwele^Z.]
Walyắ-bak, ^Hgam^H bāb dide, dla b-doṛ dide, 'əlla b-doṛ bắbe-'āwa. b-doṛ
sắwe-'āwa. kullu 'anna... kalbe. [A.H.: 'āni 'āġawāyəd Čalla ^Zwelu^Z]. he,
'āni 'āġawāyəd^18 Čalla.

11 *šodərru kəmri kutru 'āse l-qəṭla. mandelu 'əbbəd ṃāye. mā—, hənna Zāwa*
deni, ki'ətte. 'e—, ṃāye 'uṛwa... téreni bāwədwa. walḥāsəl walḷa qemi 'āni
qaṭlilu. hudāyəd pə́šwālu-ži kə́tt-u-māt 'riqālu. ^Hha-sóf^H didu lu məṭye
hənna be 'Awṛāham, be Nuwaḥ... l-Mə́ssər-ž(i). xa ^Hməšpaḥắ^H mənnu
zə́lwālu l-Məssər. 'atta lu d'ire qam kma šənne l-axxa.

---

16 For expected *gmaṭyắwa.*
17 See s.v. in the glossary for the possible origin of this phrase.
18 Shabbo usually uses the plural form *'āgāye.* He merely repeated the form that Ahiya
had just said.

In short, what on earth should we do? They took (the land) from them. **8**
Some they killed. Some they put in prison. Some fled out of fright. Some
remained. Your late grandfather and the other one, the other (one) I don't
know what his name is, they (the Jews of Challa) up (and) send them
to Bashkala before the local governor with those, um, copies and forged
contracts and trickery because they (the Kurds) have taken it (the land),
um, (by) force from them (the Jews). They also took whatever they had
in the house. Also it went. They up (and) kill whoever also spoke. And
those who did um, managed to flee, fled.

In short, they up (and) sent there your late grandfather (and) also **9**
the other one (who was) with him. I don't remember what his name
is. Look! [A.H.: The grandfather of my father. The grandfather of my
father. The grandfather of my father.] Your grandfather. Mashiaḥ, um,
was your father's grandfather. [A.H.: No, Mashiaḥ is my grandfather.] He
was your grandfather. They up (and) sent them to Bashkala before the
local governor. So at that time, in that generation, the (long) arm of the
government did not reach Challa, you know, it was a distance from them
(the residents of Challa). And as for the Kurds too, even dogs are better
than them. They are without religion, like those Arabs.

In short, by God, they sent (them) to the house of the Agha in Jola- **10**
merk. There is one there they call Husni Effendi. So he was the son-in-law
of the Vali Bey, that Husne Effendi. He (was), um, the son-in-law of the
Vali there. He was the mufti. He was the judge. He was all things. They
sent (them) there. And they used to call his father Dervish Effendi. (They
sent them there so that) those Jews should not return from there. [A.H.:
The Vali Bey was the Agha of Challa.] The Vali Bey, also his father, not in
his generation but rather it was in the generation of his father. It was in
the generation of his grandfather. All of those … dogs [A.H.: They were
the aghas of Challa.] Yes, they (were) the aghas of Challa.

They sent (them) saying the two of them should be killed. They should **11**
throw them into the water. What—, um, our Zawa (River), you know it.
That—, big (body of) water… It would be sufficient for us (here in Israel).
In short, by God, they up (and) they kill them. And the Jews who had
remained fled bit by bit. The last of them have come, um, the family of
Abraham (and) the family of Noah … to Egypt. One (other) family had
gone with them to Egypt. Now they have returned here (to Israel) a few
years ago.

12 *walḥāsəl hatxa widilu. kətte kətte 'riqālu m-qam didu. māḷu šqəllu. mxelu
'əllu. u-kullu ᴴdvarímᴴ wədlu 'əllu. 'atta ᴴgamᴴ mṭelu 'əlləd hənna qəṭla.
bāziwa b-xurṭūsa go besa pšaqliwa mād gbewa. ᶻgəmriwaᶻ... [A.H.: ...
l-Məṣṣər, Šama'ya ᶻweleᶻ.] he, he, Šama'ya... walḥāsəl ḥil tāma mṭelu ḥil
Məṣṣər. 'āni zəllu 'idəd Páras-ži zəllu. 'ā—, la-ki'axlu har lá-ki'ax ᴴysodᴴ
didu 'éka-'ile. mā pəšlu? pəšlu ḥel dór... tāma.*

13 *'áxtun-ži m-qam didu 'riqắlexun, 'anna xeta t—, basər mənnexun 'anna
t—, be 'amoyi Zawūlun. 'áni-ži zəllu. pəšlan 'axnan tāma. [A.H.: kma
wa'da basər mənnan mpəqlu? xá-šāta?] mani? 'āna ki'ənwa xa šắta-u-palge
xa məndi. he, hatxa. 'á-ži nixəd 'amoyi Zawūlun-ži mxéwālu. šodə́rwālu
xa 'Abdi ᶻgəmríwāleᶻ. xa Ṣaləḥko u-xa xeta mšudrilu bárakus dide. 'āya
mən Moṣəl kesewa. go Galli. Galli ktaxrətte? [A.H.: he, he.] ᴴ'azᴴ tāma
waḷḷa mə́rwāle 'āġa ṭas didu ġulamawás dide: qaṭlétūle Zawūlun.*

14 *zəllu l-tāma. 'āni ṭḷāha-ewa. ᴴmoḥlətluᴴ. xa kemər ta d-e xeta kemər:
xa 'áwon-la. tré-ži mxabine b-iya hudá qaṭlile. māxax xa təffaq l-'aqle.
bamrax ta 'āġa lá-ᴴmusləḥlanᴴ qaṭlaxle. 'riqāle. waḷḷa xa ᴴkadúrᴴ drelu
'əbbəd dide u-mxelu 'aqle 'aqle. mən aqle qemi ᴴpaš'ileᴴ. zəlle 'riqāle zəlle
l-Kəri. Kəri u-Maləxta 'ətwa hənna xa ᴴnəkudátᴴ hənna 'iya mā kəmrila
ᴴmištarətᴴ 'Eraqnāye l-tāma.*

5.2. THE AGHA TAKES WHAT HE WANTS

1 *u-ᴴ'azᴴ 'āya šqə́lwāle—, tmanya ḅaṛāne xilíwāle. ḥaqqeni lá-hūle. 'āni
haḷḷa haḷḷa 'aġáye-lu. mare təffáqe-lu. xa šö'i tmāni təffáqe 'ətle. šəmməd
dide—, bābe Rašíd 'Áġa-'ewa. 'ā b-gyāne Maḥammat Ṭāhər 'áġa-'ewa.
bāb dide skətle zəlle. nixəd bábi-ži nəxle. xá-yoma zəlli 'əlləd pareni l-tāma.
kemər ṭāsi: mā-gəbət?*

In short, they made them (dispersed) like this. One by one they fled   12
from before them. (The Kurds) took their property. They beat them. They
did all sorts of things to them. Also now they were, um, killed. They (the
Kurds) would go by force into a house (and) they would take whatever
they wanted. They would say—. [A.H.: ... to Egypt, it was Shemaia]. Yes,
yes, Shemaia... In short, they got as far as there, until Egypt. They also
went in the direction of Iran. As for him—, we didn't know them, in any
case we don't know what their origin is. What has become of them? They
remained till the generation... there.

Also you fled before them, those others w(ho)—, after you those   13
w(ho)—, the family of my uncle Zebulun. Also they went. We remained
there. [A.H.: How long after us did they leave? One year?] Who? I
knew (it was) something (like) a year and a half. Yes, (something) like
that. Also they (the Kurds) had beaten my late uncle Zebulun. They
had sent someone called Abdi. They sent after him (Zebulun) a certain
Ṣaleḥko and someone else. He had come from Mosul. In Galli. Galli, you
remember it? [A.H.: Yes, yes.] So there, by God, the Agha had said to his
servants: "You should kill Zebulun."

They went there. They were three. They decided. One says to the other: 14
"One: it's a sin; two: it's also a pity (that) they should kill that Jew. Let's
shoot at his foot (with) a rifle. We will tell the Agha that we didn't succeed
in killing him. He fled." By God, they put a bullet in him and shot him
in his foot. They up (and) injured him in his foot.[19] He went, he fled, to
Kiri. There was at Kiri and Malexta, um, an outpost,[20] um, what do they
call it?—the Iraqi police there.

5.2. The Agha Takes What He Wants

And so he had taken—, eight rams he had filched. He did not pay us   1
for them. They, how fortunate, are the aghas! They are rifle owners. One
has about seventy, eighty rifles. His name—, (by the way) his father was
Rashid Agha. He himself (the son), was Mahammat Taher Agha. His
father croaked (and) died. Also my late father passed way. One day I went
there for our money. He says to me: "What do you want?"

---

[19] The repetition of *'aqle* (*'aqle 'aqle*) raises the possibility of distributive meaning and
that he was shot in both his feet, though it would then be hard to explain how he fled.
[20] Lit., 'point'.

2 *mərri: tmanya ḫaṛāne 'axiwélexun²¹ 'arbi dināre 'it rešexun, qurdá! bābox le šqila-llu. 'āna ᴴmbakšənᴴ pār gyāni. kemər: ᴷjuwa ke brəsi bihn ču sar dene kawa.ᴷ ki'ət ᴴperúšᴴ má-yla? lá-ktaxrətta kurdi, ᴴnaxónᴴ? la'? [A.H.: la'.] ya'ni hudāye 'ən kpənnu, gezi reš dena tiqa. 'ána-ži mərri ṭas dide mərri: denəd hudāye hálūle! la kese reš dena tiqa. 'ako dena xləṣle ᴬxaḷaṣᴬ.*

3 *mərri: qurdá, xzi! 'āna Hekkarná-wən. u-'āhat Be Bádən-wət. u-'āhat lá-mṣət māḷeni 'axlətte. 'ən māḷeni 'āse l-'ixāla, 'it 'āǧa d-Čalla. 'it Pəncatūsa. 'it Karatūsa. 'āna mare—, mare ᴴkówaḥᴴ-'iwən, lá-xašwət? jirānatūsa ᴴmašehí 'aḥérᴴ. má-'ətwa basəmta godila bə́ž-basəmta. bale 'ən pəšla 'ənyān hənna 'iya má-kəmri ᴴnakamótᴴ, 'āhat lá-mṣət 'əlleni.*

4 *kemər: si! mā 'urṭūsəd 'itən go šallox mándila! wáḷḷa-ži ḥməlli mərri: ḫāš xa qurdáya-le mənni pəzaǧá mən Čalla. 'egā drele gopaḷta. mərri: la'. la māxətte! la māxətte! šuqle! 'axnan hudāye 'ako kpənnan gezax reš dena tiqa. kemər: he. mərri: ᴴb-sedərᴴ.*

5 *ḥmóləna! xulūl d-iya Daniyél bər Hoče 'ewa. xa zo'a bargúze-le qāmi. ᴴnáylunᴴ-ži hādax lewe. lu bəjrá. wax reš gāre l-xulūla kulleni kapaneni lu b-əǧdad bərqāda. 'é-Maḥammat Ṭāhər 'āǧa sele. 'āǧa-le. manoxe xāze julləd mani bəš tāza-l(e). monəxle monəxle monəxle. sele. nixəd bābi u-Hoče u-'āni lu 'əltəx. 'āni lu bəštá. 'axnan 'iwax reš gāre bərqāda. 'əryána-le-ži.*

6 *[A.H.: 'eka? go Čalla?] la, go Kāra. Kāra 'āt lewət xə́zya-lla. he. Kāra lewət xə́zya-lla 'āhat. [A.H.: la'. lewən...] 'ewa, 'ewa l-Kāra. sele kemər ṭāsi: má'alləm! 'ána-ži mərri: má-lox Maḥammat Ṭāhər 'āǧa? 'anna bargúze gəbe yāwəttu ṭāsi. 'ānid qāmi... [A.H.: Kāra 'Iraq ᶻwelaᶻ, lewa-). he he. [A.H.: Kāra 'Iraq ᶻwelaᶻ.] he he 'Éraq-wa...*

---

²¹ For *xilíwālexun?*

I said: "You've filched eight rams. You owe forty dinars, Kurd! Your 2
father has taken them. I request my money (for the rams)." He says: "*juwa
ke brəsi bihn ču sar dene kawa*." Do you know what the meaning is? You
don't remember Kurdish, correct? No? [A.H.: No.] That is to say, if Jews
are hungry, they go for an old debt (to collect it). I also said to him: "Hand
over (your) debt to the Jews! (Jews) don't come for an old debt. When the
debt is finished, it's over. (But this isn't a debt like that.)"

I said: "Kurd, Look! I am a resident of Hakkari and you are (a resident 3
of) Be Baden. And you cannot filch our possessions. If our possessions
should get filched, (then you should remember that) there is an agha of
Challa (who will look after us). There are those (aghas) from Pinianish.
There are those (aghas) from Kara. I am—, powerful, don't you think?
(As for good) neighborliness (that is) something else. Whatever may be
pleasant (to start off with), good relations make it even nicer. But if it
becomes a matter of, um, what do they call it?—revenge, then you cannot
best us."

He says: "Go! Whatever fart you've got in your pants, release it!" Also 4
by God, I waited (and) said (to myself): "(It is) good that it is a Kurd (that)
is with me, a village noble from Challa." So then (the village noble from
Challa) beat him with a shepherd's stick. I said: "No! Don't hit him! Don't
hit him! Leave him! We Jews, when we are hungry, we go (to collect) an
old debt." He says: "Yes." I said: "Okay."

Wait! It was the wedding feast of this Daniel son of Hoče. I am wearing 5
a woolen suit. It isn't nylon (material) like this (that I am now wearing).
(The participants in the wedding feast) are moving around. We are on the
roof at the wedding feast, all of us, our shoulders are together, dancing.
That Mahammat Tahər Agha came. He is the Agha. Looking around,
he sees whose garment is nicer. He looked around (and) around (and)
around. He came (near). My late father and Hoče are down below. They
are drinking. We (on the other hand) are on the roof dancing. Also it is
rain(ing).

[A.H.: Where? In Challa?] No, in Kara. You haven't seen Kara. Yes. You 6
haven't seen Kara. [A.H.: No, I haven't...] It was, it was in Kara. He came
(and) says to me: "Teacher!" I said: "What's with you, Mahammat Taher
Agha?" (Mahammat Taher says:) "You must give me that woolen suit."
The one that (is) on me (Shabbo)... [A.H.: Kara was Iraq, it isn't—.] Yes,
yes. [A.H.: Kara was Iraq.]... Yes, yes. It was Iraq...

7   *ắna-ži... 'ắna-ži mərri: qurdắ! 'āna ču bargūze lá-gmzabnan. lá-julli-ži
    šalxənnu m-qam gyāni yāwənnu ta—. kəm(ər): mād pāre gebət byāwənnox.
    'āna gyắni-ži 'atta byāwənnu ṭā(sox). mərri: waḷḷa gəmrən kulla 'Eraq
    gyānox yāwətta ṭāsi, 'āna julle m-qāmi lá-gšalxənnu yāwənnu ṭā(sox). 'ako
    zəlli l-besa mšadrənnu 'əllox. waḷḷa 'iya [H]mašehu 'aḥér[H]. bale l-axxa? la'!

8   'áx-geb tán-geb ṭaṃáha-geb, waḷḷa kemər: 'āna 'anna bargūze gbənnu.
    māṭo t-(h)ūwa. kmād gebət byāwən. mərre: [H]b-sedər[H]. 'atta 'əd-gyāni pšal-
    xənnu byāwənnu. mərri: la, la, mxalope let l-axxa. 'ako zəlli l-Čalla, 'āna
    mšadrənnox. kma, kmắ-la? mərri tre'sár-dināre. menəx! xāzax! menəx!
    bargūze qam xəddắ-'it?

9   'anna Karāye kullu [H]'antíka[H]-ilu. kúllu-ži. mani 'ilu? ya'ni gyānu gbela
    ṛába. wət bəxzāya mən didu? la, waḷḷa let. u-let. u-zəlli l-besa u-mšadrən-
    nox. pār gyāni šqilili. bargúze-ži lu qāmi zəllan besa. zəllan besa šlixili.
    hiwili ṭas dide. zəllu 'án-bargūze. zəlli l-tāma xá-gā xet mərri gəbən pār
    gyāni...

10 [H]az[H] 'āni zəllu tūlu go 'urxa dide. xa 'āṣərta le bisāya. 'egā bāzən Be-Búwa
    xa dūka, Be-Búwa [Z]gəmrila[Z]. tāma mədor didu gyātu go d-é-[H]'azọr[H], Be-
    Búwa. xá-le tiwa go d-iya ṭarrašta reš 'urxa. xa 'əl-'ída... xa 'əl-'ída. waḷḷa
    ṣrəxlu xá-l-e-xet: de-m-é-(i)da m-é-(i)da sāwun 'əlle! hatxa monəxle. he, xa
    təffaq-ži la mənnu. ṭḷāha náše-lu-ži bisāya. 'anna deni. 'āya 'əšta xulắme-lu
    mənnu. kutxa xa—, xa təffaq 'ənglízi-la b-kāpe. 'áya-ži xa reš kutke. hənna
    [H]'ekdáḥ[H]-ži-ila b-ṭanəšta. b-ṭanəštəd dide.

11 'āni 'riqắlu xulamawắs dide, u-'āya mokušlu m-kawənta. mokušlu m-
    kawənta. 'an bargūze d-wən mzúbna-llu ṭāse, 'āni-lu qāme. 'āni didi 'e(wa)
    ta xlūl Daniyél bər Hoče. walḥāṣəl waḷḷa mokušlu. kəmri: hay yəmmox
    silắleni! hay baxtox səllan! xāsox səllan! yəmməd bābox səllan! 'āhat ṃāḷ

As for me ... as for me, I said: "Kurd! I will neither sell any woolen suit 7
nor will I take my clothes off of myself to give them to you." (Mahammat
Taher sa)ys: "Whatever money you want I will give you. I myself will now
give it (the money) to yo(u)." I said: "By God, I say should you give me all
your very own Iraq, I shall not take off the clothes I am wearing to give
them to (you). When I have gone home, I will send them to you. By God,
this (is) something else (altogether). But here? No!"

When all's said and done, by God, (Mahammat Taher) says: "I want 8
that woolen suit. However it may be. Whatever you want I will give."
(Mahammat Taher) said: "Okay. Now I will take them off of myself, I will
give them (to you)." I said: "No, no, there is no exchanging here. When I
have gone back to Challa, I will send (them) to you." (Mahammat Taher
said:) "How much, how much is it (the price)?" I said: "Twelve dinars.
Look around! Let's see! Look around! Is there on anyone (else here) a
suit (like this)?"

Those from Kara are all old-fashioned. All of them even. Who are they? 9
That is to say, they pride themselves very much. Can you see (anything as
fine as my suit) with them? No, by God, there isn't (anything like my suit),
not at all. And (when) I have gone home, I will send you (it)." I took my
money. And we went home (with) the woolen suit on me. We went home,
(then) I took them off. I gave them to him (Mahammat Taher). That
woolen suit went (to the Agha). I went there another time (and) I said (to
Mahammat Taher): "I want my money (since I sent you my woolen suit)."

So they (a group of ambushers out to punish Mahammat Taher for not 10
paying for the woolen suit) went (and) stationed themselves on his path.
Evening is coming on. So then I will go to Be Buwa, a place they call Be
Buwa. Their mudir is stationed there in that area, Be Buwa. One (of the
ambushers) has settled himself in this thicket on the path. One on (this)
side... one on (that) side. By God, they shouted to each other: "So from
that side! From that side approach him!" Like this he looked (around).
Yes, they have one rifle. Three men are also coming (towards Mahammat
Taher). Those ones of ours. There are six servants with them. Each one (of
Mahammat Taher's servants has) an—, an English rifle is on his shoulder.
Also he (Mahammat Taher) (has) one on his knees. Um, also there is a
pistol at the side. At his side.

They, his servants, fled and (the ambushers) brought that one (Mah- 11
ammat Taher) down off the mule (he was riding on). They brought him
down off the mule. That woolen suit, which I have sold him, is on him. It
was mine for the wedding feast of Daniel son of Hoče. In short, by God,
they brought him down (off the mule). (The ambushers) say: "Hey! We

hudāyəd deni baxlətte? de mándūle qāman. 'egā kí'ət-ži mā wáxt-ile?
ḥanúkka-'ile. mā qársa-la l-tāma go ṭūra! ʿaṣə́rta-la. pu!

12 *šqəllu* ^H*makél*^H *'əlləd dide. 'üdlu b-ṣudra u-šarwāla. bas ṣudra u-šarwāla.*
    məndelu. qāman. məndelu. mxi u-mxi u-mxi u-mxi u-mxi u-mxi! ḥel wəlle
    desta, ^H*pastela*^H *reš* ^H*pas 'adamá*^H*. 'ár'a-ži xapči jmə́tta-la. tāma xanči*
    tálga-ži le 'əsya. [A.H.: . . . ^H*Ḥanukká*^H*.] he.*

13 *šāləd dide—, šāle ki'əttu má-ylu? xərxāṣe. šāləd dide 'ə́twāle xa hənna 'iya*
    mā kəmrila ^H*ḥagorá*^H *'anglizi(t) 'əd-*^H*kaṣiním*^H *hənna 'əd-*^H*ʿór*^H*. 'anna tre'.*
    'āya b-^H*əkdáḥ*^H *'āwa.* ^H*əkdáḥ*^H*dide. təffaq dide. [A.H.: dabanja.] sā'əd*
    dide. dabanja dide. 'an bargūzəd 'āna mzübniwāli ṭāse tre'sar dināre. u-
    'ə́twāle ^H*arnák*^H*-ži. šö'a—, šwa'sar dināre u-palge go* ^H*arnák*^H *dide 'ewa.*

14 *'āya mundelu l-tāma. kəmri: xzi! kalba bər kalba! 'axnan ya'ni qam 'ilāha*
    gnáxpaxin 'əlla šarwāla u-ṣúdra-ži kšalxáxwālu[22] *qāmox. qemi šoqile l-*
    tāma. šoqile l-tāma 'é-lele. 'āya pəšle l-ta(m). xulamawás dide 'riqālu zəllu.
    'anna ^H*davarím*^H*, kawənta 'anna kullu məselu. 'āya ṭarma šüqlu l-ta(ma),*
    šüqlu l-tāma u-'āni selu.

15 *'anna* ^H*davarím*^H *məselu u-selu. 'āya pəšle l-ta(m) ḥel yom basra. selu nāše*
    pədlu mən tāma kxāzele 'āya ṭárma-le l-tam. 'egā lašše le m'ubya mād
    lu máxye-lle 'əbbəd ^H*maklót*^H*. kulle lašše le piša paq'e paq'e. xa hənna go*
    hənna 'ewa—. qəwya ʿéba-le. yəmme čiqálu-lle.

16 *walḥāṣəl xá-lele 'axnan beseni. tar'eni b-léle-ži ptíxa-le. tək-u tək-u tək,*
    mxelu l-tar'a. máni-le? yəmmi ṣrəxla 'əlləd dide. kemər: Sise, Sise! tar'a
    ptuxle! Ábo-le. šəmme Ábo-le. [Y.H.: ḥukum mxelu 'əlle?] lā. 'ānid lu
    máxye-lle 'āya. ^H*ken*^H*, 'ānid əmxéwālu 'əlle. lā. d-qbə́lwāle* ^H*makót*^H*, 'ā*

---

[22] For expected *kšalxaxlu.*

fucked your mother! Hey! We fucked your wife! We fucked your sister! We fucked your father's mother! Will you filch the possessions of our Jews? Now throw it (the woolen suit) down before us." So then do you know what time of year it is? It is Hanukka. How cold it is there on the mountain! It is evening. Phew!

They took a stick to him (Mahammat Taher). They did it (to him) in 12 (his) shirt and trousers. (He was) only (in his) shirt and trousers. They threw him down in front of us. They threw him down. They beat him over and over and over again.[23] Until he is right now a portion of food, mincemeat, on the face of the earth. Also the earth is a bit frozen. Some snow has also fallen there. [A.H.: ... Hanukka.] Yes.

His belt—, you know what a *šale* is? His cummerband. His belt has, 13 um, what do they call it?—an English officers' belt, um, of leather. Those (are) the only two (weapons on the belt). It was with a pistol. His pistol. His rifle. [A.H.: *dabanja* (pistol).] His watch. His pistol. That woolen suit that I had sold him (for) twelve dinars. And he also had a purse. Seven—, seventeen and a half dinars were in his purse.

That one (Mahammat Taher) they threw down there. They say: "Look! 14 Son of a bitch! We, that is to say, before God we are embarrassed, but we are taking (your) trousers and shirt off of you." They up (and) leave him there. They leave him there that night. He remained there. His servants fled, they went away. (The ambushers) brought (back) all of those things, (including) the mule. They left that corpse (of Mahammat Taher), they left (it) there and they came (back).

They brought those things and they came. He remained there (lying 15 there on the ground) till the next day. People came, they passed by there, they see him. That corpse is there. Now then his body has swollen up (since) they have beaten it (so much) with sticks. His whole body has become pieces. A, um, in, um, it was—. It was dreadful. They tore his mother apart over it.

In short, one night we (are in) our house. And our door is open at 16 night. *Knock, knock, knock.* They knocked on the door. "Who is it?" my mother called out to him (the one who knocked). He says: "Sise, Sise! Open the door! It is Abo." His name is Abo. [Y.H.: Did the government beat him?] No, those who have beaten him, that one (are at the door now). Yes, those who had beaten him (are at the door). No, he who had received

---

[23] Lit., 'strike and strike and strike and strike and strike and strike!' (narrative imperative).

pəšle ṭarma go ṭūra. xulamāse 'riqǻwālu. tar'a ptəxla yəmmi. 'ǻna-ži qəmli manox(e). 'Ābo má-yla? le ᴴbər'ādaᴴ mənnəd zdo'səd gyāne.

17 *qurdāya má-lox? qay wetun qṭile xədda? lā, le māra. 'e kalba bər kalba xzile! yəmmax sílela(!)[24] 'əlləd dide. lá-ki'ən ᴴḥáy ᴴ-le ᴴ'oᴴ le misa. máni-le 'e kalba bər kalba? Maḥammat Ṭāhər 'āǧa. 'ahá! 'ǻga-le-ži. he. má-yla breta? y'ele hənnəd gyāne gunikəd gyāne. šqilāle. téra-ila. tera... godiwa hənna tāma. pəmma ptíxa-le 'áqqara. sele qlibāle l-tāma.*

18 *xzi! 'anna bargūze didox flāna yoma m-xlúla qāmox? 'ǻya-ži hə́nna-ži m-xlúla 'ewa. mərri: 'ewa dídi-lu. kemər: ᴷčəhú mən. čəhú mənᴷ ya'ni hudāya. hudāya kemər. 'iya dabanja. 'iya xanjar. 'iya šāla. [Y.H.: dabanja warwar?] he, he. warwar. ᴴkenᴴ. 'axnan ᶻgəmraxᶻ dabanja.*

5.3. Sufi Abraham, the Prayer Rug, and the Ḥajj

1 *walḥāṣəl zəllan 'əlləd hənna 'iya mā kəmrila zónaxin ... ᴴsmixótᴴ. zonax ᴴsmixótᴴ. 'úrreni go xá-dukkāna. šəmməd (d)e-mar dukkāna ḥajji Qǻdər-le. sele barakuseni. qbilaxle ᴴyaféᴴ. walḥāṣəl walla, de! šəmmox má-yle? kemər: ṣóf(i)-Ibrāhim. 'Áwṛaham pəšle ṣóf(i)-Ibrāhim. kutxa xa šəmma drele l-gyāne.*

2 *walḥāṣəl de ṣofi! má-'āhāt? nāš d-éka-wət? kəmri dəd Wān. 'eka bāzət? kemər: bāzən ḥajj. mašmi'! bāzət ḥajj? 'iya səswa bodaxle l-Ṣṭambul. ᴴkšeᴴ-báhar bāzən ḥajj. o! kemər: ṛāba dā'ət ṭaseni, ṛāba hiwi, d'āya 'odət ṭaseni! 'āzət reš qōr Maḥammad hənna ṛāba dā'ət ṭaseni ta-lá-'āse balāye b-rešeni, heeeee. ᴴhakol b-sedərᴴ... he he.*

3 *'egā dbəšle b-'idəd 'Awṛāham mučú mučú mučú. le bə-nšáqa-lla. kulle gəldəd 'ide hənnélle—. mərri: 'Awṛāham! go—, go ləbbi wən bimāra 'egā 'atta 'idox... ḥil bəšṭor wāwa. lá-hatxa. walḥāṣəl tūlu barqul 'ǧdāde.*

---

[24] For expected *səlla?*

blows, he (Mahammat Taher) had become a corpse in the mountain. His servants had fled. My mother opened the door. Also I got up to look. "Abo, what is it?" He is shaking from his own fear.

"Kurd, what's with you? Why, have you killed someone?" "No," he says. **17** "See that son of a bitch! Your mother fucked him. I don't know (if) he is alive or has died." Who is that son of a bitch? Mahammat Taher Agha. Aha! Moreover he is an agha. Yes. What has happened? He recognized his, um, his gunny sack. He took it. It is a large bag. A large bag... they used to make (them), um, (large) there. The mouth (of the gunny sack) opens up so big. He came, he emptied it out there.

"Look! Is this suit yours (from) such and such a day from the wedding **18** feast (that was then) on you?" This, um, was (from) the wedding feast. I said: "It is mine." He says: "*čəhú mən. čəhú mən* (My Jew. My Jew.)" That is to say, Jew. "Jew," he says. "This (is his) pistol, this (is his) dagger, this (is his) belt" [Y.H.: *Dabanja* (is) a pistol?]. Yes, yes. revolver. We say *dabanja* (pistol).

5.3. Sufi Abraham, the Prayer Rug, and the Ḥajj

In short, we went to, um, what do they call it?—to buy ... blankets. To buy **1** blankets. We entered a shop. The name of that shopkeeper is Hajji Qader. He came towards us. He received us nicely. In short, by God (he says): "So! What is your name?" (My brother Abraham) says: "Sufi Ibrahim." Abraham became Sufi Ibrahim. Each one (of us Jews) gave himself a (Muslim) name.

In short, "So Sufi! What are you? Where are you from?" They say **2** from Van. (Hajji Qader says:) "Where are you going?" (Abraham) says: "I am going on hajj." (Hajji Qader says:) "Listen! You are going on hajj?" (Abraham says:) "We will spend this winter in Istanbul. When it is spring I am going on hajj." Oh! (Hajji Qader) says: "Pray a lot for us! Lots of pleading, do a lot of praying for us! You should go to the grave of Muhammad, um, (and) you should pray a lot for us lest disaster befall us." Yessss. Everything is okay... Yes, yes.

So then he stuck (his lips) to Abraham's hand (and) *smack smack smack* **3** he is kissing it. All the skin of his hand became um—. I said: "Abraham!" In—, in my heart I am saying so now your hand... until it was better. Not like that. In short, they sat opposite each other.

4 *sele xa sayyə́dka-ži. sayyədka le bəxdāra l-ᴴnədaváᴴ. le bəxdāra l-ᴴnəda-*
váᴴ sayyədka. le xdira go d-an ᴴṣrifeᴴ kullu. ᴴba-ʿérex ʾuláyᴴ tre paṇqáṇote
u-palge pāre daqiqe ti gyāne le ṭəʿya. waḷḷa tūlu barqul ʾə́gdāde. sayyədka
šə̀mme hənna sayyəd Mā́jid-ʾile. u-ʾAvṛāham ʾāya ṣof(i)-Ibrā́him-le. u-ʾe
xeta ḥajji Qā́dər-ile...

5 *walḥạ̄ṣəl musele xa səjjāda. ʾAwṛāham mətwāle l-ʾar'a. har hatxa le bāda*
səjjāda, ptā́la-lla hatxa. b-iya ʾida le ḥmila réša-ži. hatxa le 'wida qam
ʾenəd kutru. hatxa le bāda səjjā(da). hā le māra: ʾiya səjjāda qəbla lewa
bədwā́qa-lla. he mašmi(ʾ)! qəbla lewa bədwā́qa-lla. ʾan kutru qurdāye xet,
sayyədka u-ʾe xet lu manoxe ʾəbbe, mar dukkāna. ʾe səjjāda šqilāle d'ipāle,
šqəlle xa xet. ʾá-ži mətwāle l-ʾar'a. hatxa le bāda ʾəbbəd dida... ʾíya-ži qəbla
lá-düqāla.

6 *xa ʾəṣra səjjāde ʾāni har lu manoxe ʾəbbəd dide. ʾiya—, mā qurdáya-le.*
hatxa narm u-ḥāle garməd dide. ʾiya nāša ᴴk-nər'éᴴ mən gen'edən le
ʾəsya... ʾAwṛāham... he, he. ṣof(i)-Ibrā́him. walḥạ̄ṣəl ʾáxnan-ži, ʾāna,
nixəd ʾaxoni ʾAwṛāham u-nixəd Baṣālel ʾidan pəmman ta la gaxkax. he.
kāsan əmre(ʾ)la ʾəllan mən gəxka. xa səjjāda xe ʾá-ž(i) šqilāle d'ipāle. xa xet
šqəlle məttūle l-ʾar'a. hátxa-le. ʾəl-ʾár'a. ʾíya-ži səjjāda lá-gdoqāla.

7 *hənna mar, hənna mar ᴴḥanútᴴ-ži kemər ṭas dide: ṣof(i) ʾiya má-iwət*
bāda? kemər: ʾit xa Maḥámmad-ʾā́ga m-kəslexun l-axxa le ʾəsya kəsleni.
təjjāra ʾewa. meséwāle səjjāde ʿaṣli. səjjāde ᴴtovímᴴ. mạ̄ṭod mandéwālu l-
ʾar'a qəbla gdoqíwāla. ʾanna lewu qəbla—. bābo! kemər: səjjāde mən kəsleni
gzoni, lu ʾəsye? mạ̄ṭo qəbla...?

Also a sayyid came. The sayyid is going around (begging) for a hand- 4
out. He is going around for a hand-out, the sayyid. He has gone around
in all of those huts. About perhaps, two and a half liras[25] (oops sorry, I
mean) small change he has sought for himself. By God, they sat opposite
one another. The sayyid, his name, um, is Sayyid Majid. And Abraham,
he is Sufi Ibrahim. And that other one is Hajji Qader...

In short, he brought a prayer rug. Abraham placed it on the ground. He 5
is doing just like this (to the) prayer rug (on) the ground, he is unrolling
it in this way. Also he is standing over it on this side. Like this he has done
(it) before the eyes of the two of them. He is unfolding[26] the prayer rug
like this. "Here," he is saying, "this prayer rug is not facing the qibla.[27] Yes,
Listen! It is not facing the qibla." Those two other Kurds, the sayyid and
that other one, are looking at him, the shopkeeper. He took that prayer
rug, folded it up, (and then) took another. He also placed it on the ground.
Like this he is doing to it... this one too did not face the qibla.

(After) about ten prayer rugs they still are looking at him. (They 6
think:) "This—, what (sort of) a Kurd (Abraham) this is! He is a pleasant
fellow![28] This person apparently has come from the Garden of Eden..."[29]
Abraham... Yes, yes. Sufi Ibrahim. In short, we too, I, my late brother
Abraham and the late Besalel, the hand (is on) our mouth in order that we
shouldn't laugh. Yes. Our stomach hurt us from laughter. He (Abraham)
took another prayer rug (and) folded it. He took (yet) another one (and)
placed it on the ground. It is like this. On the ground. Nor does this prayer
rug face it (the qibla).

Um, the owner, um, the shopkeeper says to him: "Sufi, what (is) this 7
you are doing?" He (Abraham) says: "There is a Maḥammad Agha of
yours here who has come to us. He was a merchant. He used to bring
genuine prayer rugs. Good prayer rugs. As soon as he would throw them
down on the ground, they would face the qibla. These do not (face) the
qibla—." (The shopkeeper says:) My God! He says: "The prayer rugs come
from us, they buy (them from us?) How the qibla...?

---

[25] Shabbo has probably anticipated the sum mentioned in § 5.3.9.

[26] Lit., 'doing'.

[27] Lit., 'the prayer rug is not grasping the qibla,' i.e., when it is unfolded and falls to the
ground, it does not point to the qibla in Mecca and thus, according to Abraham, is not
ritually satisfactory.

[28] Lit., 'His bones are so soft and the like.'

[29] They think that Abraham is truly a holy man because of his insistence that in
throwing down the prayer rug, the rug should orientate itself in the direction of the qibla.

8 *kemər: b-xudrešox ʿaziza! b-é-ḥajj ʾāzən ʾalləd dida. kemər: dax mundyālu*
   l-ʾarʾa səjjāda qəbla gdoqắwāla. ʾanna lewu bədwắqa-lla. ^A*yā ṛaḅḅi!*^A *māṭo*
   ʾiya—? ʾiya b-(ʾ)eni ^H*zaxút*^H*?" ... walḥāṣəl pa kullu səjjāde phannəlilu*
   ^H*(m)myašrilu*^H *l-ʾarʾa barqul qəbla u-mdagli reš didu. kemər: lā, ʾiya mā—,*
   dax mundyālu l-ʾarʾa, qəbla l-gyāna gdoqắwāla.

9 *ʾaxnan ʾída-la pumman.* ^A*yā ṛaḅḅi*^A *mắ-odax? (hā)dax* ^H*zmán-ʿavàr*^H*.*
   xá- ^H*smixà*^H *wax ptáxa-lla, manoxe wa—, bəďápa-lla, mattówe-lla l-*
   dūka, bə-šqāla xa xe. ^H*zmán-ʿavàr*^H*. de mā—, māṭo pūwa māṭo lá-kūwa?*
   xa b-kmá-ila? kemər: kúd-^H*smixạ*^H *ṭasexun ʾaxtun bāzetun əl-ḥajj tre*
   paṇqáṇoṭe u-palge ^H*paḥót*^H*. ʾiya* ^H*hanaxát*^H *dexun. walḥāṣəl b-íya-ʾida u-*
   yắ-ʾida pəšlan ḥil ʿāṣərta. hādax ʾắ-le bəšqāla ^H*smixót*^H *mattowe l-ʾarʾa.*
   səjjāda zöra b-xá-metər. hatxa... he he. hatxa le bāda ʾəbbəd didu. lā, qəbla
   lewu bədwắqa-lla ʾanna. ʾanna lewu. lewu mənna ḅāš.

10 *ḥil ʾe sayyádka-ži—, qómleni... ʿāṣərta drangésa-la. kemər ta sayyəd-*
   ka—. ʾegā lu bənšāqa ʾ́ǵdāde. xa xəllu ^K*sar čāwəd*^K *d-e-xéta. lu tiwe ʾāni*
   barqul ʾəǵdād. ʾaxnan wewax b-^H*ṣad*^H*. xa lu mšaboḥe ʾəl-xé, ʾAwṛāham*
   u-marəd dukkāna u-ʾé-sayyədka. sayyəda ^{Kʾ}*awlắd-e rasúl*^K*-ile. ʾāya mən*
   ^H*mišpaḥat*^H *Maḥámmat-le. hādax lu ʾwíde-lle. ʾAwṛāham bāzəl ḥajj gəldəd*
   ʾide xəllu. he, ʾāya bāl ḥajj. he, bale hiwi u-dʿāya gbewa ṭas didu. pəšle, ʾe
   xeta, sayyədka. kemər ṭas dide: qəmlan b-ʾaqle, he mbárbəzax. wax zūne.
   kutxa māḍ le zwŭna le zwina.

11 *kemər ta sayyədka, kemər: sayyəd, ʾắ-ži mərre* ^{Kʾ}*az qurbán sofyé-mən*^K*.*
   kemər: ʾāna gəbən yāwətti palpa(ṇqaṇoṭ)—, pálgəd-lira mən pārox tad
   dārənna go pāri ta baṛāxa. ḥməlle monəxle ʾəbbe. ʾide drele go jeba xa šāla le

He (Abraham) says: "Take my word for it, precious one! On this hajj 8
I am going to it (the qibla)." He (Abraham) says: "As soon as they threw
the prayer rug on the ground, it would face the qibla. These (prayer rugs)
do not face the qibla." Oh my Lord! How is this—? By virtue of what is
this?" ... In short, so all the prayer rugs, they will um them, they will
straighten them on the ground facing the qibla and they tell lies about
them. (Abraham) says: "No, this is what—, as soon as they threw it (the
prayer rug) on the ground, it would the face qibla by itself."

The hand is (on) our mouth (so we shouldn't laugh). Oh my Lord! 9
What should we do? Like this time passed: we are opening a blanket,[30]
looking at (it) and—, folding it, putting it back in place, taking another.
Time passed. So what—, what on earth will be? How much does one cost?
(Hajji Qader) says: "Each blanket for you (is) two and a half liras less
(because) you are going on hajj. This (is) your discount." In short, when
it comes down to it, we remained till the evening. Like this he is taking
blankets (and) putting them down on the ground. A small prayer rug of
one meter. Like this... yes, yes. Like this he is doing to them. No, those
(prayer rugs) are not facing the qibla. Those are not. They are not good
with regard to it (the qibla).

And until that sayyid—, we arose... it is late evening. (Abraham) says 10
to the sayyid—. So now they are kissing each other. Each declared himself
at the service of the other.[31] They have sat down opposite each other. We
were at the side. One is praising the other, Abraham and the shopkeeper
and that sayyid. The sayyid is a descendant of the Messenger.[32] He is from
the family of Muhammad. They have done like this to him. (Because)
Abraham will go on hajj, they ate the skin off his hand (from kissing it
so much). Yes, he will go on hajj. Yes, indeed, pleading and praying was
necessary for them. He remained, that other one, the sayyid. Abraham
says to him: "We have gotten up on (our) feet, yes, we should go our
separate ways.[33] We have bought (what we wanted). Each one has bought
whatever he has bought."

(Abraham) says to the sayyid, he says: "Sayyid." Also (the sayyid) said: 11
"My dear sufi (Abraham)."[34] (Abraham) says (to the sayyid): "I want you
to give me a half lir(a)—, a half lira of your money so that I can put it

---

[30] I.e., a prayer rug.
[31] Calque on Kurdish 'on the eyes'.
[32] I.e., Muhammad.
[33] Lit., 'scatter'.
[34] Lit., 'I am (your) sacrifice, my Sufi.'

qāme. xá-gdāda garšət mənne 'alpa rqā'e mnapli mənnəd dide. báz-zodāna
mən təksa, he, báz-zodāna mən təksa lá-kpeša. 'an xeta 'afəllu mbárbəzi.
'á-ži 'ida drele go jeba 'an pāre le jə́m'a-llu ᴴnədaváᴴ u-drele go 'idás
'Awṛāham.

12 'Awṛáw-ži šqilile monəxle 'əlləd didu. kemər: 'āna gəbən pálpaṇqàṇoṭ. 'āna
wən bizāla l-ḥajj. ṛāba pāre 'āna gəbən (m)bázbəzən. ṛāba pắre-ži 'ətli. bale
'āhat mən ᴷ'awlắd-e rasúlᴷ-'iwət. ᴷ'awlắd-e rasúlᴷ, ya'ni mən ᴴmišpaḥatᴴ
Maḥammad 'iwət. 'āna gəbən pálpaṇqàṇoṭ mən pārox tad dārənna go
pāri ta ᴴšamranᴴ pāri ta baṛāxa. sayyə́dka-ži kemər ṭas dide: kma gnapli
qāman? čú-məndi lewu 'anna pāre. 'atta hāwéwāli xa 'əmma tremma
paṇqáṇoṭe, yāwə́nwālox. 'āna ᴴsameaḥᴴ wənwa hādax.

13 kemər: 'āna lá-gbən. 'āna bāzən ḥajj. gəbən barbəzə—, hə́nna-la, ᴴ(m)báz-
bəzənᴴ pāre 'āna. jebi mə́lya-le. lewən 'āni. bale ham 'āhat—, wən bəxzāya
nūra le bizāla m-pāsox. 'āhət wət 'əsya mən gən'edən. 'āna gəbən ta baṛāxa
šaqlən mən pārox, he. dārənnu go pāri ta baṛāxa ta ᴴšamranᴴ pāri.

14 pə́šla ᴴb-kowaḥᴴ mābayn dide 'əd-'Awṛáham. b-íya-'ida u-yá-'ida sayyədka le māra: kullu šqullu! 'āna mərri: la… pálpaṇqàṇote. walla ᴴb-sofó šəl
davárᴴ qāyəm sayyədka max—. ᴴmáxrəhleᴴ. pār gyāne šqilile. pálpaṇqàṇoṭ hūle ṭas dide.

15 tāma ᴴ'əzórᴴ šuftíye-le. kud šuftiya 'ətlox hatxa: 'éni-əšti kiloye šö'i kiloye
… walla 'āni mədlu məndi reš 'əgdāde. si zon! kilo tré-qorūše. walḥāṣəl
'anna pálpaṇqàṇot xamši qorūše-la. 'anna 'əsri u-xamša kiloye šuftiya
basya 'əbbu. walla kúšleni mən dukkāna. 'əṛḥáqleni xor m-axxa ᶻhəlᶻ reš

(together) with my money for a blessing (alms)."[35] (The sayyid) stopped (and) he looked at him. He put his hand in the pocket of certain pants (that) are on him. (If) you pull one thread from it (the pants), a thousand patches will fall from it. No more than the waistband, yes, not more than the waistband remains (from the pants if you pull out one thread). Even those other (threads) will scatter. And he put his hand in (his) pocket (and took) that money (that) he has collected as a hand-out, and he put (it) in the hands of Abraham.

Abraham took them (the money) and looked at it. He says: "I want a 12 half lira. I am going on hajj. I want to distribute a lot of money.[36] Also I have a lot of money. However, you are from the descendants of the Messenger. Descendants of the Messenger, that is to say, you are from the family of Muhammad. I want a half lira of your money in order to put it in with my money for a blessing (alms)." The sayyid also says to him: "How much (do you think) has come my way? This money isn't (worth) anything. Now were I to have a hundred, two hundred liras, I would give (them) to you. I would have been be happy (if it were) like this."

(Abraham) says (to the sayyid): "I don't want (it). I will go on hajj. I 13 want to distrib—, um, I will distribute the money. My pocket is full. I am not poor. However, also you—, I am seeing fire going (forth) from your face. You have come from the Garden of Eden. I want to take some of your money for a blessing. Yes. I will put them (your money together) in with my money for a blessing so that I keep my money (safe and blessed)."

It was by force (this give-and-take) between him (the sayyid) and 14 Abraham. When it comes down to it, the sayyid is saying: "Take all of them (the liras)!" I said: "No… (I want only) half liras." By God, in the end, the sayyid gets up (and) for—. He forces him. (The sayyid) took (and gave Abraham) his own money. A half lira he gave him.

There is an area (for selling) watermelons there. Each watermelon 15 you have (is) like this: some sixty kilos, seventy kilos!… By God, they stretched out something on each other. Go buy (one)! A kilo (for) two piasters. In short, that half lira is fifty piasters. For them comes a watermelon of twenty-five kilos. By God, we went down out of the shop. We moved continually farther away, like from here to the road.[37] (Abraham)

---

[35] It is to be given as charity to the poor upon arriving in Mecca.
[36] To the poor upon arriving.
[37] From the room in Shabbo's house in which the story was told to the road outside his house.

^{H}kviš^H. le māra: de 'égā mā—, 'āna yəmməd d-iya hənna sayyədka lá-silāli?
kemər: de 'egā sāwun 'ázaxin pálpaŋqàṇoṭ dide yāxla b-šuftiya.

16 'ána-ži kəmrən ṭas dide: mā lewət zűna-lla—, u-šqíla-lla tad dārətta go
pārox ta baṛāxa? ki('ət) 'āna xorexun xmāra léwəna. 'āna ṭamá baxlən
pār gyāni? baxlan pār didu. ko wət šqíla-lla ta baṛāxa 'āhat! kemər:
^{H}šmor^H hənna ta ^{H}šamrax^H l-pārox! mā? 'áya ^{K}'awlắd-e rasúl^K. kemər:
'axtun, kemər: lá-ki'ətun čú-məndi. 'āna ki'ən... 'āna baxlən pār didu.
ṭamá baxlən pār gyāni?

5.4. The Death of Mighty Qoto[38]

1 walḥāṣəl məndid deni 'əšqəllu. ^{H}be'emét^H kesewa. 'e hənnəd 'iya mā kəmri
'ən hāwewa xa qəṭ'a gāla go besa 'á-ži kšaqlíwāle. pəšla ^{H}sən'á^H mābayneni.
'āni zədlu. xor baṛāze gmese tre'sar təlta'sar teške m-ə́gdāde. hādax zədlu.
'átta-ži lu piše 'āni. walḥāṣəl waḷḷa má-odi? hudāye ^{H}be'emét^H gəborím^H-
ewa.

2 bas 'āni ṛába-ilu. bāsewa dax kpə́nwālu, (b)'oriwa. qemi hudāye mpāle(')lu
l-gyānu. kutxa hudāyəd xə́dda-le. bāsewa—, 'iya məndi lətle, bāsewa 'iya
məndi gəbən. lə́tleni. de qū misi! hatxa bodax. māxéwālu. ^{H}be'emét^H selu
'iya mā kəmrila—. 'ətwa hənna Qoto.

3 Qoto bāb Šəm'on wewa. [S.B.: ^{H}ken, naxón, naxón.^{H}] Qoto bāb Šəm'on
wewa. Qoto. mā Qóto-le? hatxa dāwəqle ... Qoto wewa šəmməd dide, 'āna
wən šəmya Qoto. walḥāṣəl sele. 'ə́twāle xa 'áḡa šəmme Qárani 'ewa. sele
Qárani pəšle—. ksesa gəbe, lá-ki'ən, məšxa gəbe mād sele. Qóto-le go gūba.

---

[38] For a slightly different version of this story told on a different date, see Fassberg
2008b.

is saying: "So then what—, did I not fuck the mother of this, um, Sayyid!" (Abraham) says: "So then come on, let's go (and) spend his half lira on a watermelon.

Also I (Shabbo) say to him (Abraham): "What, have you not bought **16** it—[39] and taken it to put it with your money for a blessing?" (Abraham says:) "You kn(ow that) I, like you, am not an ass. Why should I use up my own money? I will use up their money." (Shabbo says:) "(But) you have taken it for a blessing!" (Abraham) says: "Keep it, um, so that we will keep your money." (Shabbo says:) "What? (But) he (is) the descendant of the Messenger!" (Abraham) says: "You," he says: "You don't know anything." I know... I will use up their money. Why should I use up my own money?"

5.4. THE DEATH OF MIGHTY QOTO

In short, they took something of ours. Really, they would come. That, um, **1** of what do they call it?—if there was an item of kilim rug in the house, that too they would take. There was hatred between us. They increased. Like pigs (these Kurds) bring (into the world) twelve, thirteen young (animals) all together. Like this they increased. And now they have become poor. In short, by God, what should they (the Jews) do? The Jews really were heroes.

But they (the Kurds) are many. They would come, as soon as they **2** had gotten hungry they would enter. They up (and) distribute the Jews for themselves. Each Jewish house was assigned to a particular gang of robbers.[40] (The Kurd) would come—, this thing he he hasn't got (so) he would come (and say:) "I want this thing. We don't have (it). Now up (and) bring (it)! Like this we will do (to you if you don't)!" He would beat them. Really, they came, what do they call it?—. There was, um, Qoto.

Qoto was the father of Simeon. [S.B.: Yes. Correct, correct.] Qoto **3** was the father of Simeon. Qoto. What (kind of person) is Qoto? Like this he grabs him... His name was Qoto, I have heard (about) Qoto. In short, he came. He had an agha (whose) name was Qarani. Qarani came (and) became—. He wants a chicken, I don't know, he wants cooking oil, whatever came along. Qoto is at the loom. (Qarani) says: "Now up (and)

---

[39] This is a false start.
[40] Lit., 'Each one is a Jew of someone.'

kemər: da qū mísili! 'iya b-xurṭūsa—, qaṭí'a-ži-le go 'ide, ya'ni, lá-mesət, ham māxənnox. ham gəbe mesət. ^Htov^H. [A.H.: ham pšāqəl.] he, pšāqəl.

4 *walḥāṣəl 'á-le go gūba. 'á-ži sele kemər: 'āga lətli. kemər: lətlox? ḥmol! 'atta pāwelox! mxele 'əlle. mundele qam qaṭi'a. Qóto-ži 'riqāle. 'ürre l'uwwa. Qarắni 'ürre basre. walla Qoto qāyəm dāwəqle, xor ^Hpax^H dā'əple. mundele qam kulle. hādax 'üdle 'əlləd dide. garma ṣax la', lá-šuqle go laššəd dide. [S.B.: məšəlmāna?] he, he. 'áġa-le. 'ā pəzaġáya-le. šəmmu lu dərye, la pəzaġāye. ^Htov^H.*

5 *walḥāṣəl Qoto pləṭle qam tar'a. kemər: baxxatəd 'ilāha! Qárani qṭilaxle. sāwun mxálṣüli mən go 'idás dide! hādax le 'wida l-Qárani: le mṛíċa-lle go 'əġdād. pləṭle qam tar'a. ṣrəxle: baxxatəd 'ilāha! mxálṣüli mənnəd qaṭəl! he. he. 'á-ži kemər: de xilālox. ḥmol! ta pešət nāša pešət xwaš hudāya. lewe bəḥmāla l-'aqle mād le krixa 'əbbe. le mṛíċa-lle. mṭele l-tāma. zəlle Qárani. Qárani pəšle naxwaš ḅāš. pəšle naxwaš.*

6 *'egā 'āni 'ādətəd dídu-la 'əd-'áġa. gəbe kúd-yom 'āzi 'anna t-ilu 'uṛwānəd hənna reša hənna reš hənna ^Hroš ha-mišpaḥót^H. gəbe 'āzəl yatwi 'əlləd 'oḍəd 'āga ^Hkafé^H d-^Hbokər^H šāte l-tāma. ^Htov^H. xá-yoma Qarani la zəlle, tré-yome la zəlle, ṭlá-yome la zəlle. má-le? kəmri: walla Qárani naxwaš 'ile. náxwaš-le. he. 'āga-ži xmāra lewe. lewe. 'áqəl-ile. kemər: bābo pa, mā naxoš má-yla pa la—? flānā yoma séwāle l-axxa. ču-məndi lətwāle. hādax-ži kemər: walla le zila go hudāye. ^Hyaxól lihyót^H hudāye lu wide l-axxa məndi.*

7 *kemər: bābo! sūn tāma! hatxa 'odun 'əlle! 'ən zde'le ċfəlle, yā'etun walla hudāye 'idāsu lu məṭye 'əbbe. 'ən lá-ċfəlle, ču-məndi lewa breta 'əlle. [S.B.:*

bring (it) to me!" This by force—, a stick is also in his hand, that is to say, (Qarani says:) "if you don't bring (it), I will also beat you. You should also bring (it)." Fine. [A.H.: He will also take it.] Yes, he will take (it).

In short, he (Qoto) is at the loom. And (Qarani) comes (to steal and 4 Qoto) says: "Agha, I don't have (any)." He says: "You don't have (any)? Stand still! Now you will have (some)!" He struck him. He attacked him with the stick. And Qoto fled. He entered inside (the house). Qarani entered after him. By God, Qoto up (and) grabs him, like tin (Qoto) bends him (Qarani). He beat him with everything. He did to him like this. He didn't leave an unbroken bone in his body. [S.B.: (He was a) Muslim?] Yes, yes. He is the Agha. He is a village noble. They gave themselves the name of (village nobles, but they) weren't the village nobles. Fine.

In short, Qoto went outside. He says: "For the mercy of God! Qarani 5 has beaten us up! Come rescue me from his clutches!" (Qoto) has done like this to Qarani: he has crumpled him up. (Qoto) went outside. He shouted: "For the mercy of God! Rescue me from the beating!" Yes, yes. (Qarani) says (to Qoto): "Now you've had it![41] Wait! (I beat you up) so that you should be a human being, you should be a good Jew." (Qarani) is not standing on his feet so much has (Qoto) smashed him up. He has crumpled him up. He reached there. Qarani left. Qarani became very ill. He remained ill.

Now it is a custom of theirs with the Agha. They have to go every day, 6 those who are leaders of, um, the head, um, the head, um, the head of the families. He has to go and sit in the room of the Agha to drink morning coffee there. Fine. One day Qarani didn't go (for the morning coffee), two days he didn't go, three days he didn't go. What's with him? They say: "By God, Qarani is ill. He is ill." Yes. And the Agha is not an ass. He is not. He is intelligent. He says: "By God, so then, what (is) he ill (with), what's happened, (after all) he's not—." On such and such a day he had come here. He had nothing (wrong with him). He says like this: "By God, he has gone among the Jews. It might be that the Jews have done something here."

(The Agha) says (to the heads of the families): "My God! Go there 7 (to Qarani)! Do like this to him (and poke him)! If he is afraid (and) startled, (then) you know, by God, the Jews, their hands have reached him. If he is not startled, (then) nothing has happened to him." [S.B.:

---

[41] Lit., 'you ate it' (calque on ModH? Kurdish?).

dərəst.] dərəst. gezi. de Qárani mắṭo-wət? mắṭo lewət? bābo naxwaš ʾíwəna.
ʾā gnắxəp-ži ʾāni hudắye-lu. lu mdúmbəke-lle. waḷḷa hatxa xədda, hatxa
ʾüdle ʾəlle. ā! kəmri: ʾiya ʾidəd hudāye la mṭeta ʾəbbəd dide. he.

8 waḷḷa Qárani ᴴmumšəxleᴴ ʾəbbəd ᴴmaḥalátᴴ gyāne. ᴴʾulắyᴴ xa ʾəṣrá-yome
mqulqəlle. skətle. zəlle. skətle. zəlle. ʾatta ʾegā mani hādax le ʾwida ʾəlle?
Qoto hādax le ʾwida ʾəlle. de. Qóto-ži ʾarba xamša lá-mṣe ʾəlləd dide. Qoto,
mắ-Qoto-l(e)? hatxa ʾanəškəd gyāne kud gorəd ḥāməl qam dide mandele
xamša'sár-metre.

9 walḥāṣəl xá-yoma ᴴmoḥlətluᴴ gəbe—. kəmri: gəbé nablaxle go Galli, go
Galli qaṭlaxle. he, hənna ʾiya mā kəmrila, ʾé-Galli mənne u-l-é-ʾāl xá-māsa
ʾitən Bet Kāre ᶻgəmrilaᶻ. Bet Kāre wət ʾəsya-lla? [S.B.: he, ᴴbetaḥᴴ.] mən
ʾáx-geb ʾitən tāma škaftyāsa ʾuṛwe ʾuṛwe.

10 qemi nablile xá-yoməd ʾəryāna… walḥāṣəl nobəllu l-tāma. nobəllu l-tāma.
lu zile xa ʾəsri nāše mare xanjāra. kutxa səkkinəd dide l-axxa. u-zəllu
ḥil zəllu l-tāma ʾəryāna-le bisāya. tləllu. zəllu škafta. bodi nūra. zəllu.
ʾüdlu nūra. kəmri ta Qoto: ʾāhat mesət ṣiwe! Qoto musele ṣiwe. məttūle.
drele reš—, ʾüdle nūra. ʾāni nūra mučṃelu. xá-gā xet kemər: ṭamắ wetun
mačṃóye-lle? kəmri: mắʾəqle! ʾāni—, ʾiya, ʾiya mā kəmrila, ʾāya gəbe kāyəp
t(a)-āni ḥamlile ʾəbbəd ᴴsəkkinímᴴ. kenᴴ.

11 walḥāṣəl xá-gā xet moʾləqle nūra. ʾāni mučṃelu nūra. naqəl ṭḷāha moʾləqle.
mučṃelu. waḷḷa m-é-ʾida kəple. kemər: de-mpóx ʾəbbəd paḷḷe ta pāyəš hənna
ta lāʾəq. waḷḷa kəple reš dide. mundelu qam xanjāra. qemi qaṭlile. šoqile l-
tāma u-selu. ʾāṣərta. kəmri: sāwun! Qóto-ʾile l-flāná-dūka. músūle ṭarməd
dide. le qṭila. walḥāṣəl waḷḷa Qoto zəllu muselu. qemi qorile. ʾāya zəlle. [S.B.:
qurru go Čalla?] he. he. go Čalla ᴴbetaḥᴴ.

True.] True. They go. (They say to Qarani:) "So Qarani, how on earth are you?" (Qarani says:) "My God! I am ill." He (Qarani) is also embarrassed that they are Jews (who have beaten him up). They have pummelled him. By God, like this, one (poked him), he did like this to him. "Ah," they say: "this (is the) hand of the Jews (that) has reached him." Yes.

By God, Qarani continued with his illness. Perhaps (after) about ten 8
days he kicked the bucket. He croaked. He died. He croaked. He died. So now then who (is it who) has done this to him? Qoto has done this to him. Now Qoto (is so strong that) even four (or) five (people) cannot (best) him. Qoto, what (sort of person is) Qoto? He had such elbows that any man standing next to him (if he nudged him with his elbows) he throws fifteen meters.

In short, one day they decided (saying we) should—. They say: "We 9
should lead him away to Galli to kill him, in Galli." Yes, um, what do they call it?—that Galli, beyond it on the other side is a village they call Bet Kare. Have you been to Bet Kare? [S.B.: Yes, of course.] On this side (of Bet Kare) there are very big caves there.

They up (and) lead him one rainy day... In short, they led him there. 10
They led him there. About twenty people (each one) with a dagger have gone. Each one's knife is here (at the side). And they went and by the time they got there rain is falling. They got wet. They went (to) a cave. They will make a fire. They went. They made a fire. They say to Qoto: "You should bring wood!" Qoto brought wood. He put it down. He placed it on—, he made a fire. They extinguished the fire. Once again he (lights the fire, they extinguished it and he) says: "Why are you extinguishing it?" They say: "Light it!" They—, this, what do they call it?—he has to bend down (to light the fire) so that they could attack him with knives. Yes.

In short, once again he lit the fire. They extinguished the fire. A third 11
time he lit it. They extinguished it. By God, he bent over (the fire) from that side. (One) says (to Qoto): "Now blow on the coals so that (the fire) will become, um, will catch." By God, he bent over it (the fire). They attacked him with a dagger. They up (and) kill him. They leave him there and came. (It is) evening. They say: "Go! It is Qoto in such and such a place. Bring his corpse! He has been killed." In short, by God, they went (and) brought Qoto. They up and bury him. He died. [S.B. They buried (him) in Challa?]. Yes, yes, in Challa, of course.

5.5. The Murder of a Peddler

1 *basər hādax brela ġér-ᴴmikrẹ̄ᴴ. ġer-ᴴmikréᴴ kəslexun Kāra. mašmi'! 'āna*
go ᴴṣawā́ᴴ wənwa b-é-ᴴtkufạ̄ᴴ. go ᴴṣawā́ᴴ wənwa. sele xa ʿaṭarka 'əlləd
Kāra. 'e ʿaṭarka mətle go məzgafte. qemi dārela hənnəd dide qəṭəl dide
[A.H.: 'əl-hudāye] u-qdāl Hoče nixəd xəmyāni. lá-ki'ən mani xéta-ži. mən-
nexun Karāye. [S.B.: ʿaṭarka mətle go məzgafte?] he, he mə́twāle go məzgaf-
te. de mašmi'! mə́twāle. ʿā́qəlu mpəllu. mani lu qṭíle-lle ʿaṭarka? mani lewu
qṭíle-lle? hudāye lu qṭile.

2 *l(!)-é-məzgafte xe bes be-Hóče-wa l-tāma. go palgus māsa, ᴴnaxónᴴ? [S.B.:*
'āwa qam tar beseni.] he 'əlla! jwāb mṭele l-nixəd bābi. nixəd bábi-ži ḥməlle.
kemər: mā 'iya qurdā́? xlə́ṣwālu kullu? hudāya le zila ʿaṭarka qṭíle-lle go
hənna 'iya mā kəmrila go məzgafte?

3 *waḷḷa qəmle səqle kəsəl 'āga, səqle ta hādax. kas didu maryǎ́-rešeni. ᴴmvu-*
dadímᴴ lá-waxwa. kemər 'āga: ḥál-u-masale hátxa-la. 'ā́-ži kemər: 'āhat
m-éka-wət šəmya? kəmər: 'āna l-tāma (wə)nwa. balāye lu dárye-lla b-reš
qdāl Hoče u-Mi'ər u-lá-ki'ən mani xeta. lu məxye 'əllu ko lu zile lu qṭile l-e
ʿaṭarka go məzgafte. 'ā́-ži kemər: mā 'iya hādax brela? qurdāye xlə́ṣlu? 'āga
mərre: he! hudāye 'āzi go məzgafte qaṭli?

4 *kemər 'āga: mani le 'wída-lle? xədda-, Rašo Be-Zamərná. (k)taxrətte? [S.B.:*
mā́ṭo ktaxrənne?] 'əlla xzi! waḷḷa [S.B.: 'atta lá-ktaxrənne.] hənna 'iya
mā kəmrila, Ḥajji 'Áḥmad-ži ṣrəxle 'əlləd kma ᴴbaḥurímᴴ mənnəd hənna

5.5. The Murder of a Peddler

After this another incident (of persecution of Jews) took place, another 1
incident by you (in) Kara.[42] Listen! I was in the army during that period.
I was in the army. A peddler came to Kara. That peddler died in the
mosque. They up (and) place (the responsibility of), um, his death [A.H.:
on the Jews] and (on) Hoče, my late father-in-law. I don't know (on)
whom else either. With you residents of Kara. [S.B.: The peddler died
in the mosque?] Yes, yes, he had died in the mosque. Now listen! He had
died. They fell from their senses.[43] Who on earth has killed the peddler?
(The Kurds decided that) the Jews have killed (him).

That mosque was there below the house of Hoče's family. In the middle 2
of the village, correct? [S.B.: It was there outside our house.] Yes, where
else (would it have been)? The news reached my late father. My late father
stopped. He says: "What sort of Kurd (is) this (who has been killed)? Are
all of them (the Kurds) exempt from suspicion[44] (that only the Jews are
left to blame)? A Jew has gone (and) killed the peddler in, um, what do
they call it?—in a mosque?"

By God, (Shabbo's father) up (and) appealed[45] to the Agha (Hajji 3
Aḥmad), he appealed to him over this. They (Hajji Ahmad and his family)
are angry on our behalf.[46] We were not isolated. The Agha says: "The
upshot is like this." Also he says: "From where have you heard?" (Shabbo's
father) says: "I was there. They have blamed[47] Hoče and Meir and I don't
know whom else. They have beaten them because (the Jews have) gone
(and) have killed that peddler in the mosque." And he (the Agha) says:
"What is this (that) has happened like this? Are the Kurds exempt from
suspicion (that they should now blame the Jews)?" The Agha says: "Hey!
Should Jews go into a mosque to kill?"

The Agha says: "Who is the one who has done it?" (Shabbo's father 4
answered:) "Someone (named) Rasho from Be-Zamor." Do you remember him? [S.B.: How should I remember him?] But look! By God [S.B.: I
don't remember him now.], um, what do they call it?—and Hajji Ahmad
summoned some young men from, um, from the family, his household.

---

[42] This comment was directed to Samuel Ben-Yosef from Kara.
[43] A calque on Kurdish?
[44] Or 'all of them are finished' or 'they finished all of them', i.e., have they finished with
all of them that they now turn to the Jews?
[45] Lit., 'he went up'.
[46] Lit., 'their stomach hurts over us'.
[47] Lit., 'they have put trouble on the neck of…'

mənnəd ^{H}*mišpaḥấ*^{H}, *be didu. xa Ṣalə́ḥko-'ewa, 'e Maqṣu d-godət baḥse u-xa xeta. kemər: bāba! sūn Bé-Zamòr! marun ta Rašíd-'āġằ: xāzax dəmməd d-é-'aṭarka kmá-ile ta 'āna yāwənne. ya'ni 'iya…*

5 *walḥāṣəl 'amrétūle-ži: xāzax. hə́nne-āwa 'an hudāye. hudāyéni-lu… lu qṭíle-lle 'aṭarka, pa dəmma gnāpəl 'əllan gəbe 'axnan dəmma yāwaxle. 'e hudāya t-ile nəxṛāya l-tāma, máni-le? kəmri 'ấ-ži hənna Zebarnáya-le. hudāyəd Barzāna. [S.B.: Rekanāya.] la, la Rekanāya 'əlla Barzanấ. kemər: 'ắni-ži 'amawaseni, yāl 'amawaseni-lu. farq lewa. 'ấ-ži har déni-le hudāya. walḥāṣəl qəmlu mšodərru kəsəl Rašíd 'āġa. Rašíd 'āġa-'ile, lewe hənna… 'āya qəmle zəlle*[48] *kəsəl dide. [S.B.: naxón…laḥma gyāwəlwa]…. he, he, laxma ṛāba gyāwəlwa. ya'ni 'āġa d-láxma-ewa.*

6 *walḥāṣəl qəmle zəlle l-tāma. 'axtun mani wetun?… 'axtun mani wetun? 'axnan pəzaġāyəd Čalla. yāl 'amawāsəd Ḥajji 'Aḥmad 'iwax. wax 'əsye xāzax dəmmox. kmá-le? 'āhat—, hənna 'e 'aṭarka lu qṭíle-lle. hudāye déni-lu. hudāyəd Kāra hudayéni-lu 'əd—, hənna Čalla. 'āni lu qṭile 'əlle. xāzax kmá-yle dəmme dide ta 'áxnan-ži yāwaxle. wax 'əsye mə́sye-llox dəmma.* ^{H}*tov*^{H}*. b-íya-'ida u-yắ-'ida, bāba ṣṭaġfəṛəḷḷấ. 'āya kə́rmanj-ewa. 'anna deni 'aširátte-lu. 'āġáye-lu.* ^{H}*az*^{H}*… Mirko u-hənna 'Isāxar u-Hoče 'anna lu zile lu qṭile 'aṭarka go məzgafte?* ^{H}*tov. b-sedər*^{H}*.*

7 *walḥāṣəl 'áx-geb tán-geb le b-dárd-u-balāye Rašo. má-*^{H}*avàl*^{H}*? walḥāṣəl kemər: 'āna* ^{H}*mbakšən 'ət sliḥấ*^{H}*. kəmri: lewət b-*^{H}*sliḥấ*^{H}*. 'āhat wət* ^{H}*mó'šama*^{H}*-llu 'əbbəd qəṭləd 'aṭarka go məzgafte. mā? qurdāye lu xliṣe? hudāye-ži go məzgafte qaṭli nāše? 'imal la breta 'iya xədda? hay kalba bər kalba. ḥmol! 'əlla 'aqlāsox gəbe qaṭ'axlu 'əllox 'āhat. b-íya-'ida u-yắ-'ida 'əbbəd šohad u-'áx-geb tán-geb ya'ni b-hiwiye u—… ḥel xləṣle mənnəd Ḥajji 'Aḥmad. u-'əxre … pəšla b-Rắšo. 'āna lewən mira u-lá-ki'ən* ^{H}*šəmu'ót*^{H}*. karāye lu mire u-lá-ki'ənwa.*

---

[48] Error for the plural *'āni qəmlu zəllu*.

One was Salihko, (a second was) that Maqsu about whom you talked, and (there was) another one. He says: "By God! Go to Be-Zamor. Say to Rashid Agha: 'Let's see how much the blood money of that peddler is that I should pay it.' That is to say, this..."

In short, also you should say to him: "Let's see. It was um, those Jews. 5 They are our Jews... they have killed that peddler, then the blood money falls on us (and) it is necessary for us to pay the blood money. That Jew who is a foreigner there, who is he?" They say: "He is, um, a resident of Zebar. A Jew from Barazan." [S.B.: A resident of Rekan]. No, not a resident of Rekan but rather of Barazan. (The Agha Hajji Aḥmad) says: "They are our uncles, our cousins. There is no difference. He too is still ours, the Jew." In short, they up (and) sent to Rashid Agha... Rashid is an agha, he is not, um... he up (and) went to him. [S.B. He used to give bread.]... Yes, yes, he used to give a lot of bread.[49] That is, he was (known as) the agha of bread.

In short, he up (and) went there. (Rashid Agha says:) "Who are you?... 6 Who are you?" (The three representatives of Ḥajji Aḥmad say:) "We are the village nobles of Čalla. We are the cousins of Hajji Ahmad. We have come to see (about) your blood money. How much is it? You—, um, they have killed that peddler. They are our Jews. The Jews of Kara are our Jews, of—, um, Čalla. They have killed him. Let's see how much is his blood money that we pay it. We have come (and) brought you blood money." Fine. When it comes down to it, I ask God's forgiveness! He was a Kurd. Those are our tribes. They are Aghas. So... Mirko and, um, Issachar, and Hoče, those have gone (and) killed a peddlar in a mosque? Fine. Okay.

In short, when all's said and done, Rasho is pained and troubled. 7 But what? In short, he (Rashid Agha) says: "I request forgiveness." They (the representatives of Hajji Aḥmad) say: "You aren't forgiven. You have accused them (the Jews) of killing the peddler in the mosque. What? Are the Kurds all exempt from suspicion (that they should begin accusing Jews)? Jews should kill people in a mosque? When has such a thing happened? Hey! Son of a bitch!" (The representatives say:) "Stop! We should certainly cut off your feet." When it comes down to it, (it was concluded) with a bribe and, when all's said and done, that is to say, with pleas and ... until he finished (the deal) with Hajji Ahmad. And shit... remained on Rasho (from the incident). I have not said and I don't know (the) rumors. Residents of Kara have told (me) and I didn't know.

---

[49] I.e., he would give the Jews food if they needed it.

8 ^Hʾax ʾaxar^H masale mpučkənālu, waḷḷa ʿaṭarka nobəllu qurru. muṣláya-
ewa. u-nobəllu qurru u-ʾắni-ži mənnəd ^Hʾaḥarayút mšaḥarərilu^H. mə́twāle
b-gyāne l-tāma go məzgafte. qemi dārela balāye ʾəbbəd reš hudāye ta šāqəl
mənnu pāre. [A.H.: ^Hsʿirím la-ʿazazél^H.] he, he, he.

9 walḥāṣəl waḷḷa šqəlle, šqəlle mənnəd hənna mənnəd dide pāre mād gbele. u-
mbokəšle ^Hsliḥắ^H-ži reš hənnəd ^Hʾašmát mó'šəmwāle^H hudāye. kemər xá-gā
xeta: pummox pathəṭte ʾəlla, kemər, ʾāna qaṭlənnox. čú-məndi xeta lá-godən
ʾəllox ^Hḥatixát^H kalba bər kalba. ʾāhat ^Hmá'šəmət^H hudāyeni ʾəbbəd dugle?
hudāye lu bizāla bəqṭāla qurdāye? qurdāye lu bəqṭāla hudāye! ʾāhat wət
bimāra hudāye ^Hkvar^H lu zile bəqṭāla hənna qurdāye. b-íya-masale, ʾiya
l-axxa xləṣla.

5.6. The Beating and Killing of Jews

1 hā mṭelan ʾəlləd qəṭləd Qoto.[50] qemi qaṭlile. muyde(ʾ)lu kəmri: wax qtíle-lle
flāná-dūka. sūn músūle ṭarməd dide! basər hādax ʾiya mā kəmrila kúd-
dūka-u-dūka ko dax kpə́nwālu kalbe bāsewa. kutxa bāzəlwa. hudāye pə́lye-
wa. kutxa ʾə́twāle hudāyəd gyāne. ʾé-(ʾi)ya məndi gəbən, ʾiya məndi.

2 ^Hʿesək muthəlle^H b-nixəd sāwi. ʾə́twāleni ʾaxnan ʾərxe l-tāma. ʾə́twālan besa.
ʾətwa ʾarʾāsa. mā ʾamrənnox? ʾáqqara ʾakčən məzzəd rešox. kullu šqilíwālu.
mpu... l-gyānu. [A.H.: ʿaqāre] he, he. walḥāṣəl sele xədda ^Zgəmríwāle^Z
Məṣṭo. nixəd sáwi-le go gūba le bəzqāra. sele kemər ṭas dide. məṭṭūle go
tarʾəd besa.

---

50 See § 5.4.

But after they wrapped up the story, by God, they took the peddler 8 away (and) buried him. He was a resident of Mosul. And they took him away and buried him, and they also absolved them (those Jews) of responsibility. (The peddler) had died by himself there in the mosque. They up (and) blame the Jews[51] in order to take money from them. [A.H.: Scapegoats.]. Yes, yes, yes.

In short, by God, he (Rashid Agha) took from, um, from him (Ḥajji 9 Aḥmad) money, whatever he wanted. And he requested forgiveness for, um, the accusation with which he had accused the Jews. (Ḥajji Aḥmad) says another time: "Should you open your mouth," he says, "I'll certainly kill you. I will do nothing less to you, (you) piece of a son of a bitch. You accused our Jews falsely? The Jews are going (around) killing Kurds? (On the contrary), Kurds are killing Jews! You are saying Jews have already gone killing, um, Kurds. With this matter, this here is finished."

5.6. The Beating and Killing of Jews

So (now) we have reached the killing of Qoto. They up (and) kill him. 1 They announced saying: "We have killed him (in) such and such a place. Go bring his corpse!" After this, what do they call it?—in every single place, since as soon as they got hungry, the dogs (the aghas) would come. Each one would go. The Jews had been divided up.[52] Each one (agha) had his own Jew(s). That (agha says:) "I want this thing, (I want) that thing."

The affair began with my late grandfather. We had a mill there. We had 2 a house. There were lands. What can I tell you? (We had) as much as the hairs on your head! (The aghas) took all of them. They di(vided it up) for themselves. [A.H.: landed property.] Yes, yes. In short, one came whom they called Misto. My late grandfather is at the loom weaving. (Misto) came (and) says to him(: "Give what you have for me!"). He placed it outside the house.[53]

---

[51] Lit., 'put trouble on the head of the Jews'.

[52] The aghas would divide up the Jews among themselves. Each agha would be responsible for the safety and protection of his Jews, who in turn owed him their allegiance. See Brauer & Patai 1993:223–227.

[53] I.e., give me my dues. In return for the agha's protection, the Jews had to give him whatever he demanded.

3 *ə́twālu xa ^Hginəd^H bəṣle. bə́ṣle-ži lu—, ṭima hatxa ^Hyafé^H. məsele, məttūle
   ... go tarʾa. ʾé-Məṣṭo. lá-pedetun mən d-áxxa-ži. nixəd sə́wi-ži kemər ṭas
   dide kemər: ʾāġa, kulle mənni šqə́llexun. ʾáxxa-ži let xa dūkəd xapči šətyəd
   gyāni maštən ʾəlla.

4 šqəlle gopaḷta u-mxele l-sāwi. ʾāya. sə́wi-ži ʾürre lʿuwwa. ʾürre. básbasre-
   wa. ʾriqāle m-gora. lá-mxele-lle ḅāš. waḷḷa ʾida drele ʾəl-ṣádər dide. sāwi
   ^Zgəmrənnox^Z: dəbba ʾətwa. dāwəqla hatxa. maḥməlla ʾəbbəd xá-ʾi(da)...
   he, he, he, he, he. [A.H.: bə́š-ṛomāna ^Zwele^Z mən nixəd bābox?] mani?
   ^Hbetaḥ^H. nixəd bābi ʾakčən xá-ʾidəd dide lə́twābe. walḥāṣəl moʾərre lʿuwwa.
   moʾərre lʿuwwa. (m)pəlle ʾəlləd d-iya Məṣṭo ʾegā (m)dambəkle. hādax ʾüdle
   l-Məṣṭo. Məṣṭo mṛəčle ʾəġdāde.

5 pləṭle qam tarʾa. sāwi kemər: baxxatexun! sāwun! mxalṣun ʾəlli m-idəd
   Məṣṭo! wal ^Hpolátika^H54 d-hudāye ṛába-la. walḥāṣəl selu nāše ta xāṭəreni.
   hudáye-lu. ṃāḷ didu wetun šqile-lle. hátxa-ži lá-od. kemər: de b-xá-gā xeta
   lāyəp hatxa lá-ʾāwəd, ʾəlla xá-gā xeta pqaṭʾənne. ^Hʾavál^H le ʾüda ʾəlləd dide
   lá-mṣe ʾegā ʾāzəl b-urxa, yāsəq ʾəl-bésa. waḷḷa Mə́ṣṭo-ži zəlle. Məṣṭo mpəlle.
   pəšle ʾə́-ži ṭarma pəšle. la skəṭle, bale pəšle pálgəd-nāša.

6 ʾegā... xá-yoma tré-yome kxāzewa ʾāġa kullu ʾanna ʾuṛwānəd didu lewu
   bizāla kəsle bənhe šāte ^Hkafé^H. ʾiya ʿādə́ta-la. (m)bāqərwa: flān nāša, flānkas ké-le? ṭamá lewe ʾəsya? bābo! lewe ^Hmargíš tov^H. ʾā mərre: sūn hatxa
   ʾodun ʾəlle! ʾən čfəlle... [A.H.: hudāye.] lu píče-lle. ʾən lá-čfəlle, ʾāhat—,

---

54 Apparently *politika* < MHeb פּוֹלִיטִיקָה.

They had an onion garden. Onions fetch a good price. (My grandfa- 3
ther) brought it, he placed it ... at the gate. That Misto. (He says:) "Don't
even pass by here!" My late grandfather says to him: "Agha, you took all
of it from me. There isn't here even a place (where) I can (stretch out and)
moisten a bit of my own yarn."[55]

(Misto) took a shepherd's stick and struck my grandfather. That (was 4
what he did). And my grandfather came inside. (Misto) came in. He was
right after him. (My grandfather) fled from the man. (Misto) didn't strike
him hard. By God, (my grandfather) put his hand on his (Misto's) chest.
I (will) tell you (a story about) my grandfather. There was a bear. (My
grandfather) grabs him like this. He stops it with one ha(nd)... Yes, yes,
yes, yes, yes. [A.H.: Was he taller than your late father?] Who? Of course.
My late father, (even if he were fighting with only) one hand, one couldn't
best him.[56] In short, (my grandfather) brought him inside. He brought
him inside. He fell upon this Misto (and) then he pummels him. He did
like this to Misto. He has crumpled Misto up.

(Misto) went outside. My grandfather says: "For your mercy! Come! 5
Save me from the hands of Misto!" Indeed, the craftiness[57] of the Jews is
great. In short, people came on our behalf. They are Jews. (My grandfather says to Misto:) "You (Kurds) have taken their possessions. Don't do
such a thing!" (My grandfather) says: "So then next time he should learn
not to do such a thing, but next time I will cut him (down to size)." But
he (my grandfather) has done (such) to him (that) (Misto) isn't able then
to walk in the road, to go up home. By God, Misto went. Misto fell (to his
sickbed). He became, he became a corpse. He didn't croak, but he became
half a person.

So then... (for) one day, two days, the Agha was noticing (that) all 6
those nobles of theirs were not coming to him in the morning to drink
coffee.[58] This is a custom. He would ask: "Where is such and such a
person, so and so? Why hasn't he come?" (They say:) "My God! He
isn't feeling good." (The Agha) said: "Go do like this to him!"[59] If he
is startled... [A.H.: (It's) the Jews]. (The Jews) have crushed him. If he

---

[55] The long threads for weaving were laid out on the ground, moistened, and then left
out in the sun to dry.
[56] Lit., 'My late father, the size of one of his hands, he couldn't.'
[57] Lit., 'politics'.
[58] Several of these elements appear in § 5.4.
[59] I.e., poke him with your finger.

čú-məndi lewe. 'it xa ^{H}səba^H xeta. hatxa qədyālu mənnəd didu ḥil kullu mburbəzlu.

7 *be sāwi xa ^{H}tkufá^H l-Kára-ewa. xarāye m-Kāra lu zile l-Šiwa. lu piše l-Šiwa. xarāye m-Šiwa xá-gā xet lu d'íre-wa l-Čalla. basər hənna… lu zile mən Kāra l-Šiwa. m-Šiwa xá-gā xet lu d'íre-wa l-Čalla. mā? kulle məndi didu šqəlwālu. čú-məndi lá-šüqwālu ṭāsu. 'ən xədda hāwewāle xa šálla-u-… kšaqlíwāla mənne. be-dín wewa.*

8 *walḥāṣəl tam l-é-'āl 'iya mā kəmrila qṭəllu hənne 'Āko bər Pəto, 'āna ktaxrən. ^{H}ṣa'ír^H-wa (k)taxrətte? [A.H.: lá-ktaxrən, la'.] 'āya qṭəllu Spindar-nāye. qṭəllu Spindarnāye. [S.B.:… mani wewa?] 'Āko, 'Āko. Ya'qov ^{Z}gəm-ri^Z. Yá'qo-we(wa) šəmme. ^{Z}gəmríwāle^Z 'Āko. 'āya qṭəllu. basər dide qṭəllu bāb Šmū'el [A.H.: yalunke lə́twāle.] mani? [A.H.: Pəto.] ^{H}ḥūṣ^H mənne lə́twāle čú-məndi. 'āya b-təne 'ewa. 'āya b-təne 'ewa. čú-xa xe lə́twāle. 'āya hənna 'āya zəlle.*

9 *basər hādax qṭəllu Šambi, Šámbi-ži reš pāre. 'ə́twāle denāna. zəlle mjāmə' denānəd gyāne. qemi qaṭlile. bāb Šlomo. he, he bāb Šlomo. [A.H.: 'amoyəd yəmmi.] he, 'amoyəd yəmmox. walḥāṣəl 'á-ži… nixa. 'á-ži qemi qaṭlile. [A.H.: ^{Z}damməd qam qaṭlile^Z…] 'áya-ži zəlle. [A.H.: ^{Z}qam xāzele^Z go xa wādi u-hənna xa qaṭṛa reše. zəllu m-hənna mesele…]*

10 *walḷa har tāma le qwira. lewu músye-lle… [A.H.: kulla misa 'á-ži qurru tāma.] la, lu qwíre-lle l-tāma. šüqwālu l-ṭmane'sar yome nixa qam šəmša, hənna 'iya mā kəmrila ḥel doktor məselu mən Wān reš dide. mən Wān doktor sele reš dide. la pə́šwāle, la pəsra u-la čú-məndi ^{H}ḥūṣ^H mən garme lá-pə́šwāle. kulle pšə́rwāle qam šəmša. walḥāṣəl… har Šambi qṭəllu.*

11 *'iya nixəd 'Eli 'ə́twāle brona. 'iya—, Guli. [A.H.: Yoḥānan.] Yoḥānan. 'āya bréwāle bāziwa 'əlləd hənna ^{H}brit^{H60} dide. qəmle lel xošeba ktaxrən…*

---

60 Cf. the JNeoAram $^+$barīṯ mīla (Sabar 2002:115).

isn't startled, you—, it is nothing. (Then) there is another reason (for his absence). In such a way they passed the time with him[61] until they all dispersed.

The family of my grandfather was in Kara for a period. Later they have 7 gone from Kara to Shiwa. They have remained in Shiwa. Later once again they have returned back to Challa from Shiwa. After, um… they have gone from Kara to Shiwa. From Shiwa once again they have returned back to Challa. What? (The aghas) had taken all their things. They had left nothing for them. If someone had (e.g.,) a pair of pants and… they would take it from him. They were without religion.

In short, from there on, what do they call it?—they killed, um, Ako 8 son of Pito, I remember. He was young, you remember? [A.H.: I don't remember, no.] As for him, the residents of Spindar killed him. The residents of Spindar killed (him). [S.B.: … Who was it?] Ako, Ako. They call him Ya'qov (Jacob). Yaqo was his name. They called him Ako. That one they killed. After him they killed the father of Samuel [A.H.: He didn't have children.] Who? [A.H.: Pito.] Apart from him, he didn't have anything. He was alone. He was alone. He had nothing else. He, um, he died.

After that they killed Shambi, Shambi also over money. He had 9 debtors. He went to gather together his debtors. They up (and) kill him. The father of Shlomo. Yes, yes, the father of Shlomo. [A.H.: My mother's uncle.] Yes, your mother's uncle. In short, he too… died. He too, they up (and) kill him. [A.H.: When they killed him…] He too died [A.H.: They found him in a certain wadi with, um, a boulder on him. They went from, um, they bring him…]

By God, he is buried right there. They didn't bring him (there). [A.H. 10 Every dead person they buried there.] No, they have buried him there. They had left the deceased for eighteen days in the sun, um, what do they call it?—until they brought a doctor for him from Van. From Van a doctor came for him. Nothing had remained, neither flesh nor anything (else) apart from his bones had remained. All of him had melted in the sun. In short… they also killed Shambi.

This late Eli had a son. This—, Guli.[62] [A.H.: Yochanan.] Yochanan.[63] 11 He had just been born (and) they were going to, um, his circumcision.

---

[61] Shabbo erroneously says 'with them'.
[62] 'Eli's wife.
[63] 'Eli's son.

[S.B.: *'eka bréwāle 'āwa?*] *mani?* [S.B.: *Yoḥānan.*] *Yoḥānan, Bétanūre.*
[S.B.: *'ā Bétanūre.*] *he, he l-Bétanure. mā hanne 'Eli* [A.H.: *mā bréwāle* ^{Z}*'o*^{Z}
Raḥamím, 'axón 'Eli?] [S.B.: *náxwāle.*] *'āya náxwāle. zalle* ^{H}*m'uṣbanne*^{H} *xa*
kalba. y'elox? kalba qamle gyāne maxyāle 'alle. kulle naxír dide xálwāle 'alle.
^{H}*'az*^{H} *düqle* ^{H}*kalevet*^{H} *u-... matle.* [S.B.: *lā.*] ^{H}*be'emét*^{H}*. 'āna* ^{H}*históriya*^{H}
d-kullu ki'anna... ^{H}*históriya*^{H} *d-kullu ki'anna.*

12 [A.H.: *'āna ki'an, (k)taxran, (k)taxran* ^{Z}*qam doqile*^{Z} *l-'askar. zalle drele*
quṭma go 'ene ta gyāne maštāhar...] *he, he. 'āya u-Baṣālel kutru düqíwālu.*
masale pašla. 'āya séle-wa dáre-wa quṭmad jigāre go 'ene ḥil 'ene.... xzi!
'ilu 'úde 'askar go—, 'anna lu wide 'askar go Túrkiya. 'āni ḥanna xanči
mannu lu wide go 'Eraq. xzi! māṭo šamme u-'ar'a ráqqa-lu m-aġdād! go
Túrkiya ^{H}*ḥukím*^{H} *u-'Eraq hādax 'arqa*[64]*-lu m-aġdāde.*

13 *go Túrkiya náše-lu. la, lá-hāwe, ḥanna,* ^{H}*ba'ayót*^{H} *lá-od—. lá-godi* ^{H}*ba'a-*
yót^H*.* [A.H.: *máni-lu go 'Iraq?*]... *l-axxa 'itan Ša'ya, či'atte.*[65] *wat* ^{H}*gyísa*^{H}*-*
lle 'āhat. 'āya le 'wida go 'Eraq. xaloyi Šālom le 'wida go 'Eraq. [A.H.:
^{H}*tov*^{H}*, 'āni* ^{H}*'Irāqim*^{H} ^{Z}*welu*^{Z}*.*] *la, 'egā* ^{Z}*gamrannox*^{Z}*. mannad—,* ^{H}*havdél*^{H}
'ile 'abbad ^{H}*ḥuká. ken*^{H}*. mannad* ^{H}*ḥuká*^{H}*.* [A.H.: *Šālom naxle.*] *he le nixa...*

14 *walḥāṣal ḥanne 'iya mā kamrila Šambi qṭallu.* ^{H}*be'emét*^{H} *nixad bābi-, xá-*
yoma düqlu... nablilu l-^{H}*bet sohar*^{H}*. 'áx-geb tán-geb qurdáye-lu. zallu*
hūlu šohad. kamri: 'ā ^{H}*zakén*^{H}*-ewa. xe 'avrāza le nixa. da 'jiza wat dwiqa*
'āhat. kemar: le misa. ^{H}*tov*^{H} *'āya zalle.* ^{H}*be'emét*^{H} *nixad bābi mpalle xe*
^{H}*haverím*^{H} *gyāne. 'āni d-atle qurdāye* ^{H}*haverím*^{H}*. walḥāṣal xadda... qṭál-*
wāle nixad Šambi. qṭálwāle xa qurdāya mannad mas gyáne-ži. walla nixad
bābi qāyam meselu 'é-mašpaḥà. kemar: 'imal tol babexun parqétūle? marre:
'axnan gzad'ax man ḥukum 'áx-geb tán-geb tamáha-geb. bābi kemar:

---

[64] Apparently an error for *raqqa*.
[65] See § 3.4.b n. 10.

I remember he got up on Sunday night... [S.B.: Where had he been born?] Who? [S.B.: Yochanan.] Yochanan (in) Betanure. [S.B.: Ah, Betanure.] Yes, yes, in Betanure. What (about), um, Eli? [A.H.: When was that Rahamim born, Eli's brother?] [S.B.: He had died.] He had died. He went (and) irritated a dog. Did you know? The dog up (and) hurled himself at him. (The dog) had eaten off all his nose. Then he caught rabies and... died. [S.B.: No.] Really. I know the history of everyone ... I know the history of everyone.

[A.H.: I know, I remember, I remember they seized him for the army. **12** (Eli) went (and) put ashes in his eyes so that he would go blind...] Yes, yes. He and Besalel, the two of them, they (the army) had seized them. The affair remained. He came back to put ashes in his eyes again until his eyes... Look! They have done military service in—, those have done military service in Turkey. They, um, a few of them have done (military service) in Iraq. Look! What distance from each other are the heavens and the earth! In Turkey and (in) Iraq the laws are such a distance from each other!

In Turkey they are (decent) human beings. No, there shouldn't be, um, **13** don't do—. They don't make problems. [A.H.: Who are in Iraq?]... here there is Shaya, you know him. You recruited him (for police service).[66] He did (military service) in Iraq. My maternal uncle Shalom did (military service) in Iraq. [A.H.: Fine, (but) they were Iraqis.] No, so then I tell you. With—, there is a difference in the constitution. Yes. With the constitution. [A.H.: Shalom died]. Yes, he has passed away...

In short, um, what do they call it?—they killed Shambi. Really. As for **14** my late father—, one day they seize (some Kurds)... They take them away to prison. When all's said and done, they are Kurds. They went (and) gave a bribe. They say: "He (the victim) was an old man. He has passed away at the bottom of the hard climb." (A policeman says to one of the arrested): "(You're not going to be charged with murder since) you grabbed a sick person." (The policeman) says: "He has died." Fine. He died. Really, my late father fell in (with a good bunch) of friends. Those friends he has (are) Kurds. In short... someone killed the late Shambi. A Kurd from his own village had killed him. By God, my late father up (and) brings them, that family (of Shambi). He says: "When will you avenge (the death) of your father?" (A member of the family) said: "When all's said and done,

---

[66] Ahiya was in charge of police recruitment during part of his police service.

ḥukum? ^Hʿal ʾaḥarayutí^H. ʾe xéta-ži ^Hbišúaʿ ʿavodą́^H har ʾaxtun gyānexun. kəmri ḅāš-ila.

15 waḷḷa grešla, lá-kiʾən xá-šāta, šắta-u-palge. ʾiya kalba bər kalba le ʾwida ṛəzza, ʾarʾāsa. ṛəzza le ʾúda reqa mən ^Hkfar ba-ʿérəx^H xor mən kəslexun Pisgát Zəʾév ʾaqqar rəqqa mənnəd māsa. ʾāya… [A.H.: ʾeka ^Zwele?^Z go Byadre?] la, laʾ, laʾ,laʾ. xá-māsa kəmrila Marūfa. Pənčāye… ʾāya u-baxte [A.H.: ʾāna wən hüya go Pənčāye, kiʾət?] ʾāhat? [A.H.: he. lá-kiʾət bā(bi) zálwāle xá-šāta tre šənne go Pənčāye ^Zwele^Z bābi]. ^Htov, mxubád^H wewa. kullu dukāne gbéwāle ʾāya.

16 ^Hʾaz^H waḷḷa le wida ʾarʾāsa. ʾegā kəsleni ʾətwa dahbe kesewa u-maxərwiwa. hənna—, ḅaṛāze ʾətwa. dəbbāsa ʾətwa. kesewa u-maxərwiwa dukāne [A.H.: ʾarʾāsa], ʾarʾāsa. he. ʾāya le zila reš hənna—, ṛāba ʾarʾāsa le ʾwida ṛəzza. ʾā le—, ^Hkšāmər^H ʾalləd didu qam ḅaṛāze. ḅaṛāze kesiwa. ʾətwa ^Htəlamím. ʾaz^H kxapríwālu. ʾətlu xor, xor skine… ʾallu. ṭāʿewa l-kərme. ʾāni kəxli kárme-ži.

17 walḥāṣəl ʾāya-le l-tāma. waḷḷa ʾe-^Hhavér^H u-nixəd bābi, treʾ, qəmlu zəllu. le reš qaprāna dmixa ʾāya u-baxte u-ʾətle təffaq-ži ʾətle xa-réšəd dide. ʾan xet dlá-təffaq. waḷḷa hedi zəllu. təffaq qemi šaqlila m-xa-réšəd dide. bābi kemər: baxta lá-qaṭlètūla. həšyar hāwetun. baxta lá-qaṭlètūla. lá-dāretun dəmmāhe zodāne qdāl gyānexun. həšyar hāwetun. ʾən baxta mḥokela, marun: ^Htov^H ʾāya zálle, ʾaxnan pšaqlaxlax. ʾāhat la gpešat hādax hənna ^Hmʿugenet^H mā ^Zgəmrila^Z? [A.H.: baxtāsa naqoṣe ^Zwelu^Z.] he. baxtắsa-ži naqóṣe-wa. ʾāya zálle hūle … ^Hlo ḥašúv^H.

we are afraid of the government." My father says: "The government? It's my responsibility. But apart from that, carrying out the work is only up to you." They say: "It's fine."

By God, it dragged on (until revenge was exacted for the murder of Shambi), I don't know, a year, a year and a half. This son of a bitch (the murderer) has grown rice, (in) fields. He has grown rice far from the village (of Challa), about as far as Pisgat Zeev from you (in Ma'ale Adummim[67]), about that far from the village. He... [A.H.: Where was he? In Byadre?] No, no, no, no. A village they call Marufa. (An area known as) Pinianish. He and his wife. [A.H.: I was born in Pinianish, do you know?] You? [A.H.: Yes, don't you know my fat(her) had gone away (and) for a year or two was in Pinianish?] Fine. (Your father)[68] was respected. (People) liked him everywhere.

So, by God, he (the murderer) has worked the fields. Now then there were wild animals with us (which) would come and destroy. Um—, there were pigs. There were bears. They would come and destroy places [A.H.: the fields], the fields. Yes. He has gone concerning, um—, many fields he has cultivated with rice. He has—, is guarding them from the pigs. The pigs would come. There were furrows. Then they they would dig them up. They had (tusks) like, like knives... They would hit with them to search for worms. They also eat worms.

In short, he (the murderer) is there. By God, that friend and my late father, only the two (of them), up (and) went (to avenge the murder). He (the murderer) and his wife were asleep on (top of) a hut and he has, he has a rifle under his head. Those others (the friend and Shabbo's father were) without a rifle. By God, they went slowly. They up (and) take the rifle from under his (the murderer's) head. My father says: "Don't kill the woman. You should be careful. Don't kill the woman. Don't make yourselves responsible for more bloodshed.[69] You should be careful. If the wife speaks, say: 'Fine, he is dead, but we will take you (with us). You won't remain like this,' um, a deserted wife (m'ugenet), what do they call it?" [A.H.: Women were few.] Yes, also women were few. He went (and) he gave ... It's not important.

15

16

17

---

[67] I.e., from where Ahiya lives in Ma'ale Adummim to Pisgat Ze'ev, which is a distance of several kilometers.

[68] Ahiya's father, Jacob, was a well-respected rabbi in the area. See § 1.5.

[69] Lit., 'Don't put more guilt of bloodshed on your own necks.'

18 *waḷḷa šqilālu təffaq. hedi* ^H*kané*^H *dəryālu hənna* ^H*kané*^H *dəryālu go nāsəd dide. ṭiq! waḷḷa zəlle. baxta qəmla har hatxa wədla. kemər: gyānax lá-qṭulla! 'āna* ^H*muxắn*^H*-iwən qadome bomāxəd 'āna mnablənnax.* ^H*'avál zehu*^H. *waḷḷa baxta zəlla. sele jəwāb ta nixəd bābi. kəmri: waḷḷa wax qṭílelle. šəmməd dide hənna 'Abd Raḥmanko wewa. xa baṛāza 'ewa* ^Z*gəmrən-nox*^Z ...

19 *waḷḷa 'āya u-nixəd bābi u-nixəd 'Eli mjohə́dwālu l-Bétanūre. mašmi' l-íya* ^H*siḥá!* ^Z*qam qaṭlile*^Z *'e nāša ... he, Bétanūre. bābi zə́lwāle l-Bétanūre 'əlləd hənna kud kma yarxe gezəlwa 'əl-táma qam ṣlosa,* ^H*kol miné dvarím*^H*-u, 'iya mā kəmrila, 'Eli məndele xabre. məndele xabre. kemər: lewət bāda čúməndi l-tāma, 'áx-geb tán-geb. 'áqqara lire 'é-gora—, byāwən ham 'āya nāša... 'āse l-qəṭla. 'Eli byāwəl. [S.B.: mani 'āse l-qəṭla?] 'é-məšəlmānəd nixəd bābi muqṭəlle. [A.H.: 'Eli m-eka 'ə́twāle?]*

20 *de mašmi'! [A.H.:* ^H*yatúm*^H.] *bābi 'əhmə̄lle monəxle 'əbbe kemər: 'Eli. kemər: mā? kemər: xzi ḥabibi! 'āna, kemər: 'āhat daxwás 'ile xalóx, xalóyile-ži,... har 'e... hənna soti brāt 'amód d-e Šambi 'āwa. xās Šino wāwa. Šino (k)taxrətte. xās Šino, 'āni yāl 'amawása-ewa. Šambi u-Šino, 'āni yāl 'amawása-ewa. xá-mišpaḥà-'ilu. waḷḷa 'āya kemər: xzi!... he be ḥanúkkalu.*

21 *walḥāṣəl kemər ṭas dide kemər: xzi! 'āt byāwət lire. kemər: he. kemər: 'āna lá-gmə̀hə̀mnena. kemər: 'it* ^H*havdél*^H *mābayn mḥakesa u-'wādəd* ^H*p'ulá*^H *... he, mābayn* ^H*biṣūaʿ 'avodá*^H *u-mḥakesa, 'anna—, 'it ṛāba* ^H*havdél*^H. *rə́qqa-lu m-əġdāde. 'Eli! 'āhat lewət mən gūre 'ida gdāre l-kəstox u-'āna kí'ən-ži lətlox. 'egā ṭamá mḥākət? bāse yoma 'é-masale pqaṭya. k(emər):*

By God, (my father and his friend) took the rifle. Slowly they stuck **18**
the barrel, um, they stuck the barrel in his (the murderer's) ear. Bang! By
God, he died. The wife got up (and) did just like this (grabbed a rifle, and
threatened to shoot herself). He says: "Don't kill yourself! I am ready to
take you away tomorrow, the day after tomorrow. But that's it." By God,
the woman went off (with them). My late father got his own back (for the
murder of Shambi).[70] They say: "By God, we have killed him." His name
was, um, Abd Rahmanko. I tell you, he was a pig...

By God, moreover, my late father and the late Eli had quarreled in **19**
Betanure. Listen to this conversation! They killed that person (Abd Rahmanko)... Yes, (in) Betanure. My father had gone to Betanure to, um,
every few months he would go there for prayer,[71] all sorts of things and,
what do they call it?—Eli said things.[72] He said things. (My father) says
(to Eli): "When all's said and done, you are not doing anything there.
So many liras that man—, I will also give (in order that) that person...
should be killed. Eli will give (money for the revenge)." [S.B.: Who should
be killed?] That Muslim whom my father had killed. [A.H.: From where
did Eli have it?][73]

Now listen! [A.H.: (Eli was an) orphan.] My father stood, looked at him **20**
(and) says: "Eli." He says: "What?" (My father) says: "Look, my friend!
I," he says, "just as he is your maternal uncle, so too is he my maternal
uncle ... since that... um, my grandmother was the daughter of the
paternal uncle of that Shambi." She was the sister of Shino. You remember
Shino. The sister of Shino, they were cousins. Shambi and Shino, they
were cousins. They are one family. By God, he says: "Look!... yes, they
are the Hanukka family."

In short, (my father) says to him (Eli), he says: "Look! You will give **21**
liras (for the revenge)." (Eli) says: "Yes." (My father) says: "I don't believe
(it)." (My father says): "There is a difference between talking and doing
the job... yes, between performing the work and talking, those—, there
is a big difference. They are are a distance from each other. Eli! You are
not (one) of (those) men (who) puts (his) hand in his[74] moneybag, and
I also know you don't have (any money). Now why are you talking? The

---

[70] Lit., 'The response came to my late father.'
[71] Because there were not enough men for a prayer quorum (מִנְיָן) in Challa.
[72] I.e., he spread rumors.
[73] I.e., the information that Shabbo's father had been involved in revenging the murder
of Shambi.
[74] Lit., 'your'.

'āna 'atta byāwənna. 'Éli-le-ži šxina. 'ilāha mānəxle. šaxina 'ewa. lá-mḥakesa.

22 'áx-geb tán-geb bābi lá-mḥokele. kemər: 'Eli, ^Hkodəm kol^H pšām(')ət. 'āna 'atta lá-^Zgəmrən^Z čú-məndi. pšām(')ət xa yoma. walḥāṣəl waḷḷa 'Eli šme'le. nixəd bābi basər hādax zəlle l-tāma. kemər: kma lire 'āhat mə́rwālox? 'arbi lire byāwət? 'əšti lire byāwət? u-misi xamša. da xāzax. qū misi xamša. 'an xet kullu ṭāsox. walḥāṣəl waḷḷa zəlle məšəlmāna. baxtəd díde-ži xa xeta šqilāle. 'āya zəlle.

5.7. ABRAHAM GETS DRUNK

1 masaləd 'Āko. 'Āko qṭəllu. ^Hbe'emét^H dəmməd dide qāyəm šāqəlle. selan masaləd 'əd-'Awṛáham. 'Awṛāham. 'axnan zəllan 'Amədya 'ə́na-wən u-'āya u-xá-məšəlmāna. zəllan nobəllan poṣṭa, ^Hdowar^H. nobəllan ^Hdow-ar^H. [S.B.: mən Čalla?] mən Čalla he. nobəllan ^Hdowar^H he, ta 'Amədya. ^Hdowar^H gyānu zəlle kəl qāymaqam, ^Hdowar^H gyānan msulmālan. kəmri: qadome 'āsetun šaqletun ^Htšuvá^H. 'ədyo let. ^Hb-sedər^H 'ədyo let. 'axnan zəllan.

2 ^Hbrít^H-ila go xá-besa 'əl-'Amə́dya. muzmənaxlu l-tāma. lu musye tre ṭá-nəke, 'araqin mənnəd 'Arādən. 'Arādən xəzyālox…[S.B.: la', bale wən šəmya.] he, he. surāye l-tāma. [S.B.: 'anna surāye, ^Hnaxón^H.] 'egā 'aráqin-ži. mā 'aráqin-le? kullu drelu go d-anna ṭánəke… lu músye-ll—, žang la mrupeta… mə́-le-ži qéṭa-le. qéṭa-le. waḷḷa zəllan. lá-prəqlu mənnan hudāye… walḥāṣəl muzmənaxlu. zəllan ^Hbrit^H. tāma lu 'wide ^Hsə'udá.^{H75}

3 basər ^Hsə'udá^H muselu 'araqin. 'Awṛāham déni-ži 'ida drele 'əbbəd dida bəštāya 'araqin. šaxə́nta-la. xumma. [S.B.: 'Awṛahám bər Noka?] he, he, 'Awṛāham bər Noka. 'ə́na-wən u-'āya u-xa məšəlmāna. [S.B.: 'Awṛahám

---

75 Cf. the JNeoAram forms sɩ'ōḏa, sa'ūḏ/da (Sabar 2002a:242).

day will come (and) that matter will be decided." (My father sa)ys: I will now give it (money for the murder)." Eli is hot(-headed). May God rest his soul. He was hot(-headed). No doubt about it.[76]

When all's said and done, my father didn't talk. He says: "Eli, first of all **22** you will hear (what I have to say). I now am not saying anything. One day you will hear." In short, by God, Eli heard. My late father, after this (that Shambi's murder was avenged), went there. He says (to Eli): "How may lira did you say it was? Will you give forty liras? Will you give sixty liras? (Get up now and) bring five (liras)! Now we'll see (if you'll actually do it). Get up (and) bring five (liras) and the rest (of the money) is all for you." In short, by God, the Muslim (who murdered Shambi) died. Somebody else took his wife. She (indeed) went off.

5.7. ABRAHAM GETS DRUNK

(And now) the matter of Ako. They killed Ako. Really, he up (and) spills[77] **1** his blood. We've come (now) to the matter of Abraham. Abraham. We went to Amidya: I am (there) and he and a Muslim. We went (and) brought *posta*, 'mail'. We brought mail. [S.B.: From Čalla?] From Čalla, yes. We brought mail, yes, to Amidya. Their mail went to the local governor, our mail we delivered. They say: "Tomorrow you should come take the return mail. Today there isn't (any)." Okay, today there isn't (any). We left.

There is a circumcision ceremony in a house in Amidya. They invited **2** us there. They have brought two large tin cans, arrack from Aradhin. You saw Aradhin… [S.B.: No, but I've heard (about it).] Yes, yes. Christians (were) there. [S.B.: Those (were) Christians, correct.] So then arrack also (is there). What arrack is it? They put all (sorts of things) in those large tin cans… (that) they have brought—, rust has come loose (and is floating about inside)… What's more, it's summer. It's summer. By God, we went. The Jews didn't leave us (alone)… In short, they invited us. We went (to) the circumcision ceremony. They made a festive meal there.

After the festive meal, they brought arrack. And our Abraham put his **3** hands on it (the large tin can), drinking the arrack. It is hot. (There is oppressive) heat. [S.B.: Abraham son of Noka?]. Yes, yes, Abraham son of Noka. I am (there), and (so is) he, and a Muslim. [S.B.: Abraham

---

[76] Lit., 'no talk'.
[77] Lit., 'takes'.

šatāya wewa?]. ^H*mā-še*—^H, *kšātewa, bale 'egā réše-ži lá-gpāyəšwa l-dúke.*
[S.B.: *mar: šaxina-le.*] *he, he, he. walḥāṣəl štele. məšəlmána-ži tŭrki 'ā*
le māra-lle: lá-šti! lá-šti! 'āhət lá-mṣet šātət! 'ắ-ži lu musye, lu músye-lle
məšəlmána-ži. wíde-lle ^H*'aruḥấ lə-ḥúd. 'ət ha-'emét* ^H. *'ắ-ži le tiwa mənneni.*

4   *xanči 'āna šteli 'araqin. šaxina. mani 'ibe šātele? qéṭa-ži. ču* ^H*kerah* ^H *let.*
ču talga let. [A.H.: *gdāréwāle go 'ena* ^Z*xapča* ^Z]. *mā 'ena? 'ena 'éka-la? xá-*
yoma, xá-yoma geziwa ḥil gmāṭewa l-'ena . . . walḥāṣəl waḷḷa štelan. štelan
u-xəllan.

5   *čanyāsa šqililan. 'āna zəlli. poṣṭa gyāni šqilāli,* ^H*tšuvá* ^H *mən qāymaqam.*
selan. bāzax. 'āxər 'Awṛāham le bəgxāka . . . ham (m)pəlle. ham nāpəl. he.
xúmma-le-ži. 'it xa 'ena 'əltxé(t?) ṭappá ^Z*gəmrila* ^Z-, *kāni Karačke* ^Z*gəm-*
rila ^Z. *kušlan ḥil tāma.* ^H*kim'át* ^H *'urxəd pálsā'a-la.* ^H*yridá* ^H-*ži 'ila. kúšlana*
'əltəx 'əltəx. kušleni ḥel tāma. 'Awṛāham le mənnan.

6   *waḷḷa 'Awṛāham kemər: 'āna lá-kesən. ṭamá la kesət, 'Awṛāham? kemər:*
^H*be'emét* ^H *'āna lá-kesən. qadome hənna 'ədyo xamúšeb 'ile. 'əróta-ži l-axxa*
pāwən. yom šapsa hénna-la—, godi ^H*məsibá* ^H *ṛapsa. kemər: pšātax 'araqin.*
'āh! kemər: dunya čú-məndi-le.

7   *'axnan lewax nāšəd d-axxa, ḥabibi! 'axnan lewax nāšəd d-axxa. 'axnan*
mən Túrkiya 'iwax. 'āni 'ilu go 'Eraq. 'atta 'axnan poṣṭa pšaqlaxla. 'āhat
lətlox kvar ^H*zaxút* ^H *l-axxa, pešət l-axxa.* ^H*zaxút* ^H *d-é-poṣṭa 'āhat iwət 'əsya*
l-axxa. la. 'áx-geb tán-geb tamáha(-geb) b-séfer-ṭoṛa. 'Awṛāham m-kāni
Karačke mxéle 'əlla ḥil səqle 'əl-'Amə́dya.

8   *mašmi'! [A.H.: skira?] he. səqle kemər: 'āna la kesən. 'ắna-ži—, 'ə́twāleni*
'əzla, 'əzla ṣəwya. xa hənna 'ətwa Maṣlo bron d-é-Yosef ṣawāya. 'āya 'ə́twāle
hənna ṣáwewa 'əlləd Bétanūre-ži. 'əzla—, šúqa-le l-Bétanūre. 'āna u-məšəl-
māna mxelan 'əlla. zəllan Bétanūre. zəllan Bétanūre. 'əzleni šqəllan.

was a drinker?] Whatever (he could get), he would drink, but then he would lose control.[78] [S.B.: Say: "He is hot(-headed)!"] Yes, yes, yes. In short, he drank. The Muslim is speaking to him Turkish: "Don't drink (from rusty tins)! Don't drink! You can't drink (that stuff!)" They also have brought him, they have brought him, the Muslim, too. They have made him a separate meal. (I am telling you) the truth. He too has sat down with us.

I drank a bit of of arrack. (It is) warm. Who is able to drink it (in this **4** heat)? (It is) summer. There is no ice. There is no ice. [A.H.: They used to put (the arrack) in a spring (of water) for a bit (till it cooled down).] What spring? Where is there a spring? One (whole) day, one (whole) day they used to walk until they would reach a spring... In short, by God, we drank. We drank and we ate.

We took the (mail) satchels. I went. I took my own mail, return mail **5** from the local governor. We came (to collect the mail and then) we will go. Well! Abraham is laughing... and he fell. And he falls (because he is drunk). Yes. And it is hot. There is a spring at the bottom of the hillside they call it—, the spring of Karachke they call it. We went down there. (It is) a path of almost half an hour. It is a descent. We went way down. We went down until there. Abraham is with us.

By God, Abraham says: "I am not coming." (Shabbo says:) "Why aren't **6** you coming, Abraham?" He says: "Really, I am not coming. Tomorrow, um, today is Thursday. I shall be here Friday. Saturday there is, um—they make a big party." He says: "We will drink arrack." "Ah," he says: "Nothing is happening (anyway) in the world (so I can stay)."

(Shabbo says:) "We are not people from here, my friend! We are not **7** people from here. We are from Turkey. It is they (who are) in Iraq. Now we will take the mail. You (Abraham) no longer have a right here, to remain here. You have come here by right of that mail. No. When all's said and done, (I swear) on the Torah scroll." From the spring of Karachke Abraham hit it (the road) until he went up to Amidya.

Listen! [A.H.: (Abraham was) drunk?] Yes. (Abraham) went up (to **8** Amidya) saying: "I am not coming. And I—." We had yarn, dyed yarn. There was, um, a Maslo son of that Joseph the dyer. He had, um, he used to dye for Betanure also. Yarn—, there is a market (of it) in Betanure. I and the Muslim hit (the road). We went (to) Betanure. We went (to) Betanure.

---

[78] Lit., 'but his head would not remain in its place'.

'é-lele pəšlan tam. dməxlan tam. bənhe qəmli sā‘a ’əṣṛa [S.B.: yom ’ərota.],
he, yom ’ərota, sā‘a ’əṣṛa ^Hkvar^H bésa-(wa)xwa-(’a)xnan.

9 baxte sela ^Hməskena^H ’Asmāre, kəmra: ké-le ’Awṛāham? mərri: walla le
zila l-‘Amədya kšāte ‘araqin. le piša. ’āya ^Hməskena^H murpyāla l-bəxya.
kəmra: le qṭila. ’axtun letun mára-lli. kəče, walla lewe qṭila. ’á-le zila
šāte ‘araqin. ’áx-geb tán-gəb tamáha-geb walla lá-mhomənna ’əlla. tūla
bəbxāya (m)walwole.

10 ’Awṛāham pəšle l-‘Amədya. yom xošeba mxele ’əlla. sele l-Kāra mən ‘Amədya... de-mášmi’! ’egā tāma ’é-‘urxa ’aqqar mayrəxla. mən Kāra yom
trūšeb mxele ’əlla. ’it xa ’urxa Razoke ^Zgəmrila^Z [S.B.: ki’ənna, ki’ənna.]
ki’ətta. b-é-’ida səqle hil sele reš ’enəd Səgrazoke. ’ərbəd Spindarnāye lu l-
tāma. ṭlāhá-’arba-qəṭ’e. mā—, tāma kalbe la mrāpelu⁷⁹ ’əlləd ’Awṛāham.
mašmi’! kalbe mrupyālu⁸⁰ l-’Awṛāham gəbe qaṭlile. b-íya-’ida u-yá-’ida
’anna nāše mrupyālu ’əlləd ’Awṛāham. ’Awṛāham xá-p-təne-le. xa tre
čanyása-ži lu b-xāṣe. ’áx-geb tán-geb walla qemi ’odile be-čáṛa. m-é-’ida
selu tmanya... ’an Pənčāye ’Aṿṛāham (m)poləṭlu m-go ’idás didu.

5.8. The Attempted Seduction

1 xa nə́qwa-ži lewa gurta. ’ena la dreta ’əlli. ’āna lá-ki’ən. čú-gā lewən
mhukya mənna u-lewən zíla-ži l-tāma. he, he. xzi! la go hə́nna-ži-la,
^Hm’oreset^H-la-ži. xa behna kxázənna. ’ə́twāleni xa šwāna. ’ə́twale—, xor
^Hkəbúṣ^H-ewa u-’ə́twāle ^Hparót^H u-’ə́twāle kulle məndi. ’āya šātət ’arba
lewən xázya-lle. walla qāyəm dāwəqli.

2 hiwa xanči ^Hxəm’a^H u-xanči sartuk... [Y.H.: xanči məšxa. mar: məšxa!]
he, məšxa. sartuk lewe məšxa. ’e xeta kar’a, ’it kar’a, he, kar’a ’iya hə́nna-le.

---

⁷⁹ The verbal form is difficult, yet the general context seems clear.
⁸⁰ See § 4.4.23.5.

We took our yarn. We remained there that night. We slept there. In the morning I got up at ten o'clock. [S.B.: Friday.], yes, Friday, at ten o'clock we were already (at) home.

His wife came, the poor Asmare. She says: "Where is Abraham?" I **9** said: "By God, he has gone to Amidya drinking arrack. He has remained (there)." That poor one broke out crying. She says: "He's been killed. You aren't telling me." (Shabbo says:) "Woman! By God, he has not been killed. He has gone to drink arrack." When all's said and done, by God, she didn't believe it. She began crying (and) wailing.

Abraham remained in Amidya. Sunday he hit it (the road). He came to **10** Kara from Amidya… Now listen! Now then that path there makes it so much longer. Monday he hit (the road) from Kara. There is a path (that goes by a village) they call Razoke [S.B.: I know it, I know it.] You know it. He went up in that direction until he came to the spring of Segrazoke. The sheep of the residents of Spindar are (grazed) there, three, four flocks. What—, there the dogs (residents of Spindar) let Abraham have it. Listen! The dogs let Abraham have it, they wish to kill him. When all's said and done, those people let Abraham have it. Abraham is all alone. There are one (or) two satchels on his back. When all's said and done, by God, they up (and) made him helpless.[81] Eight (people) come from that direction… Those residents of Pinianish delivered Abraham out of their hands.

5.8. The Attempted Seduction

(There was) a certain female (who) hasn't married. She has put her eye **1** on me. I was unaware. I have never spoken with her nor have I gone over there (to her). Yes, yes. Look! And she is in, um, and she is engaged. Suddenly I see her. We had a shepherd. He had—, it was like a kibbutz and he had cows and he had all sorts of things. I hadn't seen him for four years.[82] By God, he up (and) grabs me.

A bit of butter was given and a bit of cream[83]… [Y.H.: A bit of *məšxa* **2** (cooking oil). Say: *məšxa*!] Yes, *məšxa*. *sartuk* (cream) is not *məšxa*. That

---

[81] I.e., Abraham is unable to flee because of the weight of the satchels he is carrying.
[82] Lit., 'It was the fourth year I have not seen him.'
[83] Earlier in the recording he mentions that he has run out of butter and gone to the shepherd, Mustafa, for some more.

məšxa xāsa 'ile. ta d-anna ^Zgəmri^Z kar'a. ^Htov^H. tūle l-tāma gyāpe laxma. kud laxma 'āya 'akčən d-íya-^Hšulḥàn^H. məsənne ^H'aruḥát ṣohorayim^H tre sapoxe. 'xəlli...

3 *xa mamzer. xa yalunka ^Hba-'érəx^H 'ibe ^Hb-gil^H 'əšta šənne sele. šəmme Məṣṭáfa-le məšəlmāna. kemər: Məṣṭāfa-ž(i). kemər: mā? kemər: hudáya-le l-axxa? 'á-ži kemər: 'āna wən tiwa dəpən dide. bābi le mira 'āse kəsleni. xzi mā ^Hmamzerím^H-ilu! šəmməd, šəmməd bāba—, la mšudarta basri u-'āna lá-ki'ən. waḷḷa ^Htov^H. kemər: le bixāla. ko xəlle xarāye bas...*

4 [Y.H.: *la wətwa gwira?*] *ha? la, la, lá-wənwa gwira. lá-wənwa gwira. la waḷḷa lá-wənwa gwira. waḷḷa ḥel tre sapö(xe) xəlli xá-gā xeta sele 'é-bəč'a. kemər bābe le ḥmila žwanti. yom 'əróta-le-ži ya'ni gezəl xuṭba. mərri: mā? bābox lewe zila l-xuṭba?*

5 *lā kemər. qam tar didu hənna-le ṛūbar māye kāwəš. kemər: gyāne le ^Hmaxóne^H-lla. bāzəl xuṭba ^H'im ha-mamzerím^H* [Y.H.: *le maḥzore gyāne bāzəl xuṭba.*] *he, he. bāzəl xuṭba 'á-ži. xəlli tre sapöxe. qəmli. gézəna. tar'a ptíxa-le 'āna-ži zəlli.*

6 ^H*šalóm šalóm^H, 'á-la go tar'a. ké-le bābax? kəmra: wəlle reš māye. 'átta-bāse. xa julla la mtúta-lli l-tam qam ^Hḥalón^H. 'az^H zəlli tūli. 'əlli tar'a ḥləqla. ^Hbe'emét^H... 'āhat məšəlmanta, 'āna hudá. kəmra: 'āna gbannox. 'iya basər 'Azizko lu qtile 'əlle, 'ila 'iya masale. 'āna-ži mərri... 'ā düqāli murḥəqāli mən gyāni. kəmra: xzi! gəbət? mar: ken. lá-gbət 'é-baxta pṣarxa.*

7 *'é-məšəlmāna wənwa kəsəl dide, xa 'ár'a-'ila qam tar didu. 'āni lu wíde-lla ^Htiras.⁸⁴ tiras^H wetun xəzye grāwe, he hatxa grāwe. 'āya le 'əsya, le ^Hmúrgəša^H. 'əsya le 'wira go ^Htiras mul ḥalón^H. le manoxe 'əbbeni.* [A.H.: *barqul šabák*] *he, he. barqul šabbāka. 'axnan panjāre ^Zgəmráxwāla^Z.* [A.H.: *panjāre*]. *he.*

---

84 On other occasions Shabbo uses NeoAram *ganmnoke* 'maize'.

other (thing), butter (*karʾa*), there is butter, yes, butter, it is, um, butter. It is new cooking oil. They call these (things) butter (*karʾa*). Fine. He sat there baking bread. Each (loaf of) bread (is) the size of this table. He brought me lunch, two wrap sandwiches. I ate…

A bastard, a child, about six years old, came. (The shepherd's) name 3 is Mustafa, (he is) a Muslim. (The child) says: "Mustafa!" (Mustafa) says: "What?" (The child) says: "Is the Jew (Shabbo) here?" And he (Mustafa) says: "I am seated next to him." (The child says:) "My father has said he should come to us." See what bastards they are! The name of, the name of her father—, (that woman) has sent for me and I don't know (why). By God, fine. (Mustafa) says (to the child): "He is eating. Since I ate enough…

[Y.H. You hadn't married?] Huh? No, no, I hadn't married. I hadn't 4 married. No, by God, I hadn't married. By God, by the time I ate the two sandwiches, that bastard (child) came again. (The child) says his father has been waiting for me expectantly. And it is Friday, that is to say, he goes to the (Friday) sermon (in the mosque). I said: "What? Your father hasn't gone to the Friday sermon (because he is waiting for me)?"

"No," he says. Outside their door, um, descends a stream of water. (The 5 child) says: "(My father) is preparing himself." He will go to the Friday sermon with the bastards. [Y.H.: He is preparing himself to go to the Friday sermon.] Yes, yes. He also will go to the Friday sermon. I ate two sandwiches. I got up. I go. The door is open and I go (in).

"Hello, hello" (the woman says), she is in the doorway. (I say:) "Where 6 is your father?" She says: "He's right at the water. Now he will come." She has put a piece of cloth there for me in front of the window (to prevent people from looking in). So I went (in and) sat down. She locked the door on me. Really… (I say:) "You (are) a Muslim, I (am) a Jew." She says: "I love you." This is after they have killed Azizko, it is this affair. And I said:… I grabbed her (and) pushed her away me. She says: "Look! Do you want to? Say: 'Yes.' (If) you don't want to, I[85] shall shout."

(As for) that Muslim at whose place I was, there is a (plot of) land 7 outside their door. They have grown it with corn. You have seen corn growing, yes, like this it grows. He (that Muslim) has come (and) he has noticed. (He has) come (and) he has entered the corn(field) opposite the window. He is looking at us. [A.H.: In front of the *šabak* (window).] Yes, yes… in front of the *šabaka* (window). We used to call it (a window) *panjare*. [A.H.: *panjare*] Yes.

---

[85] Lit., 'that woman' (§ 4.1.7.j).

8 walḥāṣəl walla mād mərri ṭāsa la ^Hʿzərra^H ʾəlli. tarʾa la ḥlə́qta-lle. qdila la
dréta-lla go jeba. mərri: mašmeʾ! ʾāhat qurdésa-wat ʾāna hudǻya-wən. ʾāna
lá-gbənnax. lá-qqarwən ʾəbbax. kəmra: xzi! pṣarxan u-maqṭəlannox. ʾən
wət góra-ži, nǻbəlli. ʾāna ppešan hudesa. mərri: hudāye ʾəbbax lá-gzedi. lá-
ʾasyat hudǻye-ži maḥərmattu. ʾāni lu piše ḥalāle. ʾāni m-lá-ḥarmi. ʾaxnan
lá-gbax ʾəmməteni xorexun zeda ʾəbbəd ḥaramūsa.

9 walla lá-^Hʿzərra^H ʾəlli. lá-^Hʿzərra^H ʾəlli. lewa prǻqa-lli. mərri: ʾamrənnax
[Y.H.: bāba kiʾewa mən kulla...] ʾāna lá-kiʾəna. bāba lá-(we)wa l-tam.
^Hyaxol lihyot^H kiʾewa. ʾāni kəslu ʾərwāna-la mād mázəlṭi xa hudāya. ʾən
hudesa [A.H.: b-idəd məšəlmāne] šaqlila ʾodila. yaʿni ʾən kutru... mərri:
ṭamá wat ʿšə́qta-lli?

10 ^Hkodəm kol^H, ʾāhat ^Hmʾoréset^H-wat. kəmra: pšoqanne ʾāya. mərri: ṭamá?
mā masále-la? kəmra: ʾaxnan wax mbuqre. ʾaxtun hudāye gzire wetun,
yaʿni ʾodetun ʾəlleni. ʾərwǻna-la ʾodax ʾəlléxun-ži. ʾərwǻna-la. ʾən kutru
ʾalāle, ʾərwāna ^Hmšulǻš^H ʾila. kutru ʾalāle.

11 mərri: b̭ǻš-ila hatxa gəbat. mərra: he. mərri: ptox tarʾa! ʾe kaləpsa brāt
kalba. la, lá-kpatxa. walla düqāli baloʾtəd dida. mətwāli l-ʾarʾa ʾegā krox!
^Hbli raḥma(nūt), türkit türkit^H. króx-u-króx-u-króx-u-króx-u-króx-u-!
ʾegā dreli pumməd dida.

12 ʾǻ-le qam ^Hḥalón^H le manoxe. ʾāna lá-kiʾən. lewən bəxzáya-lle. qóme-ži
kərya wewa, la yarixa. he. walla hādax ʾüdli ʾəlləd dida. b-iya baṛāxa
ʾüdāli ^Hpastela^H. mə́ndyāli l-tāma. qaḥba brāt qaḥba! ʾāna hudāya u-ʾāhat
məšəlmanta. wəllu qurdāye terax ter yəmmax ter xaswāsax ter kullexun
ʾilu. ʾən gǽbat-ži nablənnax. ʾit türkāye l-axxa. ʾanna ṭlāhá-ʾarba šənne lu go
^Hṣavǻ^H. byāwənnax ʾəl-ʾídu. didax ʾáya-la. čú-ga ču ^Htaʿanót^H lá-hāwelax.

In short, by God, whatever I said to her didn't help me. She has locked **8**
the door. She has placed the key in her pocket. I said: "Listen! You are
a Kurd, I am a Jew. I don't want you. I am not coming near you." She
says: "Look! I will shout and I will have you killed. If you are a man, lead
me away. I shall become a Jewess." I said: "Through you, the Jews are not
going to increase (in number). You will not come (and) pollute the Jews.
They (Jews) have remained pure. They shouldn't become impure (now
by your becoming Jewish)! We don't want our nation to increase like you
(Kurds) through impurity!"

By God, it didn't help me. It didn't help me. She isn't leaving me (alone). **9**
I said: "I'll tell you" [Y.H.: Did her father know of all the . . . ?] I don't know.
Her father wasn't there. It is possible that he knew. With them it is a good
deed to convert a Jew. If a Jewess (falls) [A.H.: into the hands of Muslims],
they take her to make her (a Muslim). That is to say, if both of them . . . I
said: "Why have you desired me?"

(I said to her:) "First of all, you are engaged." She says: "I will leave that **10**
one." I said: "Why? What's the story?" She says: "We have inquired. You
are circumcised Jews, that is to say, you should do it to us (circumcise us).
It is a good deed that we should do (it) for you. It is a good deed. If both
sides (want it), it is a triple good deed . . . (For) both sides."

I said: "It's fine (if) that's the way you want (it)." She said: "Yes." I said: **11**
"Open the door!" That bitch! No, she doesn't open (the door). By God, I
seized her throat. I laid her down on the ground (and) so then I smashed
her.[86] Without mer(cy), Turkish, Turkish (style?). I smashed her over and
over and over again. So then I stuck my (fist) in her mouth.

He is in front of the window looking. I am unaware. I don't see him. **12**
His height was short, not tall. Yes. By God, I did like this to her. With
this blessing[87] I made mincemeat out of her. I threw her (down) there.
Daughter of a whore! (I said:) "I (am) a Jew and you (are) a Muslim. Right
now the Kurds are enough for you, enough for your mother, enough for
your sisters, enough for all of you. If you want, I will lead you away. There
are Turks here. Those (Turkish men) are in the army for three (or) four
years (and are desperate to have a woman). I shall hand you over to them.
It is yours (to decide). May you never have any complaints (since they will
satisfy your sexual desires)."

---

[86] Lit., 'So then smash!' (narrative imperative).
[87] Is Shabbo being sarcastic about the blessing over food since he is talking about
making mincemeat out of her?

13 walla qdila mən jeb dida mpolətli. tar'a ptəxli gyāni. məxyāla[88] 'əlli xá-gā
xeta basri. walla zurri 'əlləd dida ḥil 'ar'a… m-'ar'a la qəmla. mərri: da-
ḥmól! 'urxa düqāli. seli l-besa [Y.H.: bāba la mərre čú-məndi?] lewe l-besa
bāba. [Y.H.: mərrox ᶻweleᶻ ḥmila manoxe 'əbbəd panjāra…] 'āya mərra.
'e xet 'āya xá-nāša xeta… sela kəmrāli: ki'ewa. 'āni ki'ewa b-əġdād. 'āna
lá-ki'ən. walḥāṣəl walla 'iya masale zəlla. 'iya masale zəlla.

14 seli l-besa. məšxa məseli. hūli… mərri: lá-mšadrətti xá-gā xeta go qurdāye.
'ən sníqa-wət xədda sele kəslox gəbət ᴴ'azrətteᴴ, si gyānox! 'āna lá-gezən.
la mərri ṭāse čú-məndi. walla zəlla. ᴴbe'emétᴴ. mərri tas dide: b-gyānox
'āzət. lá-'amrət ṭāsi. 'āna lá-mṣən mābayn d-anna baxtāsa xadrən, la. kullu
dukāne lu bə'rāqa basri hənna. mā 'odən 'əbbu? 'āna lá-gbənnu. walḥāṣəl
walla la ᴴmurgəšleᴴ má-'it u-má-let. 'iya masale pəšla xapči ᴴšeketᴴ. zəlla.

15 xá-yoma ᴴba-'érəxᴴ… xzi! xa ṭḷá-yarxe zəlla 'əbbəd dida. 'iya nixəd 'Awṛāham zəlle mulšənne kəsəl nəxtəd yəmmi: ki'at brónax-ži le mpila basər
baxtás qurdāye? la yəmmi ki'a la bābi ko mā masále-la. lewən míra-llu-
ži. walla bábi-ži ᴴm'uxzá(v)ᴴ. le báda-lli ᴴpartsufímᴴ kol mine dəvarímᴴ.
lewe mḥakoye mənni ᴴyafé məsudárᴴ. 'áx-geb tán-geb, 'ít-xa məndi.

16 xá-yoma kəmrən ta nəxtəd yəmmi. mərri: má-lox?[89] kəmra: 'āhat pášwālox
ṭahóra-ži. zəllox basər baxtás qurdāye? mərri: m-eka ki'at? xulma wetun
xəzye? mā bréla 'əllexun? kəmra: bale, bale 'it sahāde. mərri: sahāde?
'āna ki'ən 'Awṛāham le 'əsya mulšəna ṭasexun. mərri: bášš-ila. da-ḥmól!
lá-mḥokeli. [A.H.: mar: ᶻmluqṭaᶻ] 'ā?… le māra hənna 'ŭda fasādūsa.
fasādūsa ᶻgəmriᶻ [Y.H.: mar: fasādūsa]. ᴴkenᴴ. fasādūsa.

---

[88] See § 4.4.23.5.
[89] An error for má-lax.

By God, I took the key out of her pocket. I opened the door myself. She 13
hit me once again from behind. By God, I turned around to her until the
ground... She didn't get up from the ground. I said: "Now stop!" I took
to the road. I came home. [Y.H.: Her father didn't say anything?] He isn't
in the house. [Y.H.: You said he was standing looking in at the window.]
She said it. And that other one, another person... She came (and) says to
me: "He knew." They knew (of the matter from) each other. I don't know.
In short, by God, this affair went away. This affair went away.

I came home. I brought the cooking oil (which I had originally been 14
sent to get). I gave it... I said (to my father): "Don't you send me again
among the Kurds. If you are in need (because) someone has come to you
(and) you want to help him, go yourself! I am not going." I didn't tell him
anything (about the incident). By God, it passed. Really. I said to him: "Go
yourself. Don't tell me (to go). I am not able to go around among those
women, no. They are running after me everywhere, um. What should I
do with them? I don't want them." In short, by God, he (my father) didn't
notice anything at all. This affair remained a bit quiet. (The affair) went
away.

One day about... look! About three months went by since (the inci- 15
dent). (Then) this late Abraham went (and) he informed (on me) to my
late mother: "Do you know your son has chased after women of the
Kurds?" Neither my mother knows nor my father what the incident is.
I haven't even told them. By God, my father (is) disappoin(ted). He is
making all sorts of faces at me. He is not speaking with me nicely (or
on a) regular (basis). When all's said and done, (I can tell that) there is
something (wrong).

One day I say to my late mother, I said: "What's with you?" She says: 16
"You had been pure. (But then) you went after women of the Kurds?" I
said: "From where do you know (this)? Have you been dreaming? What
happened to you?" She says: "Yes indeed, yes indeed, there are witnesses."
I said: "Witnesses? I know Abraham has come (and has) informed (on
me) to you." I said: "It's fine. Now stop!" I didn't talk. [A.H.: Say: *mluqṭa*
(he has informed against).] Huh?... He is saying, um, he has spread[90]
gossip. They say *fasadusa* (gossip). [Y.H.: Say: *fasadusa* (gossip)!] Yes.
fasadusa.

---

[90] Lit., 'done'.

17 *walḥāṣəl zəlla ʾəbba. ᴴʾazᴴ jirānəd d-e, d-é-baxta xa ᴴbaḥúrᴴ ʾətwa l-tāma. zamára ʾewa ṛāba. ᴴʾazᴴ kəsleni gyatwiwa. kudlel kesewa ᴴʾorḥímᴴ zamriwa ḥil palgədlel. ᴴba-ʿérəxᴴ sāʿa tre'sar hatxa geziwa kutxa mbarbəziwa gezəlwa l-bes gyāne. ʾé-nāša ᴴmuzmənniᴴ. ʾāhat⁹¹ xə́lwāli kəsəl dide ᴴʾaruḥə́ᴴ. u-ʾé zamára-ži ᴴmuzmənniᴴ xá-yoma. Ḥasan ᶻgəmriwāleᶻ. mərri: ʾāsət kəsleni xanči zəmrəyāsa basime ʾamrət. kemər: ᴴtovᴴ. Mə́ṣṭo-ži mesətte mən gyānox, mərri… selu kəsleni.*

18 *nixəd bābi lá-kiʾe yəmmi lá-kiʾa mā masále(-la). tūlu zmərru ḥil palgədlel. hənna-wa qurwəd ḥanukká-(w)a. waxtəd qəmlu ʾána-ži mərri ṭāse: Məṣṭo! kemər: mā? ʾə́twāle tre ʾaxawāsa. mərri: ʾāhat b-xudreš ʾaxawāsox u-bqurʿān dexun ʾəbbəd Maḥammad dexun, ʾāna gmaymənnox ᶻʾóᶻ-yoma d-āna seli kəslexun, kəslox, u-let hənna məšxa, düqənnox, lá-qbəllox ʾāzən. mərrox ḥel ᴴaruḥə́ᴴ lá-ʾaxlət kəsli lá-gezət. mə́-ʾətwa? ʾāna gəbən ʾamrət ᴴʾemétᴴ.*

19 *ḥməlle monəxle. waḷḷa qəmle ḥməlle qam nixəd bābi. kemər: xzi! ʿāwon didox ʾəd-kúlla⁹² hudāye mən kullu dukāne. kemər: qdāli hūwa. qdāl báb-u-yəmmi hūwa. reš hənna səjjādəd Maḥammad ʾāna …hatxa ʾən ʾāna mdaglənnox. kem(ər:) ḥə́l-u-masaləd bronox hatxa ʾāwa. flán-brāta lewa prə́qta-lle. le dwǘqa-lla. hāda(x) le lṭixa ʾəbba. hāda(x) le krixa ʾəbba. le wida ʾəlla ᴴḥolāᴴ. le múndye-lla l-tāma. (b-)xurṭūsa gəba—, gbāwa ʾāya dāməx mənnəd dida. tarʾa la ḥləqta ʾəlləd dide. mā le ᴴmbukšaᴴ mənna? lewa ᴴmšuḥrərartaᴴ ʾəlle. tarʾa lewa ptə́xta-lle. b- ᴴkowaḥᴴ tarʾa le ptíxa-lle u-hátxa-la. hátxa la breta. ke(mər): lewe nqiša ʾəlləd dida.*

20 *basər hādax ᴴʾazᴴ bābi mpuršəqle. kefe sele. mərri: kud ᴴčizbátᴴ⁹³ sele mən xá-dūka gyatwət mašm(ʾ)ət ʾəlləd dide… lewən sira! u-ʾidi síra-le⁹⁴ ʾaqlāsi síre-lu? lewu ysire ʾaqlāsi. ʾāna la gezən kəsəl didu. lá-gbən.*

---

⁹¹ An error for *ʾāna.*
⁹² For expected *kullu.*
⁹³ < ModH < Ar.
⁹⁴ An error for *síre-le.*

In short, (the gossip?) about it went (around?). Then there was a young   **17**
man there who (was) a neighbor of that, of that woman. He was a great
singer. So (people) would sit with us. Every night guests would come.
They would sing until midnight. (At) about something like twelve o'clock,
they would go, each one would leave (and) go to his own house. I invited
that person (the singer). I had eaten a meal at his place. And moreover
one day I invited that singer. They called him Ḥasan. I said: "You should
come to us (and) sing a few nice songs."[95] He (the singer) says: "Fine."
"You should also bring Misto (the shepherd) with you," I said... They
came to us.

Neither my late father nor my mother know what the story (is). They   **18**
sat (and) sang until midnight. It was, um, it was close to Hanukka. At the
time they got up (to leave) I said to him: "Misto!" He says: "What?" He
had two brothers. I said: "Take my word for it by the head of your brother
and by your Quran (and) by your Muhammad, I adjure you that on that
day that I came to you all, to you, by God, and there isn't, um, cooking oil,
you grabbed me (and) you didn't agree that I should go. You said: 'Until
you eat a meal with me you are not going.' What was it there? I want you
to tell the truth."

(Misto) stopped (and) looked. By God, he got up (and) he stood before   **19**
my late father. (Misto) says: "Look! Your guilt (and) of all the Jews from
everywhere," he says: "may it be upon us.[96] May the guilt be that of
my father and my mother. On, um, the prayer rug of Muhammad, I
(swear)... thus (may they do to me) if I am lying to you. He sa(ys): "The
upshot of the story of your son was like this: a certain girl hasn't left him
alone. He has grabbed her (in order to get the key out of her pocket so
that he could open the locked door). For this reason he (went up and)
struggled with her. Like th(is) he has beaten her. He has made her ill. He
has thrown her down there. (By) force she want(ed)—, wanted him to
sleep with her. She has locked the door on him. What has he asked of
her? She hasn't let him go. She hasn't opened the door. By force he has
opened the door and that's the way it is. That's the way it happened. He
sa(ys): "He hasn't touched her."

After this then my father stretched out (and relaxed). He rejoiced. I   **20**
said: "You sit (and) listen to each lie (that) comes from any place... I am
not tied up! Are my hands tied (and) are my feet tied up? My feet aren't
tied up. I am not going to them (if you need something from them). I
don't want to."

---

[95] Lit., 'say'.
[96] Lit., 'May it be (on) my neck.'

21 walḥāṣəl ʾáx-geb tán-geb... pəšla ᴴšeketᴴ. qəmlu ʾida drelu ʾəbbəd ʾaxawāsi.
    ʾanna mənni pəšlu be-hívi. ᴴtovᴴ. ʾaxawāsi—, ᴴbe'emétᴴ nixəd ʾAwrāham
    zəlle mən... ʾiya mā kəmrila ʾaxoni Ḥáyyo-ži zəlle mənne, ʾanna kutru.
    [Y.H.: la ʾüdlu ʾəllu čú-məndi?] la! ḥmol! heš lewu məṭye l-hādax ʾodi ʾəllu.
    qamāye gbe ḅāš ᴴmšaxnəxiluᴴ⁹⁷ ḅāš mazəlṭilu. xarāye ʾegā ᴴəmmʾeymiᴴ⁹⁸
    ʾəlləd didu: qaṭláxlexun ʾən lá-hatxa.

5.9. The Wife of the Mudir Repays Kindness

1 kma šənne kəsleni mədor wewa. kma ᴴtafkidímᴴ le xlipa. wakil qáymaqam
    wewa. dukāne nablíwāle. Mẓaffər ᶻgəmríwāleᶻ. ʾāna ᴴ'vərriᴴ⁹⁹ mən tāma.
    baxte xəzyāli qam tar'a... ḥel ʾiya mā kəmrila ʾáya-la qam tar'a. hatxa
    monəxla ʾəbbi. ʾāya ki'āli [Y.H.: baxtəd quṇṣuḷ?] la, bax mədor, mədor.
    [Y.H.: ʾā, bax mədor.] ʾāna mənnəd ḥənna wən bəqrāwəd Jólamerg.

2 walḷa sela. kəmra ṭāsi: m-eka wət bisāya? ʾāya ki'āli. ʾəsri, ʾəsri, ṭḷāsi šə́nne-
    wax, go Čalla wewa. ʾalpa šu'āle wax wide ṭas didu. walḥāṣəl mərri: xānəm
    walḷa ʾāna mən Moṣəl wən bisāya. kəmra: ʾaxxa ʾurxəd Móṣəl-la? mərri:
    pəšla ʾurxəd Mosəl. pəšla ʾurxəd Mosal. walla ʾāna mən Moṣəl wən bisāya.
    ʾegā gəbat mhémənat ᴴ'oᴴ čú-məndi.

3 ʾāna wən piša šəxtāna. ʾāya tmaneʾsar yome b-ʾaqle wən bisāya. tmaneʾsar
    yome. ʾegā le—, le ḥənna, sāʿa, ʾəṣra, tre'sár-sāʿe sir(e) ʾaqle. xarāye ʾegā
    yasrilox mən ʾaqlāsox u-ḥil ṣadrox ʾəbbəd ᴴʿamídᴴ.¹⁰⁰ mərri: ḥál-u-masale
    hátxa-la. ʾeka bāzət? mərri: bān Jólamerg. kəmra: Jólamerg lewa ṛāba...
    rəqqa ḥənna ṛāba réqqa-le. ʾárba xamša sāʿe māṭət Jólamerg.

4 bale ʾádlele ḥənna šapsa déxun-ila. ᴴšabátᴴ-ʾila. ʾeka bāzət? mərri: ʾətlan
    ʾaxnan ṛāba ᴴhaverímᴴ tāma. walḷa xāzeli ᴴpxatfīliᴴ. má-āhat kxašwat?
    ʾətlan ᴴhaverímᴴ ʾaxnan kullu dukāne.

---

⁹⁷ Unexpected reflex of ModH שֶׁקֶט.
⁹⁸ < *bmʾāymi.
⁹⁹ Elsewhere Shabbo uses the NENA form ʾürri.
¹⁰⁰ For expected ᴴʿamidáᴴ.

In short, when all's said and done... it became quiet. They up (and) 21
put a hand on my brothers. They despaired of me. Fine. My brothers—,
really the late Abraham went with... What do they call it?—my brother
Ḥayyo went with him, the two of them. [Y.H.: They didn't do anything
to them?] No, wait! They hadn't yet got to doing anything to them. At
first one should convince them nicely to convert. Then later they threaten
them. "We'll kill you if (it is) not like this (and you don't convert)."

5.9. THE WIFE OF THE MUDIR REPAYS KINDNESS

He was the mudir with us for a few years. He has switched several 1
positions. He was the deputy of the local governor. They used to transfer
him (to different) places. They called him Mzaffer. I passed by there. I
saw his wife outside... until, what do they call it?—she is outside. Like
this she looked at me. She knows me. [Y.H.: The wife of the consul?] No,
the wife of the mudir, the mudir. [Y.H.: Ah, the wife of the mudir.] I with,
um, I am approaching Jolamerk.

By God, she came (up to me). She says to me: "Where are you coming 2
from?" She knows me. Twenty, twenty, thirty years we (have known each
other); she was in Challa. We have done a thousand things for them. In
short, I said: "Madam, by God, I am coming from Mosul." She says: "Is
the path to Mosul here?" I said: "It became the path to Mosul. It became
the path to Mosul. By God, I am coming from Mosul. So then (if) you
want, believe (it), or not at all."

I have become dirty. It (is) eighteen days (that) I have been walking 3
on foot. Eighteen days. So then is—, is, um, my feet are tied up[101] an
hour, ten, twelve hours. Then later they tie you up from your feet until
your chest in a standi(ng position). I said: "The upshot is like this." (She
says:) "Where are you going?" I said: "I am going (to) Jolamerk." She says:
"Jolamerk is not very... a distance, um, (not) a great distance. You should
reach Jolamerk in four, five hours."

"Indeed tonight, um, is your Sabbath. It is *Shabbat*. Where are you 4
going?" I said: "We have many friends there (in Jolamerk)." By God, they
see me (and) they will snatch me up. What (else) do you think? We have
friends in all places.

---

[101] Shabbo had crossed the border illegally into Iraq, was caught, imprisoned, and
marched back to the border tied up.

5 kəmra: waḷḷa pešət kəsleni. mərri: xānəm 'āna māṭo pešən kəslexun? 'iya
šəxta? b-iya hənna hatxa la gərya? la xipa? la mxulpa? la ču-məndi? hatxa
šəxtāna b-iya ᴴmaṣávᴴ? hā, kəmra: mā? 'axnan ᴴbne 'adámᴴ lewax? didox
'áya-le. jullox masyannu. mesyannu ǵér-julle. jullox mesyannu. damxət
kəsléni-ži. kəsleni pāwət. xošeba xarāye si! xošeba si!

6 mǻ-'āhat? mərri. 'üdli—, mərri: b-iya šəxta... kəslexun? kəmra: byāxlox
ṣābun. byāxlox xa margəlta. byāxlox ṣiwe. tāma ṣiwe let. tāma 'it guniye.
'áni-maqdi. si! wəlle hənna néhra-ži-le qāmox. si reš nehra (m)šāxənnox
ṃāye. xóp-u loš julle qliwe! jullox māsaxlu.

7 māṭo? 'āhat bax mədor, masyat julli? kəmra: mā 'egā 'ána-ži ᴴbne 'adámᴴ;
lewax xor kullu? mā? 'itən piča wetun plixe ṭaseni? 'ána-ži mərri: xānəm,
'āna gnaxpən. ṭāsi 'éba-ži, 'āna hudāya u-'āhat bax mədor yatwat masyatti
julle? kəmra: xzi! 'axnan ᴴga'avanímᴴ lewax. 'aqqar šu'āle ḅāš wetun 'üde
ṭaseni. ᴴl-'olámᴴ 'axnan lá-gnāšax. ᴴtovᴴ. mərri: ᴴtodá rabáᴴ.

8 zəlla. məsela ṭāsi məšxa, kar'a, gupta, sartuk, masta. šləqla be'e go čaydanka. ki'a kullu ᴴtoxniyótᴴ deni, hudāye ki'ālu. widənna ᴴ'aruḥáᴴ. xəlli.
mərri: mǻdor-bak 'éka-le? kəmra: 'ile b-ᴴmisrádᴴ. 'áya-la u-yəmma u-xá-
brona. 'ətla xá-brona. bron 'əč'á-šənne. 'āya gezəl ᴴbet seferᴴ. 'ā u-yəmma
kpeši l-'uwwa, gor dída-ži gezəl ᴴmisrádᴴ.

9 (ma)noxe. 'iya besa hatxa ta góva-ži. 'áqəli lá-qāṭe' nāfe'. bale gāwe geb
lu 'űde-lle kulle ᴴluḥótᴴ ṣiwe ᴴyafé yaféᴴ lu wide. 'ána-ži har plətli qam
tar'a. 'ürri. 'üdli-, 'ürri. 'āya la manoxe 'əbbi la bəgxāka. mərri: mǻ-
'āhat bəgxāka? kəmra: 'ít-xa-məndi kəslox. 'áqqara bə'wāra bəplāṭa bə'wāra
bəplāṭa. xa məndi 'it.

She says: "By God, you should remain with us." I said: "Madam, 5
how should I remain with you? (With) this filth (on me)? In this, um,
unshaven (state) like this? Unwashed? Unchanged? (Without) anything?
Dirty like this, in this state?" "Here," she says: "What? Aren't we human
beings? It (our house) is yours. I'll wash your clothes. I'll bring you other
clothes. I'll bring your clothes. And you should sleep with us. You will be
with us. (On) Sunday finally go! Go (on) Sunday!"

"What (are) you?" I said. "I did—," I said: "In this filth… with you?" 6
She says: "We will give you soap. We will give you a cauldron. We will give
you pieces of wood (to heat up the water)." There aren't pieces of wood
there. There are brambles there. They burn (them to heat up the water).
(She says:) "Go! Right now, um, the river is in front of you. Go to the
river (to get water and) I'll warm up water for you. Wash and wear clean
clothes! We'll wash your clothes."

(I said:) "How so? You, (are) the wife of the mudir. You should wash 7
my clothes?" She says: "What, I too am a human being; aren't we like
everyone? What? Is it a little thing (what) you have done for us?" I
also said: "Madam, I am embarrassed. It is also a disgrace for me, I
a Jew, and you the wife of the mudir that you should sit (and) wash
clothes for me." She says: "Look! We are not proud. You have done so
many good things for us. We never forget." Fine. I said: "Thank you very
much."

She went. She brought me cooking oil, butter, cheese, cream, (and) 8
yoghurt. She poached eggs in a teapot. She knows all our customs,[102] she
knows the Jews. She made me a meal. I ate. I said: "Where is the mudir
bey?" She says: "He is in (the) office." She is (there in the house along
with) her mother and a son. She has one son. The son (is) nine years old.
He goes (to) school. She and her mother remain inside and her husband
goes (to the) office.

(I am) looking (around). And this house, like this, (is) a stall. My mind 9
doesn't comprehend (how it) suits (them). But on the inside they have
made it all wood panels. They have made (it) very nice. I went outside.
I just went in and out. I did—, I entered. She is looking at me, she is
laughing. I said: "Why are you laughing?" She says: "There is something
(funny) about you. So much entering, leaving, entering, leaving. There is
something (funny about it)."

---

[102] Lit. 'plans'.

10 *xa ᴴ**ḥeder**ᴴ xéta-ži 'ǝtlu. tre ᴴ**ḥǝdarím**ᴴ lu ᴴ**b-sax ha-kól**ᴴ. 'ürri l-táma-ži.*
plǝṭli. kǝmra: ṭamá 'āhǝt bāda? mǝrri: gǝbe gāwe xá-mǝndi ti gyāni. yārūsa
*'üdli 'ǝbba. kǝmra:. . . māt gǝbǝt. ᴴ**be'emét**ᴴ séli-wa. xlǝṣli monǝxli zurri*
basǝr bes didu. mǝnnu l-é-'āl-ži ṛūbar ṃáye-le. mǝrri: mǝdor 'imal bāse?
kǝmra: sā'a tre'sar.

11 *. . . mǝrri mašme'! gǝbǝn nablǝnnax mǝn d-axxa. ḥmǝlla. monǝxla 'ǝbbi.*
kǝmra māṭo nablǝtti mǝn d-axxa? mǝrri mašme'! 'āna hudāya. wǝn bisá
*m-ᴴ**bet sohar**ᴴ. 'āhat tūla(x) mselax julle ṭāṣi. mǝsǝnnax julle. 'āna zǝlli*
*xǝpli. mxolǝpli. 'āna 'iya ᴴ**tǝmurá**ᴴ gǝbǝn mad'ǝrǝnna 'ǝllax.*

12 *kǝmra mā bodan? mǝrri xze! 'ǝn gǝbat dá'rat-wa 'ǝl-Čalla—. 'āhat go qaṣra*
*watwa tre ᴴ**qomót naxón**ᴴ? ktaxrat? kǝmra he. [A.H.: tre ṭabāqe]. he tre*
*ṭabāqe u-'arba ᴴ**ḥedarím**—ᴴ**ewa l-'ǝlǝl, 'árba-ži l-'ǝltǝx. ᴴ**naxón**ᴴ? kǝmra*
*ᴴ**naxón**ᴴ. mǝrri 'āhat lewat ᴴ**mat'imá**ᴴ l-axxa hūwat.*

13 *ᴴ**be'emét**ᴴ 'ǝn ba'yat, la', xamša'sar yomāsa xet 'āhat la pūwat 'axxa. 'ǝn la*
ba'yat-ži 'āwon dīdax u-'ǝd-górax b-qdalexun. kǝmra māṭo nablǝtti? mǝrri
xze! 'āhat 'āya šüqla ṭāṣi māṭo nablǝnnax. 'atta bāse gorax. 'āya gora wakil
*qāymaqam wewa. mǝdor wewa. 'ǝmma dukāne le zila. 'ǝmma ᴴ**tafkidím**ᴴ*
gṃalēwa. 'āya ki'e kullu dukāne.

5.10. The Art of Stealing While on a Moving Train

1 *walḷa mǝn tāma mǝn Ṣṭambul kud ᴴ**taḥanǝ́d**ᴴ gezaxwa, mesewa mǝndi*
gǝmzabniwa. 'áx-geb tán-geb bāmǝrwa: halu! halu! pšāqǝlwa u-pšāqǝlwa
*u-pšāqǝlwa. marawāse lu 'ǝltǝx 'ǝl-'ár'a. 'áya-le go ᴴ**rǝkevet**ᴴ.*

2 *xamši paṇqáṇoṭe xá-yoma mpulṭāle. ᴴ**bakašá**ᴴ. hā šqol ḥaqqox! ḥabibi*
xá-šawa 'āna mzabnǝn xamši paṇqáṇoṭe lá-kā'eli.¹⁰³ 'egā 'āhat byāli¹⁰⁴

---

¹⁰³ See § 3.3.c.
¹⁰⁴ Apparently a contracted form from the verb *yhw(l)*.

They also have another room. They are two rooms all together. I also 10
entered there. I went out. She says: "Why (are) you doing (that)?" I said:
"There must be something in it for me." I made a joke with her. She
says…: "Whatever you want." Really, I had come (and gone and come
and gone). I finished, I looked, (and) I went around behind their house.
From them on in that direction there is a stream of water. I said: "When
is the mudir coming?" She says: "Twelve o'clock."

… I said: "Listen! I want to take you away from here." She stopped. She 11
looked at me. She says: "How can you take me away from here?" I said:
"Listen!" I (am) a Jew. I am coming from prison. You sat (and) washed
clothes for me. You brought me clothes. I went (and) washed. I changed
(my clothes). In exchange I want to return this favor to you."

She says: "What shall I do?" I said: "Look! If you want to return 12
to Challa—. You were in a mansion that had two floors, correct? You
remember?" She says: "Yes." [A.H.: Two floors.] Yes, there were two floors
and four rooms upstairs, and four rooms downstairs. (I said to her:)
"Correct?" She said "Correct." I said: "You don't fit here."

Really, if you want (me to arrange the transfer, then) no, you won't 13
be here in another fifteen days. And if you don't want (me to arrange
it), then you and your husband are responsible. She says: "How will you
transfer me?" I said: "Look! You leave it to me how I transfer you. Now
your husband will come." That man was the deputy local governor. He
was the mudir. He has gone (for work) to a hundred (different) places.
He filled a hundred positions. He knows all the places.

5.10. The Art of Stealing While on A Moving Train

By God, from[105] there, from Istanbul, (at) every station which we went 1
to, they (sellers) would bring something and would sell. When all's said
and done, he (Abraham) would say: "Hallo! Hallo!" He would take and
take and take. The owners (of the merchandise) are below, on the train
platform.[106] He (Abraham) is (up above them) in the train.

One day (Abraham) took out (of his wallet) fifty liras. (He says:) 2
"Please. Here take your due!" (The seller says:) "My friend, I sell (during
an entire) week and (yet) I don't get fifty liras (by the end of the week).

---

[105] Error for 'to' as is apparent from the rest of the story.
[106] Lit., 'the ground'.

xamši paṇqáṇoṭe? pa da-ḥmól. mpartǝxǝnna. bāzǝlwa mǝn tam ḥāmǝlwa go—, let ᴴrǝkevet. rǝkevetᴴ zǝlla.

3 ᴴbe'emétᴴ *xá-qorūṣ mǝn tāma ḥel sele l-Ṣṭambul. xá-qorùṣ 'ā—, mād šqǝlle kulle baláš. mād šqǝlle kulle balåš. 'iya ḥāleni-l... Baṣālel lewe wida 'án-šu'āle. Baṣālel* ᴴbe'emétᴴ *[S.B.:* ᴴ*ze nikrá gezǝl*ᴴ.*] 'ā!* ᴴ*gezǝl*ᴴ *kǝsǝl dide čú-mǝndi lá-ewa.*

4 *xá-yoma mǝselu xa* ᴴmagášᴴ *kǝsyāsa, xa ṭḷāsi ṭḷāsi u-xamša kǝsyāsa mbušle. 'axnan wax go* ᴴrǝkevetᴴ *wax bizāla. walḷa sele le bǝṣrāxa. mǝrre: kǝsyāsa! hǝnna* ᴴmagášᴴ-*ile rešreš dide. kǝsyāsa lu gāwa. ksesa 'ǝbbǝd lira u-palge mbušalta. 'á-ži kemǝr: hal tre'!... 'Awṛāham, he... la, l-tāma, l-tāma go* ᴴrǝkevetᴴ *yom bizāla ta Ṣṭambul. kemǝr: hal tre'! 'á-ži hūle. hūle tre'.*

5 *'āni nāše xapči* ᴴmvugarímᴴ. *mxabdilu*ᴴ *ṛāba. kǝslu 'ítǝna* ᴴkavódᴴ *'aṣmí*ᴴ. *walḷa kemǝr ṭas dide: hal tre'! šqǝlle tre. báxte-ži kǝmra: gmaxlǝt ṭarefa l-yalunke? kem(ǝr): de 'āhat lá-mḥakyat! kemǝr hǝnna: 'āhat lá-mḥakyat! baxli baxli! 'á-ži mhomǝnna ko bmāxǝl l-yalunke.*

6 *walḷa hǝnna kǝsyāsǝd gyānan mǝtwile l-tāma. mar! kǝsyása-ži 'ǝltǝx reš* ᴴpas rǝkevetᴴ *ile mzabone. mzobǝnne ḥil—. xa 'ǝṣra daqiqe* ᴴrǝkevetᴴ *ḥamla báz-zodāna la bāza. walḥāṣǝl hǝnna-la ṣrǝxle. kemǝr:* ᴴdod, dodᴴ, *xāzax pārǝd kǝsyāsa. mpulṭāle xamši paṇqáṇoṭe, düqále. 'egā ṭḷāhá-'arba metre ṛomána-ile 'āya mǝn dide.* ᴴbakašáᴴ *šqol ḥaqqox!*

7 *manoxe le māra: ḥabibi! 'arba* ᴴmagašímᴴ *'āna mzabnǝnwa b-zoṛ māṭe l-xamši paṇqáṇoṭe. m-eka yāwǝnnox? kem(ǝr): pa da-ḥmól. 'atta mpartǝ-xǝnna 'ǝllox. sele l-é-'āl go* ᴴrǝkevetᴴ. *walḷa* ᴴrǝkevetᴴ *zǝlla.* ᴴrǝkevetᴴ *zǝlla. mašmi'! zǝllan xapči l-é-'āl. 'egā kǝsyāsa lu l-tāma.*

So now you'll give me fifty liras? (Abraham says:) "So just wait. I will get change for it." (Abraham) would go from there (inside the train in order to get change), (and the seller) would wait on (the train platform)—, there is no train! The train departed (and the seller is left without his goods and without his change)!

Really, (Abraham didn't spend) a piaster from there until he came to Istanbul. (Not) a piaster did he—, whatever he (Abraham) took, it (was) all free. Whatever he took, it (was) all free. This (was) our situation... Beşalel[107] hasn't done those (sorts of) things. Beşalel really [S.B.: This is called robbery.] Ah! Robbery is nothing for him (Abraham). 3

One day they brought (around) a tray of hens, about thirty, thirty-five cooked hens. We are in the train (and) we are moving. By God, (a seller) came (and) is shouting. He said: "Hens!" Um, the tray is right above him (the seller).[108] Hens are on it. A hen for a lira and half, cooked. He (Abraham) also says: "Give (me) only two (of them)!"... Abraham, yes... no, there, there in the train the day we (are) going to Istanbul. He (Abraham) says: "Give (me) only two!" He gave him (them). He gave him two. 4

They (the sellers) (are) somewhat older. They respect them greatly. They have self respect. By God, (Abraham) says to him (the seller): "Give (me) only two (hens)!" He (Abraham) took two. And his wife says: "Are you feeding the children non-kosher meat?" (Abraham) says: "Now don't you talk!" He says, um: "Don't you talk! They will eat (it), they will eat (it)!" Also she believed that he will feed the children (non-kosher meat). 5

By God, um, (the seller) placed our hens there (on the tray). Say! He is also selling the hens on the railway track below. He sold until—. About ten minutes more the train stands (and) won't depart. In short, um, (the seller) called out. He says: "Uncle, uncle, let's see the money for the hens." (Abraham) took out fifty liras (and) grabbed it (the tray). Now then he (Abraham) is three to four meters higher than him (the seller). (Abraham says to the seller:) "Please, take your due!" 6

Looking (at Abraham) he is saying: "My friend! Were I to sell four trays, it would hardly come to fifty liras. From where should I give you (change)? (Abraham) sa(ys): So wait. Now I will make change for you." (Abraham) came to the other side of the train (pretending to look for change). By God, (in the meantime) the train departed. The train departed. Listen! We went a little to that side. Now then the hens are (still) there (on the train). 7

---

[107] Abraham's brother.
[108] I.e., he is holding the tray up high over his head.

8 *báxte-ži la manoxe 'əbbe. la māra: mmaxlət ṭarefa l-yalunke? la, kemər:
'āhat lá-mḥakyat! ṣo'ərre 'əlləd dida. ṣo'ərre 'əlləd dida. walḥāṣəl kemər: lā,
lā, 'āhat lá-mḥakyat! lá-m'amṛat!*

9 *walla šqilāle xa ksesa. qəṭ'a kəsəl dida düqāle. zurre go ^{H}rəkevet^H kem(ər)
ksesa ksesa ta ^{H}ḥayalím! ḥayalím^H məšša-lu go ^{H}rəkevet^H. ta ^{H}ḥayalím^H.
xá-lira u-palge wən zwũna-lla, xá-lira u-palge ṭasexun.*

10 *walla sele. xa šqilāle… de mašmi'! sele. zəlle l-xeta. 'á-ži mzübnāle har
hādax. kemər: ṭamá? gzonax jigāre gzonax ^{H}dvarím 'aherím^H. 'ən snəqlan
tāma baxla(x) m-pār gyānan. baxlax mənnəd didu.*

11 *walla zəllan ^{H}taḥaná^H d-basra. xədda sele bəmzabone čāy. 'āni šö'á-^{H}nafa-
šòt^H-ilu. walḥāṣəl 'á-le, u-baxte u-xamša yalunke. walḥāṣəl walla kemər:
de-hál! mar—, 'atta mare čāy. xá-ta Moše u-xá-ta Nuwaḥ u-xá-ta Bārux
u-xá-ta Səmḥa u-xá-ta d-e-xét, xá-ta d-e-xét. šö'a čāye šqəlle. qatxe didu
zóre-lu. walḥāṣəl tūlu bəštá. [A.H.: 'əstakāne]. he. tūlu bəštá. walḥāṣəl čāy
xləšla. šəṭyālu. qátxe-ži pəšlu l-tāma. mare čáy-ži har le mzabone. ^{H}kos^H
b-'əṣra qorūše. ^{H}tov^H.*

12 *mṭele 'əlləd hənna kemər: bāba. hallu! qatxi u-pāri! 'atta ^{H}rəkevet^H jó-
žāle.^{109} ^{H}rəkevet^H ṣraxla ^{H}kvar^H. 'á-ži mpoləṭle xamši pəṇqáṇoṭe… har 'é-
xamši pəṇqáṇoṭe. čú-məndi xet let. har 'é-xamši pəṇqáṇoṭe. 'á-ži le māra:
bāba m-eka 'āna mesənnox xamši—, ^{H}'odef^H xamši pəṇqáṇoṭe yāwənnox?
xá-šawa ^{H}šalém^H 'āna mzabnən čāy xamši pəṇqáṇoṭe lá-kese b-'idi. ^{H}az^H
m-eka? 'ā kemər: pa da-ḥmól mpartəxənna.*

13 ^{H}rəkevet benatayim^H *zəlla. 'iya bron dide Moše, wət xázya-lle? [S.B.: mani?]
Moše bron dide. [S.B.: la ki'ənne…] 'Aḥiya ki'ənne… walḥāṣəl 'á-ži kemər
ṭas dide: … ka-'égā čāy šəṭyáleni. 'anna qatxe…hənna múd'əra-llu 'əlləd
didu. məskena. čāy dide ḥaqqa lá-hūlan. qatxəd díde-ži pəšlu ṭaseni…*

---

^{109} For expected *jujla?*

Also his (Abraham's) wife is looking at him (Abraham). She is saying: **8**
"Will you feed the children non-kosher meat?" "No," he says: "Don't you
talk!" He cursed her. He cursed her. In short, he says: "No, no, don't you
talk! Don't give orders!"

By God, he took a hen. He grabbed a piece of it. He went around on **9**
the train say(ing): "A hen, a hen for soldiers!" There are many soldiers on
the train. (He calls out:) "(Hens) for soldiers!" (He says to the soldiers:)
"I have bought it (the hen) for a lira and a half, for you (at the same price)
a lira and a half."

By God, he came. He took one (hen)... Now listen! He came (to **10**
one soldier). He went to another (soldier). He (Abraham) sold it just
like this. (Abraham) says: "Why (do I do this)? We buy cigarettes, we
buy other things. If we need to (buy things once we arrive) there, we
will use our own money. (But now) we will use their (other people's)
money.

By God, we went to the next station. Someone came selling tea. They **11**
are seven people. In short, he is (there), his wife, and five children. In
short, by God, he (Abraham) says: "Now give (me some tea). (The tea-)
seller—, now the tea-seller. One for Moses, and one for Noah, and one for
Baruch, and one for Simha, and one for that other, one for this other." He
(Abraham) took seven (glasses of) tea. Their glasses are small. In short,
they began drinking. [A.H.: *ǝstakāne* (small glasses for tea.)] Yes. They
began drinking. In short, the tea was finished. They drank it. And the
glasses remained there (with Abraham). The tea-seller is still selling (tea).
A glass for ten piasters. Fine.

(The tea-seller) came to, um, he says: "By God! Give them! My glasses **12**
and my money!" (Just) now the train moved. The (whistle of the) train
already called (out to go). He (Abraham) takes out fifty liras... the same
fifty liras (as before). There is nothing else (as simple as that). The same
fifty liras. He also (the tea-seller) is saying: "By God! From where should
I bring you (change for) fifty—, give you change (for) fifty liras? I sell
tea (for) a whole week (and) I (still) don't earn fifty liras. So from where
(should I get change)?" (Abraham) says: "Then wait that I make change
for it."

Meanwhile the train departed. This son of his, Moses, have you seen **13**
him? [S.B.: Whom?] Moses, his son. [S.B.: I don't know him...] Ahiya
knows him... In short, he (Moses) says to him (Abraham, his father):
... since then we drank the tea... those glasses... um, returned them
to them. Poor fellow. We didn't give (him) the price of his tea. And his
glasses remained with us...

14   *he, he, de-máśmi'! ṣofi 'Avṛáham-le, mā ṣofi? hənna ṣof(i)-Ibráhim-le.*
     walḥāṣəl qatxe pəšlu. 'á-ži kemər waḷḷa qatxe híwā-llu 'əlləd didu. 'áwon-ila.
     məskena. čáy-ži šətyālan qátxe-ži pəšlu. k(əmər:) 'āt wət 'əsya pešət sahāda
     rešeni?

15   *xa gopáḷta-la go 'ide. šqilāle l-Moše... Moše brone. kemər: 'āt wət 'əsya*
     pešət sahāda rešeni? mā? 'āna wən mbaqore mənnox? čáy-ži pšātaxla
     qatxe-ži peši ṭaseni. kemər: 'āhat lišānox yaríxa-le. Moše pappūka' ā xəlle
     máša-xuṭṭe. zöra 'ewa. 'ā kemər—, ᴴgilᴴ šö'á-tmanya šənne wewa. waḷḷa
     xəlle xuṭṭ(e).

16   *mərri: 'Awṛāham. kemər: mā? ke(mər:) 'āna xorexun 'affandi lewən.*
     yā'at.[110] *'āna baxlən m-pār didu. lá-kəxlən m-pāreni. 'āya kúd-dūka-u-*
     dūka lu masoye ᴴ'ugiyót, mā—, kol mine dvarímᴴ. 'āya har le bəšqāla.
     he, xamši paṇqáṇote-ži lewe mpúrtəxa 'əlle. xləšla. ᴴma'aséᴴ b-xamši
     paṇqáṇote ḥil mṭéleni l-Ṣtambul. 'iya ḥāleni hátxa-ewa.

5.11. Shabbo Decides to End
Business Dealings with His Kurdish Neighbors

1   *[A.H.: kma sā'e 'izāla ᶻwelaᶻ m-Čalla l-tāma?] ᴴba-'erexᴴ 'arba sā'e. 'arba*
     sā'e. nāša qalūla 'āzəl 'arba sā'e. 'ən la, garša xamša, xamša u-palge. [A.H.:
     Nerwa ṭḷāha sā'e.] Nerwa 'urxa bə́š-ᴴyašàraᴴ 'āwa. tāma gbe košiwa l-
     'əqər dunye. təhóme-awa tāma. walḥāṣəl waḷḷa zəlli xá-gā xet. mərri ṭas d-é
     qurdāya: wetun wide ᴴtováᴴ. bax 'axoni ṛāba yarxe l-axxa 'āwa. wetun
     ᴴmtupleᴴ 'əbba. 'áxnan-ži wax ᴴzireᴴ 'əllexon ᴴmtupleᴴ. 'anna ḥaqqəd
     gyānan.

---

[110] See § 4.1.6.d.

Yes, yes, now listen! He is Sufi Abraham,[111] what Sufi? Um, he is Sufi **14** Ibraham. In short, the glasses remained (with us). He (Abraham) even says that, by God, (the tea-seller has) given them the glasses. It's a sin. The poor fellow (the tea-seller). We both drank the tea and the glasses remained (with us). (Abraham says to his son Moses:): "You have come to be a witness against us?"

There is a shepherd's stick in his (Abraham's) hand. He attacked Moses **15** with it...[112] Moses, his son. (Abraham) says (to Moses): "Have you come to be a witness against us? What? Am I asking you (for anything)? We will both drink the tea and the glasses will remain with us." (Abraham) says (to Moses): "You are cheeky."[113] The poor Moses suffered[114] a lot of (blows with) sticks. He was young. He says—, he was aged seven (or) eight years. By God, he suffered blows.

I said: "Abraham." He says: "What?" (Abraham) sa(ys:) "I am not a **16** gentleman like you (people). You should know. I shall spend their money. I don't spend our money." He (Abraham), every single place they are bringing cookies, what—, all sorts of things. He is just taking. Yes, he (Abraham) did not make change for him for fifty liras. It's finished. (This was) the story of (how we lived on) fifty liras until we arrived in Istanbul. Our situation was like this.

5.11. SHABBO DECIDES TO END
BUSINESS DEALINGS WITH HIS KURDISH NEIGHBORS

[A.H.: How many hours walking was it from Čalla to there (Kara)?] **1** About four hours. Four hours. A quick person should go in four hours. If not, it drags out to five, five and half. [A.H.: Nerwa (was) three hours.] The path was more direct to Nerwa. One had to descend there to the bottom of the world. It was an abyss there. In short, by God, I went once again. I said to that Kurd: "You have done a favor. My brother's wife was here many months. You have taken care of her. We too have helped you, (have) taken care (of you). Those are our obligations towards you."

---

[111] See § 5.3.
[112] Lit., 'He took it to Moses.'
[113] Lit., 'You've got a long tongue.'
[114] Lit., 'he ate'.

2 *xá-gā xet d'ərre l-é-xabra. mərri:* ^{H}*b-sedər*^{H}*. ḥmol! mosox qam xāṣi nāpəl*
   'ən 'āna lá-m'almənnox, go ləbbi. seli l-besa. ^{H}*beznəs*^{H} *qətyāli m-qurdāyəd*
   ^{H}*'azór*^{H} *deni.* ^{H}*šúm-davàr*^{H}*. la* ^{H}*masá*^{H} *u-la* ^{H}*matán*^{H}*. har selu u-zəllu har*
   selu u-zəllu. lá-gleli ṭásu-ži má-'āna gəbən.

3 *xá-yoma pəšlu veza, ki'ət? kulla 'ənyān dídu-lu*[115] *go 'ideni. kesən l-besa.*
   mā kesən u-ménxəna? kullu ^{H}*roše*^{H} *hənna* ^{H}*švatím*^{H} *'ilu 'əsye kəsleni. xa*
   'əč'a 'əṣra muxtáre-lu-ži mənnu. lu 'əsye beseni. lu mulye-lle. xāṣu lu híwe-
   lle— [Y.H.: ^{Z}*besoxun*^{Z} *b-Čalla?*] *he, l-Čalla. xāṣu lu hiwe-lle l-gūda qam*
   qalunke. 'āt (k)taxrəttu qalunke? [A.H.: *he, he.*] *m-axxa byātūwa qalunka*
   mayráxwāle l-tāma [Y.H.: *'amoyi Šəlo 'ilāha mānəxle gewədwāle.*] ^{H}*'az*
   zehu.^{H} *walḥāṣəl lu bəgrāša. kullu xāṣu le l-gūda.*

4 *'āna 'ürri b-tar'a. walla qəmlu kəmri: 'éka-wətwa ḥel 'atta? 'an majbili,*
   majbili. mərri: xa hənna xa ^{H}*pakíd*^{H} *'əd-*^{H}*'esəkím*^{H} *mābaynəd dide. gəbən*
   'āzən xalṣənnu. mərri ta yəmmi: méselu təttun l-axxa. walla ṣópa-ži-la
   qāmu. qalunku mən garšila mayrəxilu kud duksəd gəbe. 'āna zəlli. mesyattu
   'ixāla u-čāy u-kullu. čú-məndi lá-hāwe ^{H}*hasér*^{H} *'əlləd didu.*

5 *u-'āna zəlli. mərru xá-məndi. mərri: 'atta bāse u-'átta-ži bamrənnu 'āna*
   'ətli šūla. 'atta bāzən u-bāsən. walla zəlli. zəlli 'āna. gyāni muḍi'āli 'əlləd
   didu ^{H}*ba-'érex*^{H}*. 'āni har pəšlu. pəšlu ko 'āna dá'rən-wa. 'āna lá-d'ərri.*
   ^{H}*s(v)ivót*^{H} *sā'a 'əṣra hatxa mərri: bāzən besa. 'atta kullu lu zile. čú-xa lewe.*
   lewe piša.

---

[115] For expected -*le*, apparently by attraction to the preceding *didu*.

Once again he returned to that matter.[116] I said: "Okay. (He said:) **2**
"Wait! I'm responsible for your death, in my heart, if I don't inform you
(that I am planning on leaving Challa)."[117] I came home. I cut off business
with the Kurds of our area. Nothing. No (business) negotiations (with
them at all). (The Kurds) still came and went, still came and went. I didn't
reveal to them what I intend (to do).

One day they became like this, you know? All their (business) affairs **3**
are in our hands. I come home. I come and I see what? All the heads,
um, of the tribes have come to us. About nine, ten mukhtars are also
with them. They have come to our house. They have filled it. (They sat
there with) their backs to the wall—[118] [Y.H.: Your house in Challa?]
Yes, in Challa. They (sat there) with their backs up against the wall in
front of the narghiles. Do you remember the narghiles? [A.H.: Yes, yes.]
One would sit here (and) would extend the narghile (all the way) over
there. [Y.H.: My paternal uncle Shilo, may God rest his soul, used to do
it.] So that's it. In short, they are smoking. All of them, their back is to the
wall.

I entered through the door. By God, they got up (and) say: "Where **4**
were you until now?" I answered them, I answered them. I said: "A
certain, um, an official, with whom (there is) some business." I want to
go get rid of them. I said to my mother: "Bring tobacco here for them.
By God, the stove is in front of them. Let them smoke their narghiles
(and) lengthen them (to) whatever place they want." I went. (I said to my
mother:) "You should bring them food and tea and everything. Nothing
should be lacking to them."

And I went (away). They said something. I said (to myself): "Now they **5**
will come and now I will also say to them: 'I have work (to do). Now I
will go and come (back).'" By God, I left. I left. (I thought that) I had just
about rid myself of them. (But) they still remained. They remained since
I would return back, (but) I didn't return. Around ten o'clock I said like
this: "I will go home. Now all of them have gone. There is no one. No one
remains."

---

[116] I.e., a story (§ 5.2) Shabbo had told earlier about how an agha expropriated his
property.
[117] Lit., 'Your death will fall on my back, if I don't inform you.'
[118] Lit., 'They have given their back to it (the wall).'

6 kesən besa u-menxən kullu. kútxa-le dūkəd gyane. xə́dda-ži lewe zila.
[Y.H.: [H]'avál[H] zəllox, ma 'üdlox [Z]damməd[Z] zəllox?] zəlli xdərri. [Y.H.:
'ah! [H]stam[H] xdərrox.] he, he. lá-gbən 'odən [H]'esəkím[H] mənnu. la pəšta
'əlli [H]nəm'ás[H]. kāsi la mre'ta mənnu. waḷḷa késəna. har xzeli. qəmle xədda
tar'a ḥləqle. tar'a ḥləqle. kəmri: tū mābayneni! tūli. kemər: má-yla? mə́-
[H]səba[H]-la [H]beznes[H] letun bāda mənneni? lá-gzonetun, lá-gmzabnetun, lá-
gzaqretun, lá-kəmḥaketun, lá-kxadretun. mə́-[H]səba[H]-ila? mə́-'it?

7 xa kalba bər kalba xa məndi le 'wida xa məndi le mira? xa dūka har
kāsox 'ila mre'ta, hudə́. mərri: 'amrə́nnexun. kəmri: mā? mərri: flāna māsa
ki'étūla? kəmri: he. mərri: 'ako mən tāma 'āya māṣe[119] [H]šālət[H], mạ̄leni l-
axxa 'āxəlle. 'āna go Tűrkiya. 'āya go 'Eraq, 'iya xa'. 'āna hudāyəd 'āġa
d-Čalla. 'ə́-ži bāb dide 'āna ktaxrən. 'əsri naqle bābi le mira [H]haré[H] beseni
xá-gā l-Kāra 'ewa. bābi le də́rya-lle ('ax)xa kutkākəd gyāne.

8 bābəd dide Rāšo [Z]gəmríwāle[Z]. tāma le piša 'atta 'āġa. 'āya 'āxəl mạ̄li. 'āna
lá-gyatwən l-axxa qurdāye. lele-'ile qurwəd sā'a 'əṣra 'əṣra u-palge kəmri:
'āya sāyəlla yəmmeni u-bas. u-qəmlu. bas 'iya xabra. 'āya sāyəlla yəmmeni
u-bas. qəmlu zəllu kəmri: [H]maspík[H] šme'lan.

9 waḷḷa qəmlu u-zəllu u-tūlu go 'urxəd dide ṭḷāha nāše b-xá-təffaq. xá-təffaq-
la. xá-yoma kese Maḥammat Ṭāhər 'āġa 'əšta xulāme kutxa xa 'anglízi-
la l-kāpəd dide, m-anna kərye. [Y.H.: he, he.] he. u-'āya b-gyáne-ži xa
'anglízi-la reš kutkākəd[120] dide. rakáwa-le l-xa kawənta xazina 'anglízi-
la xese [Y.H.: [H]karabín, lo? rové karabín[H]; A.H.: [H]lo, ze mark for[H]... təffaq
'anglizi.] he, [H]ze[H] təffaq 'anglizi. [A.H.: 'it xamša fišake]. la 'əṣra, 'əṣra
šaqli. 'əṣra. u-xá-ži go [H]bet bli'ə́[H] 'anna xade'sar.[A.H.: [A]'aywa, 'aywa [A].]
kem(ər): walḥāṣəl...

---

[119] See § 4.4.28.15 n. 210.
[120] Error for kutkāpəd, perhaps under the influence of kutkākəd in § 5.11.7.

I come home and look at all of them. Each one is (in) his own place. **6**
No one has gone. [Y.H.: But you left. What did you do when you left?] I
left (and) I walked about. [Y.H.: Ah! You simply walked about.] Yes, yes.
I don't want to do business with them. I've had it.[121] My stomach hurts
from them. By God, I come. I still see (them). One got up (and) locked the
door. He locked the door. They say: "Sit among us." I sat. He says: "What
is it? What is the reason you all aren't doing business with us? You don't
buy, you don't sell, you don't weave, you don't talk, you don't go around.
What is the reason? What is there?"

"Has a son of a bitch done something or said something? Somehow **7**
your stomach still hurts, Jew." I said: "Let me tell you." They say: "What?"
I said: "Do you know such and such a village?" They say: "Yes." I said:
"When from there he is able to control (us), he filches our posessions
here. I (am) in Turkey. He (is) in Iraq, this (is point) one. I (am) a Jew
of the Agha of Čalla. I also remember his father. My father has told me
(about him) twenty times since our house was once in Kara. My father
has borne a grudge against him here.[122]

They called his father Rasho. He has now become the Agha there. He **8**
filches my possessions. I'm not staying here (anymore), Kurds." It is night,
close to ten o'clock, ten-thirty (and then) they say: "He should fuck our
mother and (we've had) enough!" And they got up. Just this statement.
"He he should fuck our mother and (we've had) enough!" (The Kurds)
up (and) went saying: "We heard enough (and now we're going to take
action on your behalf)."

By God, they up and went and three people with one rifle sat in his **9**
(Rasho's)[123] path (waiting to ambush him). There is one rifle. One day
Mahammat Taher Agha[124] comes (with) six servants (and) each one (has)
an English (rifle) on his shoulder, of those short ones (rifles). [Y.H.: Yes,
yes.] Yes, and as for himself, there is also an English (rifle) on his shoulder.
(Mahammat Taher Agha) is a rider on a mule, (with) an English cashbox
underneath him. [Y.H.: A carabine, no? A carabine rifle.; A.H. No, it's a
'Mark Four' (rifle)... an English rifle.] Yes, it's an English rifle... [A.H.:
It has five bullets.] No, they (those rifles) take ten (bullets). Ten. And
another one in the chamber (makes that) eleven. [A.H.: Yes, yes.] He
sa(ys:) In short...

---

[121] Lit., 'It has become for me despicable.'

[122] Lit., 'My father has placed him here, all his teeth.'

[123] The one who has caused problems for Shabbo.

[124] He is the son of Rashid, who is mentioned in the previous paragraph. See also § 5.2.

5.12. The Death Threats over Leaving Challa for Israel

1   *walḥáṣəl 'atta 'ənyān Čalla. 'ənyān Čalla. zəlli. əṢṭambul séli-wa. ^Haz^H 'iya
^Htoxnít^H 'údwālu. sele xa məšəlmāna mirənne. ki'ewa lu wide tagbir. 'ətlu
^Hḥašáš^H 'axtun mən d-axxa bāzetun. ^Haz^H bāse reš Zāwa qemi 'əllexun.
kullu 'anna 'uṛwe (q)qaṭlilu yalunke nablilu u-bāzi. 'egā xzi! 'iya—. bale
báḥse-ži lá-odən. mərri mənne baḥs šəmme lá-od(ən). ki'ewa pqaṭlili.*

2   *'āna zəlli 'é-naqləd mənnəd hənna seli mən Moṣəl, ^Hemét^H hənna zəlli kəsəl
xa məšəlmāna. kātəb wewá-(hə)nna 'ewa. mərri: xa hənna 'iya mā kəmrila
^Hbakašá^H ksūli! ksūle ṭāsi xa 'arzūḥal. nobəlli hūli l-wāli b-'idi. ksūli l-tāma
^Hmá-(h)a-toxnìt^H lu wide hənne kurdināye ṭaseni. kemər palṭa(x) m-tāma
pqaṭlilan 'áx-geb tán-geb. 'ürreni ṭas dide.*

3   *kemər: 'āhat hudáya-wət? mərri: ^Hken^H wāli. kemər: ṭamá zad'əwāne
wetun 'axtun? wa'dūsa kemər 'əlli: 'ən bāre xá-məndi, 'iya 'əpra, kəmər:
dārənne l-'ərbāla maxəlta. mərri: pāša, mā? ko drelox 'ərbāla maxəlta
ya'ni, 'axnan 'ən qṭilaxle ya'ni mā? mā ^Hmurvəḥlan^H mən d-iya? 'āna
gəbən lá-'asya b-rešan čú-məndi, lá-hāwe ^Hkašé^H l-ḥukum. ^Htov^H. reš d-iya
'arzuḥál—, u-mšádərre ta mədor 'āhat 'əbbəd ^Hdowar^H dexun ko yoməd
'āna palṭən tāma yā'eli[125] ^Hmištará^H. yā'eli mḥáfəza m-'Eráq. pləṭlan
m-tāma ^Hmitaḥat la-šmirá^H.*

5.13. The Seizure of Shabbo's Brother
and Attempted Forced Conversion

1   *walḷa 'iya 'axoni Mədo mpəlle b-'idəd didu. qemi doqile. (b-)xurṭūsa qemi
məšəlmile. wədlu qurdá. 'axnan 'é-yoma zəllan. 'axoni 'Awṛāham šuqwāle
reš ^Hḥovót^H. zəllan mṭelan Txūma. zəllan b-urxa b-urxa. mərwāli: 'āsetun
ḥamletun 'əlləd flāná-dūka.*

---

¹²⁵ See §3.3.c.

5.12. The Death Threats over Leaving Challa for Israel

In short, now the matter of Čalla. The matter of Čalla. I left. I came back to **1**
Istanbul. Then (the Kurds) made this plan. A certain Muslim came (and)
told me. He knew they have conspired. (He said:) "There is a fear you
will leave here. So they (the Kurds) will go to the Zab (River) to rise up
against you. They should kill all of the grown-ups, lead away the children,
and leave. So then look! This—. (He said) also however that I shouldn't
make mention of him. I said I wouldn't mention his name. He knew they
will kill me.

I went at that time when I came from, um, from Mosul, truly, um, I **2**
went to a certain Muslim. He was a clerk, he was an, um. I said: "Write
for me a, um, what do they call it?—a request!" He wrote out a petition
for me. I took it away (and) gave it by hand to the Vali. I wrote there what
the plan (was that) they have made, um, the Kurds, for us. (The Vali) says
we should leave there (since the Kurds) will kill us when all's said and
done. We entered into his (presence).

He says: "You are a Jew?" I said: "Yes, Vali." He says: "Why are you **3**
cowards?" He makes me a promise: "If something happens, this soil," he
says: "I will put it through a coarse sieve (and) a fine sieve (looking for
the killer[s])." I said: "Pasha, (so) what? That you put (all the soil through)
a coarse sieve (and) a fine sieve, that is to say, as for us, if (a Kurd has)
killed us, that is to say, (so) what? What have we benefited from this? I
want that nothing should happen to us, that it should not be difficult for
the government (to protect us). Fine. Concerning this petition—, and
you send it to the mudir in your post office that on the day I leave there,
he should give me a police (escort). He should give me protection from
Iraq." We left there under guard.

5.13. The Seizure of Shabbo's Brother
and Attempted Forced Conversion

By God, this brother of mine, Mido, fell into their hands. They up (and) **1**
seize him. (By) force they up (and) convert him to Islam. They made him
a Kurd. We went that day. My brother Abraham had left behind debts.
We went (and) we reached Tekhuma. We went along the way. I had said:
"You should come (and) wait at such and such a place."

2 ʾətli ^Hhaském^H mənnəd quṇṣulya ^Hyisraʾelí(t)^H go hənna Ṣṭambul. gəbe
yāwən ^Hmivrák^H b-(ʾ)eni sāʿa ʾāna pləṭli mən Čalla u-kma ^Hnafašót^H-
ilu mənni. ʾāna zəlli ʾalləd ^Hdowar^H. ʾāni zəllu. zəllan b-é-duksəd mə́rwāli
ṭāsu. ʾāni jandərme. ṭḷāha jandərme mənnan wewa. ḥmile. šöʾa kərāčíye-ži
dawāre mənnan. lu ḥmile tam manox(e). ʾaxoni lewe l-tam.

3 kəmrən ta yəmmi: ké-le Mədo? kəmra: lá-kiʾan.¹²⁶ lá-čiʾan. ^Htov^H. ʾé-lele
zəllan Txūma. mən tāma yom basra muṭʿənnan zəllan go Zāraž, go Zāraž.
xa māsa xet ʾətwa ʾurxəd xa sáʿa rəqqa mən dūkəd lele ʾaxwa, l-dūkəd
Txūma.

4 tāma ʾətwa télafon. ^Htulfənni^H ta ʾAnwar, he. ʾAnwar ^Zgəmrənnox^Z: …
mərri: ʾaxoni wetun dúqe-lle. kma šənne, kma ʾəmmāhe šənne ʾaxnan
^Hʿabadím^H dexun l-axxa qurdā? wetun dúqe l-ʾaxoni. wən gəlya ʾəlle. gleli.
hūli ^Hsimán^H ta ʾAwṛāham. mərri: gezəlwa l-flāná-besa. si l-tāma! balkit
xa ^Hsimán^H pxāzət.

5 waḷḷa zəlle l-tāma. ^Hsimán^H xzele: kusise u-gopaḷte təlye-wa b-xá-səksa
l-tāma. mərre ta ^Hbaʿalát bayit^H. gūre zə́lwālu xazdiwa ^Htiras^H. baxta
pə́šwāla l-besa. kəmra: lewan xə́zya-lle byamyannox. byamyatti ʾəlle? waḷḷa
séle-wa mirənnu.

6 mərri: ʾatta nābəl xa hənna ^Hšotér^H mən gyānox ʾāzət əl-tám. xāzax má-
ylu wíde-lle. ʾən le qṭila, ^Hgufát^H dide. ʾənʾ ile ^Hḥay^H, (m)paḷtile. waḷḷa
^Hšotér^H nobəlle u-zəlle. zəlle l-tāma. har gopaḷta hənna lu l-tam. ksise. xzi!
ʾən ʾilāha xədda moḍiʿāle ʾəlle, lá-mṣe ʾāwəd čú-məndi. ʾāni lewu wide ḥazur
maḍiʿilu.¹²⁷ kəmri: la, ʾaxnan lewax xə́zye-lle u-maʾrqile nablile l-ʿEraq.
hádax-ži lá-mṣaxwa ʾodaxwa čú-məndi əlləd dide.

7 waḷḷa šodərri ʾAwṛāham ʾalləd didu. zəlle. kemər ta baxta, kemər: ʾéka-
le gora? kəmra: ʾəl-flána dūka lu bəxzāda. ke(mər): mšādər basre ʾāse!

---

¹²⁶ k is realized as [kʸ].
¹²⁷ For expected maḍiʿile.

I have an agreement with the Israel consulate in, um, Istanbul. I need 2
to send a telegram (informing them) as to which hour I left Čalla and
how many people are with me. I went to the post office. They went (with
us, i.e., the police protection sent by the Vali to protect them from the
Kurds). We went to that place which I had mentioned to them. They
(are) policemen. Three policemen were with us. (They have) stopped.
Seven muleteers (with) their mules (were) with us. They have stopped
there (and are) looking around. My brother isn't there.

I say to my mother: "Where is Mido?" She says: "I don't know. I don't 3
know." Fine. That night we went (to) Tekhuma. From there, the next day
we loaded (the animals and) went into Zaraj, in Zaraj. There was another
village, a journey of one hour's distance from the place we were during
the night, to the place Tekhuma.

There was a telephone there. I phoned Anwar,[128] yes. "Anwar," I say to 4
you: . . . " I said: "You have seized my brother. How many years, how many
hundreds of years (have) we (been) your servants here, Kurd? You have
seized my brother. I have found it out. I found it out. I gave Abraham
a sign." I said: "(Mido) used to go to such and such a house. Go there!
Perhaps you will see a sign (of him)."

By God, he went there. He saw a sign: his hat and his shepherd's stick 5
had been hung on a peg. He spoke[129] to the mistress of the house. The
men had gone (and) were harvesting the corn. The wife had remained at
home. She says: "I haven't seen him, I will swear to you." (Abraham says
to her:) "You will swear to me concerning him? By God, they said to me
that he came back."

I said (to Abraham): "Now take a policeman (there) with you. You 6
should go there. Let's see what they have done to him. If he has been
killed, (let's see) his corpse. If he is alive, let them bring him out." By
God, he led the policeman and he went. He went there. The shepherd's
stick, um, still is there. (And) his hat. Look! If God has made someone go
missing, it is not possible to do anything. (But) they have not estimated
(that) they would notice that he was missing. They say: "No, we haven't
seen him" (but) they should smuggle him out (and) take him away
to Iraq. In that case we wouldn't have been able to do anything for
him.

I sent Abraham to them. He went. He says to his wife, he says: "Where 7
is (your) husband?" She says: "At such and such a place they are harvest-

---

[128] He was in charge of the post office See § 5.13.15.
[129] Lit., 'he said'.

(m)šodərra basre. gor dida sele. kemər: ʾiya nāša mare d-iya gopáḷta-u ksísa ʾāna gbənne.

8 kemər: ʾaffandi, byāmaxlox. ʾaxnan lewax xəzye ʾəlle. ᴴba-ʿérex ʾuláyᴴ qam xá-yarxa séwāle. ʾā u-broneni ᴴḥaverímᴴ wewa. lewət xázya-lle? kemər: la. kemər: si! si-ḍból! byāmət. kemər: he, byāmən. ʾəṣra naqle.

9 walḥāṣəl məsele. (m)šodərre—, gyāne ḍbilāle. türkāye hādax godi. qamāye byāme de-bázi ḍabli xarāye. sele kemər: de-ymí! b-iya qurʾān! ké-le yāla? kemər: byāmənnox b-iya qurʾān lewax xázya-lle. lu dərye-lle go gova. šöʾá-govāne. ʾətwa xa basər xa tarʾa lu ḥliqe-llu l-reš dide ta-lá-ʾārəqla. ᴴtovᴴ. waḷḷa ke(mər).

10 ymele ʾəbbəd qurʾān ko lewe xázya-lle. kemər: baxta ʾətlox? kemər: he. kemər: de-ymí b-ṭaláqox-ži. ymele ṭaláqe-ži, he! kemər: ʾatta lewət xázya-lle ᴴnaxónᴴ? la, lewən xázya-lle ʾaffandi. ʾən wali(!) xázya-lle bamrənwālox.

11 xa ṭaṛka šqəlle ʾəlləd dide. ṭaṛke mə́šša-lu. mese ṣiwe ta səswa. gázra-wa l-tāma. xa ṭaṛka šqəlle ʾəlle. kemər: ᴬbə-smi-llāhi raḥmán u-raḥímᴬ. traq-u traq-u traq! tāma ᶻgəmrənnoxᶻ, türkāye ᴴmuthəllu, ᴴ hafs(aka) ᴴ, hənna ᴴhafsakáᴴ let. hādax ʾüdlu[130] ʾəlləd dide ḥil (m)pəlle. (m)pəlle. har le bəṣrā-xa, le bimāra: baxxatəd ʾilāha! ʾe türkáya-ži le māra ta ʾAwṛāham, má-yle māra? ʾile bəṭlāba baxxatəd ʾilāha.

12 kemər: ʾilāha? la ʾatta ymele ʾəbbəd dide b-dugle? ʾegā má́-gəbe mən ʾilāha? ʾatta le bəṭlāba baxxatəd ʾilāha. txərre ʾəlləd ʾilāha, ᴴnaxónᴴ? kenᴴ. le yəmya ʾəbbe b-dugle. ʾatta ᴴkol ʿodᴴ ʾilāha lá-mšādər... kemər: ᴴkol ʿodᴴ ʾilāha lá-mšādər xa malʾax ʾāmər: ᴴšáḥrərūleᴴ!... ᴴkol ʿodᴴ ʾilāha lá-āmər: (m)šādər xá-malʾax ᴴmáfsikᴴ—. ʾā har le māra baxxatəd ʾilāha. ʾən ʾilāha bāʾe ᴴmšaharərənneᴴ, bəš xa lá-māxənne. ʾilāha məlyone malʾāxe ʾətle.

---

[130] For expected ʾüdle.

ing." (Abraham) sa(ys): "Send (someone) after him that he should come!"
She sent (someone) after her husband. He came. (Abraham) says: "I want
this person, the owner of this shepherd's stick and hat."

(The husband) says: "Effendi, we will swear to you. We have not seen 8
him. Perhaps about a month ago he had come. He and our son were
friends." (Abraham says:) "You haven't seen him?" (The husband) says:
"No." (Abraham) says: "Go! Go have a ritual bath (and then) you will
swear!" He says: "Yes, I shall swear. Ten times."

In short, he brought him. He sent—, he had a ritual bath. Like this the 9
Turks do (it). At first they will swear, later they will go to have a ritual
bath.[131] He came, (Abraham) says: "Now swear! On this Quran! Where
is the child?" He says: "I shall swear to you on this Quran we haven't seen
him." (But) they have (actually) put him in a stall. There were seven stalls.
There was one after the other. They have locked the door on him lest he
flee. Fine. By God, he sa(ys).

He swore on the Quran that he hasn't seen him. (Abraham) says: "You 10
have a wife?" He says: "Yes." (Abraham) says: "Now also swear on your
divorce!" He swore also (on) the divorce, yes! (Abraham) says: "Now you
haven't seen him, correct?" (He says:) "No, I haven't seen him, Effendi. If
I had seen him, I would have told you."

(Abraham) took a stick to him. There are many sticks. They bring wood 11
for winter. There was a pile of chopped wood there. He took a stick to
him. He says: "In the name of the Merciful and Just God." Thwack and
thwack and thwack! There, I tell you, (once) the Turks began (to hit),
stoppi(ng)—, um, there is no stopping. He did to him like this until he fell
down. He fell down. He is still screaming, he is saying: "For the mercy of
God!" That Turk is saying to Abraham, what is he saying? He is requesting
the mercy of God.

He says: God? Didn't he swear now by him falsely? So now what does 12
he want from God? Now he is requesting the mercy of God. (Now) he
remembered God, correct? Yes. He has sworn by him falsely. Now as long
as God does not send..." (Abraham) says: "As long as God does not send
an angel (that) says: 'Free him!'... As long as God does not say: 'Send an
angel (that) he should stop—,' he is still saying: 'for the mercy of God!'
But if God wants me to free him, I won't beat him a single (blow) more.
God has millions of angels."

---

[131] Shabbo has reversed the order: he should have a ritual bath before taking an oath
as in the preceding paragraph.

13 *(m)šādər xá-maḷ'ax—, ^H'avál mafsík^H—, hənna ^Htafsík^H, 'āna pšaqlənne*
^Hmakél^H didi mándənne l-tāma bəš xet ^Hrašút^H lətli. ^Hkol ʿod šə^H-'iláha lá-
'āmər, (m)šādər čú-xa ko 'āna ^Hmáfsəkən^H, 'āna har kkarxən 'əbbe. hādax
'üdle 'əlləd dide. səqle 'egā reš kāse 'əbbəd potine. potine didu 'ətlu bəzmāre
hatxa l-'əqru ta-háyya lá-māxe. hādax 'üdle 'əlle. dəmma (m-)pəmme u-
šərme se(le).

14 *xarāye ṣrəxle: baxxatəd 'ilāha, ta xāṭər 'ilāha! sa ploṭ! (g)maqṭələnnox. 'āhət*
lá-ki'ət mā sela b-reši. 'ən gbəttan ta dineni, 'ilāha, sa ploṭ mxáləsli! 'ən la,
sa-, si qloʿ! si mən d-axxa! kemər: ḥil 'atta la xzéwālox. 'atta ymelox b-
dugle 'əbbəd ṭalāqəd báxtox-ži. 'əbbəd qúrʿān-ži. pa 'egā 'eka wewa 'iya?
^H'az^H 'ətlan m-de 'áškara.

15 *sele 'Awṛāham télafon-ži. ^Hyom šalém^H reš télafon-le. waḷḷa kemər: waḷḷa*
xzeli ḥál-u-masale hátxa-la. 'āna dbəšli 'əbbəd 'Anwar. 'Anwar ^Hmnahél
dówar^H-ile. mərri: qurdāye (m)šádrūle yāla zöra! lā, kemər: le piša qurdá.
yoməd ^Kḥašr u-našr^K ki'ət, yoməd din 'āya bāzəl pšāke 'əlleni. bāmər 'āna
gbənwa pešənwa qurdá. balé hā qurdāye lá-qbəllu. 'egā din dide nāpəl
rešeni. 'axnan (p)pešax ^Hḥayavím^H. Maḥámmad-^H(m)mʿānəšlan ^H!¹³²

16 *'iya qurdá—, 'āna bāzən dūka ṛapsa. 'āna bāzən dūka ṛapsa. 'axtun*
(p)pešetun go Čalla. 'āna 'axoni har pšaqlənne. lá-'amretu: lewən mira.
mā mərre ṭāsi? kemər: ^Kčāwən. čāwən^K yaʿni 'eni. ^Kčāwən^K. kemər: 'ən 'āhət
mṣelox 'axonox šqəllox mənneni, 'axnan 'iya ^Hazór^H kulleni baxtaseni
byāxlu ṭāsox!

17 *'āna mṭeli l-Jólamerg hənna ta Hakkāri. ^Hmogəšli bakašá la-bét məšpát^H.*
'ətwāli ^Hḥaverím^H türkāye l-tam. šme(')lu selu. má-yla breta? mərri: hátxa-
la. kəmri ṭāsi: ḥmol! 'axnan 'atta bāzax ^Hbadqax ḥok. 'az ha-ḥók^H mā
^Zgemər^{Z A}qāḍi^A? 'ən 'ətlox ^Hzaxút^H (m)ḥākət 'əbbəd dide, u-lətlox ^Hzaxút^H
'atta bamrənnox. 'ən ^Hpaḥót^H-ile m-tre'sar, hés-ile xe 'idox 'ətlox ^Hzaxút ^H.
'ən la, ^Hʿvərre^H tre'sar, ^H'aṣma'í^H-le. lətlox ^Hzaxút ^H (m)ḥākət 'əbbəd dide.

---

¹³² Shabbo actually says [ma'ḥamman ʿa:n'ɪʃlan].

"Should (God) send an angel—, but stopping—, (saying) um, 'Stop!' 13 (then) I will take it, my stick, (and) I will throw it down there (because then) I do not have any more permission (to beat him). (But) as long as God does not say, (i.e.,) send anybody (saying) that I should stop, then I shall keep on bashing him." He did like this to him. He trod on his stomach with boots. Their boots have nails like this at their bottom in order not to strike quickly. He did to him like this. Blood ca(me out from) his mouth and his ass.

Finally he screamed: "For the mercy of God, for the sake of God! Come 14 on out! You are having me killed. You don't know what has happened to me. If you love our religion, God, come on out! Save me! If not, come—, go to hell!" (He said to Abraham, who was beating him): "Go away from here!" (Abraham) says: "Until now you hadn't seen him. Now you also swore falsely on (the) divorce of your wife. On the Quran too. So then where was he? So we have (this affair) now in the open."

And Abraham came (to) the telephone. He is on the telephone a whole 15 day. By God, he says: "By God, I saw (that) the upshot is like this." I stuck to Anwar. Anwar is the head of the post office. I said: "Kurds! Send the young child!" "No," he says, "he has become a Kurd. ḥašr u-našr, you know, (on) the Day of Judgment, he will go complain against us. He will say: 'I wanted to remain a Kurd but then the Kurds didn't agree.' So then his religion will be our responsibility. We shall become guilty. Muhammad will punish us."

This Kurd—, I am going to a large place. I am going to a large place. 16 "You will remain in Challa. I will yet take my brother. Don't say: 'I haven't said.' What did he say to me? He says: 'čawən.' čawən, that is to say 'my eye.' čawən. (Anwar) says: "If you are able to take your brother from us, we, all of us (in) this area, we will give you our wives!"

I reached Jolamerk, um, Hakkari. I handed in a request to the court. 17 I had Turkish friends there. They heard (and) came. (They said:) "What has happened?" I said: "It's like this." They say to me: "Wait! We will go now (and) check the law." So regarding the law, what does the judge say?: "If you have the right to speak with him, (fine). And if you don't have the right, now I will tell you. If he is less than twelve, he is still under your authority (and) you have the right. If not (and) he has passed twelve, he is independent. (Then) you don't have the right to speak with him. He has the right (to make up his own mind)."

GLOSSARY

The following contains all Aramaic lexemes found in the recordings of Shabbo 'Amrani, a few additional words contributed by Ahiya Hashiloni (when they differ from the JZakho koine he speaks and it appears that they do reflect Challa) as well as some words culled from Ahiya's father, Rabbi Jacob Hashiloni, when reciting the Passover *haggada* (from the printed JAmid version and only when he deviates from what is written there). Words found only in the oral recitation of the *haggada* often reflect an older literary register and are marked in the glossary as *haggada*. Verbs are listed by root as abstracted from the form of the Subjunctive. The entries are listed according to the alphabetical order ʾ ʿ *a/ā b ḅ č č̣ d ḍ e ə f g ġ h ḥ i j k l ḷ m ṃ n o/ö p p̣ q r ṛ s ṣ š t ṭ u/ū ü/ṻ v w x y z ẓ ž*. The reconstructed singular of words attested only in the plural are marked by an asterisk. When the reconstruction of the singular form is difficult because of conflicting evidence from other Neo-Aramaic dialects, the word is listed in the plural. The gender of nouns is marked only when it is explicit in the text in which it occurs.

Square brackets contain earlier Aramaic evidence of the lexemes and occasional etymological information. Sometimes reference is made to a particular Aramaic dialect or dialects, other times to a phase of the Aramaic language (according to Fitzmyer's 1979 classification), and often the siglum ClAram (Classical Aramaic) has been used to indicate that the lexeme is found in at least two of the three vocalized Aramaic corpora (Biblical Aramaic, Targums Onqelos and Jonathan, and Syriac). Cross-references to relevant paragraphs in the grammar are sometimes noted.

Borrowings from other languages with which Jewish Challa was in contact in Kurdistan are also noted. The loans that penetrated the dialect prior to Shabbo's arrival in Israel come from either Kurdish (Kermanji), Turkish, or Arabic, languages which Shabbo spoke fluently. The ultimate origin of many of the loanwords is undoubtedly Arabic, but it is often difficult to tell whether a given loanword entered Jewish Challa through Kurdish, Turkish, or Arabic, or more than one of the languages. Older Hebrew borrowings from before Shabbo came into contact with Modern Hebrew are marked with the siglum H, and borrowings from Modern Hebrew are marked by ModH. The latter are included when Shabbo has inflected them as Aramaic, e.g., the verb עזר 'help' ('zərru 'they helped')

or the noun *dapé* 'pages'.[1] At times one cannot be certain if the lexeme
is a reflex of the older Aramaic lexeme or a borrowing from the Modern
Hebrew cognate.

In order to highlight the relationship of the lexicon of JChalla to that of
other *lishana deni* dialects, constant reference is made to the dictionary
of Sabar (2002a), which contains data from JAmid, JDohok, the JNerwa
texts, and JZakho, and to the glossary in Mutzafi (2008a), which contains
data from JBetan. For the sake of brevity Sabar's dictionary is referred
to simply as Sab and Mutzafi's glossary as Mutz (e.g., Sab174 = Sabar
2008a:174, Mutz398 = Mutzafi 2008a:398). When the lexeme takes the
same form in other *lishana deni* dialects as in Jewish Challa, the relevant
page in the two books is noted. If the Jewish Challa realization or meaning differs from those found elsewhere in *lishana deni* dialects, then the
other realizations are noted by "cf." When unattested in either Sabar or
Mutzafi, but found in Maclean (1901)'s dictionary, the latter is also noted
as well as other relevant works on Neo-Aramaic.

VERBS

ʾ

ʾby   [ClAram √עבי; Sab89] D *mʾabya* 'swell up'

ʾlq   [Ar. √علق; cf. *ʿlq* and *ʾlq* Sab250 and Mutz335] G *ʾaləq* '(search and) find,
         earn'; C *maʾləq* 'kindle'; see *lʾq*

ʾmr   [ClAram √אמר; Sab97; Mutz332; § 4.4.27.1] G *ʾamər* 'speak'; *xanči zəm-
         rəyāsa basime ʾamret* 'you should sing a few nice songs'; see *ʾmər*, *ʿmr*,
         maʾmúr

ʾrgn   [ModH אִרְגֵּן] Q *mʾargən* 'organize'

ʾrq   [ClAram √ערק; Sab101; Mutz333; § 4.4.28.7] G *ʾarəq* 'run' *ʾrəqli* 'I ran';
         'flee' (with dummy 3 f.s. obj. suff.) *ʾriqāli* 'I fled' C *maʾrəq* 'make run,
         chase away, smuggle out'

ʾsy   [ClAram √אתי; Sab101–102; Mutz333; § 4.4.28.8] G *ʾāse* 'come'; marking
         passive voice: *ʾən māḷeni ʾāse l-ʾixāla* 'if our possessions get filched'; C
         mese 'bring'

ʾšm   [ModH הֶאֱשִׁים] C *maʾšəm* 'blame, accuse'

ʾwd   [ClAram √עבד; Sab90–91; Mutz333; § 4.4.28.1] G *ʾawəd* 'do, make,
         spend (time)'; *ʾāni lu wíde-lla* ᴴ*tiras*ᴴ 'they have grown it with corn'; *le
         māra hənna ʾúda fasādūsa* 'he is saying, um, he has spread gossip'; cf. *ʿbd*

ʾwr   [ClAram √עבר; Sab91; Mutz333; § 4.4.28.1] G *ʾawər* 'enter'; C *māʾər*
         'bring in'; cf. *ʿvr*

---

[1] Cf. ClAram דַּפָּא 'column, board'.

’xl   [ClAram √אכל; Sab95; Mutz333; § 4.4.27.1] G *’āxəl* ‘eat, spend, suffer, filch’; *baxla(x) par gyānan* ‘we will spend our money’; *’ā xəlle mə́ššaxuṭṭe* ‘he suffered a lot of (blows with) sticks; *axlət māḷeni* ‘you filch our property’; C *māxəl* ‘feed’

’ym   [ModH אִיֵּם] D *m’āyəm* ‘threaten’

’zl   [ClAram √אזל; Sab92; Mutz333; § 4.4.28.9] G *’āzəl* ‘go’; fig. ‘die’; *si* ‘go!’

ʿ

ʿbd   [ModH עִבֵּד] D *mʿābəd* ‘cultivate, till’

ʿks   [IrAr √عكس ‘stop, block’ Clarity et al. 2003:318; cf. ‘be cross’ Sab249] G *ʿākəs* ‘stop, block’

ʿll   [ModH הִתְעַלֵּל] D *mʿāləl* ‘torment’

ʿlm   [Ar. √علم; C ‘teach’ Sab249] D *mʿāləm* ‘teach, inform’; see *maʿalləm*

ʿmr   [Ar √امر; Sab250; Mutz335; § 3.3.d] D *mʿāmər* ‘boss around, give orders’; see *maʿmū́r, ’mr, ’əmər*

ʿnš   [ModH הֶעֱנִישׁ] D *mʿānəš* ‘punish, fine’

ʿsk   [ModH הִתְעַסֵּק] D *mʿāsək* ‘deal with’

ʿṣbn   [ModH עִצְבֵּן] Q *mʿaṣbən* ‘irritate’

ʿṣr   [Ar √عصر; Sab251; Mutz335] G *ʿāṣər* ‘squeeze’

ʿšq   [Ar √عشق; Sab252] G *ʿāšəq* ‘desire’

ʿvr   [ModH עָבַר; Sabar 1975:495] G *ʿāvər* ‘pass by, cross over’; C *maʿvər* ‘take across’; cf. *’wr*

ʿyf   [ModH הֵעִיף] C *māʿəf* ‘fly (tr.), throw out’

ʿyš   [Ar √عيش; Sab249] G *ʿāyəš* ‘live’

ʿzr   [ModH עָזַר] G *ʿāzər* ‘help’

b

b’y   [ClAram √בעי); Sab103; Mutz335] G *bā’e* ‘want, wish, love’; *gəbe* ‘it is necessary’

bhn   [ModH בָּחַן; cf. Syr ܚܢܐ ‘try, test’] G *bāhən* ‘examine’

bkh   [ModH הִתְוַכֵּחַ; § 3.1] D ‘argue’ *mbākəh*

bl’   [ClAram √בלע; Sab110; Mutz339] G *bāle’* ‘swallow’

blbl   [ClAram √בלבל; Sab110; Mutz339] Q *mbalbəl* ‘search, look for’

bny   [ClAram √בני; Sab112] G *bāne* ‘build’

bqr   [ClAram √בקר; Sab113; Mutz340] D *mbāqər* ‘ask, inquire’

brbz   [LAram √בזבז Sab114; √בזז Mutz340] Q *mbarbəz* ‘scatter’; cf. *bzbz*

bry   [ClAram √ברי; Sab114; Mutz340] G *bāre* ‘happen, be born’

brx   [ClAram √ברך; cf. *brx* ‘bless’, ⁺*brx* ‘dedicate a house, greet with a gift’ Sab115, *brx* ‘bless, congratulate, wed bride and bridegroom’ Mutz341] D *mbārex* ‘bless’; see *barāxa*

brz   [Ar √برز?; cf. ‘dry, dry up, fear greatly’ Maclean 1901:39, ‘be dry’ Sab114, ‘dry up, be stiff’ Mutz340] G *bārəz* ‘fear greatly’

bsm   [ClAram √בסם; Sab112; Mutz341] G *bāsəm* ‘be pleasing’; D *mbāsəm* ‘make pleasing’; see *basima bšl*   [ClAram √בשל; Sab116; Mutz341] G *bāšəl* 'cook (intr.)'; D *mbāšəl* 'cook (tr.)'

bṭl   [ClAram √בטל; Maclean 1901:30,153; Sab107; Mutz341] G *bāṭəl* 'be cancelled, nullified'; D *mbāṭəl* 'cancel, nullify'

bxy   [ClAram √בכי; Sab110; Mutz341] G *bāxe* 'cry'

bzbz   [ModH בִּזְבֵּז] Q *mbazbəz* 'squander'; cf. *brbz*

č

čfl   [Ar √جفل; Sab132; Mutz342] G *čāfəl* 'be startled'

čyk   [K; Sab131; Mutz342] G *čāyək* 'stick in, poke'

čyq   [Ar √شقق; Sab131 and 2006:169 n. 57] G *čāyəq* 'tear out'

čyr   [K; Khan 1999:552 and 2004:582; Mutzafi 2004:220] G *čāyər* 'move around'

ç

çmy   [√סמי Mutzafi 2005:92–93 and 2008a:342; Sab132] G *çāṃe* 'be extinguished'; C *maçṃe* 'extinguish'

çym   [ClAram √טמם Mutz342 and 2006a:88–89; Sab131] G *çāyəm* 'close (eyes)'

d

d'g   [ModH דָּאַג] G *dā'əg* 'be worried, take care of'

d'p   [Syr ܐܪܚܒܕ, حبج; *d'p* Mutz343; Sab136] G *dā'əp* 'fold (tr.)'

d'r   [Ṭur and Mlaḥ *d'r* Mutz343 and 2004:221; cf. Ar √دور Maclean 1901:59; Syr √ܪܥܕ Sab137] G *dā'ər* 'return (intr.)'; C *mad'ər* 'return (tr.)'

d'š   [ClAram דוש? Sab141; Mutz343; or conflation of ClAram דוש + Ar دعس?] G *dā'əš* 'tread on'

d'y   [Ar √دعو; cf. G 'pray, plead, curse,' C 'demand, sue, pray' Sab143, D 'plead, pray, curse, demand rights acording to marriage contract' Mutz343] G *dā'e* 'pray'; D *mdā'e* 'demand (rights)'

dbḥ   [Ar √ذبح; cf. ClAram √דבח; cf. *d/dbḥ, zbḥ* Sab147, *dbḥ* Mutz344] G *dābəḥ* 'slaughter'; see *dabāḥa*

dbš   [denom. < ClAram דבשא 'honey' Sab138; Mutz344] G *dābəš* 'stick to'

dgl   [ClAram √דגל; Sab138; Mutz345] D *mdāgəl* 'lie'; see *dugle*

dġy   [K, T Maclean 1901:60; Sab138] G *dāġe* 'be branded, cauterized'

dḥy   [ModH דָּחָה] G *dāḥe* 'postpone'

dmbk   [cf. K *dinbilik* 'drum' Rizgar 1993:257, IrAr *dumbug* 'drum' Clarity et al. 2003:59; Eng 'drum into someone'] Q *mdambək* 'pummel'

dmdm   [ClAram √דם?; cf. 'bleed, cup, howl' Maclean 1901:159, 'grumble, bleed' Sab142–143] Q *mdamdəm* 'stuff, fill'

dmx   [ClAram √דמך; Sab143; Mutz345] G *dāməx* 'sleep'; C *madməx* 'put to sleep'

drmn   [denom. < *dərmāna* 'medicine, remedy' < K, T; Sabar 1982:162] Q *mdarmən* 'medicate'; see *dərmāna*

drš   [ModH דָּרַשׁ] G *dārəš* 'ask, request, demand'

drx   [ModH דָּרַךְ, הִדְרִיךְ] G *dārəx* (1)'tread', (2) 'cock (a gun)'; C *madrəx* 'instruct'

dry   [ClAram √דרי Mutz346; Sab145] G *dāre* 'put, put in, insert'; *drele gopalṭa* 'he beat him with a walking stick'; *dreli pumməd dida* 'I stuck my (fist) in her mouth'

dwq   [ClAram √דבק; Sab139–140; Mutz346] G *dāwəq* 'hold, grasp, seize'; *'iya-ži qəbla lá-düqāla* 'this one too does not face the qibla' (lit. 'does not grasp the qibla'); *'urxa düqāli* 'I took to the road' (Meehan & Alon 1979:183 n.38); C *mādüq* 'cause to grasp, seize'

dxl   [Ar √دخل; Sab142] G *dāxəl* 'enter'

ḍ

ḍbl   [ClAram √טבל; Sab170] G *ḍābəl* 'have a ritual bath'

ḍy'   [Ar √ضيع; cf. *ẓ/⁺dy'* Sab271, *ðy'* Mutz347] G *ḍāye'* 'be lost, disappear' C *māḍə'* 'cause to lose, miss'

f

f'l   [ModH הִפְעִיל] C *maf'əl* 'activate'

fhm   [Ar √فهم; Sab262; Mutz347] G *fāhəm* 'understand'

fsd   [ModH הִפְסִיד; cf. JBetan (< Ar √فسد) D 'disclose secretly or without permission' Mutz347] C *mafsəd* 'lose'

g

gdr   [ModH גָּדַר] D *mgādər* 'fence off'

glgl   [LAram אִתְגַּלְגַּל; ModH הִתְגַּלְגֵּל; cf. NeoAram Q 'make a round shape' Sabar 1982:155] Q *mgalgəl* 'roll around (intr.)'; cf. *gndr*

gly   [ClAram √גלי; Sab122; Mutz349] G *gāle* 'reveal'

gndr   [ClAram √גנדר; Sab123] Q *mgandər* 'roll down (tr.)'; cf. *glgl*

gnw   [ClAram √גנב; Sab123; Mutz349] G *gānu* 'steal'; see *ganāwa*, *ganawūsa*

gny   [LAram √גני; Sab123; Mutz349] G *gāne* 'set (sun)'

gr'   [ClAram √גרע; Sab123; Mutz350] G *gāre'* 'shave'

grgš   [ClAram √גרש; Sab124 and 1982:162; Mutz350] Q *mgargəš* 'drag, pull behind'; see *grš*

grš   [ClAram √גרש; Sab125; Mutz350] G *gārəš* 'drag, pull, last (drag out time), smoke' (*jəgāra*); see *grgš*

gwr   [denom. < Aram גַּבְרָא; Sab120; Mutz350] G *gāwər* 'marry (intr.)'; C *māgur* 'marry off'; see *gwira*

gxk   [LAram √גחך; Sab122; Mutz350] G *gāxək* 'laugh'; see *gəxka*

gyr   [ModH? LAram √גיר; denom. < ClAram גִּיּוֹרָא; Sab122] D *mgāyər* 'convert to Judaism (tr.)'

gys   [ModH גִּיֵּס] D *mgāyəs* 'draft, recruit'

gzr   [ClAram √גזר; Sab121; Mutz351] G *gāzər* 'circumcise'; see **gzira*

ġ

ġrġr [onomat. or Ar √غرغر?; Ar √غور? Sab135] Q *mġarġar* 'be hoarse'
ġrq [Ar √غرق; Sab135] G *ġaraq* 'sink' (intr.)'

h

hjm [Ar √هجم; Sab149] G *hājam* 'attack'
hnnl [filler *hanna* + *l*-; Sab52,151; Mutz352; Rubin 2005:78–79 n.46; §4.4.28.11] irreg. 'do, um'; *hannálle* 'he did, um-'; see *hanna*
hwy [ClAram √הוי; Sab149; Mutz352] G *hāwe* (1) 'be', (2) 'be born'
hymn [ClAram √הימן < PrAram C *ʾmn; Sab150; Mutz352; §4.4.28.13] Q *mheman* 'believe'
hyr [TJ and JBA√יהר 'overbearing'? Syr √ܝܗܪ 'annoy'? cf. D and C Sab150, D Mutz352–353] G *mhāyar* 'dare'

ḥ

ḥdr [Ar √حضر; cf. *ḥz/dr* Sab168, *hdr* Mutz353] G *hādar* 'be ready'; C *mahdar* 'make ready'
ḥkm [Ar √حكم; Sab166; Mutz353] G *hākam* 'rule'; C *mahkam* 'appoint as ruler'
ḥky [Ar √حكى; cf. D and C Sab166; D (rare) and C Mutz353] D *mhāke* 'speak'; see *mhakesa*
ḥkr [ModH חָקַר] G *hākar* 'investigate'
ḥlḥl [ModH חִלְחֵל] Q *mhalhal* 'permeate'
ḥlk [ModH חִלֵּק] D *mhālak* 'divide'
ḥll [H חִלֵּל; cf. C Sab165] D *mhalal* 'desecrate'; see *hyl*
ḥlq [Ar √غلق; cf. *ġlq, xlq* Sab135, *hlq* Mutz354] G *hālaq* 'lock, close (door)'
ḥlt [ModH הֶחְלִיט] C *mahlat* 'decide'
ḥml [Ar √حمل; Sab166–167; Mutz354] G *hāmal* 'stand, wait, stop'; C *mahmal* 'make one stand, stop'; *hamlile ʾabbad* ᴴ*sakkiním*ᴴ 'that they attack him with knives'
ḥrm [Ar √حرم; Sab168] G *hāram* 'be polluted'; C *mahram* 'pollute, impurify, ban, confiscate'; see *harám(a), haramūsa*
ḥsl [ModH חִסֵּל] D *mhāsal* 'finish off, eliminate'
ḥyl [H חִלֵּל; C Sab165] C *māhal* 'desecrate'; see *hll*
ḥyš [Ar √حشى; Sab165; Mutz354] G *hāyaš* 'insert (tr.)'
ḥyw [ModH חִיֵּב] D *mhāyu* 'obligate'
ḥzk [ModH הֶחְזִיק] C *mahzak* 'hold'

j

jhd [Ar √جهد; Sab127; Mutz354] D *mjāhad* 'argue, quarrel'; cf. *nṣy*
jmʿ [Ar √جمع; Sab128; Mutz355] G *jāma* 'gather (tr. and intr.)'; D *mjāma* 'gather (tr.)'
jrm [Ar √جرم; cf. Sab129] D *mjāram* 'impose a fine, punish'

jrmṭ   [Ar √شرمط?; cf. šrmṭ Sab304] Q mjarmaṭ 'be entangled'

jry   [Ar √جرى; cf. ⁺jry Sab129] G jāre 'flow'

jwb   [Ar √جوب; cf. D and C Sab126–127, D Mutz355] C mājab 'answer'; see
         jawāb, jwāb

jwj   [LAram √שבש Mutz355; JBA זוז? Sab127] G jāwaj 'move'

k

kbs   [Ar √كبس; Sab181] G kābas 'conquer'

kfṣ   [ModH קָפַץ; cf. TO, JBA, and JPA √קפץ] G kāfaṭṣ 'jump'

klt   [ModH קָלַט] G kālat 'absorb'

kpn   [ClAram √כפן; Sab188; Mutz357] G kāpan 'become hungry'; see kapna,
         kpina

krd   [Ar √كرد; Sab188] G kārad 'drive away'

krkm   [denom.; Syr √ܟܘܪܟܡ; LEAram כּוּרְכְּמָא 'saffron'; Sab189; Mutz358] Q
         mkarkam 'to make yellow'

krx   [ClAram √כרך 'wrap around'?; cf. G 'go round, be wrapped round,
         surround,' D and C 'shroud, wrap up' Maclean 1910:140,177, G 'be
         attached,' D 'shroud' Sab189] G kārax 'smash someone, wrestle'

kry¹   [LEAram √כרי; Sab189; Mutz358] C makre 'shorten'; see karya

kry²   [Ar √كرى; cf. ⁺kry Sab189] C makre 'rent out'

ksb   [K, Ar √كسب; cf. ks/zb Sab187, ksb Mutz358] G kāsab 'earn'

ksw   [ClAram √כתב; Sab190; Mutz358] G kāsu 'write'; C maksu 'dictate' (<
         ModH הכתיב)

ksy   [ClAram √כסי; Sab187; Mutz358] D mkāse 'cover'

kvˁ   [ModH קָבַע] G kāva' 'determine'

kwš   [ClAram √כבש; Sab184; Mutz359] G kāwaš 'descend'; C mākuš 'cause to
         descend'

kym   [ClAram √אכם; Sab185; Mutz359] G kāyam 'become black'; see koma

kyn   [ModH הֵכִין] C māxan 'prepare'

kyp   [ClAram √כפף; Sab185; Mutz359] G kāyap 'bend (intr.)'; C mākap 'bend
         (tr.)'

l

lʾq   [Ar √علق] G lāʾaq 'be kindled, burn (intr.)'; see ʾlq

lqy   [ClAram √לקי; Sab208; Mutz360] D mlāqe 'punish (God)' (haggada)

lšn   [ModH? or earlier H הִלְשִׁין?; JPA and JBA √לשן < MishH] C malšan
         'slander, inform against'

lṭx   [Ar √لطخ; Sab205] G lāṭax 'stick (intr.), be attached'

lxlx   [ModH לְכְלֵךְ] Q mlaxlax 'dirty (tr.)'

lwš   [ClAram √לבש; Sab205; Mutz360] G lāwaš 'wear'

lyp   [TO √אלף, Syr √ܡܠܦ < PrAram *אלף; cf. lyp, ylp Sab206, lyp Mutz360]
         G lāyap 'learn'; C mālap 'instruct'

lzy   [K; Sab206] G lāze 'hurry (intr.)'

m

mḥy   [Ar مَحَا, ModH מָחָה; Sab215; Mutz363] C *mamḥe* 'erase, wipe out']

mly   [ClAram √מלי; cf. ⁺*mly* 'fill,' *mly* 'be sufficient' Sab219 and Mutz364,366]
          G *māle* 'it is sufficient'; see *ṃly*

mnx   [blend of *m'yn* (√עין) + *mānəx* (√נוח) Mutz363; √נוח? Sab51,232; <
          √עיני? Meehan & Alon 1979:180, n. 27; cf. LWAram and WNeoAram
          'yny] C *menəx* 'look, look around'

mpl   see *npl*

mpx   see *npx*

mr'   [ClAram √מרע; Sab224; Mutz364] G *māre'* 'be in pain'; *kāsan əmre(')la
          'əllan* 'our stomach hurt us'

mṛč   [ClAram √מרס; ⁺*m-r-č* Sab224] G *māṛəč* 'crush'; *mṛəčle 'əġdāde* 'he crum-
          pled him up'

msy   [LEAram √מסא; Sab221; Mutz365] G *māse* 'wash (tr.)'

mṣy   [ClAram √מצי; Sab223; Mutz365; §4.4.28.15] G *mṣe* 'be able'

mšx   [ModH הִמְשִׁיךְ] C *mamšəx* 'continue'

mṭy   [ClAram √מטי; Sab215–216; Mutz365] G *māṭe* 'arrive'; marking passive
          voice: *'atta* ᴴ*gam*ᴴ *mṭelu 'əlləd hənna qəṭla* 'Also now they were, um,
          killed' (§4.4.20.c); C *mamṭe* 'cause to arrive, bring'

mxy   [ClAram √מחי; Sab218; Mutz365] G *māxe* 'strike, hit'; *mxele 'urxa* 'he
          hit the road' (cf. *mxēle l/b'urxa* "he hit the road' Sab218); *mxele 'əlla* 'he
          hit it (the road)'; *gyāne məxyāle 'əlle* 'he hurled himself at him'; *məxyāla
          'əlli* 'she hit me'; see *maxisa*

myd   [Ar √مدد; Sab216] G *māyəd* 'line up (tr.)'

mys   [ClAram √מית; Sab217; Mutz365] G *māyəs* 'die'; *mətle* 'he died' (§3.1.b);
          see *misa, mosa*

ṃ

ṃly   [ClAram √מלי; cf. ⁺*mly* 'fill,' *mly* 'be sufficient' Sab219 and Mutz364,366]
          G *ṃāle* 'fill'; see *mly*

n

n'l   [IrAr √نعل < √لعن 'curse' Clarity et al. 2003:463; cf. 'curse' Maclean
          1901:183, 'marry off (pejorative of gentile marriage)' Sab233] D *mnā'əl*
          'marry off' (pejorative for non-Jews)

nbl   [ClAram √יבל; cf. *nbl, byl, ybl* Sab229, *nbl, lbl* Mutz366; §§3.7;4.4.28.16]
          C *nābəl* 'lead away'; *nobəlle* 'he led him away'

ndy   [ClAram √נדי; cf. *ndy, nyd* Sab230, *ndy* Mutz366] C *mande* 'throw
          down/away'; *pehna mande* 'kick (lit. throw a kick)'; *mundele qam qaṭi'a*
          'he beat him with a stick'; *mundele qam kulle* 'he beat him with every-
          thing'

nf'   [Ar √نفع; Sab233; Mutz367] G *nāfe'* 'be useful, benefit, suit'; also *nāpe'*

ng'   [ModH הִגִּיעַ] C *māgə'* 'deserve' (< 'reach')

ngš   [ModH הִגִּישׁ] C *māgəš* 'hand in'

nhl   [ModH נִהֵל] D *mnāhəl* 'manage'

np'   see *nf'*

npl   [ClAram √נפל; cf. *n/mpl* Sab233–234, *npl* Mutz367] G *nāpəl* 'fall,' *(m)pəl-le basər* 'follow' (lit., 'fall [in line] after'); C *mampəl* 'cause to fall'

npx   [ClAram √נפח; cf. *n/mpx* Sab233; *npx* Mutz367] G *nāpəx* 'blow'; *mpox* 'blow!' (§ 3.6.d)

nqm   [ClAram √נקם; Sab235] G *nāqəm* 'take revenge'

nqṣ   [Ar √نقص; Sab235] G *nāqəṣ* 'lessen' (intr.); C *manqəṣ* 'lessen' (tr.); see *naqoṣa, nqiṣa*

nqš   [ClAram √נקש; Sab235; Mutz367] G *nāqəš* 'touch'

ns'   [ModH הִסִּיעַ, נָסַע] G *nāsə'* 'travel'; C *māsə'* 'transport'

nṣy   [ClAram √נצי; Sab234; Mutz368] G *nāṣe* 'fight, quarrel'; see *naṣūṣa*; cf. *jḥd*

nšq   [ClAram √נשק; Sab235; Mutz368] G *nāšəq* 'kiss'

nšy   [ClAram √נשי; Sab235; Mutz368] G *nāše* 'forget'; C *manše* 'cause to forget'

nṭr   [ClAram √נטר; Sab232; Mutz368] G *nāṭər* 'keep, guard'

nwx   [ClAram √נבח; Sab231] G *nāwəx* 'bark'; C *manwəx* 'cause to bark'

nxnx   [onomat.?; cf. 'mumble threats, breathe heavily on one's neck' Sab233] Q *mnaxnəx* 'mumble threats'

nxp   [ClAram √נכף; Sab233; Mutz368] G *nāxəp* 'be embarrassed'; see *nəxpūsa*

nyx   [ClAram √נוח; Sab232; Mutz363] G *nāyəx* 'rest'; fig., 'pass away'; C *mānəx* 'give rest'; *'ilāha mānəxle* 'May God rest his soul'; see *nixa*

p

pčkn   [K *pêçan* 'pack, wrap' Rizgar 1993:144?; cf. 'go bad (gum)' Sabar 1982: 169] Q *mpačkən* 'finish, wrap up'

pg'   [ModH פָּגַע] G *pāgə'* 'injure'

pl'   [ClAram √פלג; cf. *pl', ply* Sab256, *pl'* Mutz369] G *pāle'* 'divide'; D *mpāle'* 'distribute'

plṭ   [ClAram √פלט; Sab256] G *pāləṭ* 'go out'; D *mpāləṭ* 'take out'; *mpoləṭlu pássaporṭ* 'they issued a passport' (calque on ModH הוֹצִיא דַּרְכּוֹן/פַּסְפּוֹרְט)

plx   [ClAram √פלח; Sab256; Mutz370] G *pāləx* 'work'; C *mapləx* 'employ'; cf. *falxa*

pnčr   [ModH פִּנְצֶ'ר < Eng 'puncture'; Sabar 1990:55] Q *mpančər* 'cause a flat tire'

pq'   [ClAram √פקע; Sab257; Mutz370] G *pāqe'* 'burst' (tr. and intr.)

prns   [ModH פִּרְנֵס; LEAram √פרנס] Q *mparnəs* 'manage, provide for'

prpr   [Syr √ܦܪܦܪ 'flutter, quiver'; cf. 'spin, whirl' Sabar 1982:169] Q *mparpər* 'agonize, writhe'

prpṭ   [LEAram √פרט; Sab259 and 1982:169; Mutz370] Q *mparpəṭ* 'agonize, writhe'; cf. *prṭ*

prq   [ClAram √פרק; Sab250; Mutz370] G *pārəq* 'desist, leave'; D *mpārəq* 'redeem, revenge'; see *tola*

prs   [ClAram √פרס; Sab259; Mutz370] G *pārəs* 'spread (tr.)'

prš   [ClAram √פרש; Sab259; Mutz370] G *pāreš* 'separate' *pršq*   [LEAram √פשק; Sab260 and 1982:159; Mutz370] Q *mparšəq* 'stretch, straighten (tr.)'

prṭ   [ClAram √פרט; Sab259; Mutz370] 'tear, rip up'; see *priṭa, prpṭ*

prtx   [Syr √ܦܪܬܟ 'split'; Kamil 1963:17; Sab260] Q *mpartəx* 'make change (money)'

prx   [ClAram √פרח; Sab259; Mutz370] G *pārəx* 'fly' (intr.)

pṣʿ   [ModH פְּצַע] G *pāṣə* 'injure' (tr. and intr.)

pšr   [ClAram √פשר; Sab260; Mutz371] G *pāšər* 'melt' (intr.)

ptl   [Syr √ܦܬܠ; Sab261; Mutz371] G *pātəl* 'roll, twist'

ptpt   [Syr √ܦܬܦܬ; Sabar 1982:170; Mutz371] Q *mpatpət* 'shred, cut up'

pṭr   [ModH פטר?; ClAram √פטר; cf. G Maclean 1901:249] D *mpāṭər* 'finish, leave (tr. and intr.)'

ptx   [ClAram √פתח; Sab261; Mutz371] G *pātəx* 'open (tr. and intr.)'

pyč   [K *pičan* 'break' Chyet 2003:454; in related NENA dialects 'crush with a foot, trample' Mutzafi p.c.] G *pāyəč* 'crush'

pyd   [Syr √ܦܝܕ; cf. *pâ -it, fâ -it* Maclean 1901:246, *pyd* Sab255, *pyð* Mutz371] G *pāyəd* 'pass by'; C *māpəd* 'cause to pass by'

pyš   [LEAram √ פוש; Sab255; Mutz371] G *pāyəš* 'remain, be'; *'āna ppešan hudesa* 'I will become a Jewess'

pyx   [ClAram √פוח; Sab255] G *pāyəx* 'become cool'; attested only with *ləbbe*: *ləbbe pəxle* 'he felt relieved'; C *māpəx* 'cool' (tr.); *ləbbe mopəxle* 'it relieved him'

pzr   [ModH פֻּזֵר; cf. ClAram √בדר] D *mpāzər* 'distribute'

q

qbl   [ClAram √קבל; Sab273; Mutz373] G *qābəl* 'accept, agree, allow'

qḍy   [Ar √قضى; cf. 'finish, be finished' Maclean 1901:269; 'provide (need), fulfill, wish' Sab282 and Mutz373; §4.4.23.5] G *qāḍe* 'finish, complete, spend time'

qlʿ   [Ar √قلع; cf. 'go away, go to hell, cause harm by casting the evil eye' Sab279] G *qālə* 'go away, drive away'

qlb   [Ar √قلب; Sab279; Mutz374] G *qāləb* 'overturn'

qlql   [denom. < JBA קלקלתא 'trash heap' Mutzafi p.c.; cf. 'despise, make little of' Maclean 1901:195;] Q *mqalqəl* 'kick the bucket' (used for non-Jews); cf. *skt*

qlw   [denom. < Syr ܩܠܒܐ 'mould, pattern'?; Sab279; Mutzafi 2004:238] G *qālu* 'be clean'; D *mqālu* 'clean'

qnʿ   [Ar √قنع; Sab281; Mutz374] G *qānə* 'be content, convinced'

qrm   [ClAram √קרם; Sab283] G *qārəm* 'cover'

qrmṭ   [LEAram √קמט; cf. 'wrinkle' Sab283 and 1982:170] Q *mqarməṭ* 'seize, grasp'

qrpč   [?; cf. *qrpč, qrčp* Sab284 and 1982:170] Q *mqarpəč* 'snatch'

qrw   [ClAram √קרב; Sab282] G *qāru* 'approach'

qrx   [ClAram √קרח; Sab283; Mutz374] C *maqrəx* 'whiten, make shine'

qry   [ClAram √קרי; Sab283; Mutz374] G *qāre* 'call, read, study'; G *maqre* 'teach'

qṭ' [ClAram √קטע; Sab277; Mutz374] G qāṭe' 'be cut, cut off, be resolved';
qəṭya 'cut'; see 'āqəl

qtl [ClAram √קטל; Sab277; Mutz375] G qāṭəl 'kill, beat up badly'; C maqṭəl
'have killed'; see qəṭla, qaṭəl, qaṭola

qty see qṭ'

qwr [ClAram √קבר; Sab276; Mutz376] G qāwər 'bury'

qyd [ClAram √יקד; cf. yqḍ, qyd Sab178, yqð Mutz376] G qāyəd 'burn' (intr.);
qədla kāse 'he got angry' (§4.4.27.5); C māqəd 'burn (tr.)'; see yuqdāna

qym [ClAram √קום; Sab278; Mutz376] G qāyəm 'stand up, arise'; qemi xaprile
'they up (and) dig it' (§4.4.24); C māqəm 'set up'

r

r'y [ClAram √רעי; Sab286; Mutz376] C mar'e 'to take to pasture'

r'š [ClAram √רגש; Sab286; Mutz376] C mar'əš 'awaken'

r'd [ModH רָעַד] G rā'əd 'tremble'

r'l [ModH הִרְעִיל] C mar'əl 'poison'

rgš [ModH הִרְגִּישׁ] C margəš 'feel, notice'

rhq [ClAram √רחק; Sab289; Mutz377] G rāhəq 'go far, be far away'; C marhəq
'remove'; cf. rəqqa, reqa

rkw [ClAram √רכב; Sab290; Mutz377] G rāku 'ride'; see rakāwa

rkx [ClAram √רכך; Sab290; Mutz377] C markəx 'soften'; see *rakixa

rpy [ClAram √רפי; cf. D 'throw, let go' Maclean 1901:200; +rpy G 'be set free
against, attack and D 'dispatch,' rpy C 'make loose, weak' Sabar 2002:291;
rpy G 'be released' and C 'release' Mutz377] D mrāpe 'loosen, release,
attack'; 'anna nāše mrupyālu 'əlləd 'Awrāham 'those people let Abraham
have it'; C marpe 'release'; 'āya ᴴməskenaᴴ murpyāla l-bəxya 'that poor
one broke out crying'

rqd [ClAram √רקד; Sab292; Mutz377] G rāqəd 'dance'

rvh [ModH הִרְוִיחַ] C marvəh 'earn'

rzdg [K, P; cf. +rzdg, rzk, rzg Sab288] Q mrazdəg 'arrange (table)' (haggada)

ṛ

ṛhm [H רֶחֶם, Ar √رحم; Sab289; Mutz378] D mṛāhəm 'have mercy'; see maṛ-
hāma, mrahmāna

ṛwy [ClAram √רבי; Sab288, Mutz378] C ṛāwe 'grow, grow up'; C marwe
'raise, bring up'

ṛym [ClAram √רום; cf. +rym, yrm Sab289, ṛym Mutz378] C māṛəm 'lift';
māṛəm télefon 'call on the phone' (calque on ModH הֵרִים טלפון); see
romāṇa

s

sbl [ModH סָבַל; also ClAram √סבל] G sābəl 'bear, suffer' (tr. and intr.)

sdr [ModH סֵדֶר 'arrange,' הִסְתַּדֵּר 'manage, get along'] D msādər 'arrange,
manage, get along'

skm   [ModH הִסְכִּים] C *maskəm* 'agree'

skn   [Ar √سكن; Sab240; Mutz380] G *sākən* 'dwell'

skr¹ [ModH הִשְׂכִּיר] C *maskər* 'rent out'

skr² [Ar √سكر; cf. ⁺*skr* Sab240, *skr* Mutz380] C *maskər* 'intoxicate'

skt   [Ar. سكت? cf. *sqṭ* (< Ar سَقَطَ) 'to die, used of a dog or a bad man, esp. of Mussulmans' Maclean 1901:230] G *sākət* 'croak' (used for non-Jews); cf. *qlql*

slb   [Ar √سلب; Sab240] G *sāləb* 'rob'

slm   [Ar √سلم; Sab240] D *msāləm* 'deliver, hand over'

smḥ   [ModH שִׂמַּח] D *msāməḥ* 'make happy'

smq   [ClAram √סמק; Sab241; Mutz380] G *sāməq* 'become red'

smx   [ModH הִסְמִיךְ] C *masmax* 'authorize, empower'

snq   [Syr √ܣܢܩ; Sab242; Mutz380] G *sānəq* 'need'; see *sniqa*

sny   [ClAram √סני; Sab241] G *sāne* 'hate'

spk   [ModH הִסְפִּיק] C *maspək* 'manage, succeed'

spq   [ClAram √ספק; Sab242; Mutz381] G *sāpəq* 'be empty'; D *msāpəq* 'empty (tr.)'; see *spiqa*

spr   [ModH סִפֵּר] D *msāpər* 'tell'

sqṭ   [Ar √سقط; Sab243] G *sāqəṭ* 'fall, land (fly on food)'

srq   [ClAram √סרק; Sab244; Mutz381] G *sārəq* 'comb'

sxy   [ClAram √סחי; Sab240; Mutz381] G *sāxe* 'bathe, swim'

syl   [?; cf. MishH√סלל 'act lewdly' Sab12 n.50, 239] G *sāyəl* 'fuck'

ṣ

ṣ'r   [ClAram √צער; Sab269; Mutz381] D *mṣā'ər* 'curse'; see *ṣo'rāsa*

ṣdr   [Ar √صدر] D *mṣādər* 'confiscate'

ṣfr   [Ar √صفر; Sab270] D *mṣāfər* 'whistle'; see *ṣfera*

ṣfṣf [ModH צִפְצֵף] Q *mṣafṣəf* 'utterly disregard'

ṣlḥ   [ClAram √צלח G and C 'succeed'; ModH הִצְלִיחַ; Ar √صلح 'reconcile'; Sab269] D *mṣāləḥ* 'reconcile'; *maṣləḥ* C 'succeed'

ṣlm   [ModH צִלֵּם] D *mṣāləm* 'photograph'

ṣly   [ClAram √צלי; Sab269; Mutz382] D *mṣāle* 'pray'

ṣpy   [Ar √صفو; Sab270; Mutz383] G *ṣāpe* 'be clear, untroubled (mainly liquid)'

ṣrx   [ClAram √צרח; Sab270; Mutz383] G *ṣārəx* 'call, shout, summon'; C *maṣrəx* 'call for, summon'

ṣw'   [ClAram √צבע; Sab267; Mutz383] G *ṣāwe* 'dye, color'; see *ṣawā'a*, *ṣəwya*

ṣyḥ   [Ar √صحح; Sab268] C *māṣəḥ* 'examine, check'

š

šbḥ   [ModH שִׁבַּח] D *mšābəḥ* 'praise'

šdd   [ModH שָׁדַד] G *šādəd* 'rob'

šfṭ   [ModH שָׁפַט] G *šāfəṭ* 'judge'

šḥrr [ModH שִׁחְרֵר] Q *mšaḥrər* 'free, release'

škl   [Ar √شكل; Sab298–299; Mutz386] G *šākəl* 'begin'

škn [ModH שִׁכֵּן] D mšākən 'settle (tr.)'

šky [Ar √شكو; Sab298; Mutz386] G šāke 'lodge a complaint'

šlm [ClAram √שלמ; cf. D 'pay' < ModH שִׁלֵּם; C 'become or make a Mussulman' Maclean 1901:203, C 'convert to Islam' Sab300] D mšāləm 'pay'; C mašləm 'convert (tr. and intr.) to Islam'

šlq [ClAram √שלק] G šāləq 'boil (tr. and intr.)'

šlx [ClAram √שלח; Sab300; Mutz386] G šāləx 'take off (clothes)'; see šulxāya

šm' [ClAram √שמע; Hoberman 1989:219; Sab300; Mutz386 and 2002a:485] G šāme' 'hear'; šəmya 'heard'; C mašme' 'listen, pay attention'

šmd [ModH הִשְׁמִיד] C mašməd 'destroy'

šmn [LAram √שׁמן; Sab301] G šāmən 'be fat'

šmr [ModH שָׁמַר] G šāmər 'guard, keep'

šmy see šm'

šny [ClAram √שׁני 'change'; Sab301–302; Mutz386] D mšāne 'change residence, move, depart'

šql [ClAram √שׁקל; Sab303; Mutz387] G šāqəl 'take'; šqəlle baxta 'he took a wife'

šrt [ModH שֵׁרֵת] D mšārət 'serve'

šrṭ [Ar √شرط; Sab303] D mšārəṭ 'stipulate'

šry [ClAram √שׁרי; Sab303] G šāre 'untie'

štf [ModH שִׁתֵּף; ClAram < Akk] D mšātəf 'let participate'

šthr [*Gt אשתהר; LAram √שהר 'keep a vigil'; Sab305; Mutz387] Q məštāhər 'go blind'; see šahāra

šty [ClAram √שׁתי; Sab305; Mutz387] G šāte 'drink'; C mašte 'give drink, water, moisten'; 'ən 'āna pešən Záwa-ži, baxtasexun 'āna lebi maštənnu kullu 'Even if I should become the Zawa (River), I can't moisten all of your women'

štx [ClAram √שׁטח; cf. G in Maclean 1901:304, Sab297, and Mutz387 (also štḥ)] C maštəx 'spread out'

švk [ModH שׁוּק] D mšāvək 'market'

šwq [ClAram √שׁבק; Sab296; Mutz388] G šāwəq 'leave, abandon'

šxn [ClAram √שׁחן; Sab299; Mutz388] D (m)šāxən 'warm up' (tr.); see šaxina

šxnx [ModH שִׁכְנַע; § 3.3.e] Q mšaxnəx 'persuade'

šy' [ClAram √שׁוע or שׁעע; cf. šy' Sab297] G šāyə' 'plaster'

šydn [denom. < šidana 'crazy' < ClAram שֵׁדָא 'demon'; Sab297; Mutz388] Q mšedən 'become crazy, make crazy'; see mšidəna, šidāna, šidanūsa

t

tfq [Ar إتَّفَقَ < √وفق; Sab312; Mutz389] G tāfəq 'occur, happen'

thl [ModH הִתְחִיל; Hoberman 1989:79] C mathəl 'begin'

tkf [ModH הִתְקִיף] C matkəf 'attack'

tkl [Ar إتَّكَل < √وكل; Syr ܬܟܠ; Sab309] G tākəl 'trust'

tkn [ModH תִּקֵּן] D mtākən 'fix'

tll [Syr √ܬܠܠ; Sab310; Mutz389] G tāləl 'get wet'

tly [ClAram √תׁלי; cf. tâlî Maclean 1901:321, tlty, tly Sab310 and Mutz389–390] G tāle 'hang (tr.)'; see təlya *tmx* [ModH תָּמַךְ] G *tāməx* 'support'

tpl [ModH טִפֵּל] D *mtāpəl* 'take care of'

tql [ClAram √תקל; Sab312] G *tāqəl* 'weigh (tr.)'

tvʿ [ModH תָּבַע] G *tāvəʿ* 'sue'

twr [ClAram √תבר; Sab307–308; Mutz390] G *tāwər* 'break (tr.)'; see *tūra*

txnn [ModH תִּכְנֵן] Q *mtaxnən* 'plan'

txr [ClAram √דכר; < Gt *ʾtdkr*/*ʾdkr*?; Sab309; Mutz390; §3.2.d] G *tāxər* 'remember'; C *matxər* 'remind'

tym [ClAram √תמם; Sab308; Mutz390] G *tāyəm* 'finish (intr.)'

ṭ

ṭʾn [ClAram √טען; Sab170; Mutz391] C *maṭʾən* 'load'

ṭʾy [ClAram √טעי; cf. *ṭʾy* Sab170 and Mutz391] G *ṭāʾe* 'search, look for'

ṭlb [Ar √طلب; Sab172; Mutz392] G *ṭāləb* 'request'

ṭlq [Ar √طلق; cf. G and D Sab173] D *mṭāləq* 'divorce'; see *ṭalāqe*

ṭpr [Anatolian Ar *ṭpr* 'catch fever'; Maclean 1901:113,325; Sab174] G *ṭāpər* 'burn (intr.)' (*haggada*)

ṭpy [LEAram √טפי; Sab174; Mutz392 and 2005:101] G *ṭāpe* 'stick (tr.), kindle, be inflamed'

ṭrp [ClAram √טרף; cf. 'strike, overthrow' Maclean 1901:114, 'applaud' Sab175, 'attack' Mutz392] G *ṭārep* 'attack, fall upon'

ṭry [ClAram √טרי; Sab175; Mutz392] G *ṭāre* 'drive (a car), set in motion'

ṭrs [ClAram √תרץ; cf. *tāriṣ* Maclean 1901:327, ⁺*trs* Sab313, *ṭrs* Mutz392] G *ṭārəs* 'be healthy, become healthy' see *ṭrosa*

ṭšy (ClAram √טשי; Sab175; Maclean 2008:392] D *mṭāše* 'hide'

ṭwʾ [ClAram √טבע; Sab171; Mutz393] G *ṭāweʾ* 'fall asleep'

ṭwy [ClAram √טוי; Sab171; Mutz393] D *mṭāwe* 'roast' (tr.)

w

wlwl [Ar √ولول; Hozaya & Youkhana 1999:253] Q *mwalwəl* 'wail'

x

xbd [ModH כִּבֵּד] D *mxābəd* 'honor'; see *kāwód*

xdr [ClAram √חדר; cf. cf. *x/ġd/dr* Sab192, *xðr* Mutz395] G *xādər* 'go around'

xdy [ClAram √חדי; Sab192; §4.4.23.5] G *xāde* 'rejoice'; with dummy 3 f.s. obj. suff. *xədyālu* 'they rejoiced'; see *xədyūsa*

xll [ClAram √חלל; Sab197; Mutz396] D *mxaləl* 'wash'

xlp [ClAram √חלף; cf. D (tr.) Sab197, G (intr.), D (tr.) Mutz396] G *xāləp* 'change, exchange' (tr.); more commonly D *mxāləp* 'change, exchange' (tr.)

xlq [Ar √خلق; Sab197; Mutz396] G *xāləq* 'create'

xlṣ [Ar √خلص 'finish, save'; Sab197; Mutz396] G *xāləṣ* 'finish, be saved, get rid of'; D *mxāləṣ* 'save'

xlw [ClAram √חלב; Sab197; Mutz396] G *xālu* 'milk'

xm'   [ClAram √חמע; cf. G 'be leavened, C 'leaven (tr.)' Sab198; G 'be leavened' Avidani 1959:46 and Alfiye 1986:55] C *maxme'* 'become leavened' (*haggada*)

xpq   [ClAram √חבק; cf. *xp/bq* Sab199] G *xāpəq* 'embrace, hug'

xpr   [ClAram √חפר; Sab199; Mutz397] G *xāpər* 'dig'

xrḥ   [ModH הִכְרִיחַ] C *maxrəḥ* 'force'

xrw   [ClAram √חרב; Sab200; Mutz397] G *xāru* 'be ruined'; C *maxru* 'destroy'; see *xarbé*

xṛxṛ   [K; Sab200] Q *mxaṛxəṛ* 'have pity'

xrz   [ModH הִכְרִיז] C *maxrəz* 'declare'

xss   [ClAram √חדת; Sab202] D *mxasəs* 'renew'; see *xāsa*²

xšx   [ClAram √חשח < Akk *ḫašāḫu*? Kaufman 1974:54; Sab201] G *xāšəx* 'be (religiously) proper'

xšw   [ClAram √חשב; Sab201; Mutz397] G *xāšu* 'think, consider'

xtf   [ModH חָטַף] G *xātəf* 'seize, snatch'

xtm   [ModH חָתַם; cf. ClAram √חתם 'seal, end'] G *xātəm* 'sign'

xtr   [Syr √ܚܬܪ; cf. G Maclean 1901:108 and Sab202] D *mxātər* 'boast, be proud'

xṭr   [ClAram √חטר; Sab195; Mutz397] G *xāṭər* 'beat, hit'; see *xuṭṭa*

xwr   [ClAram √חור; Sab194; Mutz398] C *maxwər* 'whiten'; see **xwāra*

xyk   [LEAram √חכך; Sab196] G *xāyək* 'scratch'

xyp   [ClAram √חפף; Sab196; Mutz398] G *xāyəp* 'wash oneself'

xyy   [ClAram √חיי; Sab196; Mutz398] G *xāye* 'live'

xzd   [ClAram √חצד; cf. *ġ/xẓd* Sab135, *xāzəd*, *ġāzəd* Mutz398] G *xāzəd* 'harvest'

xzy   [ClAram √חזי; Sab195; Mutz398] G *xāze* 'see, find'; C *maxze* 'show'

y

y'y   [ClAram √ידע; Sab176; Mutz399; §4.4.28.19] G *yā'e* 'he may know'; *y'elox* 'you know'; *'āna lá-ki'ən* 'I am unaware'; *lá-či'ətte* 'you don't know him'(§4.4.9.c); C *mayde'* 'inform, announce, notify'

yd'   see *y'y*

yhw(l)   [ClAram -ל + √יהב; Sab176; Mutz399; §4.4.28.20] G *yāwəl* 'give, pay'; *hiwa* 'given'

ymy   [ClAram √ימי; Sab178] G *yāme* 'swear'; C *mayme* 'adjure'; see *momāsa*

ypy   [ClAram √אפי; Sab178; Mutz99] G *yāpe* 'bake'

yrq   [ClAram √ירק; Sab179; Mutz399] G *yārəq* 'become green'

yrx   [ClAram √ארך; Sab179] G *yārəx* 'be long'; C *mayrəx* 'lengthen'; see *yarixa*

ysq   [ClAram √סלק; Sab178; Mutz399] G *yāsəq* 'ascend'; C *māsəq* 'bring up'

ysr   [ClAram √אסר; Sab178; Mutz399] G *yāsər* 'bind, tie'

yšr   [ModH יָשֵׁר] D *myāšər* 'straighten'

ytw   [ClAram √יתב; Sab179; Mutz399] G *yātu* 'sit'; inchoative verb in *ytw* + *b* + Gerund; C *mattu* 'put, place'; *mətwáli* 'I placed her'

ywš   [ClAram √יבש; cf. *wyš*, *ywš* Sab154, *wyš* (JBetan < JZakho) Mutz393] G *yāwəš* 'dry up (intr.)'

z

zbn   see *zwn*

zbr   [ModH הִסְבִּיר colloquially *hizbir*] C *mazbər* 'explain'

zd'   [ClAram t-stem of √זוע; Nöldeke 1868:195] G *zāde'* 'fear'; see **zad'ə-wāna, zde'sa, zdo'sa*

zgr   [ModH הִסְגִּיר colloquially *hizgir*] C *mazgər* 'hand over'

zky   [ClAram √זכי?; Ar أَزْكَى?; cf. G 'deserve,' D 'let someone possess a merit' Sab159] C *mazke* 'grant merit'; *'ilāha mazkela* 'May God grant her merit' (cf. *'ilāha mzākēlexun* Sab159); see *zxy*

zlṭ   [K *zrṭ*? cf. *zrṭ* 'prahlen mit reden (etwa vor dem kampf), ausschelten' Ritter 1990:228]; C *mazlə̣ṭ* 'convert (tr.)'

zmn   [ModH הִזְמִין] C *mazmən* 'invite'

zmr   [ClAram √זמר; Mutz400] G *zāmər* 'sing'; see *'mr, zəmrəyāsa*

zqr   [ClAram √זקר; Sab160; Mutz400] G *zāqər* 'weave'

zr'   [ClAram √זרע; Sab160; Mutz400] G *zāre'* 'sow, seed'

zrm   [ModH זֶרֶם] G *zārəm* 'flow'

zwn   [ClAram √זבן; Sab156; Mutz401] G *zāwən* 'buy'; D *mzābən* 'sell'

zwr   [K; Sab156; Mutz401] C *zāwər* 'go around'; C 'turn (around) (tr.)'

zxy   [ModH זָכָה] G *zāxe* 'deserve, merit'; see *zky*

zyč   [?] G *zāyeč* 'squeeze out, pull out'

zyd   [Ar √زيد; Sab158; Mutz401] G *zāyəd* 'increase (intr.)'; see *zodāna, bə́z-zodāna*

ẓ

ẓlm   [Ar √ظلم; cf. D (tr.) *zlm*, ⁺*ḏlm* Sab271, G (tr.) *ẓlm* Mutz401] G *ẓālem* 'oppress, force'

Nouns, Adjectives, and Particles

ʾ

ʾā	see ʾāya
ʾabla	[T Hony 1957:1] f. 'older sister'
ʾabrəsəm	[LEAram < P; Sab89] m. 'silk'
ʾádlele	[ʾd + lele; Jastrow 1990:101; cf. ʾɪdlal Sab90, ʾədlel Mutz118] adv. 'tonight'; see lele
ʾafəllu	[H אֲפִלּוּ; Sab99; Mutz128] conj. 'even'
ʾaffandi	[T < Gr; Sab99] m. 'effendi, official'
ʾāġa	[T, K, P; Sab88; Mutz328] m. 'master, agha'; pl. ʾāġāye
ʾāġātūsa	[ʾāġa + K. abstr. suff. -at + abstr. suff. -ūsa] f. 'masterdom, state of being an agha'; bodi ʾāġātūsa 'they perform the duties of the agha'
ʾahāli	[Ar أَهَالِي; Sab90] pl. tant. 'population, people'
ʾāhat, ʾāt	[ClAram m.s. (ה)אנת, f.s. (י)אנת; Hoberman 1988 and 1990; Jastrow 1990; cf. ʾāhət m.s. and ʾāhat f.s. Sab88; Mutz328] indep. prn. 'you (c.s.)'
ʾakčən	[? + אך; cf. akhchûn, akhchünta 'in so far as, whenever' Maclean 1901:8, ʾɪxjɪn, ʾɪkčɪn, ʾɪqčin, qčɪn, maxčɪn 'the size of' Sab95] 'the size of'; ʾakčən xa tora 'the size of a bull'; ʾakčən məzzəd rešox 'as many as the hairs on your head'
ʾako	[K] conj. 'when'; see čukun, ko
ʾāla	[K; Sab88; Mutz328] f. 'side, direction'; pl. ʾalāle; l-é-ʾāl 'in that direction'; mən d-axxa u-l-é-ʾāl 'from here on'; mənne u-l-é-ʾāl 'from there on'; tam l-é-ʾāl 'from there on,' ʾatta-u-l-é-ʾāl 'from now on' (cf. JZakho mɪn ʾɪdyo ulēʾāla Sabar 2005:202)
ʾaláy	[K, P, T; cf. ʾalāy ⁺qomandar 'the chief of Staff' Sab96] 'military regiment'
ʾalla	[Ar الله; Sab96] m. 'God'; see ʾilāha, ʾišalla, walla
ʾalpa	[ClAram אַלְפָּא; Sab96; Mutz328] 'thousand'; pl. ʾalpe
ʾamita	[Ar عَمِيد?] 'civilian police'
ʾamoya	[K amo, IrAr ʿammu < Ar عَم; Sab97; Mutz328] m. 'paternal uncle'; pl. ʾamawāsa; ʾamoyi 'my paternal uncle'; ʾamód d-é Šambi 'the paternal uncle of that Shambi'; ʾamo 'Uncle! (voc.)'; see ʾamta
ʾamra	[ClAram עַמְרָא; Sab97; Mutz328] 'wool'; cf. marʿaz
ʾamta	[Syr ܚܡܬܐ; Sab97; Mutz328] f. 'maternal aunt'; see ʾamoya
ʾan	see ʾanna
ʾāna	[ClAram אֲנָא; Hoberman 1988 and 1990; Jastrow 1990; Sab89; Mutz328] indep. prn. 'I (c.)'
ʾanəšk(a?)	[K Chyet 2003:7] f. 'elbow'; attested only in ʾanəškəd gyāne 'his own elbow(s)'
ʾanglisnāya	see ʾənglisnāya
ʾanglizi	[Ar أَنْكَلِيزِي; cf. inglézi Maclean 1901:15, ʾ/ʾɪnglēzi Sab98 and 1990: 59] m. 'English'; see ʾənglisnāya

'āni [JBA הְנֵּא, Syr ܗܢܘܢ; PNENA *ahnin, āni* Hoberman 1988:569; Hoberman 1990; Jastrow 1990; Sab89; Mutz382] indep. prn. 'they (c.)'

'anna, 'an [JBA הְנֵּא, Syr ܗܢܘܢ; cf. *'a/ınna/e/i* Sab97–98, *'anna* Mutz328; Jastrow 1990] dem. prn. 'these, those (c.)'

'aqalta see *'aqla*

'aqla, 'aqalta [ClAram עקל; Krotkoff 1985:130–131; Sab99; Mutz328] f. 'foot'; pl. *'aqle, 'aqlāsa*

'aqqar, 'áqqara ['ad + Ar قَدْ; cf. *'oqad(da), 'oqat, 'aθqa(da)* Sab91, *'oqad, 'óqad-da* Mutz333] adv. 'so much, to such an extent'; see *qadər, qudrəta*

'aqubra [TO and JBA עֻכְבְּרָא, Syr ܥܘܩܒܪܐ; Sab99; Mutz328] 'mouse'

'ar'a [ClAram אַרְעָא; Sab99; Mutz329] f. 'land, earth, field'; *'ar'āya (haggada = הארץ)*; pl. *'ar'āsa, 'ar'āne*

'arba [ClAram אַרְבְּעָא; Sab100; Mutz114] 'four'; *kút'arbeni* 'the four of us'; see *'arba'sar, 'arbamma, 'arbi, 'arbūšeb*

'arba'sar [Syr ܐܪܒܥܣܪ; cf. *'arba'sar* Sab100, *'arbá'əssar* Mutz115] 'fourteen'; see *'arba, 'arbamma, 'arbi, 'arbušəb*

'arbamma ['arba + *əmma*; cf. *'arbe'ma, 'arba-'ımmāye, 'arba 'ımma* Sab100; *'arbá'əmma* Mutz329; §4.3.3] 'four hundred'; see *'arba, 'arba'sar; 'arbi, 'arbūšeb*

'arbi [ClAram אַרְבְּעִין; cf. *'arbi, 'arbı'i* Sab100, *'arbi* Mutz115] 'forty'; see *'arba, 'arba'sar, 'arbamma, 'arbūšeb*

'arbūšeb [LAram ארבעא בשבא; cf. *'arbōšıb, 'arbūšıb* Sab100, *'árbošeb* Mutz117] 'Wednesday'; see *'arba, 'arba'sar, 'arbamma, 'arbi*

'arməlsa [ClAram אַרְמַלְתָּא; Sab101; Mutz329] f. 'widow'

'arye [ClAram אַרְיָא, pl. אַרְיָוָתָא; Sab100; Mutz329] pl. 'lions'

'arzūḥal, 'arzuḥál [T *arzuhál* < Ar عَرْض حَال] m. 'written request, petition'

'askanāne [?] pl. 'type of cake'

'áškara [K, P; Sab101; Mutz329] adv. 'openly, publicly'

'āt see *'āhat*

'atta [*hā danta < עִדָּנָא Mutz329; Sab101; cf. BiblAram כְּעַן, כְּעֶנֶת] adv. 'now'; *'atta-u-l-é-'āl* 'from now on'; *m-atta* 'from now'

'atxa see *hatxa*

*'aṭrušnāya [GN *Aṭruš* + gent. suff. *-nāya*] 'resident of Atruš (Iraqi Kurdistan)'; f. *'aṭrušnesa*

'avrāza [K; Sab89] 'steep slope, hard climb'

'awwal [Ar أَوَّل; Sab91; Mutzafi 2004:168] ord. num. 'first'; *yom 'awwal* 'first day'

'ax- see *'axxa*

'āxər [Ar أَخِير; cf. *âkher, âkhir* 'well!, to be sure!, at last' Maclean 1901:8] excl. 'well!'

'axnan [ClAram אֲנַחְנָא; Hoberman 1988 and 1990; Jastrow 1990; Maclean 1901:8; cf. *'axni, 'axnēni, 'axnan* Sab96, *'axnan, 'axni* Mutz-329] indep. prn. 'we (c.)'

'axona [ClAram אַח + dim. suff. *-ona*; Sab95; Mutz329] m. 'brother'; pl. *'axawāsa*; see *xāsa¹*

'axtun [ClAram אַנְתּוּן; Hoberman 1988; Jastrow 1990; cf. 'axtun, 'áxt/
nōxun Sab96, 'axtoxun, 'axtun Mutz329] indep. prn. 'you (c. pl.)'

'axūsa [LEAram אֲחוּתָא < ClAram אח + abstr. suff. א־וּתָ־? < *ʾaxwsā?] f.
'brotherhood'

'axxa, 'ax- [ClAram הָכָא; Sab95; Mutz330] adv. 'here'; l-axxa 'here, to here',
mən 'axxa, m-axxa, mən d-axxa, 'from here'; 'áx-geb tán-geb
(ṭamáha-geb) 'when all's said and done, eventually'

'āya, 'ā [TO and TJ הַהִיא; Hoberman 1990; Jastrow 1990; cf. 'āwa 'he',
'āya 'she' Sab88 and Mutz40] indep. prn. 'he, she, it'; also dem.
prn. 'that (one; c.)'

'ayāha [Sab92; Mutz330] dem. prn. 'that one over there'

'e [TO and TJ הַהִיא; Sab92; Mutz330] dem. prn. 'that (c.)'; see 'egā

'eda [Syr ܥܐܕܐ; Sab92; Mutz330] pl. 'edawāsa 'holidays'

'egā ['e + gā; Sab92; Mutz330] adv. 'so then, now then'

'eka [ClAram אֵיכָא; Sab93; Mutz330] adv. 'where?'; m-eka 'from
where?'; see ke¹

'ena [ClAram (Bibl Aram עֵינָא, Syr ܥܝܢܐ, TO עֵינָא); Sab94 and Mutz-
330] f. (1) 'eye', (2) 'spring, well'; pl. 'ene 'eyes'; 'enāsa 'springs,
wells'; go 'eni 'willingly' (calque on Ar عَلَى عَيْنِي); cf. kāni

'eni [Syr ܐܝܢܐ; cf. énî Maclean 1901:10, 'ēmi Sab94, 'ema Mutz330]
interr. prn. 'which?'; adj. 'éni-əšti kiloye, šo'i kiloye 'some sixty
kilos, seventy kilos'

'era [Ar أَيْر; Sab94; Mutz330] 'penis'

'ewa see wewa

'əbb-, 'əbbəd see b-

'əčˊa [ClAram תִּשְׁעָה; Sab90; Mutz115] 'nine'; see 'əčˊa'sar

'əčˊa'sar [Syr ܬܫܥܣܪ; cf. 'əčˊa'sar Sab90, 'əčˊá'əssar Mutz115] 'nineteen';
see 'əčˊa

'əd- see d-, 'ədyo, 'ádlele

'ədyo ['d + yoma; Jastrow 1990:101; Sab90; Mutz331] adv. 'today'; see
yoma, palgədyo

'əgdād, 'əgdāde [*ḥad + ḥad; LEAram Kutscher 1964:124; cf. 'ıxdāde, 'ıx/ġzāze,
'ıxde Sab95, 'əxðe Mutz332] reciprocal prn. 'one another, together'; m- əgdād(e), l-əgdād(e), go 'əgdād, reš 'əgdāde

'əl-, 'əlləd see l-

'ələl see l-'ələl

'əlˊuwwa [ClAram לְגֹו; < *lᵊ-ġawwāya Mutz23; cf. (l)gâ-wâ-î Maclean
1901:46, lo'a Khan 1999:573, (l)'ōya Sab247, lawġəl, lawġul Tezel
2003:246, lo'a Mutzafi 2004:229 and 2005:96, 'oya, l-'oya Mutz-
23] prep. 'inside'; cf. go, gaw-

'əlisa [TO אַלְיְתָא, JBA אַלְיְתָא, Syr ܐܠܝܬܐ; cf. 'ülīta, 'ılīta Sab96] f. 'fat
tail'

'əlla [ClAram אֶלָּא < לָא + אֵן; Sab96, Mutz331] conj. 'except, but
rather'; adv. 'certainly' see 'ən

'əl-táma see tāma

'əltəx [ClAram תְּח(וֹ)ת; cf. txēt/txe, xēt, xē Sab309, 'əltəx Mutz331] adv.
'below, beneath'; 'əltəx 'əltəx 'way below'; see 'əltxé(t?), xe

ʾəltxé(t?)   [ClAram תח(ו)ת; Sab309] prep. 'under'; see ʾəltax, xe

ʾəmər   [Ar أَمْر; cf. ʾımır, ʿımır Sab97] m. 'order'; see ʾmr, ʿṃṛ, maʿṃúṛ

ʾəmma   [ClAram מאה; Steiner 1995; Hoberman 2007:149; cf. ʾımma, pl.
                 ʾımmawāta, ʾımmāye/-he Sab97, ʾəmma, pl. ʾəmmāhe Mut331]
                 'hundred'; pl. ʾəmmāhe; -mma when enclitic to number, e.g.,
                 šöʾámma 'seven hundred'

ʾəmməta   [K, T < Ar أُمَّة; cf. ʾümmıta Sab97] f. 'nation'

ʾəṃbāši   [T onbaşı Hony 1957:275; cf. umbāši Spitaler 1967:89] m. 'cor-
                 poral'

ʾənglisnāya, ʾanglisnāya   [K, Ar < Eng + gent. suff. -nāya; cf. ʾ/ʿınglıznāya Sab98,
                 ʾənglıznāya Mutz334] m. 'Englishman'; see ʾanglizi

ʾən   [ClAram אֵן; Sab97; Mutz331] conj. 'if, or'; ʾən la 'if not'; see ʾəlla

ʾənwe   [ClAram עֵנְבָא; Sab98; Mutz331] pl. 'grapes'

ʾəpra   [ClAram עַפְרָא; Sab99; Mutz331] m. 'earth, soil'

ʾəqra   [ClAram עֵקָרָא; Sab99; Mutz331] 'bottom, base'

ʾərba   [LEAram: JBA ארבא, ערבא, Syr ܚܘܿܬܐ; Sab100; Mutz331–332] f.
                 'sheep'; pl. ʾərbe

ʾərbāla   [ClAram עֵרְבְּלָא; Sab100; Mutz332] 'coarse sieve'; pl. ʾərbāle

ʾərota   [LAram ערובתא; Blau & Hopkins 2006:439; Sab100; Mutz332;]
                 f. 'Friday'

ʾərwāna   [Syr ܚܘܿܬ̈ܐ Mutzafi (p.c.); Sab100] m. 'kindness, charity, good
                 deed'

ʾəryāna   [Syr ܚܘ̈ܐ; Mutz332] m. 'rain'

ʾərxe   [ClAram רחֵיָא; cf. ʾırxe Sab100, ʾərxe Mutz332] 'mill'

ʾəspa   [ClAram √אסף Sab98; יזף < אסף? Mutz332] m. 'loan'; b-əspa 'on
                 loan'

ʾəsri   [ClAram עשרין; Sab99; Mutz115] 'twenty'; see ʾəsṛa

ʾəstakāne   [K < Russian Chyet 2003:286] pl. 'small glasses for tea'

ʾəsṛa   [ClAram עשרא; cf. ʾısra(?), ʾıṣra Sab99, ʾəṣṛa Mutz332] 'ten'; see
                 ʾəsri

ʾəškāsa   [LAram אשכתא; cf. pl. (ʾe)škāṭa, reškāsa Sab101, ʾəšəkϑa, pl. ʾəškā-
                 ϑa Mutz332] pl. 'testicles'

ʾəšta   [LWAram אשתא < ClAram שֶׁתָּא; Sab101; Mutz114] 'six'; see ʾəštaʾ-
                 sar, ʾəšti

ʾəštaʾsar   [Syr ܥܣܪ̈ܐ(ܐ); cf. ʾıštaʾsar Sab101, ʾəštáʾəssar Mutz117] 'six-
                 teen'; see ʾəšta, ʾəšti

ʾəšti   [TO שְׁתִין, Syr ܥܣ̈ܬܐ, ܥܣ̈ܬ̈ܐ; Sab101; Mutz115] 'sixty'; see ʾəšta,
                 ʾəštaʾsar

ʾəštár   [ModH?; (א)שְׁטָר) Ben-Yaacob 1985:195 < H, Aram < Akk; cf.
                 šaṭṭar Sab297] 'document'

ʾəšvaṭ   [ClAram שְׁבָט/שְׁבַט; cf. ishwâṭ Maclean 1901:21, (א)שְׁבָט) Ben-
                 Yaacob 1985:189, šavaṭ Sab294, šawaṭ Mutz385] 'month of She-
                 vat'

ʾətwa   see ʾit

ʾəxre   [LEAram חריא; Sab96; Mutz332] pl. tant. 'excrement, shit'

ʾəzla   [Syr ܚ̈ܠܐ; Sab92; Mutz332] m. 'yarn'; pl. ʾəzlāle

ʾəzza   [ClAram עֵזָּא; Sab92; Mutz332] f. 'goat'; cf. marʿaz

'ib-   see 'it

'ida   [LAram אידא < ClAram יְדָא; Sab92; Mutz330–331] f. 'hand, side, direction'; pl. 'idāsa; b-íya-'ida u-yắ-'ida 'when it comes down to it, at any rate' (lit. 'in this hand and this hand'); 'āni zəllu 'idəd Pắras-ži 'They went (in) the direction of Persia too'

'ilāha   [ClAram אֱלָהָא; cf. 'i/īlāha, 'ilā(ha) Sab93, 'ilāha Mutz331] m. 'God'; see 'aḷḷa, 'išaḷḷa, waḷḷa

'ilāna   [ClAram אִילָנָא; Sab93; Mutz331] 'tree'

'ile, -ile, -le, -yle   [Sabar 93; Mutz50; § 4.4.6.1] 3 m.s. present copula

'imal   [ClAram אמתי; cf. 'īman, 'īmal Sab94, 'imal Mutz331] interr. adv. 'when?'

'išaḷḷa   [K < Ar إِنْ شَاءَ اللّٰهُ; Sab95] 'God willing'; see 'aḷḷa, 'ilāha, waḷḷa

'it, 'itən, 'ítəna   [ClAram אית; cf. 'īt, 'ītın, 'īs, 'īsın Sab95, 'iϑ, 'iϑən, 'íϑena Mutz-331; § 4.8.1] predicator of existence 'there is'; 'ətwa 'there was'; 'ibi (< אית בי; § 4.8.2) 'I can'; 'ibe ᴴb-gilᴴ 'əšta šənne 'He is six years old'; 'ətwāba 'she contained'; cf. let, letən

'ixāla   [ClAram √אכל; Sab93; Mutz331] 'eating, food'

'iya, yā-   [cf. 'a/ıyya(n) Sab92, 'iyya Khan 1999:563] dem. prn. 'this (c.)'; b-íya- 'ida u-yắ-'ida 'when it comes down to it, at any rate'; filler 'iya mā kəmrila 'what do you call it?—' (lit. 'this is what they call it')

'o   [JZakho 'o] dem. prn. 'that'

'oḍa   [Ar أوضَة < T; cf. ⁺ōda Sab91, 'oda Mutz333] 'room'; pl. 'oḍe

'ogā   [JZakho 'o + gā] adv. 'at that time'; see gā

'ordi   [T; cf. ûrdû Maclean 1901:6] f. 'army'

'osmoḷḷi   [T Osmanlı < Ar عُثْمَان; cf. ⁺'osmalli Sab91] m. 'Ottoman'

*⁺'umra   [Syr ܥܘܡܪܐ; cf. 'umṛa Mutz333] 'monastery, church'

'uramarnāya [GN 'Uramar + gent. suff. -nāya] m. 'resident of Uramar (Turkish Kurdistan)'

'urxa   [ClAram אוּרְחָא; Sab91; Mutz333] f. 'road, way; b-'urxa b-'urxa 'along the way' (cf. 'urxa 'urxa Mutz294, 322); 'urxa düqāli 'I took the road (= I left)'; mxele 'urxa 'he hit the road'

'uṛwa   ['urwa < *rurwa Mutzafi 2006:126–127; cf. ClAram רַבָּא; Sab91, 288; cf. 'əṛwa Mutz332;] m. 'big, important, grown-up'; xa besa 'uṛwa 'a big house'; f. ṛapsa; dūka ṛapsa 'large place'; pl 'uṛwe; baṛāne 'uṛwe 'large rams'; škaftyāsa 'uṛwe 'uṛwe 'very large caves'; təjjāre 'úṛwe-lu 'they are important merchants'; see *'uṛwāna, 'uṛwanūsa, ṛāba

*'uṛwāna   ['uṛwa + suffix -āna] m. 'leader'; pl. 'uṛwāne; kúllu-ži 'āġáye-lu 'uṛwáne-lu 'all of them are aghas, they are leaders'; see 'uṛwa, 'uṛwanūsa, ṛāba

'uṛwanūsa   [cf. rürwanūṯa Sab288] f. 'greatness'; see 'uṛwa, ṛāba

'ušya   [K ûṣî 'bunch of grapes' Chyet 2003:632] 'cluster (of grapes)'

ʿ

ʿabba [Ar عِبّ; cf. ʿubba Sab247, ʿoppa Spitaler 1967:82] 'inner pocket
of garment'

ʿačāyəb [T acayib < Ar عَجَائِب; cf. ʿajab 'wonder,' pl. ʿajābe, ʿajaby/wāta,
ʿajabāta Sab247, ʿajabāða 'miracles, wonders' Mutz334] excl.
'how strange!'

ʿādəta [K < Ar عَادَة; cf. ʿâdat, ʿâditâ, ʿâdé, ʿadât Maclean 1901:235, ʿāde
Sab246 and Mutz334] f. 'custom'

ʿamaliya [Ar عَمَلِيّة; Sab250] f. '(medical) operation'

*ʿamənnāya [GN ʿAmədya + gent. suff. -nāya; cf. ʿamıdnāya Sab250, ʿaməd-
nāya Mutz334] m. 'resident of Amidya'; pl. ʿammənnāye

ʿāni [H עָנִי; Sab251] inv. 'poor person'

ʿanjil [K, T, Ar < Gr; cf. ʾ/ʿınjil Sab98 and 1990:59, ʾənjil Mutz331]
'Gospels'

*ʿaqār [K, Ar عَقَار; Sab251] 'immovable property'; pl. ʿaqāre

ʿāqəl [Ar عَقْل; cf. ʿāqıl, ʿaqil Sab246, ʿāqəl Mutz334] m. 'reason, mind,
knowledge'; mād ʿáqəli qāṭe 'as far as I find reasonable'; ʿáqəli lá-
qāṭe' 'my mind doesn't find (it) reasonable'; ʿáqəlu mpəllu 'they
fell from their senses'

ʿaqida [Ar عَقِيد 'colonel'] m. '(military) leader'

ʿāra [Ar عَار; cf. ʿār Maclean 1901:243] m. 'shame'

*ʿarabāya [Ar عَرَب + gent. suff. -āya; Sab252; Mutz334] m. Arab; pl. ʿarab-
āye

ʿaraqin [K, Ar عَرَق; cf. ʿaraqin, ʿaraqi Sab252, ʿaraqin Mutz334] m. 'arrack'

ʿaskar [K, T, Ar عَسْكَر; cf. ʾaskar, ʿaskar Sab98, ʿaskar Mutz334] m.
'army, soldier'; lu wide ʿaskar 'they have done the army (service)'
(calque on ModH עָשָׂה צָבָא?)

ʿasəl [K, T, Ar أَصْل; ʿaṣıl Sab251] m. '(good) origin'; see be-ʿáṣəl, *ʿaṣlāya, ʿaṣli, māra (mare ʿaṣəl)

*ʿaṣlāya [K, T, Ar أَصْل + gent. suff. -āya; ʿaṣlāya Sab251] m. 'of good
origin'; pl. ʿaṣlāye; see ʿaṣli, ʿaṣəl, be-ʿáṣəl, māra (mare ʿaṣəl)

ʿaṣli [K, T, Ar أَصْلِي] inv. 'genuine, of (good) origin'; see *ʿaṣlāya, be-
ʿáṣəl, māra (mare ʿaṣəl)

ʿāṣərta [Ar عَصْر; cf. ʿāṣırta, ʿāṣır Sab246, ʿāṣər, ʿāṣərta Mutz334] f. 'evening'

ʿaširat [K, T, Ar عَشِيرَة; cf. ʿašīrıta, pl. ʿašīrıtyāta, ʿašrıyāta Sab252; ʿaširat,
pl. ʿaširatte Mutz334] tribe, clan'; pl. ʿaširatte

ʿaṭarka [Ar عَطَّار + K suff. -k; cf. ʿŭṭâr Maclean 1901:238, ʿaṭāra Sab248]
m. 'peddler'

ʿāwon [H עָוֹן; Sab247; Mutz334] 'sin, guilt'; see qdāla

ʿaziza [Ar عَزِيز; Sab248] m. 'beloved, dear'

ʿeba [Ar عَيْب; Sab248; Mutz334] m. 'disgrace'

ʿeġəl [H עֵגֶל; Sab247] 'the Golden Calf'

ʿel 'family' [Ar عِيّل; cf. ʿéyâl (< عِيَال) 'family' Maclean 1901:238, ʿēl
'(tribal Arab) populace' Sab249] 'family'

'eraqnāya   [Gn *Eraq* + gent. suff. *-nāya*] m. 'Iraqi'; pl. *'eraqnāye*

'ǝnād   [Ar عِنَاد; cf. *'ınyad* Sab251] 'mutual resistance'

'ǝnyān   [H, LAram עִנְיָן; Sab251] 'matter, affair'

'jiza   [Ar عَجِيز; cf. *'jiza* Mutz334] m. 'tired, weary'; pl. *'jize*

*'ujna   [Ar √عجن; cf. *'ıjna* Sab247] 'batch or bowl of dough'; pl. *'ujne*;
             'ujne paṭire 'batches of unleavened bread' (= עֻגּוֹת מַצּוֹת; *haggada*)

'umbāre   [Ar عَنْبَر, أَنْبَار; cf. *+'ümbar*, *'üm/nbāre* Sab250, *'ambāre* Avidani
             1959:41] pl. storehouses (*haggada*)

'urṭūsa   [Syr ܥܘܪܛܐ; cf. *'urṭīta* Sab248; *'rṭ* Mutz335; Steiner 1995:54–
             56] f. 'fart'

b

b-, 'ǝbb-, 'ǝbbǝd   [ClAram -בּ; Sab103; Hoberman 2007:149; Mutz335] 'in, at, on'

bāba   [Syr ܒܒܐ; T, K, Ar بَابَا; Sab103; Mutz335] m. 'father'; *bába-u-
             yǝmma* 'parents'; pl. *babawāsa*; excl. *bāba*, *bābo* 'Father!, my
             God! (voc.)'

badal, m-badal   [Ar بَدَل; cf. *mbâdâl*, *mbǎdâl* 'instead of' Maclean 1901:153]
             prep. 'in place of'

*baġdannāya   [GN *Baġdad* + gent. suff. *-nāya*; cf. *baġdad(n)āya*, *baġdannāya*
             Sab104; § 3.6.b] m. 'resident of Baghdad'; f. *baġdannesa*

bahar   [K; Sab106; Mutz336] 'spring season'

*bahūra   [Syr ܒܗܘܪܐ; Sab105; Mutz336] 'bright'; pl. *bahūre*

bahwarūsa   [K + abstr. suff. *-ūsa*; cf. *bahwari/ūta* Sab105] f. 'faith, trust'

baḥḥar   [K, Ar بَحْر; cf. *baḥ(ḥ)ar* Sab107, *baḥḥar* Mutz336] 'sea, lake'

baḥs   [K, T, Ar بَحْث; Sab107; Mutz121,336] 'report, talk, mention';
             godǝt baḥse 'you make mention of him' (cf. *me:so:ye baḥsox* לדבר
             עליך Avinery 1988:218)

bak   [T, K, Ar بِيك; cf. *bag, beg, bek* Maclean 1901:24, *bag* Sab104 and
             Mutz336] m. 'bey, lord'

bāla   [ClAram בָּלָא; Sab103; Mutz336] m. 'attention'

balamina   [Ar بَرِّيمَة < P? Lane 1863:195; Almkvist 1891:273 n. 2; Vollers
             1896:628–629] 'iron pole for making holes in stones to insert
             dynamite'; pl. *balamine*

baláš   [IrAr; cf. *(b)balaš, mbalaš* Sab111, *baláš* Mutz336] adv. 'for free'

balāye   [K, Ar بَلَاء; cf. s. *bala*, pl. *balıtyāta*, *balāye*, *balwıtyāta* Sabar
             2002a:110, s. and pl. *balāye* Mutz336; § 4.2.3.1.d] f.s. and pl.
             'trouble(s), disaster(s)'; see *dard*

bale, balé   [K, Ar بَلَى; cf. *bale* 'yes indeed, however, moreover' Sab111, *balé*
             'yes as answer to negative question' Mutz336] conj. 'yes, indeed,
             however'

balki(t)   [K, T; cf. *balki(d/t), balku/in* Sab111, *balki* Mutzafi 2008a:336]
             adv. 'perhaps'

balo'ta   [LEAram בְּלוֹעָא; Sab111; Mutz336] f. 'throat'

bamba   [K < Eur; cf. *+bımba* Sab111] 'bomb'

bāqe   [Ar بَقّ; LEAram בַּקָּא; cf. *bāqa* Sab104, *baqta* Mutz337] pl. 'mos-
             quitoes'

*baqqa   [K; baqqa, pl. baqqe Sab113l, baqqa, pl. baqqe, baqqaϑa Mutz-
                  336; Avidani 1959:36 פקאסָא] 'frog'; pl. baqqe (haggada)
bárakus   [K ber + קובל(?) + abstr. suff. -ūsa(?); also in JDohok] prep. 'in
                  front of, opposite'; bárakus dide 'opposite him'; see barqul
bárawanūsa   [? + abstr. suff. -ūsa] f. 'separation'
bárbara   [K; cf. bârâbâr 'together' Maclean 1901:38, barbar 'towards'
                  Sabar 2002:114] adv. 'together'
barda   [ClAram בְּרְדָא; cf. barda, barabarda Sab114] 'hail'
bargūze   [K; cf. bargūza, bargus Sab114, bargūza Mutz336] pl. 'suit, tra-
                  ditional Kurdish men's homespun woolen jacket and trousers'
barqul   [K ber + ClAram לקבל Sab116; K ber + קובל Mutzafi 2008a:336–
                  337] prep. 'in front of, opposite'; see bárakus
bārux-xábba   [H בָּרוּךְ הַבָּא; cf. bārux-xábba Sab114] excl. 'welcome!'
barwāra   [K; Sab114] 'shortcut route'
barzanāya   [GN Barzan + gent. suff. -āya] m. 'resident of Barzan (Iraqi
                  Kurdistan)'
baṛāxa   [H בְּרָכָה; cf. +birāxa Sab155, baṛāxa Mutz337] f. 'blessing'; see
                  brk
bas, bassa   [K, T, P, IrAr; cf. bas(sa) Sab112, bas Mutz337] adv. 'enough';
                  bassa bassa 'more than enough'
basər   [ClAram בָּתַר < OAram באתר; Sab116; Mutz337] prep. 'after';
                  adv. basər hādax 'afterwards'; see básbasər
básbasər   [בתר + בתר; cf. báϑ-baϑər Mutz121] prep. 'right after'; básbasre
                  'right after him'; see basər
basima   [ClAram בַּסִימָא; cf. bassīma Sab112, basima Mutzafi 2008a:337]
                  m. 'pleasing'; f. basəmta; pl. basime; see bsm
*baškalnāya, *ḅaškalnāya [GN Baškala + gent. suff. -nāya] m.s. 'resident of
                  Bashkala (Turkish Kurdistan)'; pl. baškalnāye, ḅaškalnāye
baxbāba   [bax + bāba; Sab110] 'stepmother'; see baxta, baxtūsa
baxta   [Sefire בכתה? Fitzmyer 1995:81–83; Syr ܒܟܬܐ? Krotkoff 1985:
                  131–132; Sab110; Mutz337] f. 'woman, wife'; cst. bax; bax mədor
                  'the wife of the mudir'; 'é-baxta 'I (lit., 'that woman'); pl. baxtāsa;
                  see baxbāba, baxtūsa
baxtūsa   [baxta + abst. suff. -ūsa] f. 'wifehood'; see baxbāba, baxta, gora
                  (u-baxtūsa)
baxxat   [IrAr, P; cf. báxad īlá Meehan & Alon 1979:192 n.79, bax(x)at
                  'ilāha Sab110] 'mercy'; baxxatəd 'ilāha 'for the mercy of
                  God!'
be   [ClAram בִּית; EgAram, JPA, Syr abs. בִּי; Sab110; Mutzafi 2008a:
                  338] cst. 'family, household'; be 'amoyi 'my (paternal) uncle's
                  family'; be 'āḡāye 'family of aghas'; see besa
be'ta   [ClAram ביעתא; Sab104; Mutz338] f. 'egg'; pl. be'e
be-'áṣəl   [K be 'without' + Ar أَصْل (good) origin] inv. 'bad origin'; see 'aṣəl,
                  'aṣlāye, 'aṣli, māra (mare 'aṣəl)
beb   [ClAram בֶּה בְּ- Mutz121,338; K? Sab108] prep. 'together with'
be-čára   [K be 'without' + K čare 'remedy' Maclean 1901:138] inv. 'help-
                  less'

be-dáda   [K *be* 'without' + K, T, *dād* 'justice' Maclean 1901:60] inv. 'without justice'

be-dárd   [K *be* 'without' + K 'pain'] adv. 'painlessly'; see *dard*

be-dín   [K *be* 'without' + Ar دِين 'religion'] inv. 'religionless'; see *din*[1]

behna   [K; cf. *behna*, *bıhen* Sab105] 'moment'; *xá-behna* 'in a moment, suddenly'

be-hívi   [K *be* 'without' + K *hivi* 'hope'; Sab108] inv. 'hopeless'; see *hivi*

besa   [ClAram ביתא; Sab110; Mutz338] 'house'; pl. *bāte*; see *be*

be-námus   [K *be* 'without' + K, T, Ar نَامُوس < Gr; *nāmus* 'proper behavior' Sabar 2002:228] 'improper behavior'

bəndaqiya   [Ar بُنْدُقِيَّة, K; cf. *banüqtâ* 'small gun' Maclean 1901:34] f. 'rifle'; pl *bəndaqiye*

bənhe   [ClAram גהא(ו)ה + ב; cf. *bı'ınhe*, *bınhe*, *bine* 'morrow, tomorrow' Sabar 2002a:104, *bənhe* 'tomorrow' Mutz339] 'morning'

bənjūka   [T Redhouse 1890:411] 'bead to avert the evil eye'

bər   [ClAram בר; Nöldeke 1910:137–139, Fassberg 2008a; Sab114; Mutz339] cst. 'son'; *kalba bər kalba* 'son of a bitch!'; *xmāra bər xmāra* 'what an ass!'; see *brona*, *brāta*

bərqa   [ClAram בּרְקָא; Sab116; Mutz339] m. 'lightning'

*bəṣla   [ClAram בּצְלָא; Sab113] 'onion'; pl. *bəṣle*

bəš   [K; Sab116; Mutz339] adv. 'more'; see *bə́š-ṛab*, *bəš́ṭor*, *bə́z-zo-dāna*

bə́š-ṛab   [K *bə́š* + *ṛāba*; cf. *bıš/ž-⁺rab* Sab116, *bə́š-ṛab* Mutzafi 2008a:339] adv. 'more'; see *bəš*, *ṛāba*

bəš́ṭor   [K *baṣṭir* Mutz339; cf. *bıšṭo(f/m)* Sab116] adv. 'better'; see *bəš*

bəxya   [cf. ClAram בכיתא; cf. *bikhyâ* Maclean 1901:32, *bxeṭa* Sab110] 'crying'

*bəzmāra   [K < Ar مِسْمَار < Aram מסמר; Sab107; Mutz339] '(metal) nail'; pl. *bəzmāre*

bəzza   [ClAram √בזז Sab107] m. 'wretched person'

bə́z-zodāna   [K *bə́š* + *zodāna*; cf. *bə́š-zodāna* Mutz339] adv. 'more'; see *bəš*, *zodāna*, *zyd*

bəẓẓoṭe   [K; cf. *⁺bızzəṭa*, *⁺bızzodka*, pl. *⁺bızzōte*, *⁺bızzotkat* Sab107] pl. 'torches'

bomāxəd   [*b* + *'o* + *yoma* + *xeta*; cf. *bōmaxín/d/t* Sab106, *bomaxət* Mutz340] 'the day after tomorrow'

brāta   [ClAram ברתא; Nöldeke 1910:137–139; Fassberg 2008a; Sabar 2002:113; Mutz340] f. 'daughter'; pl. *bnāsa*; *kaləpsa brāt kalba* 'what a bitch!'; see *bər*, *brona*

brona   [Syr ܒܪܘܢܐ < OAram בר + dim. suff. -*ona*; Nöldeke 1910:138; Fassberg 2008a; Sabar 202:114; Mutz340] m. 'son'; cst. *bron*, e.g., *bron 'āġa* 'son of the agha'; pl. *bnone*; see *bər*

ḅ

ḅaṇḳ   [Ar بَنْك, T < Eur; Sabar 1990:59 and 2002:112] 'bank'; see *paṇqá-ṇoṭ*

*ḇarāna   [K; cf. ⁺barāna Sab113, barāna Mutz336] 'ram'; pl. ḇaṛāne
ḇaṛāza   [K; cf. bırāza, pl. ⁺bırāze Sab113, ḇaṛāza Mutzafi 2008a:341]
               'boar, pig'; pl. ḇaṛāze
ḇāš   [K; cf. ⁺bāš Sab104, bāš Mutz337] inv. 'good'; adv. 'well, very';
               pəšle naxwaš ḇāš 'he became very ill'
*ḇaškalnāya   see *baškalnāya
ḇəč̣'a   [T, K; cf. ⁺bıč̣'a Sab104, bəč̣'a Mutz338] m. 'bastard'; cf. mamzer

č

ča   [K Chyet 2003:82] adv. 'well, c'mon' (with imperative); ča méselu
               xanči m̥āye 'C'mon (and) bring them some water!'
čådəra   [K, T; čādıra Sab130] 'tent'
čakke   [K; Sab131; Mutz341] pl. tant. 'weapons'
čalnāya   [GN Čalla + gent. suff. -nāya] m. 'resident of Challa'
čamča   [K; cf. 'ladle' Sab131, 'spoon' Mutz341] f. 'spoon'
*čanta   [K, T; Ar شَنْتة; cf. čanta, pl. čanyāta Sab132, čanta, pl. čanāϑa
               Mutz341] 'satchel'; pl. čanyāsa
čāpole   [K; cf. châpûla Maclean 1901:137] pl. 'slaps'
čappar   [K; Sab132] f. 'palisade'
čappe   [K; Sab132; Mutz341] 'left'; only in 'ida čappe 'to the left (= left
               hand)'
čāwəš   [T; Sab130] m. 'sergeant'
čāy   [Ar, K, T, P; cf. chai Maclean 1901:129, čāy(i) Sab130, čāye
               Mutz341] f. 'tea'
čaydanka   [K, T; cf. chaidân Maclean 1901:130] 'teapot'
čayxāna   [K, T; cf. čāyixāna Sab130] m. 'tea house'
čenike   [K čenek 'little' Rizgar 1993:55?] pl. 'pieces'; see čənye
čeri   [ClAram תשרי < Akk; Sab131; Mutz91,342] f. 'autumn'
čəčūke   [K çûçik 'bird' Rizgar 1993:58] pl. 'birds(?)'; cf. čūka
čənye   [K çênî 'in small portions' Rizgar 1993:56] pl. 'pieces'; cf. čen-
               ike
čəpka   [K; cf. čəppəkϑa Mutz342; Sab132] f. 'drop'
čəxra   [ClAram √שׁחר; cf. ⁺šıxra Sab299] 'soot, ground charcoal'; see
               šəxxoṛa
čiroke   [K; cf. ⁺čīrōke Sab131] f. 'story, folktale'
ču   [K; ču Mutz342; Sab130; Correll 1974] 'no, not, not any'; čú-gā
               'never,' čú-xa 'no one, anyone,' čú-məndi 'nothing'
čūka   [K; 'chick' Mutz342] 'bird(?)'; cf. čəčūke
čukulāte   [ModH, Eur] pl. 'chocolates'
čukun, čuku, čunku [K, T, P; cf. chünki Maclean 1901:128, Sabar čınki, čıki/un
               2002:132, čukun Mutz342] conj. 'because'; see 'ako, ko

č̣

č̣o'a   [ClAram √שׁעע; Sab130] m. 'smooth'; pl. č̣o'e

d

-d, d-, 'əd-	[ClAram -ד/די; Sab136; Mutz343; §4.1.8] possessive-relative particle; see *dla, mād, tad*
da	see *de*
dabāḥa	[Ar √ذبح; cf. ClAram √דבח] m. 'ritual slaughterer'; see *dbḥ*
dabanja	[T, K; cf. *+d/ṭabanja* Sab137] 'pistol'
dāda	see *be-dáda*
dahba	[K, Ar دَابّة; Sab138; Mutz343] 'animal'; pl. *dahbe*
dāna	[ClAram עִדָּנָא; Sab136; Mutz343] 'time'; pl. *dāne*; conj. *kud dān* 'whenever'
*dapá	[ModH דַּף] 'page'; pl. *dapé*
daqiqa	[K, T, Ar دَقِيقَة; Sab144; Mutz344] f. (1) 'thin', (2) 'minute (of time)'; pl *daqiqe*; see *pāre*
darbəta	[K, T < Ar ضربة; cf. s. and pl. *darbīye* Sab144 based on Avidani 1959:36–39; cf. s. זַרְבָּא, pl. זַרְבָּתִיסָא Alfiye 1986:47] f. 'blow from God (one of the ten plagues)'; pl. *darbiye* (*haggada*)
dard	[K, T; Sab144] 'pain'; *dárd-u-baláye* 'pains and troubles'; see *be-dárd*
darga	[K; Sab144; Mutz344] 'gate'
*darham	[K, T, Ar دِرْهَم < Gr; cf. *dɪrhɪm* Sabar 1990:60 and 2002:145, *darham* Mutz344] 'dirham'; pl. *darhāme*
darwéž	[K, T, P, Ar دَرْوِيش; cf. *darwēš(a)* Sab145] m. 'dervish'
dašta	[K; JBA דַּשְׁתָּא; QAram דחשת; Greenfield & Shaked 1972:38–39; Mutz344] f. 'field'
dawāra	[K, T; Sab138; Mutz344] 'riding animal'; pl. *dawāre*
dawla	[Ar دَوْلَة; cf. *dâ-wiltâ* 'wealth, riches, government, the State, prosperity, good fortune' Maclean 1901:63] 'state'
dax, daxwās-	[Syr ܐܟܘܬܐ; cf. *dɪx, dax* Sab142, *dax, daxwáϑ-* Mutz344] prep. 'like'; *dax* before nouns; *daxwās-* before suffixes; *daxwaseni*; adv. *dax* 'as soon as'; *dax mundyálu l-'ar'a* 'as soon as they threw it on the ground'
daxla	[K 'grains' < Ar دَخْل 'income'; Sab142; Mutz344] 'crop'
daxwās-	see *dax*
de, da	[K, T; cf. *dî, dé, dâ* Maclean 1901:59, *dɪ, day, de(h)* Sab140, *də* Mutz345] adv. 'so, now, well then'; *de mā 'odax?* 'So what should we do?'; *de qū misi* 'So get up (and) bring (it)!'; *da* before gutturals: *da-ḥmól* 'So wait!'
de'sa	[ClAram (דִּיעֲתָא; Syr ܕܘܥܬܐ) Sab137; *de'ϑa* Mutz344] f. 'sweat'
de'sāna	[*de'sa* + suff. *-āna*] m. 'sweaty'
dehna	[LEAram דּוּהְנָא; *dehna* Sab138] 'fat'
dehwa	[ClAram דַּהֲבָא; Sab138; Mutz344] 'gold, goldpiece'
dena	[K, Ar دَيْن; cf. *dēna, dehna* Sab141, *dena*, pl. *dene* Mutz344] m. 'debt'; pl. *dene*
denāna	[*dena* + suff. *-āna*; Mutz344] 'debtor'; pl. *denāne*
desta	[Syr ܕܣܬܐ < P; cf. *dasta* Sab143] f. 'portion of food given to guests'

dəbba   [ClAram דְּבָּא; Sab137; Mutz345] f. 'bear'; pl. *dəbbāsa*

dəd   see *did-*

dədwe   [LEAram דידבא; Sab138; Mutz345] pl. 'flies'

dəmma   [ClAram דְּמָא; Hoberman 2007; cf. *dɪmma*, pl. *dɪmmāhe*, *dɪmm-*
               āye, *dɪmmāta* Sab142; *dəmma*, pl. *demmāhe* Mutz345] m.
               'blood, blood money'; pl. *dəmmāhe* 'guilt of bloodshed': *lá-dāre-*
               tun dəmmāhe zodāne qdāl gyānexun 'don't put additional guilt
               of bloodshed on your necks'

dənga   [?; cf. *danga* 'big wooden mallet' Sab143] 'punch, blow'; pl. *dənge*

dəpna   [LEAram דפנא; cf. *dɪpna*, *dɪpɪnta* Sab144, *dəpna* Mutzafi 2008a:
               345] 'side'; prep. *dəpən*, *l-dəpən* 'next to'

dəqna   [ClAram דְּקְנָא; Sab144; Mutz345] m. 'beard'

dərəst   [K; cf. *darsa(')ad*, *darset* Sab145, *dərəst* Mutz345] adv. 'correct,
               straight, straightaway'

dərmāna   [K, T; cf. *dɪrmāna* Sab145, *darmāna* Mutz344] 'medicine, rem-
               edy'; see *drmn*

dəžmən   [K, T; cf. *dɪžmɪn*, *dušmɪn* Sab140, *dəžmən* Mutzafi 2008a:345]
               'enemy'

did-   [דִּי + ל? דִּי + יד?; Sab141; Mutz41] indep. genitive prn. 'of'; *didi*
               'mine', *didox* 'yours (m.s.)', *didax* 'yours (f.s.)', *dide* 'his', *dida*
               'hers', *deni* 'ours', *dexun* 'yours (c.pl.)', *didu* 'theirs'; *dəd Wān* 'from
               Wan'

din[1]   [K, T, Ar دِين Sab141; Mutz345] m. 'religion'; see *be-dín*

din[2]   [H דִּין; Sab141] 'judgment'; *yoməd din* 'Day of Judgment'

dinar   [Ar دِينار < Lat, Gr; cf. ⁺*dīnar* Sab141 and 1990:60, *dinár* Mutzafi
               2008a:345] 'dinar'; pl. *dināre*

dla   [ClAram לָא + דְּ; Mutz345] prep. 'without'; conj. 'lest'; see *d-*

doktor   [T, K, Eur; cf. ⁺*d/tuxtor* Sab138] m. 'medical doctor'

domóz   [K, T Chyet 2003:163] 'pig'

dor   [H דור; ⁺*dōr* Sab140] m. 'generation'

*drangāya   [K; cf. *drangi* Sab145] adj. 'late'; f. *drangesa*

dugle   [Syr ܕܘܓܠܐ; Sab138; Mutz346] 'lie(s)' adv. *b-dugle* 'falsely'

dūka, duksa [ClAram דְּכָא, דְּכְתָא; Sab139; Mutz346] f. 'place'; pl. *dukāne*;
               dūkəd xlāṣa 'place of refuge'

duksa   see *dūka*

dukkāna   [Ar دُكَّان; TJ דֻּכָּן; cf. *dɪk(k)āna* Sab142] 'shop, store'

dūma   [K; Mutz346] m. 'tail'

dumāyik   [K; cf. *dūmāy/hɪk* Sab139] adv. 'at the end'

dúnume   [Ar دُونُم, T *dunum*] pl. 'dunams'

dunye   [K, T, Ar دُنْيا; Sab139; Mutz346] f. 'the world, earthly existence'

dūra   [ModH דּוּרה, Ar ذُرَة] 'durra'

dūša   [ClAram דֶּבְשָׁא; Sab141; Mutz346] m. 'honey'

f

falaq   [T, Ar فَلَق; *falaq* Sab263] 'bastinado'

falda   [< Ar فِلْدَة 'piece (of meat)'] 'strip of meat placed in cholent'

falxa	[colloquial ModH < Ar] 'work in the field'; cf. *plx*
faqír	[T, Ar فقير; cf. *faqīr(a)* Sab264, *faqir* Mutz347] inv. 'poor' (but also pl. *faqirím* [H pl. suff.])
farq	[Ar فرق; cf. ⁺*farq* Sab265] 'difference'
farqūsa	[*farq* + abstr. suff. -*ūsa*] f. 'distinction, discrimination'
fasādūsa	[Ar فَسَاد + abstr. suff. -*usa*; cf. 'gossip' Yona 1999א:361, 'corruption' Sab263] f. 'gossip'; see *'wd*
feka	[K, Ar فَاكِهَة; Sab262; Mutz347] 'fruit'
fišaka	[K, Ar فشَك < T; Sab263; Mutz347] 'bullet, cartridge'
flān, flāna	[K, Ar فُلَان; cf. ClAram פְלָן; cf. *flān(a)*, *flānkas* Sab263, *flán-*, *flāna* Mutz347; § 4.1.12.d] 'such and such, a certain'; *flān* is used with humans: *flān brāta* 'such and such a daughter', *flān nāša* 'such and such a person'; *flāna* is used with non-humans: *flāna māsa* 'such and such a village', *flāna dūka* 'such and such a place'; see *flānkas*
flānkas	[Sab263; Mutz347; § 4.1.12.e] 'so and so, a certain person'; *flānkas ké-le* 'Where is so and so?'; see *flān(a)*

g

gā	[K; cf. *gāha, gaha, ga* Sab118; *gā* Mutz347] f. 'time'; *xá-gā* 'once'; *xá-gā xet(a)* 'once again'; *čú-gā* 'never'; *'é-gā* 'so then, when'; *'atta gā* 'now'; *xarāye gā* 'the last time'; see *'egā, 'ogā, gār*
gāla	[Syr ܓܠܐ; cf. גְּלָא Yona 1999א:85, *gāla* Sab18a and Mutz 347] 'kilim rug'
gali	[K; Sab122] 'valley'
gamiya	[T; Sab123] 'ship'
ganāwa	[ClAram גַּנָּבָא; Sab123; Mutz348] m. 'thief'; pl. *ganāwe*; see *gnw, ganawūsa*
ganawūsa	[*ganāwa* + abstr. suff. -*ūsa*; Sab123] f. 'thievery'; see *gnw, ganāwa*
ganmoke	[K; Mutz348] pl. tant. 'maize'
gār	[K, Ar كَرَّة; cf. גָּרָא, גְּרִי Yona 1999א:91, *garra, -gar* Sab123] 'time'; attested only in *čú-gār* 'never' (less frequent than *čú-gā*) and *gárgāra* 'from time to time'; see *gā, gárgāra*
garáč	[ModH גְּרָז', T, K, Eur; Yona 1999ב:253] 'garage'
gardāna	[K; Sab124] 'heavy gold or silver necklace' (*haggada*)
gāre	[ClAram אַגְּרָא < Akk; Sab118; Mutz348] 'roof'; pl. *garawāsa*
gárgāra	[*gār + gār*] adv. 'from time to time'; see *gā, gār*
garma	[ClAram גַּרְמָא; Sab124; Mutz348] 'bone'; pl. *garme*
*garūsa	[ClAram √גרס; Sab124; Mutz348] 'large'; pl. *garūse* 'large (vegetables)'
gaw-	see *go*
gazeṛa	[H גְּזֵרה; cf. ⁺*gazēra* Sab121, *gazeṛa* Mutz348] f. '(evil) decree'
gdāda	[LEAram גְּדָדָא; Sab119; Mutz348] 'thread'; pl. *gdāde*
geb	see *geba*
geba	[ClAram גִּבָּא; cf. *gēba* Sab121, *geb(a)* Mutz348] 'side, direction'; *'eka geb zəlle* '(in) which direction did he go?'; *'áx-geb tán-geb*

(ṭamáha-geb) 'when all's said and done, eventually' (lit. 'here side, there side, way over there side)'; cf. JZakh *maxxa laxxa* Sabar 2005:195; JBetan *m-é-'āla m-é-'āla* 'for various reasons' Mutz207; JBetan *mən d-axxa l- d-axxa* 'eventually' Mutz330; *'áx-geb* 'hither' and *tám-geb* 'thither' Mutz34; Palestinian Arabic *min hōn la-hōn* 'when all's said and done' Elihay 2005:159)

gehənnam   [TO and JBA גּיהנּם < H גּיהנּם; cf. *gēhinnām, gēhinna, gēhanna* Sabar 2002:122, *gehənnam* Mutz348] 'hell'; *gehənne gehənnam* 'hell of hells' (Mutz348)

gen'edən   [H גּן עֵדֶן; cf. גּן-עֵדֶן Yona 1999א:90, *gan-'ēḏin* Sab123, *gan'edən* Mutz348] 'Garden of Eden'

gera   [K; Sab122] f. 'threshing'

gəlda   [ClAram גּלְדָא; Sab122; Mutz349] m. 'skin'

gəlla   [ClAram גּלָּא; Sab122; Mutz349] 'grass, plant, herb'; pl. *gəllāle*

gənāhe   [K; cf. *günāha, gunah* Sab123] pl. 'sins' (*haggada*)

gərāni   [K; Sab124] f. 'famine'

gərūsa   [LEAram גּוּרבָּא < P; cf. *gɪ/urūṭa*, pl. *gɪ/urwe* Sab124, *gərūϑa*, pl. *gərwe* Mutz349] f. 'sock'; pl. *gurwe*

gərūwer   [K; cf. גּורוֹבֵר Yona 1999א:79, *gɪruvír* Sab124] inv. 'round-shaped'

gəšra   [LAram < Akk; cf. ⁺*gɪšra* Sab125, *gəšra* Mutz349] 'bridge'

gəxka   [LAram גחך Sab122; Mutz349] f. 'laughter'; see *gxk*

gəzra   [ClAram √גזר; Sab121; Mutz349] m. 'pile of chopped wood'

giska   [K; cf. *gizkâ, giziktâ* Maclean 1901:49, *gīsɪka* Sab122] 'young goat'

go, gaw-   [ClAram גּו < PrAram *gaww; cf. *go, ko* Sab119, *gu* Mutz350] prep. 'in, within, among'; with suffixes *gaw-*, e.g., *gawexun*; cf. *'əl'uwwa*

gob'ena   [גו + בית + עינא Mutz350; גו +ב + אינא? Sab119] 'forehead'

gopāla, gopalta   [K; cf. ⁺*gōpāla*, ⁺*gōpalta* Sab120] m. and f. 'shepherd's stick'

gora   [ClAram גּבְרָא; Sab120; Mutz349] m. 'man'; pl. *gūre, gurāne*; *gora u-baxtūsa* 'husband-wife relationship (= being married)'

*goranāya   [GN *Gorāni* + gent. suff. -*āya*] m. 'resident of Gorani (Iraqi Kurdistan)' pl. *goranāye*

gorūsa   [LAram גּבְרוּתָא;] f. 'manliness (bravery)'

gova   [K < גּבָּא?; cf. גּוֹבָא Yona 1999א:75, *gowa* Mutz349] 'stall, den'; pl. *govāne*; see *govka, gūba*

*govka   [K *gov* + *k*] 'stall, den'; pl. *govke*; see *gova, gūba*

*goza   [Syr ܓܘܙܐ < P?; Sab119; Mutz350] 'walnut'; pl. *goze*

gūba   [ClAram גּבָּא 'pit'; Maclean 1901:45; Sab119; Mutzafi 2008a:350] 'pit, loom (located in the pit)'; see *gova*

gūda   [LEAram גּוּדָא; Sab119; Mutz350] 'wall'; pl. *gudāne*

gulange   [K? cf. pl. *gulāge, gulangi* Brauer 1993:413, גּוּלָגָּא Yona 1999א:76; *gulāga* Sab120] pl. 'sidelocks (of orthodox Jew)'

gulpanyāsa   [ClAram גּפָּא; cf. *gulpa* Sab120] pl. 'wings' (*haggada*)

gumrək   [T; cf. *gümrüg* Maclean 1901:47, *gumrɪk* Sab120] 'customs'

guniya   [K; cf. *gâ-wân* 'thorn for lighting fires, bramble' Maclean 1901:

47, *guniya* 'gunny sack' Sab120 and Mutz350] f. 'bramble, kindling twigs'; pl. *guniye*

guník   [K *gûnîk, gînîk* Chyet 2003:230] 'gunny sack'

gupta   [TJ גּבְנָא, Syr ܓܒ݂ܶܬ݁ܐ, ܓܒ݂ܶܬ݁ܐ; cf. *gup/bta* Sab120, *gupta* Mutz-350, *gupta ~ gubta < gubbᵊtā < *gubnᵊtā* Talay 2008:58 n. 98] f. 'cheese'

gwira   [ClAram √גבר] m. 'married'; f. *gurta*; see *gwr*

gyāna   [K; cf. *gyāna, gāna*, pl. *gyānāṯa* Sab121, *gyāna*, pl. *gyanāϑa* Mutz350–351] f. 'self, soul'; *gyāni* 'myself'; pl. *gyanāsa* 'souls' (*haggada*)

gzira   [ClAram √גזר] m. 'circumcised'; pl. *gzire*; see *gzr*

ġ

ġazab   [Ar غَضَب; cf. *ġazab*, ⁺*xazab* Sab135, גְּדָאב Avidani 1959:38–39, גֵּזֵב Alfiye 1986:47] 'anger' (*haggada*)

ġer   [Ar غَيْر; cf. ⁺*ġēr* Sab134, *ġer* Mutz351] 'another'; *ġer dūka* 'another place'

h

hā   [ClAram הָא; Sab148; Mutz351] adv. 'here, so, then'; *hā šqol haqqox* 'Here take your due!'

hādax   [ClAram הָא + ד + איך Sab148; הָדָּא, הַדָ + הָךְ, אִימַה + ܗܳܕ݂ Mutzafi 2008a:351] adv. 'thus, so, like this'; *qam hādax* beforehand,' *basᵊr hādax* 'afterwards'; see *hatxa*

halla halla [K, P; ⁺*hallā*-⁺*hallā* Sab150] excl. 'how fortunate!'

ham   [K, T, P; Sab151; Mutz351; Blau & Hopkins 2006:455] adv. 'also'

har   [K, T, P; Sab151; Mutz351] adv. 'always, still, in any case, after all, just'; *har hatxa* 'just like this'

hatk   [K, Ar هَتْك; cf. הַתִּיכָא Yona 1999א:118, *hatīke* Sab152] m. 'disgrace'

hatxa, 'atxa [ClAram הָא + ד + איך Sab149; cf. *had/txa* Sab149; *hād* + *kā* Mutz351] adv. 'so, such, like this'; see *hādax*

hawūsa   [*yhawūϑa?* Mutz351; *hawa* (< T *heva*) + abstr. suff. -*ūsa* Maclean 1901:72] f. 'favor'

hay   [T, K; Sab149; Cohen 1995:398] excl. 'hey!'; see *he²*

hayāma   [K < Ar أَيَّام; cf. *hayam* Sab150, *hayāma* Mutz351] adv. 'period of time'

hayya   [QAram הי, Sam Aram הי, JBA הייא, חיי Sokoloff 2002:375–376; Sabar 2002:149–150; Mutz352] adv. 'quickly, early'

he¹   [ClAram הֵן, אֵן; Sab149; Mutz352] adv. 'yes'

he²   [ModH הֵי?; Mutz352] excl. 'hey!'; see *hay*

hedi   [K < Ar هَادِئ; Sab150; Mutz352] adv. 'slowly'; *hedi hedi* 'very slowly'

hekkaratūsa [GN *Hekkāri* + K abstr. suff. -*at* + abstr. suff. -*ūsa*] pl. 'residents or region of Hakkari (Turkish Kurdistan)' *hekkarnāya* [GN *Hekkāri* + gent. suff. *-nāya*] m. 'resident of Hakkari (Turkish Kurdistan)'

hermike [K; Sab152] pl. 'pears'

heš [K; cf. *hēš(tan)* Sab150, *heš* Mutz352] adv. 'yet, still'

hənna [Syr ܗܢܐ, Ṭur *hnố*; cf. *hin-nâ, hin-nî* Maclean 1901:78, *hınna* Sabar 2002a:151; Rubin 2005:78–79 n. 46; *hənna*, pl. *hənne* Mutzafi 2008a:352; Hoberman 2007:140] filler 'um, whatchamacallit'; see *hnnl*

həšyar [K; cf. *hıšyar, hıššar* Sab152, *həššar* Mutz352] inv. 'careful, awake'

hivi, hiwi [K; cf. *hīvi, hīwi*, pl. *hīvīye* Sab150, *hiwi*, pl. *hiwiye* Mutz352] 'hope, plea, pleading'; pl. *hiwiye*; see *be-hívi*

hudắ, hudāya [ClAram יְהוּדְיָא; Sab149; Mutz352; § 3.15.a] m. 'Jew'; f. *hudesa*, pl. *hudāye*

ḥ

ḥabibi [ModH, Ar حَبِيب; Sab163; Mutz353] m. 'my beloved'

ḥafla [ModH, Ar حَفْلَة] 'party'

ḥajj [Ar حَجّ; cf. *hij* Maclean 1901:92] 'the haj (pilgrimage to Mecca)'

ḥajji [K, P, T, Ar حَاجّ; Sab163; § 4.2.3.10] 'hajji, pilgrim (who has been to Mecca)'; pl. *ḥajjāye*; *'edəd ḥajjāye* 'pilgrim festival'

ḥākəm [K, T, Ar حَاكِم; cf. *ḥākım, ḥēkım* Sab163, *ḥākəm* Mutz353] m. 'judge'

*ḥakoma [Ar √حكم; Sab165; Mutz353] 'ruler'; pl. *ḥakome*

ḥāl [K, T, Ar حَال; Sab163; Mutz353] f. 'situation, condition'; *ḥāl-u-masale* 'the upshot' (cf. Mlaḥsô *ḥāl w masale* Jastrow 1994:76; JZakho *ḥāl-u- qıšta* Sab163; JAradh *ḥāl-u-ḥwāl* Mutzafi 2002: 486); *narm u-ḥāle* 'soft and the like' (see *garma*)

ḥalāla [K, T, Ar حَلَال; cf. *halāl(a)* Sab166, *ḥalāla* Mutz353] m. 'kosher, lawful'; f. *ḥalalta*; pl. *ḥalāle*

ḥambaqisa [conflation of Ar √حبك + ClAram חנק√? JNerwa *ḥabbaqisa* 'dense smoke, dusty weather'; JAmid *ḥambaqiϑa* 'dense smoke,' JBetan *ḥambaqiϑa* 'dense smoke, suffocating smoke' and *ḥanbaqiϑa* 'suffocating smoke' Mutzafi p.c.] f. 'dense smoke'; *ḥambaqisəd tənna* (haggada; cf. תְּנָא חַבַּקִיסִיד = עָשָׁן-תִּמְרוֹת Avidani 1959: 35)

ḥanukka [H חֲנֻכָּה; cf. *ḥanu/ıkka* Sab167, *ḥanukka, ḥanukkoye* Mutz353] 'Hanukka'

ḥaqq [K, T, Ar حَقّ; cf. Sabar *ḥaq(qa)* 2002:168, *ḥaqqa* Mutz353] m. 'right, true, salary, due'; pl. *ḥaqqāne*

ḥarắm, ḥarāma [K, T, Ar حَرَام; cf. *hârâm, ḥarâmâ* Maclean 1901:79,106, *ḥarāma* Sab168] m. 'forbidden'; f. *ḥaramta*; see *ḥaramūsa, ḥrm*

ḥaramūsa [*ḥarām* + abstr. suff. *-ūsa*; Sab168] f. 'prohibition, impurity'; see *ḥarắm, ḥrm*

ḥarb [T, Ar حَرْب; Sab168] '(international) war'

ḥāxắm [H חֲכָם; cf. *ḥāxām, xāḥām* Sab166, *ḥāxam* Mutz353] m. 'rabbi'

ḥāxắm bāši	[H חָכָם + T *baş*; Sab166] m. 'Chief Rabbi (of the Ottoman Empire)'
ḥayyāwe	[H חִיָב; cf. *ḥayyāv* 'guilty' Sab165] pl. 'obligated'
ḥel	see *ḥil*
*ḥewan	[K, T, Ar حَيَوَان; cf. *ḥēwan, ḥaywan* Sab165, *ḥewan* Mutz353] 'animal'; pl. *ḥewāne*
ḥəzur, ḥə́zura	[K, Ar حَزْر; cf. ⁺*ḥızur* Sab164] 'estimation, conjecture'; pl. *ḥə́zure, ḥəzūre; 'üdli ḥə́zure* 'I estimated'
ḥil, ḥel	[LWAram לְהִל; cf. *hā/l, hī/ıl, ḥīl* Sab148, *həl, ḥəl* Mutz23] prep. and conj. 'until'
ḥudud	[T, Ar حُدُود; Yona 1999א:136] 'border (geographical, political)'
ḥukum	[Ar حُكْم; cf. *ḥukum, ḥıkum* Sab164] f. 'government'; see *ḥukūma, ḥukumiya*
ḥukūma	[Ar حُكُومَة; Mutz354] 'government'; see *ḥukum, ḥukumiya*
ḥukumiya	[*ḥukum* + *iya*] 'government'; see *ḥukum, ḥukūma*
ḥušta	[Ar حُجَّة; Sab164; Mutz354] f. 'excuse, pretext'
ḥūt	[K, Ar حُوت; Sab164] 'large fish'

j

jalab	[Ar جَلَب; Sab128] 'herd'
jamadāni	[K; cf. *jımıdāni* Sab128] f. 'checkered kerchief or keffiya'
jandərma	[K, T, IrAr < Fr; Sab129 and 1990:60; Mutz354] m. 'gendarme'; pl. *jandərme*
jawāhər	[Ar جَوَاهِر; cf. ⁺*jawāhır* Sab126] 'gemstone' (*haggada*)
jeba	[Ar جَيْب; cf. *jēba*, pl. *jēbābe* Sab127, *jeba*, pl. *jebāne* Mutz354] 'pocket'; pl. *jebābe*
jema'	[IrAr; Sab128] 'mosque'; cf. *məzgafte*
jeza, jezá	[Ar جَزَاء; cf. *jı/uza* Sab127] 'penalty, fine'
jəgāra	[IrAr, T, K < Eur; cf. ⁺*jıgāra, jəgāra* Mutzafi 2008a:354] f. 'cigarette'; pl. *jəgāre*; see *grš*
jəns	[Ar جِنْس < Lat; Sab129] 'type, sort'
jəwāb, jwāb	[K, Ar جَوَاب; cf. *jıwāb* Sab126, *jwāba* Mutz355] m. 'answer, response'; see *jwb*
jəzdān	[IrAr, K, T; cf. ⁺*jızdān* Sab127] 'purse, wallet'
jigra	[T, P, Ar √جكر; cf. ⁺*jıgra, jıkra* Sab126, גִּגְרִי Avidani 1959:38–39, גִּגְרּ Alfiye 1986:47] 'wrath' (*haggada*)
*jirān	[K, Ar جِيرَان; cf. *jīran, jīranta*, pl. *jīrāne* Sab128] 'neighbor'; pl. *jirāne*; see *jirānatūsa*
jirānatūsa	[*jirān* + K abstr. suff. *-at* + abstr. suff. *-ūsa*] f. 'neighborliness'; see *jirāne*
jmətta	see **jmida*
*jmida	[Ar √جمد] m. 'frozen'; f. *jmətta*
julla	[K, Ar جُلَّة; Sab127; Mutz355] 'article of clothing'; pl. *julle*
jwāb	see *jəwāb*

k

ka- [K; *ke* Wahby 1966:72] conj. 'when, since'; only in *ka-ʾégā* 'since then'

kaččala [K; cf. *kâchâlâ* Maclean 1901:131, *kaččala* Sab181] m. 'bald'

káfil, kafíl [K, T, Ar كَفِيل; cf. *kafil* Sab188] m. 'guarantor'

kāfər [K, T, Ar كَافِر; Sab180] m. 'heretic, infidel'; cf. **kapora*

*kāka [ClAram כָּכָּא; Sab180; Mutz356] 'tooth'; pl. *kāke; le dárya-lle (ʾax)xa kutkākəd gyāne* 'he has borne a grudge against him here' (cf. דרילו כאכא Sab180)

kalamča [K; Sab186] f. 'handcuff'

kalba [ClAram כַּלְבָּא; Sab186; Mutz356] m. 'dog'; pl. *kalbe; kalba bər kalba* 'son of a bitch!'; *kálbe-u-malbe* 'dogs and the like' (see *m-* in doublets Sab209); see *kaləpsa*

kaləpsa [ClAram כַּלְבְּתָא; cf. *kalıb/pta* Sab186; § 3.22.b] f. 'bitch'; *kaləpsa brāt kalba* 'what a bitch!'; see *kalba*

kallax [K; cf. *kallax, kallaš* Sab186] 'corpse'; pl. *kallāxe*

kaməsre [Syr ܟܡܬܪܐ, ܟܡܬܪܐ; cf. *kâmitrâ* 'pear' Maclean 1901:135; *kamisre* 'a fruit tree' Brauer 1993:416] pl. 'pears'

kāni [K; Mutz356] 'spring'; *kāni Karačke* 'spring of Karačke'; cf. *ʾena*

kāpa [JBA כַּפָּא, כַּתְפָּא < ClAram כַּתְפָּא; Sab180 Mutz367] f. 'shoulder'; pl. *kapāne*

*kapora [Syr ܟܦܘܪܐ; *kapora Sab188 and Mutz356] m. 'faithless, cruel'; pl. *kapore*; cf. *kāfər*

kar'a [Syr ܟܪܥܐ; *kar'a* Mutz356] 'butter'

karatūsa [GN *Kāra* + K abstr. suff. *-at* + abstr. suff. *-ūsa*] pl. 'residents or region of Kara (Iraqi Kurdistan)'; see **karāya*

*karāya [GN *Kāra* + gent. suff. *-āya*] m. 'resident of Kara (Iraqi Kurdistan)'; pl. *karāye*; see *karatūsa*

karb [K < Ar كَرْب; cf. *karba* Sab188] 'anger' (*haggada*)

karta [Syr ܟܪܬܐ; Sab189; Mutz356] f. 'load, burden'

kāsa [ClAram כְּרְסָא; Sab180; Mutz356] f. 'belly, stomach'; *kāsu qədla* 'they got angry'

kašxe [IrAr; cf. *kašxa* 'show-off' Sab189] pl. 'fine, impressive'

kātəb [K, Ar كَاتِب; cf. *kātıb(či)* Sab181] m. 'secretary'

kavra [K *kevir* 'rock' Chyet 2003:808] 'cliff'; pl. *kavre*

kawdənta, kawənta [ClAram כּוּדַנְ(י)א; Bar-Asher 1998:136–137; cf. *kawdınta, kōzınta, kodıne* Sab182, *koðənta*, pl. *koðəne* Mutz357] f. 'mule'; pl. *kódəne, kawdəne*

kāwód [H כָּבוֹד; cf. *kāvōḏ, kawóḏ* Sab181, *kāvoḏ* Mutz356] f. 'honor, respect'; *kāwóḏ ṛapsa* 'great respect'; see *xbḏ*

kawənta see *kawdənta*

kčəkčab [K?] m. 'type of rifle'

ke-¹ [ClAram כָּא; Sab93; Mutz356] *ké-le* 'Where is he?'; see *ʾeka*

ke² [K; Sab184] adv. (used with imperative) 'c'mon, please!'; *ke sa* 'c'mon!'

kef, kefa	[K, T, Ar كَيْف; cf. *kef* Sab185 and Mutz3565] 'joy'; *māṭo kefox* 'How are you?'; *kefox sele* 'you rejoiced'
kelka	[K *kelek* 'dry stone wall' Wahby 1966:73] m. 'stone wall'; *kelkəd ḥudud* 'stone wall marking the border'
kepa	[ClAram כֵּיפָא; Sab185; Mutz357] m. 'stone'; pl. *kepe*
kəče	[K; cf. *kichî*, *kachâ*, *kichâ* Maclean 1901:131, *kaččē* Sab181] f. 'woman! (voc.)'
kəl	see *kəsəl, kəskəsəl*
kəliliye	[onomat.; cf. *kılīlīyat* Sab186, *kililiye* Mutz104] pl. 'ululations' (*haggada*); *mxāya kəliliye* 'make ululating sounds' (cf. *d-r-y kılīlī-yat* Sab186)
kəndāla	[K; Sab187] m. 'steep slope'
kəpna	[ClAram כַּפְנָא; Sab188; Mutz357] 'hunger, famine'; see *kpn, kpina*
kəppur	[H כִּפּוּר; Sab177; Mutz357] '(Day of) Atonement'
kəra	[K, T, Ar كِرَاء; cf. ⁺*kıre* Sab188] m. 'rent'
kərāčiye	[K; cf. *kerajo* 'donkey-driver' Rizgar 1993:108] pl. 'muleteers'
kərma	[K; cf. *kırmıkṭa* 'worm,' pl. *kırmıkyāṯa, kırmıyāna* 'wormy' Sab189; *kərməkϑa* 'worm,' pl. *kərməkyāϑa* Mutz357] 'worms'; pl. *kərme*
kərmanj	[K *kirmanc* 'Kurd, peasant' Chyet 2003:325] m. 'Kurd, peasant'
kərya	[LAram √כרי] m. 'short'; see *kry*¹
kəs	see *kəsəl, kəsəkəsəl*
kəsəl	[< *kislā* 'loin' Mutz357 and 2006:93–97; cf. Sab187] 'to, with, by'; *kəslu; mən kəsəl, kəsəl dide, kəl* before nouns: *kəl muxtar* 'with the mukhtar,' *kəl xmāse* 'with his mother-in-law,' *kəl Rəḥovot* 'at Rehovot'; *kəs spindarnāye* 'with the residents of Spindar'; see *kəsəkəsəl*
kəsəkəsəl	[*kesel + kesəl*] prep. 'right with'; *kəsəkəsleni* 'right with us'; see *kəsəl*
kəsta	[JBA and Mand כִּיסְתָא; Sab188; Mutz357] f. 'small bag, money-bag'; see *kis*
kətte	[K; cf. *kətte* Sab190, *katte* Mutz356] 'one (of two or of a group)'; see *kətt-u-mát*
kátt-u-māt	[cf. *kətt-u-māṭ* Sab190] 'odds and ends, bit by bit'; see *kətte*
ki'e	see *y'y*
kilo	[T, Ar, ModH < Eur; cf. *kēlo*, pl. *kēlōyat* Sab184] 'kilo'; pl. *kiloye*
kilometər	[T, Ar, ModH < Eur; § 3.18.a] 'kilometer'; pl. *kilometre*
kis	[Ar كِيس; Sab184] m. 'moneybag, pocket'; see *kəsta*
kma	[ClAram כְּמָא; Sab186; Mutz357] interr. adv. 'how much?'; *b-kma* 'for how much'; indef. prn. 'some'; *kma qorūše* 'some piasters'
knəšta	[ClAram כְּנִשְׁתָא; cf. *k(ı)nıšta*, pl. *knıšyāṯa* Sab187, *knəšta*, pl. *knəšyāϑa* Mutz357] f. 'synagogue'; pl. *knəšyāsa*
ko	[K rel. prn. and conj. *ko* Chyet 2003:328] conj. 'because, that, since'; see *'ako, čukun*
kódəne	see *kawdənta*

kolāna [K; cf. *kōlāna, kōlanka* Sab182, *kolāna* Mutz357] 'alley, path'; pl. *kolāne*

kolka [K?] m. 'hovel'

koma [ClAram אֻכָּמָא; Sab183; Mutz357] m. 'black'; f. *kumta*; see *kym*

kotakki [K, T; cf. *kōtak, kōtakki, kōtakūta* Sab184] 'hardship'

kpina [ClAram √כפן] m. 'hungry'; pl. *kpine*; see *kpn, kəpna*

ksesa [Syr ܟܣܣܐ; cf. Sab190; 2008:358; Mutz358] f. 'hen'; pl. *kəsyāsa*

ksisa see *kusisa*

kud, kut- [כול + ד; Sab181–182; Mutz358] 'each'; *kúd-lel* 'every night'; *kúd-yom* 'every day'; *kutxa* 'each one'; *kút-xa-u-xa* 'each and every one'; *kútreni* 'the two of us'; *kútrexun* 'the two of you'; *kutru* 'the two of them'; *kútlāhun* 'the three of them'; *kút'arbeni* 'the four of us'; *kutkāke* 'all the teeth'; see *kull-, kuššat*

kuləkyāsa [K; cf. *kullıkṭa, -ake* "ulcer", *kulıkyāṯa* 'hemorrhoids' Sab183] pl. 'ulcers'

kull- [ClAram כל; Sab182; Mutz358] 'all'; *kulle* 'all of him'; *kulla* 'all of her'; *kullu* 'all of them'; see *kud, kuššat*

kur [K, T; cf. *kürâ, kürrâ* Maclean 1901:128, *kōra* Sab183] 'blind'

kūra [K; Sab183] m. 'young goat'

kurdi [ModH כּוּרְדִי, Ar كُرْدِي; cf. LEAram קֻרְדֻוָיא; cf. *qûrdath, qûrdit* Maclean 1901:274, *kurdi* Sab183; *kurdi* = Jewish Neo-Aramaic, a term which arose in Israel Mutz358] 'Jewish Neo-Aramaic'; see *qurdəski*

kurdināya [*kurdi* + gent. suff. *-nāya*; cf. 'a Kurd' Sab183, 'Kurdistani Jew' Mutz358] m.s. 'Kurdistani Jew'; pl. *kurdināye*; see *qurdāya, qurd-əski, qurdawūsa*

kursi [K, Ar كُرْسِي < ClAram כּוּרְסְיָא < Akk; Sab184; Mutz358] 'chair'

kurtāke [K; Sab184] pl. 'garments'

kusisa [Syr ܟܘܣܝܣܐ; cf. *kusisa* Sab183, *kusiϑa* Mutz358, *ksila* Khan 1999:572 and 2004:607; § 3.18.a] f. 'hat'

kuššat [כול + ד + שת; Sab181; Mutz358] adv. 'every year'; see *kud, kull-*

kut- see *kud*

kutka [K *kodk* Jaba 1879:347] f. 'knee'

kutwa [Ar كَثَّة; cf. *kı/ütwa* Sab190] m. 'thorn'; pl. *kutwe*

kutxa see *kud*

ḳ

ḳappāṛa [H כַּפָּרָה; cf. ⁺*kappāra* Sab188, *kappāra* Mutz356] 'expiation'

l

l-, 'əl-, 'əlləd [ClAram -ל; Sab203; Hoberman 2008:149; Mutz123,359] prep. 'to, at, for', object marker

l-'əlal [ClAram לְעֵיל; *'ıl'ēl* Sab93, *'əlal* Mutz331] adv. 'above'

la, lā, la' [ClAram לָא; Sab203; Mutz359; § 4.7.4] adv. 'no'; *lā* and *la'* are emphatic

lākən	[K, T, Ar لاكِن; cf. *lâkin, lakin* Maclean 1901:149] conj. 'but'
lastike	[IrAr, T < Eng *elastic*; cf. *lāstik* 'elastic rubber string' Sab203 and 1990:60] pl. 'sandals (made from tire tubes)'
lašša	[K; Sab209; Mutz359] m. '(human) body or corpse'; pl. *lašše*
laxma	[ClAram לַחְמָא; Sab207; Mutz359] m. 'bread'
lāzəm	[K, T, Ar لازِم; Sab203; Mutz359] 'necessary'
leb-	see *let*
lele	[ClAram לֵילֵי; cf. *lele*, pl. *lēlıwāṭa* Sab206, *lele*, pl. *lelawāϑa* Mutz-360] m.s. and pl. 'night'; *tre lele* 'two nights'; *kúd-lel* 'every night'; see *'ádlele, palgədlel*
let, letən, létəna	[ClAram לֵית < לָא אִית; cf. *lēt, lēs, lē/ītın, lēsın* Sab207, *liϑ, liϑən, líϑena* Mutz360; § 4.8.1] negator of existence 'there is not'; *lətwa* 'there was not'; *lebi* (< לֵית בִי; § 4.8.2) 'I cannot'; see *'it*
ləbba	[ClAram לְבָּא; Sab203; Mutz360] m. 'heart'
ləbne	[Ar لِبْن; cf. ClAram לבינתא; cf. *lubna, lubınṭa*, pl. *lūne, lubne* Sabar 2005] pl. 'bricks' (*haggada*)
lətwa	see *let*
lira	[T < Eur < Lat; Sab206; Mutz360] f. 'Turkish pound (gold coin)'; pl. *lire*
lišāna	[ClAram לְשָׁנָא; Sab 206–207; Mutz360] m. 'tongue, language'; *lišāna deni* 'Jewish Neo-Aramaic'
lö'a	[ClAram לוֹעָא; cf. *lo'ta* 'chewing gum' Sab204 and Mutz360] 'jaw'

ḷ

ḷappa	[K; Sab207] 'lump, handful'

m

m-	see *mən*
mā	[ClAram מָא; Sab209; Mutz361] interr. prn. 'what?'; *má-le*, 'what's with him?'; see *kma, mād*
ma'alləm	[Ar مُعَلِّم; Sab222; Mutz361; § 3.20.d] m. 'teacher' (who functioned also as rabbi, ritual slaughterer, cantor); *má'alləm!* (voc.); pl. *ma'almine*; see *'lm*
ma'aš	[Ar مَعَاش; Sab222–223] m. 'income, salary'
ma'būde	[Ar مَعْبُود; Sab222] pl. idols, gods (*haggada*)
ma'ṃúṛ	[T, Ar مَأْمُور; cf. *ma'mur* Sab210] m. 'officer-in-charge'; see *'ṃr, 'mr, 'əmər*
*ma'qūl	[K, Ar مَعْقُول; cf. מעקול, pl. *ma'qūle* Sab222, *māqul*, pl. *māqūle* Mutz362] pl. *ma'qūle* 'nobles'
mābayn	[Ar مَا بَيْن; cf. *mā-bayni/bēn, nābēn* Sab209,228, *mabáyn* Mutz-361] prep. 'between, among'; *mābayn nāše* 'among the people'; *mābayneni* 'between us'; *mābaynəd didu* 'among them'
mād	[ClAram מָא + דְ; Sab209; Mutz361] rel. prn. 'that which, whatever, as regards'; see *d-, mā*

madắm [T, K, IrAr < Eur] f. 'Madam'

mādắm [Ar مَا دَام; cf. מְדֶם Yona 1999א:229, *mādām* Sab209; *mādắm* Mutz361] conj. 'since, as'

máfəra [K *mefer* Chyet 2003:368; Ar مَفَرّ *mɪfar* Sab223] 'opportunity, escape'

mahājər [Ar مُهَاجِر; Yona 1999א:231] m. 'refugee'; pl. *mahájəre*

mahafūza see *muḥáfəza*

máhkama [T, Ar مَحكَمَة; Sab215; Mutz361] 'court'

mal'ax [H מַלְאָךְ; cf. *mal(')ax, mal'āxa* Sab218, *mal'ax* Mutz361] m. 'angel'; pl. *mal'āxe*

malla [K < Ar مَوْلَى; cf. *mawlāyi* 'my Master' Sab213, *malla* Mutz361] 'mullah'; pl. *mallāye*

malbe see *kalba*

malək [K, T, P, Ar مَلَك; cf. 'headman' Maclean 1901:179, 'king' Sab219] m. 'chieftain'; pl. *malkāne*

mamnún [T, Ar مَمْنُون; Sab220] inv. 'grateful'

māma [K; cf. *māmo* Sab210, *māma* Mutz361] m. 'uncle'; *māmo* 'uncle! (voc.; term of respect)'; pl. *mamāni* 'my uncles' (§ 4.2.3.2 n. 50)

mar'az [Ar عَمَر عِزّ > مِرعِز *Sab225] m. 'cloth made of fine goat-wool'; cf. *'amra, 'əzza*

māra [ClAram מְרֵא; Sab210; Mutz362] 'master, owner'; cst. *mar, mare*; pl. *marawāsa, mar'āsa*; *mari* 'my Master'; *mare gora* 'married woman'; *mare Hkowaḥ H* 'powerful', *mare 'aṣəl* 'possessing a good nature', *mar dukkāna* 'shopkeeper'

margəlta [Syr ܡܪܓܠܬܐ and ܡܪܓܠܐ < Ar; cf. *marəgla* Sab224; *marəgla* 'cauldron' (larger than *margəlta*), *margəlta* Mutz362] f. 'cauldron'

maroknāya [GN *Maroko* (< ModH) + gent. suff. -*nāya*] m. 'Moroccan'; f. *maroknesa*; pl. *maroknāye*

marhāma [T, Ar مَرحَمَة] 'mercy, compassion'; see *rhm, mrahmāna*

māsa [ClAram מְתָא < Akk; Sab210; Mutz362] f. 'village'

masale [K, T < Ar مَسألَة; Krotkoff 1982:135; Mlaḥsô *mắsăle* Jastrow 1994:182;] f. 'matter, affair'; *hāl-u-masale* 'upshot'; *'iya masale zəlla* 'this matter ended'

masta [K; Sab221; Mutz362] 'yoghurt'

maṣraf [K, T, Ar مَصرَف; Sab223] 'expense'

māše [K; Sab210; Mutz362] pl. 'beans'

māt see *kəttu-māt*

maṭắr [Ar مَطَار] f. 'airport'

māṭo [*mā* 'what' + *ṭev* 'report' Nöldeke 1868:162; *mā* + *ṭev* + possible influence of *ṭo < טב Mutz362; cf. *māṭo(f/v)* Sab209, *māṭo* Mutz362] interr. adv. 'how?'; *māṭod* 'as soon as'

māṭod see *māṭo*

maṭbax [K, T, Ar مَطبَخ; Sab215] 'kitchen'

maxəlta [LEAram מחולתא, מהולתא Sokoloff 2002:644; Sab218] f. 'fine sieve'; pl. *maxəlyāsa*

maxisa [ClAram √מחי; Mutz363] f. 'blow, hit'; see *mxy*

mazwāda [ModH מִזְוָדָה?, Ar مِزوَد?] 'suitcase'; pl. *mazwāde*

mazza	[K, T, Ar مَزَّة; Sab214; Mutz363] m. 'appetizers taken with alcoholic drinks'
mažbur	[K, T, Ar مَجْبور; cf. *majbūr* Sab211, *majbur* Mutz361] inv. 'forced, reluctant'
m-badal	see *badal*
*mbušla	[ClAram √בשל] m. 'cooked'; pl. *mbušle*; see *bšl*
metər	[K, ModH מֶטֶר < Eur; cf. *mētar* Sab217 and 1990:61, s. *metər*, pl. *metre* Mutz363; § 3.18.a] 'meter'; pl. *metre*
*məbisa	[ClAram √בות]; m. 'food cooked overnight'; pl. *məbise* (*haggada*)
mədor	[K, T, Ar مُدير; cf. *mudur* Sab212] m. 'mudir, Turkish governor of a subdistrict'; pl. *mədore*
məl	see *mən*
məlkəta	[T *mülkiyet*?; Ar مِلْكِيَة?; cf. *mılk*, *mılkīni* Sab219] f. 'property, possessions'
məlləta	[K, T, Ar مِلَّة; cf. *mıllıta*, *mıllate* Sab219, *məllat* Mutz2002:363] f. 'ethnic group'
*məlyón	[K, T, ModH < Eur; cf. *mılyon* Sab219, *məlyón* Mutzafi 2008a: 363] 'million'; pl. *məlyone*
mən¹, m-	[ClAram מֶן; Sab220; Mutz124] prep. 'from, with'; *mənne u-l-ál* 'from here on'
mən², məl	[§ 4.4.7.e] jussive particle: *mən hāwe* 'let it be'; *məl 'āzəl* 'let him go';
məndi	[PrAram *madda'; TO and TJ מִדְּעָם; Syr ܡܸܕܸܡ; JBA מִידִי; Mand מינדא, מינדאם; reanalyzed as *mən + di*?; Tal 1975:16–17; Sab220; Mutz363] 'thing'; *kulle məndi* 'all sorts of things'; *ču-məndi* 'nothing'
mərrūta	[K; Sab225] '(sullen) face,' pl. *mərrūte*
məskena	[ClAram מסכן < Akk; cf. *mıskın* Sab221, *məskenūϑa* 'poverty' Mutz363] m. 'poor fellow'
məṣṣər	[K, T, Ar مصر; Sab223] 'Egypt'
məṣwâ	[H מִצְוָה; cf. *mıṣwa* Sab223] f. 'religious duty, good deed'
məšəlmāna	[Syr ܡܫܠܡܢܐ; cf. *mušılmāna* Sab213, *məšəlmāna*, *mušəlmāna* Mutz364] m. 'Muslim'; f. *məšəlmanta*; pl. *məšəlmāne*
məšpāḥa	[H מִשְׁפָּחָה; Mutz364] f. 'family'; pl. *məšpāḥe*; also attested with H pronunciation *məšpāḥá*.
məšša	[K *miše* Chyet 2003:392] inv. 'many'
məšxa	[ClAram מְשְׁחָא; Sab226; Mutz364] 'liquid butter, cooking oil'
məzāda	[Ar مَزَاد; cf. *mazâdâ* Maclean 1901:166, *mızād* Sab214] 'auction'
məzgafte	[K < Ar مَسْجِد; cf. *mızgafte* Sab214, *məzgaft*, *məzgafte* Mutz364] f. 'mosque'; cf. *jema'*
məzze	[LEAram מזיא < מעזיא? Sokoloff 2002:652; Sab214; Mutz363–364] pl. 'hairs'
mḥakesa	[NeoAram √ḥky < Ar √حكى; cf. *maḥakēṭa*, *mḥakēṭa* Sab215] f. 'talk, tale, story'; see *ḥky*
*milāna	[Syr ܡܝܠܟ < P; Krotkoff 1985:129; Sab216; Mutz363] 'blue'; pl. *milāne*

misa   [ClAram מִיתָא; Sab217; Mutz363] m. 'dead'; pl. *misāne*; see *mys*

momāsa   [ClAram מוֹמְתָא; Sab213; Mutz364] f. 'oath'; see *ymy*

mosa   [ClAram מוֹתָא; Sab214] 'death'; see *mys*

moxa   [ClAram מוֹחָא; Sab213; Mutz364] 'brain'

m-qam   [ClAram מִן קֳדָם; Sab280; Mutz124–125] prep. 'due to'; *m-qam*
              qaračke 'due to highway robbers'; see *qam, qamqam*

mraḥmāna   [ClAram (מ)רַחֲמְנָא); Sab225; Mutz365] m. 'merciful'; *'ilāha mraḥ-*
              māna- le 'God is merciful'; see *rḥm, marḥāma*

mšidəna   [NeoAram √šydn] m. 'crazed'; see *šydn, šidāna, šidanūsa*

mučču   [onomat.] 'smack! (sound of kissing)'

mufti   [T, Ar مُفْتِي; Sab213] m. 'mufti'

muḥáfəza, mahafūza   [T muhafaza Hony 1957:245, K mihafeze, muhafeze Chyet
              2003:385,398, Ar مُحَافَظَة] f. 'guarding'

muḥtāj   [K, T, Ar مُحْتَاج] inv. 'in need'; *lewu muḥtāj* 'they weren't in
              need'

muṣlāya   [GN Mosəl + gent. suff. -āya; cf. *mōṣɩlnāye* Sab213] m. 'resident
              of Mosul'; pl. *muṣlāye*

mutaṣarrəf [T, Ar مُتَصَرِّف; cf. *mûtaṣarîp* Maclean 1901:165, *mɩtaṣarrif* Khan
              1999:575] m. 'provincial governor'

muxtar   [K, T, Ar مُخْتَار; Sab213] m. 'mukhtar, headman of a village'; pl.
              muxtāre

mxabine, xabine [K, Ar غبن?; cf. *(m)ġabīne, mxabīne* Sab134] excl. *(m)xabine*
              'what a loss!'; *xabinox* 'what a loss for you!'

ṃ

ṃāḷ   [K, T, Ar مَال; cf. ⁺*mal* Sabar 2004:112, *māl* Sab209, *māḷ* Mutz365]
              'property, possessions, wealth'

ṃamzer   [H מַמְזֵר; ⁺*mamzēr* Sab220] m. 'bastard'; cf. *bəč'a*

ṃāye   [ClAram מַיָּא; Fassberg 1997; cf. ⁺*māya,* ⁺*māye* Sab209, *māye*
              Mutz365] pl. tant. 'water'

n

nāmus   see *be-námus*

naqda   [Ar نَقْد; cf. *naqda, niqda* Brauer 1993:111, *nəqda* Mutz367] 'bride
              price'

naqətta   see **naqida*

*naqida   [ClAram √נקד; Sab235; § 3.6.b] m. 'thin'; f. *naqətta*

naqla   [K, Ar نَقَل; Sab235; Mutz366] 'time'; pl. *naqle; naqəl ṭlāha* 'third
              time'

naqoṣa   [Ar √نقص; Sab235; Mutz366] 'minus, less, lacking, few'; pl. *na-*
              qoṣe; tre'sar naqoṣ 'əṣra, ruba' '11:50, 11:45 a.m./p.m.'; see *nqiṣa,*
              nqṣ

nar'a   [LEAram נרגא; Sab235; Mutz366] 'axe'

narm   [K nerm Chyet 2003:409] inv. 'gentle, soft'; *narm u-ḥāle garməd*
              dide 'He is a pleasant fellow' (lit., 'his bones are soft and the like'

(cf. *garme xafife/yaqūre* He is pleasant/unpleasant [lit., his bones light/heavy] Sab124); see *ḥāl*

nāsa   [pl. of ClAram אִדְנָא; Mutz366 and 2005; Sab230] 'ear'; pl. *nas-yāsa*

naṣūsa   [ClAram מְצוּתָא; Sab234; Mutz366; < *naṣwsā? f. 'fight'; pl. *naṣ-wāsa*; see *nṣy*

nāša   [ClAram אנשא; Sab228; Mutz366] m. 'person'; pl. *nāše*

našāma   [H נְשָׁמָה; cf. ClAram נשמתא, *nıšāma* Sab235, *našāma* Mutz366] f. 'soul'

nawāga   [P; Sab230; Mutz366] m. 'grandson'; f. *nawagta* 'granddaughter'

nāwí   [H נָבִיא; *nāvi* Sab229, *nāw/vi* Mutz18 n.42, 366] m. 'prophet'

naxira   [ClAram נְחִירָא; Sab233] m. 'nose'; pl. *naxire*

naxwaš   [K; Sab232; Mutz366] inv. 'ill'; see *xwaš*

nečir   [K; ClAram נחשר < P Greenfield 1970:183; cf. *nēčīr* Sab232] 'hunting'

nehra   [ClAram נַהֲרָא; Sab230; Mutz367] m. 'river'; pl. *nehrawāsa*

nerwāya   [GN *Nerwa* + gent. suff. *-āya*] m. 'resident of Nerwa' (Iraqi Kurdistan); f. *nerwesa*; pl. *nerwāye*

nəqwa   [ClAram נִקְבְּתָא; cf. *nüqwa, nüqva, nüq(q)ūṯa* Sab231, *nəqwa* Mutz367] f. 'female'; pl. *nəqwe*

nəxpūsa   [ClAram √נכף + abstr. suff. *-ūsa*; Sab233] f. 'embarrassment'; see *nxp*

nəxrāya   [ClAram נוּכְרָיָא; cf. *nuxrāya, nıxrāya* Sab231, *nəxrāya* Mutz367] m. 'foreigner'

nəxta   see *nixa*

nəzima   [K?; cf. *nızım* Sab231] m. 'low, inferior'

*nəžda   [K, Ar نَجْدَة; cf. נֶשְׁדָא Yona 1999א:327, *nıj/žda* Sab229] 'gang'; pl. *nəžde*

nixa   [ClAram √ניח; Sab232] 'the late' (lit., 'rested' = euph. for 'dead'); *nixəd sawoyi* 'my late grandfather'; f. *nəxta*; see *nyx*

nqiṣa   [Ar √نقص; Maclean 1901:218] m. 'lacking'; see *naqoṣa, nqṣ*

nūra   [ClAram נוּרָא; cf. *nūra, ⁺nūra* Sab231, *nūra* Mutz368] m. 'fire'

p

pa   [K; Mutz368] adv. 'so, then'

palga   [ClAram פֶּלְגָא; Sab256; Mutz368] 'half'; *tré-u-palge* 'two and a half'; *šāt-u-palge* 'a year and a half'; see *pálsā'a, palgədlel, palgədyo, pálpaŋàǹoṭ*

palgədlel   [*palgeh* + *d* + *lele*; cf. *palgıd lēle, palgızlal* Sab256, *palgədlel* Mutz-368] 'midnight'; see *palga, lele*

palgədyo   [*palgeh* + *d* + *yom*; cf. *palgıd yōm* Sab256, *palgədyom* Mutz368] 'noon'; see *palga, yoma*

palgūsa   [*palg(a)* + abstr. suff. *-ūsa*; Sab56; Mutz368] f. 'middle, center'; *palgus māsa* 'center of the village'

pálpaŋàǹoṭ [*palg(a)* + *paŋqánoṭ*] f. 'half lira'; pl. *pálpaŋqàǹoṭe* 'half liras'; see *palga, paŋqánoṭ pálsā‘a*   [*palg(a)* + *sā‘a*] 'half an hour'; see *palga, sā‘a*

panjāre   [K, T; cf. *panjârâ* Maclean 1901:254, *panjarīye* Sab256] f. 'window'

pappūka   [K; cf. *pappūka/-ūke* Sab257, *papūka* Mutz368] m. 'pitiful'

paq’a   [LEAram פקעא; cf. *piq‘â, piqyâ* Maclean 1901:256] 'crack'; pl. *paq’e*

pāre   [K, T; Sab253; Mutz368] pl. tant. 'money'; *pāre daqiqe* 'small change'

*parsnāya [ClAram פרס + gent. suff. *-nāya*; פרסנאיא Sab259; § 3.22.d] m. 'Persian'; pl. *parsnāye*

pāsa   [ClAram פָּאתָא; Sab253; Mutz369] f. 'face'

pāša   [T, K; cf. ⁺*pāša* Sab253, *pāša* Mutz371] m. 'pasha'

pastela   [ModH פַּסְטֵל < Judeo-Spanish Nehama 1977:416] 'pie'

*paṭira   [ClAram פַּטִירָא; Sab254; Mutz369] 'unleavened bread'; pl. *paṭire (haggada)*; see **‘ujna*

payṭūna   [Eur *phaeton* < Lat, Gr] m. 'carriage'

pehna   [K; Sab253] 'kick'; pl. *pehne*; see *ndy*

pelafta   [K; cf. *pēlavta* 'slipper' Sab255] f. 'shoe'; pl. *pelāwe*

pəmma, pumma [ClAram פֻּמָּא; Nöldeke 1910:177–178; cf. *pɪ/ümma, kɪmma* Sab256, *pu/əmma* Mutz369] m. 'mouth'

pənčāya   [GN *Pənča* + gent. suff. *-āya*; cf. *pənšāya* Mutz369] m. 'resident of Pinianish (Turkish Kurdistan)'; pl. *pənčāye*; see *pənčatūsa*

pənčatūsa   [GN *Pənča* + K abstr. suffix *-at* + abstr. suff. *-ūsa* 'residents or region of Pinianish'; see *pənčāya*

pəsra   [ClAram בִּשְׂרָא; cf. *pɪsra, pɪṣra?* Sab257, *pəsra* Mutz369] m. 'flesh, meat'

pəšūke   [T يشجك 'little gnat or musquito' Redhouse 1890:450; cf. K *pêšî, pêšûle* 'gnat, mosquito' Chyet 2003:452, Syr ܟ̈ܫܫܐ, MishH פִּשְׁפֵּשׁ] pl. 'gnats'

pəzaǵāya   [K *pis* 'son' + ’*āǵa* 'agha'?] m. 'village noble'; pl. *pəzaǵāye*

piča   [K *pič* Wahby 1966:108] 'small quantity, a little'

pis   [K; cf. *pīs, pīsaka, pīsake* Sab255, *pis* Mutz369] inv. 'filthy, dirty'; see *pisyatūsa*

pisyatūsa   [K *pis* + K abstr. suff. *-at* + abstr. suff. *-ūsa*] 'filthiness'; see *pis*

potine   [T, K < French *bottine*; cf. *pōtine* Sab254 and 1990:55] pl. 'boots'

poxa   [Syr ܦܘܿܚܐ; cf. *pōxa, pūxa* Sab254, *poxa* Mutz370] m. 'wind'

prāge   [Syr ܦܪܓܐ; Brauer 1993:422; Mutz370] pl. tant. 'millet'

priṭa   [ClAram √פרט] m. 'torn'; see *prṭ*

prəzla   [ClAram פַּרְזְלָא; Sab258; Mutz370] 'iron'

pṭixa   [Ar √فطح?; cf. *pṭōxa* Sab254 and Mutz371] m. 'wide'

pumma   see *pəmma*

ṗ

paləstināye [ModH פְּלֶסְטִינַאי < Eur] pl. 'Palestinians'

*paḷḷa   [K; Sab256; Mutz371] 'live coal'; pl. *paḷḷe*

paṇqánoṭ   [K banqanot, panqanot < Eng banknote Chyet 2003:23,430; cf. banqanōṭ Sab112] f. 'lira, paper money'; pl. paṇqánoṭe; f.s.?: mpulṭāle xamši paṇqánoṭe (§ 4.4.23.5); see baṇk; pálpaṇqàṇoṭ

pássaporṭ   [T, K < Italian; cf. ⁺passaport, ⁺pastapor Sab257] 'passport'

poṣṭa   [K, T < Eur; Sab254] f. 'post, mail'

q

qabǝl   [Ar قَبْل; cf. (m)qabıl Sab273, qabǝl Mutz372] prep. qabǝl mǝn 'before'; conj. qabǝl mǝn 'before': qabǝl mǝn ʾaxnan ʾāsaxwa 'before we used to come'; adv. qabǝl hādax 'beforehand'

qačax   [K, T; cf. qačax/ġ 'smuggler' Sab273, qačāġa 'robber' Mutz372] m. 'smuggled goods'; see qačāxa

qačāxa   'smuggler'; see qačax

qaddiš   [H קַדִּישׁ; Sab273] 'memorial prayer'

qadǝr   [Ar قَدْر; cf. qadra, qadır, qadda Sab273–274, qadar Mutzafi 2008a:372] 'size, quantity'; see ʾaqqar, qudrǝta

qadome   [ClAram √קדם; Sab273; Mutzafi 2002:482] 'tomorrow'

qahwa   [K, T, Ar قَهْوَة; cf. qahwa, qahwe Sab274, qahwa Mutz372] 'coffee'

qaḥba   [Ar قَحْبَة; cf. qaḥba/e, qaḥbıke Sab276, qaḥba Mutz372] f. 'daughter of a whore!'

qāla   [ClAram קָלָא; Sab272] m. 'voice, sound'

qalāma   [K, Ar قَلَم; Sab278] m. 'pen'

qalʾa   [K, Ar قَلْعَة; Sab278; Mutz372] f. 'fortress'

qalūla   [Syr ܩܠܝܠܐ; Sab279] m. 'quick, fast'

qalunka   [K; Sab279; Mutz372] m. 'narghile'; pl. qalunke

qalya   [ClAram √קלי; Sab279] 'fried and heavily salted meat; meat cooked for the winter'

qam   [ClAram קֳ(ו)דָם; Sab280; Mutz372] prep. 'before (temporal and spatial); xa zoʾa bargūze le qāmi 'I am wearing a woolen suit'; qam tarʾa 'outside'; qam hādax 'beforehand'; see m-qam, qam-qam

qamāya   [ClAram קֳדְמָיָא; cf. qamāya 'first, before' Sab280, qamāya 'first' Mutz372] m. 'previous'

qamāye   [ClAram בקדמיתא; cf. qamāye Sab280, qamāye Mutz372] adv. 'at first'

qamqam   [ClAram קֳ(ו)דָם; qắma-qam Mutz372] prep. 'right before' (spatial); qámqāman 'right before us'; see qam, m-qam

*qāna   [ClAram קַרְנָא; Sab272; Mutz372] 'horn'; pl. qanāne 'horns'

qānun   [Ar قَانُون < Gr; Sab273] 'law'

qaprāna   [K; Sab281; Mutz372] 'hut, booth'; pl. qaprāne

qapṭán   [K, T < Eur; cf. qapṭan Sabar 1990:62 and 2002:281] 'captain'

qarantina   [T karantina, Ar كُرَنْتِينَة, ModH קָרַנְטִינָה < Eur] 'quarantine'

qaraqól   [T; qaraqōl 'head of robbers' band' Sab284] 'garrison'

qarǝtta   see qarire

*qarira   [ClAram קְרִירָא; Sab283; Mutz372; § 3.6.i] 'cold, cool'; f. qarǝtta; pl. qarire

qarsa   [Syr ܩܰܪܣܳܐ; Arnold 2008:309–310; cf. *qarta* Sab284, *qarṯa*
               Mutz373] f. 'cold, cold weather'

*qaṛačāya   [K, T + gent. suff. -*āya*; cf. *qaṛačāya* Sab282, *qaṛačāya* Mutz372]
               'gypsy, highway robber'; pl. *qaṛačāye*; see *qaṛačke*

*qaṛačka   [K, T + suff. -*k*] 'gypsy, highway robber'; pl. *qaṛačke*; see *qaṛa-*
               čāya

qaṣra   [K, Ar قَصر; Sab282; Mutz373] m. 'mansion, palace'; pl. *qaṣ-*
               rāne

qāṣud   [K *qasid*, Ar قَاصِد; Sab272] 'messenger' (*haggada*)

qāša   [Syr ܩܰܫܳܐ; Sab272; Mutz373] m. 'priest'

qatxa   [Syr ܩܰܕܚܳܐ, K, T, < Ar قَدَح; cf. *qatxa, qaṭxa, qadxa* Sab284] m.
               'cup, glass'; pl. *qatxe*

qaṭəl   [Ar قَتل; cf. NENA *qəṭla* 'beating'; cf. *qṭl, qəṭla, qaṭola*

qaṭi'a   [Syr ܩܰܛܝܥܳܐ; Sab277; Mutz373] m. 'stick'; see *ndy*

qaṭola   [ClAram קְטוֹלָא; Mutz373] m. 'killer'; pl. *qaṭole*; see *qṭl, qaṭəl,*
               qəṭla

qaṭra   [Syr ܩܰܛܪܳܐ; Sab277; Mutz373] 'rock, boulder'

qaṭwāsa   [Syr ܩܰܛܘܐ, ܩܛܘ; Sab272] pl. 'cats'

qay   [cf. *qay, qawi, qavi* Sab277–278] interr. adv. 'why?'

qāymaqam   [K, T < Ar قَايِم مَقَام; Sab272] m. 'local governor'

qāzi   [K, Ar قَاضِي; cf. *qāẓi* Sab272] m. 'qadi'

qdāla   [ClAram קְדָלָא; Sab273; Mutz373] f. 'neck'; *'āwón didox b-qdālox*
               'you are responsible for it'

qdila   [Syr ܩܕܝܠܐ < Gr; cf. *qḍīla* Sab273; *qðila* Mutz373] f. 'key'

qeṭa   [ClAram קֵיטָא; Sab278; Mutz373] m. 'summer'

qəbla   [Ar قِبلَة; Maclean 1901:269] f. 'qiblah'

qəṭ'a   [Ar قطعَة, ClAram קְטְעָא; Sab277] 'piece, item, flock'; pl. *qəṭ'e*;
               'ərbəd Spindarnāye lu l-tāma, ṭlāha 'arba qəṭ'e 'the sheep of the
               residents of Spindar are there, three, four flocks'

qəṭla   [ClAram קְטְלָא; Sab277; Mutz374] 'killing, murder'; *sele qəṭla*
               and *mṭele 'əlləd qəṭla* 'he was killed'; *qəṭəl dide* 'the killing of him';
               see *qṭl, qaṭola, qaṭəl*

qəṭma   [ClAram קְטְמָא; Sab277; Mutz374] 'ashes'; *qəṭma go reše* 'May
               ashes be on his head!'

*qəṭya   [ClAram √קטע] m. 'broken'; f. *qṭe'ta*; see *qṭ'*

qəwya   [Ar. √قوى; cf. *qūya, quwya, quyva* Sab275; § 3.14]. m. 'strong,
               harsh'; f. *qwita* (*haggada*); pl. *qəwye* (*haggada*); see *qəwyūsa*

qəwyūsa   [cf. *quwwəta* 'power, strength' Sab275; § 3.14] f. 'strength' (*hag-*
               gada)

qida   [ClAram √יקד] m. 'burnt'; f. *qədta*, pl. *qide*; see *qyd*

*qliwa   [√qlw] m. 'clean'; pl. *qliwe*; see *qlw*

qolčiye   [T *kolcu* Hony 1957:206] pl. 'custom-house guards'

qólordi   [T *kolordu* Hony 1957:207] m. 'army corps'

qoma   [Syr ܩܘܡܐ; Sab275] f. 'stature'

qora   [ClAram קַבְרָא; Sab276; Mutz374] 'grave'; pl. *qorāsa*

qorbāna   [ClAram קֻרְבָּנָא; cf. *qûrbânâ* Maclean 1901:274, +*qurban, qurbon*
               Sab282] 'sacrifice'

qorúš	[K, Ar قِرْش; cf. qirûsh, qürûsh, qrûsh Maclean 1901:285, qɪruš Sab283] 'piaster, small coin'; pl. qorūše, qoruške
qotiya	[K, T; Sab276] m. 'small box'
qozzəlqorṭ	[T; cf. ⁺qɪzzɪl/rqōt Sab276] excl. 'hell!, disgusting!'
qudrəta	[K < Ar قُدْرَة; Sab274] f. '(Divine) omnipotence'; see ʾaqqar, qadər
qūjəke	[K; cf. qūja Mutz375] pl. 'martens'
quṇṣuḷ	[K, T, Ar قُنْصُل, ModH קוֹנסוּל < Eur; cf. qünṣûl, qünṣûr Maclean 1901:273; ⁺qunsor Sab275] m. 'consul'
quṇṣulya	[ModH קוֹנסוּליָה, Ar قُنْصُلِيَّة, < Eur; cf. qünṣûlkhânâ Maclean 1901: 273] f. 'consulate'
qurʿān	[K < Ar قُرْآن; cf. qurʾan Sab276] 'Quran'
qurdá, qurdāya	[qurd + gen. suff. -āya; LEAram קֻרְדָּיָא; Sab276; Mutz375; § 3. 15.a] 'Kurd'; f. qurdesa; pl. qurdāye; see kurdināya, qurdawūsa, qurdəski
qurdawūsa	[qurdá (?) + abstr. suff. -ūsa] pl. 'Kurds'; see qurdāya, qurdəski, kurdināya
qurdəski	[*qurdāʾiṯ + K suff. -ki; cf. kurdi Sab183, qurðəϑ, qurðəϑkí Mutz-375] 'Kurdish (language)'; lišāna qurdəski 'Kurdish language'; see kurdi
qura	[K; cf. qurra, qurrōna Sabar 202:276, qura Mutz375] m. 'boy'; quró 'boy! (voc.)'
qurwa	[LEAram קוֹרבה; cf. qûrbâ Maclean 1901:274, qɪrwa Sab282, qərwa Mutz373] 'vicinity, nearness'; prep. 'near'; qurwəd tāma 'near there'; qurwəd ḥanukka 'near Hanukka'
quṣur	[K, Ar قُصُور; cf. qɪṣûr Maclean 1901:283, qɪṣūr(i) Sab281] 'defect, deformity'
qūṭa	[Sab274] 'vagina'
qwita	see quwya
qyāmǝta	[K < Ar قِيَامَة; Sab278] 'resurrection'

r

raḥat	[K, Ar رَاحَة; Sab289; Mutz376] adv. 'calmly, relaxed'
rakāwa	[ClAram רַכָּבָא; Maclean 1901:293] m. 'rider'; see rkw
*rakixa	[ClAram רַכִּיכָא; Sab290; Mutz376] m. 'soft'; f. rakəxta; see rkx
rakəxta	see *rakixa, rkx
ramazán	[T, Ar رَمَضَان; Maclean 1901:294] 'Ramadan'
rašādi	[T Reşad < Ar رَشَاد] 'gold lira (minted by the Ottoman Sultan Mehmed V (Mehmed Reşad)'
rekanāya	[GN Rekan + gent. suff. -āya] m. 'resident of Rekan (Iraqi Kurdistan)'; pl. rekanāye
reš	[ClAram רֹאשׁ, רֵישׁ; calque on K ser 'head, upon' Khan 2002:239, Mutz125; cf. rɪš/ž Sab290, reš Mutz376] prep. 'on, upon'; ʾit rešexun 'you owe'; see reša, rešreš
reša	[ClAram רֵאשׁא, רֵישׁא; Sab290; Mutz376] 'head'; pl. reše; xa tremma reše 'about two hundred head (of cattle)'; reše reše 'from one end to the other'; see reš, rešreš

rešreš   [ClAram ראש, ריש; cf. *réša-reš* Mutz125, 376] prep. 'right above';
              see *reš, reša*

rə'ola   [ClAram √רעל; Sab286] 'shivering' (*haggada*)

rəqqa, reqa   [LEAram רוחקא; cf. *riqqâ, raḥqa, raqqa* Sab289, *rəqqa* Mutz24,
              378] 'distance' *m-rəqqa* 'from afar'; cf. *rḥq*

riviya   [K *rîvî, rêvî,rovî* Chyet 2003:523; cf. *rūvīka* Sab287] m. 'fox'

rqā'e   [LEAram רוקעתא; cf. pl. *raqā'e* Sab292, pl. *rqā'e* Mutz377] pl.
              'patches, rags'

ruba'   [Ar رُبْع; cf. ClAram רִבְעָא; cf. *rübɪ', rub'/'a* Sab287] 'quarter'; *xá-
              ruba'* 'a quarter'; *rúba'-sā'a* quarter of an hour'; see *naqoṣa*

rūt   [K; Sab288] inv. 'naked, bare'

ruxta   see *rwixa*

rwixa   [LEAram רויחא; cf. *rwixa* Sab288, *ṛwixa* Mutz378] m. 'wide,' f.
              ruxta

ṛ

ṛāba   [ClAram רבָּא; cf. *⁺rāba* Sab286, Mutz377 and 2006:126–127]
              adv. 'many, much, very'; *ṛāba nāše 'uṛwe* 'many important peo-
              ple'; see *'uṛwa, 'uṛwāne, bəš-ṛab*

ṛabbi   [Ar يَا رَبِّ] *yā ṛabbi* 'My Lord!'

ṛadyo   [T, K, IrAr < Eur; cf. *⁺rādıyo* Sab286] 'radio'

ṛapsa   see *'uṛwa*

ṛaṣṭe   [K, T; cf. *raṣṭî, raṣṭî* Maclean 1901:294, *⁺rāsṭ* Sab286] 'right' (as
              against 'left'); only in *'ida ṛaṣṭe* 'to the right (= right hand)'

ṛeṃa   [P; Sab290] 'pus'

ṛəzza   [K, P, Ar رُزّ; cf. LAram ארוזה, אורז, ܐܘܪܙ, ܐܪܘܙܐ; cf. *⁺rɪzza* Sabar
              2002:288; *ṛəzza* Mutz378] 'rice'

ṛomāna   [ClAram √רום + suff. *-āna*; cf. *⁺rō/ūmāna* Sab288, *romāna*
              Mutz378] m. 'high'; f. *ṛomanta*; pl. *ṛomāne*; see *ṛym*

ṛūbar   [K; cf. *rōbar, rūbar* Sab287, *ṛūbar* Mutz378] 'stream'

s

sā'a   [Ar سَاعَة; cf. *sā'a, ṣa''a* Sab236, *sā'a* Mutz378] f. 'hour'; pl. *sā'e*;
              see *pálsā'a*

sahāda   [ClAram סְהֵדָא; cf. *sahda* Sab237, *sahða, sahāða* Mutz378] m.
              'witness'; pl. *sahāde*

salāmat   [T, K, Ar سَلامَة; cf. *sâlâmat* Maclean 1901:226; cf. *salāme*, pl.
              salāmatīye Sab240] 'welfare, prosperity'; *b-salāmat* 'safely'

sahma   [Ar سَهْم; Sab237; Mutz378] m. 'portion, lot'

sántimetər   [ModH סֶנְטִימֶטֶר < Eur; cf. *santín* Mutz379] 'centimeter'

*sapöxa   [ClAram √ספ?; cf. *sapōya* Sab242; contamination with *laxma*
              'bread'? Mutzafi p.c.] 'wrap sandwich'; pl. *sapöxe*

sartuk   [K; cf. *sartīke* Sab244, סְרְטִיכֶּה Yona 1999:341, *sertika, sertun,
              sertur* Brauer 1993:425] 'cream'

sāwa   [ClAram סָבָא; cf. *sāwa* Sab236, *sawoya* Mutz379] m. 'grandfa-
              ther'; *sāwi* 'my grandfather'; see *sota*

sayyəd, sayyəda   [K, T, Ar سَيِّد; cf. *sayyıd, sayda* 'sir' Sab239] m. 'sayyid, descen-
                    dant of Muhammad'; see *sayyədka*

sayyədka   [K, Ar سَيِّد + suff. *-ka*] m. 'sayyid, descendant of Muhammad';
                    see *sayyəd, sayyəda*

se'ra   [ClAram סֶעְרָא; Sab236; Mutz379] 'goat hair'

séfarṭoṛa   [H סֵפֶר תּוֹרה; cf. *sēfar +tōra* Sab243, *sefərṭoṛa* Mutzafi 2008a:379]
                    'Torah scroll'

sepa   [ClAram סִיפָא; Sab239; Mutz379] 'sword'

setira   [K *se* 'three' + *tir* 'shot'] 'long three-shot rifle'

səfərṭās   [T, Ar سَفَر طَاس; Sab243] m. '(traveling) lunch box'

səjjāda   [K, T, Ar سِجَّادَة] f. 'prayer rug'

səkkina   see *skina*

səksa   [ClAram סִכְּתָא; Sab240; Mutz379] f. 'peg'

səmbela   [K, Ar سنبل; Sab241] 'mustache'; pl. *səmbele*

sənjāqe   [K, Ar سَنْجَق < T; Sab241] pl. 'flags, banners'

səpsa   [ClAram סֶפְתָא; Sab243; Mutz380] f. 'lip, edge'; *səpsəd 'ar'əd gy-
                    ānu* 'the edge of their land'

səswa   [ClAram סֶתְוָא; Sab245; Mutz380] m. 'winter'

skina, səkkina   [ClAram סַכִּינָא; cf. MishH סכין; cf. *skīna, sikkına* Sab240, *skina*
                    Mutz380] 'knife'; pl. *skine, səkkine*

sməxta   [ClAram √סמך; Sab241; Mutz380] f. 'pregnant'; pl. *smixe*

smoqa   [TO סְמוֹקָא, סָמוֹקָא; Sab241; Mutz380] m. 'red'

sniqa   [Syr ܣܢܝܩܐ] m. 'needy'; pl. *sniqe*; see *snq*

sota   [LAram סבתא; Sab238; Mutz380] f. 'grandmother'; see *sāwa*

sparəgla   [LEAram אספרגלא; Sab243; Mutz380] 'quince'; pl. *sparəgle*

spindarnāya   [GN *Spindar* + gent. suff. *-nāya*] m. 'resident of Spindar (Iraqi
                    Kurdistan)'; pl. *spindarnāye*

spiqa   [ClAram √ספק; Sab242] m. 'empty'; see *spq*

spisa   [probably ClAram Mutz381; NeoAram √sps < Gr? Sab242] m.
                    'rotten'

*sqila   [LEAram √סקל 'polish'; Sab243; Mutz381] m. 'beautiful'; f. *sqəlta*

surāya   [Syr ܣܘܪܝܐ; Rollinger 2006; cf. *sōrāya, surāya* Sab238, *surāya*
                    Mutz381] Christian'; f. *suresa*; pl. *surāye*

sūsa   [TO סוּסְיָא, Syr ܣܘܣܝܐ; cf. *sūse, sūsa* Sab238, *sūsa* Mutz381] m.
                    'horse'; pl. *sūse*

swa'ta   [ClAram סבעא; Sab237] f. 'satiety, satisfaction'; *xəllox swa'tox*
                    'you ate your fill'

*swi'a   [ClAram √סבע; Sab237; Mutz381] m. 'satiated'; pl. *swi'e*

ṣ

*ṣa'arta   [ClAram סְעָרְתָא; cf. +*sa'arta*, pl. +*sa'āre* Sab242, *ṣa'arta*, pl. *ṣa'āre*
                    Mutz382] 'grain of barley'; pl. *ṣa'āre* (1) 'grains of barley', (2)
                    'barley'

ṣabo'ta   [ClAram צבעתא(א); Sab266; Mutz382] f. 'finger'

ṣābun   [T, K, Ar صَابُون < Gr; Sabar 1990:62 and 2002:266; Mutz382]
                    'soap'

ṣadra | [T, Ar صَدْر; cf. ⁺ṣadra Sab267, ṣadra Mutz382] m. 'chest'; cf. ṣudra

ṣaqāṭe | [Ar سَقَط; cf. ⁺ṣaqat, ṣaqaṭōka, ṣaqaṭōke Sab243] pl. 'cripples'

ṣawā'a | [LEAram צַבָּעָא; cf. ṣabāġa Sab266, ṣawā'a Mutz382] m. 'dyer'; see ṣw', ṣəwya

ṣāx | [K, T; Sab266; Mutz382] inv. 'healthy, alive, intact, well'

ṣəḥya | [ClAram √צחי; cf. ṣeḥya, ṣehya, ṣiḥya Sab268, ṣəḥya Mutz382] m. 'thirsty'

ṣəwya | [ClAram √צבע; § 3.14] m. 'dyed, colored'; see ṣawā'a, ṣw'

ṣfera | [Ar صَفِير; cf. ṣafīra Sab270] 'whistle'; see ṣfr

ṣiwa | [LEAram צִיבָא; Sab268; Mutz382] m. 'tree, wood'; pl. ṣiwe

ṣlosa | [ClAram צְלוֹתָא; Sab269; Mutz382] f. 'prayer'

ṣo'rāsa | [Syr ܨܘܥܪܐ 'invective'; cf. ṣu'irta, ṣı'urta, pl. ṣu'rāṯa Sabar 2002a:267] pl. 'curses'; see ṣ'r

ṣofi | [K, T, Ar صُوفِي; cf. ṣōpî Maclean 1901:263, ṣōfīka Sab267] m. 'sufi, ascetic'; pl. ṣofyāne

ṣopa | [K, T; cf. ṣūpa 'ante-room' Sab267, ṣopa, zopa 'stove' Mutz383] f. 'stove'

*ṣrifa | [ModH צְרִיף] 'hut'; pl. ṣrife

ṣtaġfərəllá | [K < Ar أَسْتَغْفِرُ اللّٰه] excl. bāba ṣtaġfərəllá 'I ask God's forgiveness!'

ṣudra | [Ar صُدْرَة; Sab267; Mutz383] f. 'shirt, vest'; cf. ṣadra

ṣulḥe | [K, Ar صُلْحَة; cf. ṣulḥ Sab267] s. or pl? 'peaceful reconcili-ation(s?)'; 'axnan ču ṣulḥe la godax 'we won't make any peaceful reconciliation(s)'

ṣurta | [K, P, Ar صُورَة; Sab268] f. 'face'; pl. ṣuryāsa 'cheeks'

š

šafqa | [IrAr < Russian; Sab302] f. 'hat (with a brim)'; pl. šafqe

šahāra | [LAram √ שהר 'be vigilant'; cf. ša/ıhāra Sab294, šahāra Mutz-384] m. 'blind'; f. šaharta; see šthr

šākar | [Syr ܫܟܪܐ, ܣܟܪܐ, JBA שכר < P; K, T; Sab293 and Mutz384] 'sugar'

šāla | [K, Ar شَال < P; Sab293] m. 'fabric shawl used by men as belt'; pl. šāle

šalla | [K; Sab299; Mutz384] m. 'Kurdish woven pants of fine wool, worn usually together with *šapukta'

šapsa | [ClAram שַׁבְּתָא; cf. ša/ıbṭa, šab/psa Sab294, šabϑa Mutz384] f. 'Sabbath'

šamina | [ClAram שַׁמִּינָא; Sab301; Mutz384] m. 'fat'; pl. šamine

*šaqfa | [Ar شَقَفَة 'piece (of land)' Sab303] 'piece'; pl. šaqfe 'pieces (of fur)'

šaqisa | [Syr ܫܩܝܬܐ; cf. šaqqīta Sab302, šaqiϑa Mutz384] f. '(water) channel'; pl. šaqyāsa

šaqqa¹ | [Ar شَقّ; cf. shaqâ 'slap, half' Maclean 1901:311, šaqqa 'half' Sab302] 'half, section'

*šaqqa² | 'slap'; pl. šaqqe 'slaps'; see šaqqāme

*šaqqāma | [K; cf. šıqqāma Sab302, šaqqāma Mutz384] 'slap'; pl. šaqqāme 'slaps on face'; see šaqqa²

šar'a | [Ar الشَّرْع; cf. šar' Sab304] f. 'religious law'; pl. šar'e

šargūme	[LEAram שַׁלְגָּם Sokoloff 2005:1146; Sab303] pl. 'turnips'
*šarṭ	[Ar شَرْط; Sab303] 'covenant'; *šarṭəd mila* 'covenant of circumcision' (= ברית מילה) (*haggada*)
šarwāla	[BAram סַרְבָּל, Syr ܣܪܒܠܐ < P; cf. ⁺*šarwāl* Sab303, *šarwāla* Mutz-384] f. 'long underpants, trousers'; pl. *šarwāle*
šaṛūsa	[ClAram שְׁרוּתָא; cf. *šarūta* Sab303, *šaṛūϑa* Mutz384] f. 'lunch'
šāta	[ClAram שַׁתָּא; Hoberman 2007; cf. *šāta, šınna* Sab293, *šāta* Mutz385] f. 'year'; pl. *šənne*
šaxina	[Syr ܫܚܝܢܐ; Sab298; Mutz385] m. 'warm'; f. *šaxənta; šaxína-le* 'he is hot(-headed); see *šxn*
šawa	[ClAram שַׁבְעָא; cf. *šō'a, šawwa* 'seven, week' Sab295] 'week'; pl. *šawe; šawəd basra* 'the week after'; cf. *šō'a, šö'amma, šö'i, šwa'sar*
šes-béš	[K, T, P; Sab304] 'backgammon'
šex	[K, T, Ar شَيْخ; cf. *šex,* pl. *šēxyāne* Sab297 and Mutz385] m. 'sheikh'; pl. *šexāye*
šəmma	[ClAram שְׁמָא; Hoberman 2007; Sab300; Mutz385] m. 'name'
šəmme	[ClAram שְׁמַיָּא; Hoberman 2007; cf. *šımme,* pl. *šımmāhe* Sab300–301, *šəmme* Mutz385] pl. tant. 'sky, heavens'
šəmša	[ClAram שִׁמְשָׁא; Sab301; Mutz385] 'sun'
šənsa	[ClAram שְׁנַתָא; Sabar 202:302] f. 'sleep'
šəqya	[JBA שִׁקְיָא* Sokoloff 2002:1174; Mutz386] 'glue'
šərika	[K, Ar شَرِيك; Sab304; Mutz386] m. '(business) partner'
šərma	[Syr ܫܪܡܐ; Sab304; Mutz386] f. 'ass, buttocks'; pl. *šərme*
šərṭa	[Ar شُرْطَة; cf. *šurṭa/i* Sab296, *šərṭa* Mutz386] 'policeman'; pl. *šərṭe*
šəryoxa	[Ar شِراك?; Sab304] m. 'shoe-string'
šətya	[ClAram שְׁתִיָא; cf. *šı/atya* Sab305, *šətya* Mutz386] 'warp'
šəxda	[ClAram שׁוּחְדָא; cf. *šıx/ġda* Sab298, *šəxða* Mutz386] 'good tidings'
šəxta	[Syr ܫܚܬܐ 'sediment, secretions'; Sab299; Mutz386] f. 'dirt, filth'; see *šəxtāna*
šəxtāna	[*šəxta* + suff. -āna; Sab299; Mutz386] m. 'dirty'; pl. *šəxtāne*; see *šəxta*
šəxxoṛa	[ClAram √שחר; cf. ⁺*šı/axōra* Sab298, *šəxxoṛa* Mutz386] 'coal, charcoal'; see *čəxra*
šidāna	[calque on K, P; ClAram שֵׁדָא 'demon' + suff. -āna; Sab294; Mutz385] m. 'crazy, mad'; pl. *šidāne;* see *mšidəna, šidanūsa, šydn*
šidanūsa	[*šidāna* + abstr. suff. -ūsa; Sab294] f. 'craziness'; see *šydn, mšidəna, šidāna,*
škafta	[K; cf. s. *škafta,* pl. *škafyāϑa* Sab299 and Mutz386] f. 'cave'; pl. *škaftyāsa*
šohad	[H שֹׁחַד; cf. *šōhaḏ* Sab295] 'bribe'
šö'a	[ClAram שְׁבְעָא; cf. *šō'a, šawwa* Sab295, *šo'a* Mutz386] 'seven'; see *šawa, šö'amma, šö'i, šwa'sar*
šö'amma	[*šö'a* + *əmma*; cf. *š(o)wa'ma,* Sab295, *šo'á'əmma* Mutz396; §4.3.3] 'seven hundred'; see *šawa, šö'a, šö'i, šwa'sar*

šöʾi [ClAram שבעין; Sab295; Mutz386] 'seventy'; see *šawa, šöʾa, šöʾ-amma, šwaʾsar*

šuftiya [K *ṣiftî* Chyet 1993:581; *šəftiyya, šəptiyya* < Beduin Ar *dəbšiyya*? Talay 2008:61 n.106; cf. *shiptîyâ, shaptîyâ* Maclean 1901:310; *šiftiya* Khan 1999:581] f. 'watermelon'; pl. *šuftiye*

šūla [Syr ܫܽܘܓ݂ܠܳܐ < Ar شُغْل; *šūla, šuʾ(ā)la?* Sab296, *šūla* Mutz387] 'work, deed, affair'; pl. *šuʾāle*

šulxāya [ClAram √ שלח + suff. -*āya*; Sab296; Mutz387] m. 'naked'; pl. *šulxāye*; see *šlx*

šūqa [ClAram שׁוּקָא; Sab296; Mutz387] 'market'

šwaʾsar [Syr ܚܕܰܥܣܰܪ; Sab295; *šuwáʾssar, ʾəšwáʾəssar* Mutz115] 'seventeen'; see *šawa, šöʾa, šöʾamma, šöʾi*

šwāna [K; cf. *šivāna, šüvān, šüwān* Sab294, *ʾašwān, šwāna* Mutz329] m. 'shepherd'

t

ta, ṭas, ti [Syr ܠ, ܠܬ; cf. *ṭla, ta, da, ṭlāṭi, ṭāṭi* Sab172; *ta, ṭāli, ṭālox* Mutz388] prep. 'to, for'; conj. 'in order to'; *ta-lá* 'lest'; *ṭas dide, ṭāse* 'to him'; *ti gyāne* 'for himself'; see *tad*

tābur [T, Ar طَابُور; cf. *ṭâbûr, tâbûr* Maclean 1901:109, *tābur* Sab306] battalion'

tad [Mutz388] *ta* + *d*; conj. 'in order to' see *ta*

tagbir [K, Ar تَدْبِير; cf. *tag/kbir* Sab306, *tagbir* Mutz388] 'counsel, conspiracy'; *ʾüdlu tagbir* 'they conspired'

taḥqiqå̄t [Ar تَحْقِيقَات; Sab308] pl. 'investigations'

talga [ClAram תַּלְגָּא; Sab309; Mutz388] m. 'ice, snow'

talma [Syr ܛܰܠܡܳܐ; Sab310] m. 'water-jug'

talya [LEAram תליא 'part of stomach' Sokoloff 2002:1209; cf. 'entrails' Sab309] '(human) lung'

tāma, tam, ʾəl-tắma, ʾəl-tám, tan- [ClAram תַּמָּה; cf. *tāma, tam, ltam, mɪn tam, tangɪb/tangēba* Sab306, *tam, tāma, l-tam, l-tāma* Mutz388] adv. 'there, to there'; *ʾáx-geb tán-geb (ṭamắha-geb)* 'when all's said and done, eventually'; *tam lé-ʾāl* 'from there on'; see *ʾaxxa, geba, ṭamắha*

tan- see *tāma*

tangāwi [K; Maclean 1901:323] f. 'distress'

tarʾa [ClAram תַּרְעָא; cf. JPA תרא Kutscher 1967:70 n. 64; cf. *tarʾa, tara* Sab312, *tar-, tarʾa* Mutz389] m. 'door'; pl. *tarʾāne; qam tarʾa* 'outside'

tārix, ṭārix [ModH תַּאֲרִיךְ, Ar تَأْرِيخ; cf. *târikh* 'history, an account, date of event' Maclean 1901:326, *t/ṭārīx* 'length of time, period' Sab306–307] f. 'date'

tawərta [ClAram (TO תּוֹרְתָא, Syr ܬܰܘܪܬܳܐ); Sab308; Mutz389; § 3.22.b] f. 'cow'; pl. *toryāsa*; see *tora*

tāxa [K; Sab306] 'quarter of town'; pl. *tāxe*

tāza [K, T; inv. Sab306 and Mutz389; *tāza* and *tāze* Nöldeke 1868:135] c. 'new, fresh, precious'; pl. *tāze*

telafon, telefon [K, T, ModH טֶלֶפוֹן < Eur; cf. *telefun* Sab310 and 1990:62] m. 'telephone'; see *rym*

tena [ClAram תֵּי(נ)תָא; cf. *te'na*, *tēna* Sab306, *te'na* Mutz389] f. 'fig'; pl. *tene*

ter [K; Sab308] 'sufficient'; *wəllu qurdāye terax ter yəmmax ter xas-wāsax ter kulléxun-'ilu* 'Right now the Kurds are enough for you, enough for your mother, enough for your sisters, enough for all of you'

tera [K; cf. *tér* Maclean 1901:320, תירא Sab309] f. 'large bag, saddle-bag'

*teška [?; cf. תִּישְׁכָּא Yona 1999א:434, *tēšika*, *tēška* Sab309] 'whelp'; pl. *teške*

təffaq [K; cf. *tfang*, *tfakke* Sab311, *təffaq* Mutz389] f. 'rifle'; pl. *təffāqe*

təhome [H תְהוֹם; cf. *tɪhōm* Sab307, pl. tant. *təhome* Mutz389] pl. tant. 'abyss'

təjjāra [Ar تُجَّار (pl.); *tɪjjar*, *tājɪr* Sab306, *təjjāra* Mutz389] m. 'merchant'; pl. *təjjāre*

tək [onomat.] 'knock (on door)'

təksa [ClAram תִּכְתָא; Sab309] 'waistband'

təlqūna [T, K, Ar تَلْقِينَ] 'final rites at a funeral'

təlta'sar [TO תְּלָת עֲשַׂר, Syr ܬܠܵܬܥܣܲܪ; cf. *tɪlta'sar*, ⁺*talta-sar* Sab310, *təltá'əssar* Mutz115] 'thirteen'; see *ṭlāha*, *ṭlāsi*, *ṭlāhūšeb*

təlya [ClAram √תלי] m. 'hung'; f. *tleta*; see *tly*

təmmal [TO תְמָלִי, Syr ܐܬܡܠ; Hoberman 2007; Sab310; Mutz389] 'yesterday'

təne, b-təne [K, P; cf. *b-tɪne* Sab310, *təne*, *b-təne* Mutz389] adv. 'alone, only'

tənna [ClAram תננא; cf. *tənna*, *tehna* Sab310, *tənna* Mutz389] m. 'smoke'

təqla [ClAram תִּקְלָא; Sab312] 'weight'

tərte see *tre*

təttun [T, K; cf. *tütün*, *tɪtūn* Sab308, *tuttun* Mutz390] 'tobacco'

ti see *ta*

tiqa [ClAram עַתִּיקָא; cf. *'atɪqa* Sab103, *'atiqa* Mutz329; §3.17.d] m. 'old'; f. *təqta*; pl. *tiqe*

tmanya [ClAram תְּמָנְיָא; Sab310; Mutz114] 'eight'; see *ṭmāne'sar*, *ṭmāni*

tola [K; cf. *tûlâ* Maclean 1901:317, *to'la* Mutz390] f. 'revenge'; *tola mpārəqlax* 'you take revenge'; *tol babexun* 'revenge for your father'

tona [T, K, ModH < Eur] 'ton'; pl. *tone*

tora [ClAram (Syr ܬܘܪܐ, BAram and TO תּוֹרָא); cf. *tōra*, *tawra* Sabar 2002a:308, *tora* Mutz390] m. 'ox'; pl. *tore*; see *tawərta*

traq [onomat.; Sab175] 'thwack! (sound of beating)'

tre, tre' [ClAram תְּרֵי(ן); Sab312; §4.3.1.e] 'two'; *tre'* 'only two (pausal)'; f. *tərte* (*haggada*); *kutru* 'two of them'; see *tre'sar*, *tremma*, *trūšeb*

tre'sar [TO תְּרֵי עֲשַׂר, Syr ܬܪܲܥܣܲܪ; cf. *tre'sar* Sab313, *tré'əssar* Mutz115] 'twelve'; see *tre*, *tremma*, *trūšeb*

tremma	[*tre* + *'əmma*; cf. Mutz390 *tré'əmma*; § 4.3.3] 'two hundred'; see *tre, tre'sar, trŭšeb*
trŭšeb	[LAram תרי בשבא; cf. *trušěba, trōšıb, trūšıb* Sab313, *trošeb* Mutz-117] 'Monday'; see *tre, tremma, tre'sar, trŭšeb*
tūkəla	[K? cf. *tekeltû* 'saddle-cloth of felt' Wahby 1966:143] m. 'piece of clothing'
tūsa	[LAram תּוּתָא; Sab308; Mutz390] 'mulberry tree'
tūsi	[K?] 'type of thorn'
tuxma	[K, P, T; cf. *tuxum* Sab307, *tuxma* Mutz390] 'type, kind'; *tuxməd xorox* 'type like you'
tŭra, twira	[ClAram √תבר] m. 'broken'; see *twr*
türkāya	[*Türk* + gent. suff. *-āya*; cf. *tırkāya* Sab313] m. 'Turk'; pl. *türkāye*
türki	[K; cf. *tırki* Sab313, *turki* Mutz390] 'Turkish (language)'
twira	see *tŭra*

ṭ

*ṭabāqa	[T, Ar طَبَقَة; Sab170; Mutz391] 'story, floor'; pl. *ṭabāqe*
ṭahora	[ModH or H טָהֹר] m. 'clean, pure'
ṭalāqe	[Ar طَلَاق; cf. *ṭalāqe* Sab173] 'divorce'; see *ṭlq*
ṭamá	[*ta* 'for' + *mā* 'what'; cf. *ṭ(l)amá(ha)*, טָה מַה תֵּמָא Sab172, *ṭamá* Mutz391] interr. adv. 'why?'
ṭamāha	[ClAram תֵּמָּה; cf. *tamā/ōha* Sab306, *ṭamāha* Mutz391] adv. 'way over there' in phrase *'áx-geb tán-geb ṭamáha-geb* 'when all's said and done' (lit. 'here side, there side, way over there side'); see *tāma*
ṭánəke	[K, T, Ar تَنَك; cf. *tanîkâ, ṭŭnîkâ* Maclean 1901:323, *tanak, tanıkāye* Sab311] pl. 'large tin cans'
ṭanəšta	[K *teniṣt, ṭeniṣt* Chyet 2003 605] f. 'side'; pl. *ṭanəšyāsa*
ṭappá	[Syr ܛܦܐ 'side'; cf. *ṭappāya, ṭappēta* Sab174, *ṭapoya* Mutzafi 2002:483; § 3.15.a] 'hillside'
ṭāpu	[K, T; Sab170] m. 'title deed'
ṭaraf	[T, Ar طَرَف; Sab175] 'side, part'; only in *mən ṭaraf ḥukum* 'on the part of the government'
ṭarefa	[H טְרֵפָה Ben-Yaacob 1985:78; Sab175] 'non-kosher meat'
ṭārix	see *tārix*
ṭarka	[K *teriḳ* 'green stick' Rizgar 1993:183; *terik* 'wet firewood' Chyet 2003:608] m. 'stick'; pl. *ṭarke*
ṭarma	[K; Sab175] m. 'corpse'; pl. *ṭarme*
ṭarrašta	[Syr ܛܪܫܐ; Sab175; Mutz391] f. 'thicket, bush'; pl. *ṭarrāše*
ṭas	see *ta*
ṭayyāra	[Ar طَيَّارَة; Sab172] 'airplane'
ṭe'na	[ClAram טַעְנא; Sab170; Mutz391] m. 'load'
ṭélgəraf	[K, T < Eur; cf. *⁺telǧrāf* Sab309 and 1990:62] 'telegraph'
ṭélgəram	[K,T < Eur; cf. *⁺telǧrām* Sab309] m. 'telegram'
ṭera	[Syr ܛܝܪܐ; cf. 'bird, fowl' Sab172; 'hoopoe' Mutz391] 'fowl, bird'

*ṭəyarāya   [GN Ṭəyāra + gent. suff. -āya] m. 'resident of Tiari (Turkish Kurdistan)'; pl. ṭəyarāye; see ṭəyarnāya

ṭəyarnāya   [GN Ṭəyāra + gent. suff. -nāya] m. 'resident of Tiari'; see *ṭəyarāya

ṭima   [ClAram טימא < Gr; Sab172] 'price, cost'

ṭina   [ClAram טִינָא; Sab172; Mutz391] 'mud'

ṭiq   [onomat.] 'bang! (sound of gunshot)'

ṭlōxe   [ClAram טל(ו)פחיא; Sab172; Mutz392] pl. 'lentils'

ṭlāha   [ClAram תְּלָתָא; cf. ṭlā(ha) Sab172, ṭlāha Mutz391] 'three'; kúṭlā-hun 'the three of them'; see ṭlāhúšeb, ṭlāsi, təlta'sar

ṭlāhúšeb   [LAram תלתא בשבא; cf. ṭlāhošıb, ṭlāhúšıb, ṭlāhúšab Sab172, ṭlá-hošeb Mutz117] 'Tuesday'; see ṭlāha, ṭlāsi, təlta'sar

ṭlāsi   [ClAram תְּלָתִין; cf. ṭlāṭi, ṭlāsi, ṭlāhi Sab172, ṭlāϑi Mutz115] 'thirty'; see ṭlāha, təlta'sar, ṭlāhúšeb

*ṭmira   [ClAram √טמר; Sab173; Mutz392] m. 'hidden'; pl. ṭmire; (haggada)

ṭmāne'sar   [Syr ܬܡܢܥܣܪ; cf. tmāne(-)'sar, ⁺tmāne'sar Sab310, ṭmāné'əssar Mutz115] 'eighteen'; see ṭmāni, tmanya

ṭmāni   [ClAram תמנין; cf. tmāne, ⁺tmāne Sab310, ṭmāni Mutz115] 'eighty'; see tmanya, ṭmāne'sar

ṭrambel   [K < Eur automobile + T tulumba; Sab175 and 1990:56,63] 'automobile, bus'; pl. ṭrambele

ṭrosa   [LAram √תרץ; cf. ⁺trōṣa Sab313, ṭrosa Mutz392] 'truth, true'; marri ṭrosa 'tell me the truth!'; lewe ṭrosa 'it is not true'; see trs

*ṭupra   [ClAram טפרא (BAram טִפְרָא, TO טוּפְרָא, Syr ܛܦܪܐ); cf. ṭüpra Sabar 2002a:172, ṭupra Mutz392] 'nail, claw'; pl. ṭuprāsa

ṭūra   [ClAram טוּרָא; Sab172; Mutz392] 'mountain'; pl. ṭurāne

v

veza   [K wisa Chyet 2003:647] adv. 'so, in such a way, like this'

w

-wa   [K -hawa; Mutzafi 2004:85–86; §4.4.26] repetitive-reversive postverbal particle 'back, again'; lu d'íre-wa 'they have returned back'

wa'dūsa   [Ar √وعد + abstr. suff. -ūsa; Sab155] f. 'promise'

wājəbūsa   [Ar واجب + abstr. suff. -ūsa; Sab153] f. 'obligation' (haggada)

wakil   [K, Ar وكيل; Sab154] m. 'agent, deputy, substitute'

wal   [Polotsky 1967:111; Sab154] adv. 'indeed, surely'

walāya   [Ar وَلَايَة; Maclean 1901:81] f. 'valayet'

walhāṣəl   [Ar وَالْخَاصِل; Sab154; cf. Mlahso warhaṣel Jastrow 1994:193] adv. 'in short'

wāli, walya   [Ar والي; Sab153] m. 'vali, (Turkish) governor'; walyá-bak 'the Vali Bey' (< T vali aǧabey 'His Honor the Governor'?)

waḷḷa [Ar وَٱللَّٰه; cf. ⁺*walla*, ⁺*wallahi*, *wü/ınne* Sab153, ⁺*wulla* Sabar 2005: 176,178, *waḷḷa* Mutz393] excl. 'By God!', 'indeed'; see *ʾaḷḷa*, *ʾilāha*, *ʾišaḷḷa*

wānesa [GN *Wān* + adj. suff. -*esa*] f. 'resident of Van'

warāqa [Ar وَرَقَة; cf. ⁺*warāqa* Sab155] f. 'paper, document'; pl. *warāqe*

waxt, waxta [K < A وَقْت; cf. *waxt, waqt* Sab155] m. 'time'; pl. *waxte*

warde [TJ, LAram < P; Sab155; Mutz393] pl. 'roses, flowers'

wewa, ʾewa, -ewa, -wa [Mutz52; § 4.4.6.4] 3 m.s. past copula

wəl- [*u* + *əlla* Mutz 57–58,393; Hoberman 1989:33; § 4.4.6.3.a] deictic copula; *wəlle* 'he is right here'; *wəlla* 'she is right here'

wəždān [K, A وِجْدَان; cf. *wıj/ždān* Sab153] 'conscience'

wiza [T, K < Eur; Maclean 1901:81] 'visa'

x

xa¹, xa' [ClAram חַד; cf. *xa, xa'* Sab191, *xa, xa'* Mutz114,393–394] 'one'; indef. prn 'a(n), a certain'; *xá-yalunka* 'a certain child'; *xa'* 'a single one, only one (pausal)'; *pə́šwāle xa'* 'it remained the only one'; preceding a numeral adv. 'about, approximately'; *xa 'əṣra 'alpe* 'about ten thousand'; *xá-gā* 'once'; *xa-b-xa* 'one by one'; multiplicative; *xá-u-tre* 'double'; *xá-u-ʾarbaʿ* 'fourfold'; *xá-u-šö'a* 'sevenfold'; see *xədda*, *xade'sar*, *xošeba*

xa-² see *xe*

xabine see *mxabine*

xabra [K, T, Ar خَبَر; Sab192; Mutz394] 'thing, word'; pl. *xabre*

xabūša [LEAram חַבּוּשָׁא; Sab192; Mutz394] 'apple'

xade'sar [TO חַד עֲשַׂר, Syr ܚܕܥܣܪ; cf. *xade'sar* Sabar 202:192, *xadé'əssar* Mutz115] 'eleven'; see *xa, xədda*

xaloya [Syr ܚܠܐ; Sab197; Mutz394] m. 'maternal uncle'; *xaloyi* 'my maternal uncle'; *xalóx* 'your maternal uncle'; see *xalta*

xalta [Syr ܚܠܬܐ; Sab197; Mutz394] f. 'maternal aunt'; *xalti* 'my maternal aunt'; see *xaloya*

xalwa [ClAram חַלְבָּא; cf. *xalwa, xılya* Sab197, *xalwa* Mutz394] m. 'milk'

xam [K, Ar غَم; cf. *kham, gham, ghâm* Maclean 1901:101] m. 'care, trouble,'; *b-xāmox* 'in your care'

xamša [ClAram חַמְשָׁא; Sab198; Mutz394] 'five'; see *xamša'ar*, *xamšamma*, *xamši*, *xamūšeb*

xamša'sar [Syr ܚܡܫܥܣܪ; cf. *xamša'sar* Sab198, *xamšá'əssar* Mutz115] 'fifteen'; see *xamša, xamši, xamūšeb*

xamšamma [*xamša* + *ʾəmma*; cf. *xammıšma, xamša ʾımmāye* Sab198, *xamšá'əmma* Mutz394; § 4.3.3] 'five hundred'; see *xamša, xamša'sar, xamši, xamūšeb*

xamši [ClAram חֲמִשִׁין; Sab198; Mutz115] 'fifty'; see *xamša, xamšamma, xamša'ar, xamušeb*

xamūšeb [ClAram חַמְשָׁא בְּשַׁבָּא; cf. *xamšūšıb* Sab198, *xámšošeb* Mutz117] 'Thursday'; see *xamša, xamšamma, xamši*

xamxāme	[P; Maclean 1901:134] pl. 'steep places'
xanči	[NeoAram *xa* + K *pič*?; *xanči* Sab199] indef. prn. 'some, a few'; *xanči qṭililu* 'some they killed'; *xanči zəmrəyāsa basime 'amrət* 'you should sing some nice songs'; cf. *piča, xapči*
xānəm	[K, T; cf. *khânim* Maclean 1901:103, *xānɪme* Sab191] f. 'Madam'
xanjar, xanjāra	[K, T, Ar خَنْجَر; cf. *xanjar* Sab198 and Mutz394] m. 'dagger'; pl. *xanjāre*
xanuqta	[ClAram √חנק; cf. *khânüqtâ* 'neck' Maclean 1901:103, *xunuqta* 'throat' Sab194] 'throat'
xapči	[NeoAram *xa* + K *pič*?; cf. *xapča* Sab199 and Mutz394] adv. 'a bit, slightly'; *'iya masale pəšla xapči* ^H*šeket*^H 'this affair remained a bit quiet'; cf. *piča, xanči*
xarāye	[ClAram חריתא(א); cf. *x(a/ɪ)rāye* Sab199, *xaṛāye* Mutz395] adv. 'later, finally'
xarbé	[K *xirbe* Rizgar 1993:200, Ar خَرَابَة; cf. *xɪrābi* Sab199, *xarābe* Mutz394] pl. tant. 'ruins'
xāsa[1]	[ClAram חָתָ(א); Sab191; Mutz395] f. 'sister'; pl. *xaswāsa*; see *'axona*
xāsa[2]	[ClAram חדתא; cf. Sab191, Mutz395] 'new'; f. *xasta*; pl. *xāse*; see *xss*
xāṣa	[ClAram חרצא, חצא; Sab191; Mutz395] m. 'back'; *pəšlu xa xāṣa* 'they were of one opinion'; see *xərxāṣa*
xāṭər	[Ar خَاطِر; Sab191; Mutz395] 'sake, wish'; *ta xaṭərexun* 'for your sake'; *ta xāṭər 'ilāha* 'for the sake of God'
xāye	[LEAram חַיֵי); Sab191; Mutz395] pl. tant. 'life'
xazina	[Ar خَزِينَة; cf. *xɪzēna, xazīne* Sab195] m. 'treasure, safe, cashbox'
xe[1], *xes-*, *xa-*	[ClAram ת(ו)חת; cf. *txēt/txe, xēt, xē* Sab309, *xe, xeθ-* Mutz395] prep. 'under, beneath'; *xese* 'under him'; *xa* before *reš* (Sab200): *xa-réšəd dide* 'under his head', *m-xa-réšəd dide* 'from under his head'; see *'əltəx, 'əltxé(t?)*
xe[2]	see *xeta*
xes-	see *xe*[1]
xet	see *xeta*
xeta, xeta, xe[2]	[BiblAram אָחֳרִי, TO אָחֳרִנְתָא, Syr ܐܚܪܢܐ; cf. *xēta, xɪ/et* Sab196, *xeta, xət* Mutz395; §4.1.10.b] inv. 'other'; *xá-gā xet(a)* 'once again'; *xa xet šqəlle* 'he took another'; *xa səjjāda xe* 'another prayer rug'; *ṣrəxlu xá-l-e-xet* 'they shouted to each other'; *xa lu mšabohe 'əl-xé* 'One is praising the other'
xədda	[ClAram חֲדָא; Fassberg 1985; cf. *khdhâ* Maclean 1901:92, *ḥda* Jastrow 1988:90, *xda, xɪdda* Sab192; Hoberman 2007:149] indef. prn. 'someone'; see *xa*
xəddamta	[Ar خَدَّامَة; cf. *xɪddamta* Sab192] f. 'maidservant'
xədyawāsa	[ClAram חֲדְיָא; cf. pl. *xɪdyɪwāṯa* Sab192, *xəðyawāθa* Mutz395] pl. 'breasts'
xədyūsa	[ClAram חֲדוּתָא; Sab192; Mutz 2008:395] 'joy' (*haggada*); see *xdy*
xəlya	[ClAram חֲלְיָא; Sab197; Mutz395] 'sweet'; pl. *xəlye* (*haggada*)
xəmyāna	[Syr ܚܡܝܢܐ; Sab198; Mutz395] m. 'father-in-law'

xəpyāya   [Syr ܒܦܢܐ; Sab199; Mutz396] m. 'barefoot'

xərxāṣa   [K xir + xāṣa; Sab200; Mutz396] 'cummerbund'; see xāṣa

xəška   [Syr ܚܫܟܐ; Sab201; Mutz396] m. 'darkness'

xətna   [ClAram חתנא; Sab202; Mutz396] m.'bridgeroom, son-in-law'

xətta   [ClAram חטא; cf. xıṭṭīta, pl. xıṭṭe Sab195, xəṭṭiϑa, pl. xəṭṭe Mutz-
             396, xiṭṭa, pl. xıṭṭe Khan 1999:585] 'grain of wheat'; pl. xəṭṭe
             'wheat'

xəyyāra   [K, T, Ar خِيَار; cf. xıyyāra Sab196] f. 'cucumber'; pl. xəyyāre

xəzma   [K, T; Sab195] m. 'in-law'; pl. xəzmawāsa

xiṭka   [K?; K xeṯ Chyet 2003:657, Ar خَط 'line' + suff. -k?] m. 'bar
             indicating military rank on a uniform'

xlima   [LAram חלימא 'healthy'; Sab197; Mutz396] m. 'thick'; pl. xlime

xlūla, xulūla [Syr ܚܠܘܠܐ, JBA and Mand הילולא; Nöldeke 1875:118 n. 2; cf.
             h/ḥ/xılūla Sab150–151, xlūla Mutz396; § 3.18.a] m. 'wedding
             feast'

xmāra   [ClAram חמרא; Sab198; Mutz396] m. 'ass, donkey'; pl. xmāre;
             xmāra bər xmāra 'what an ass!'; see xmarūsa

xmarūsa   [ClAram חמרא + abstr. suff. -ūsa; Sab198; Mutz396] f. 'stupidity';
             see xmāra

xmāsa   [ClAram חמתא; Sab198; Mutz397] f. 'mother-in-law'

xola   [ClAram חבלא; Sab194; Mutz397] 'rope'

xor   [ClAram חברא; cf. xōr Sab194, xur Mutz397;] prep. 'like'; see
             xora, xorūsa

xora   [ClAram חברא; cf. xōra, xōra Sab194, xūra Mutz397] m. 'friend';
             see xor, xorūsa

xorūsa   [ClAram חברא + abstr. suff. -ūsa; Maclean 1901:91] f. 'friend-
             ship'; see xor, xora

xošeba   [LAram חד בשבא; cf. xu/ošēba Sab195, xošeba Mutz117] 'Sun-
             day'

xruwiye   [K; cf. khrüryé 'millet' Maclean 1901:106, xro:win 'buckwheat'
             Krotkoff 1982:155, xrowiye 'sorghum' Mutz397] pl. tant. 'sor-
             ghum'

xudreš   [חיי דראש Sab191; Tezel 2003:99,112] 'Take my word for it!' (= [I
             swear by] the life of the head of-'); b-xudrešox; see xāye, reša

xulāma   [K, Ar غُلاَم; cf. +gulāma Sab134, xulāma Mutz397] m. 'servant';
             pl. xulāme, xulamawāsa

xulma   [ClAram חלמא; cf. xı/ulma Sab197, xulma Mutz397] 'dream';
             'āna ki'ən xulma lu xəzye xulma lewu xəzye 'Do I know if they
             have dreamt or not?'

xulūla   see xlūla

xumma   [TO חומא; LEAram חומא; cf. xımma Sab197, xəmma Mutz395]
             m. 'heat'

xurga   [LAram חורגא; Sab194] m. 'step-son'

xurṭ   [K; cf. כורט Yona 1999א:172, +xurt, xurıt Sab195] inv. 'aggres-
             sive'; see xurṭūsa

xurṭumāne   [Syr ܚܘܪܛܡܢܐ, ܚܘܪܛܘܡܢܐ; cf. xurṭmāne Sab195, xurṭumāne
             Mutz398] pl. 'chickpeas'

xurṭūsa   [*xurṭ* + abstr. suff. *-ūsa*; cf. כּוׂרטוׂסָא Yona 1999א:172, ⁺*xurtuṭa* Sab195] f. 'force'; *b-xurṭūsa* 'forcefully'; see *xurṭ*

xuṭba   [T, Ar خُطْبَة] f. '(Muslim Friday) sermon'

xuṭṭa   [ClAram חוּטְרָא; cf. *khüṭrâ* Maclean 1901:94, *xıṭra* Sab195] 'stick, rod'; pl. *xuṭṭe*; see *xṭr*

xuwwa   [TO חִוְיָא, חִוְיָא; Hoberman 2007:140 cf. *xuwwe* Sab193, *xuwwa/e* Mutz398] m. 'snake'; pl. *xuwwe*

*xwāra   [ClAram חִוָּרָא; Sab193; Mutz398] 'white'; pl. *xwāre*; see *xwr*

xwaš   [K *xweš* Chyet 2003;674; cf. *xōš* Sab195; *xoš* Mutz397] inv. 'good'; see *naxwaš*

xwazí   [K; cf. *xwazī, xuzzī* Sab193] excl. 'would that!'

y

yā-   see *'iya*

ya'ni   [K, T, Ar يَعْنِي; cf. *yânî* Maclean 1901:121, *ya'ni, ya'nu, ya'nix* Sab178, *ya'ni* Mutz398] adv. 'that is to say'

yāla   [ClAram יַלְדָּא ?עוׂל; Ar عِيَال?; Sab92; Mutz399] m. 'child'; pl. *yāle, yalunke*; *yāl 'amawāsa* 'cousins'; *kalbe yāl kalbe* 'sons of bitches!'; see *yalunka*

yalunka   [*yāla* + dim. suff. *-ūn + ka*; Sab92; Mutz399] m. 'child'; pl. *yalunke*; see *yāla*

yāma   [ClAram יַמָּא; Sab176; Mutz399] 'sea'

yarixa   [ClAram אֲרִיכָא; Sab179; Mutz399] m. 'long'; f. *yarəxta*; pl. *yarixe*; *lišāna yarixa* 'cheeky' (lit. 'long tongue'); see *yrx*

yarxa   [ClAram יְרְחָא; Sab179; Mutz399] m. 'month'; pl. *yarxe*

yārūsa   [K; cf. *yārūsa* Sab176 and Mutz399] f. 'camaraderie'; *b-yārūsa* 'jokingly'

yatumta   [ClAram יְתֵמָא; Sab179; Mutz399] f. 'orphan'

yəmma   [ClAram אִמָּא; Sab177; Mutz399] f. 'mother'

yoma   [ClAram יוׂמָא; Sab177; Mutz399] m. 'day'; pl. *yomāsa, yome*; *yoməd din* 'Day of Judgment'; *ḥil yoma gənya* 'until the sun (has) set' (§ 4.4.16.g); *yom basra* 'the next day'; *kúd-yom* 'every day'; see *palgədyo*

yuqdāna   [Syr ܝܩܕܢܐ; Sab177] 'conflagration' (*haggada*); see *qyd*

z

*zad'əwāna   [NeoAram *zado/u'a*? + suff. *-āna*; Maclean 1901:83] 'fearful, cowardly'; pl. *zad'əwāne*; see *zd', zde'sa, zdo'sa*

zamāra   [LAram זַמָּרָא; Sab159; Mutz400] m. 'singer'

zanqa   [Syr ܙܢܩܐ < P; 'flesh under the chin, the larynx' Maclean 1901:88; 'chin' Sab160] f. 'chin'

zaviya   [K; cf. *zawīya, zavīya* Sab157] f. 'field'

zaxonāya   [GN Zāxo + gent. suff. *-nāya*; Sab156, Mutz400] m. 'resident of Zakho'

zde'sa, zdo'sa   [ClAram אזדעזע; cf. *zde'ta, zdo'ta* Sab156, *zdo'ϑa* Mutz400] f. 'fear'; see *zad'əwāna, zd'*

zdo'sa   see zde'sa
zebarnāya   [GN Zebar + gent. suff. -nāya] m. 'resident of Zebar (Iraqi
                    Kurdistan)'; pl. zebarnāye
zəbla   [Ar زِبِل; Sab156] 'garbage'
zəmrəyāsa   [TO זְמַר; Syr ܙܡܪ̈ܐ; cf. zmârâ, zmârtâ Maclean 1901:87, zɪm-
                    murta Sab159, zəmra Mutz400] pl. 'songs'; see 'mr, zmr
zindān   [T, K; cf. Syr ܙܢܕܢ 'jailer' < P; cf. zɪndāna Sab160] 'dungeon,
                    prison'
zo'a   [LAram זוגא < Gr; Sab157; Mutz400] 'pair'; pl. zo'e
zodāna   [Ar √زيد + suff. -āna; Sab157; Mutz400] m. 'more, additional';
                    pl. zodāne; see bə́z-zodāna, zyd
zoma   [K; Sab157] 'summer camp'
zozān   [K; cf. zōzān(a) Sab157] f. 'mountain (summer) pasture'; pl.
                    zozāne
zöra   [LWAram זעור and Syr Kutscher 1976:23–25; cf. z'ōra, zōra Sab
                    2002a:156, zora Mutz400] 'small, little, young'; f. zürta; pl. zöre
zūna   [ClAram זמנא < P < Akk; cf. zūna, zōna Sabar 2002:157, only
                    m(ən)- zūna Mutz401] 'time'; attested only in m-zūna 'long ago'
zūna, zwina   [ClAram זבן√] 'bought'; see zwn
zyāṛa   [K, T, Ar زِيَارَة; cf. +zyāra, +zyarta Sab158, zyāṛa Mutzafi 2008a:
                    401] f. 'visit to a shrine'; 'edəd zyāṛa 'Feast of Weeks, Pentecost
                    (שבועות)'

ẓ

ẓoṛ   [K, T, Ar زُور; cf. zōr, +bɪzzōr Sab157] 'force'; b-ẓoṛ 'forcefully,
                    reluctantly'

ž

žang   [K Chyet 2003:809] f. 'rust, rusty'; pl. žange
-ži, -ž   [K; cf. ši(n), šɪk(ēne), žī(g) Sab297, -ši Mutz385; Cohen 2008b]
                    conj. 'also, too, even'
žwanta   [K jivan 'rendez-vous, date, appointment' Chyet 2003:292] 'ex-
                    pecting, waiting for'; bābi le ḥmila žwanti 'my father has been
                    expecting me'; Hbet kvarótH la ḥməlta žwantox 'the cemetery has
                    been expecting you'; (cf. צפה' חְמַל-היביתא Yona 1999ב:405)

BIBLIOGRAPHICAL REFERENCES

Alder, Marcus N. 1907. *The Itinerary of Benjamin of Tudela: Critical Text, Translation and Commentary*. London: Henry Frowde.

Alfiye, Shabtay. 1986. הגדה של פסח בשפה כורדית זאכוית. Jerusalem: n.p.

Almkvist, Herman. 1891. *Kleine Beiträge zur Lexikographie des Vulgärarabischen*. Leiden: Brill.

Arnold, Werner. 1990. *Das Neuwestaramäische*. Vol. V: Grammatik. Semitica Viva 4/V. Leiden: Harrassowitz.

Arnold, Werner and Helmut Bobzin, editors. 2002. *"Sprich doch mit deinen Knechten aramäisch, wir verstehen es!" 60 Beiträge zur Semitistik. Festschrift für Otto Jastrow zum 60. Geburtstag*. Wiesbaden: Harrassowitz.

Assaf, Simha. 1934. "לתולדות היהודים בקורדיסטאן ושכנותיה." *Zion* 6:קיג-פה.

———. 1943. *Beoholei Ya'akov: Essays on the Cultural Life of the Jews in the Middle Ages*. Jerusalem: Mossad Harav Kook [Hebrew].

Avidani, ʿAlwan. 1959. סדר הגדה של פסח עברי - כורדי. Jerusalem: n.p.

———. 1977. סדר הגדה של פסח עברי כורדי. 2nd edition. Jerusalem: n.p.

Bar-Asher, Moshe. 1977. *Palestinian Syriac Studies: Source-Texts, Traditions and Grammatical Problems*. Jerusalem: n.p. [Hebrew].

———. 1998. "The Syropalestinian Version of the Bible." *Lěšonénu* 61:131–43 [Hebrew].

——— and Moshe Florentin, editors. 2005. *Samaritan, Hebrew and Aramaic Studies Presented to Professor Abraham Tal*. Jerusalem: Bialik Institute [Hebrew].

Bauer, Hans and Pontus Leander. 1927. *Grammatik des Biblisch-Aramäischen*. Tübingen: Max Niemeyer.

Ben-Ḥayyim, Ze'ev. 1954. *Studies in the Traditions of the Hebrew Language*. Madrid: Instituto Arias Montano.

———. 1976. *The Literary and Oral Tradition of Hebrew and Aramaic Amongst the Samaritans*. Vol. III, Part II: The Recitation of Prayers and Hymns. Jerusalem: Academy of Hebrew Language [Hebrew].

———. 2000. *A Grammar of Samaritan Hebrew Based on the Recitation of the Law in Comparison with the Tiberian and Other Jewish Traditions*. With assistance from Abraham Tal. Jerusalem: Magnes.

Ben-Yaacob, Abraham. 1980. *Kurdistan Jewish Communities*. 2nd edition. Jerusalem: Kiryath-Sepher [Hebrew].

———. 1985. *Hebrew and Aramaic in the Language of the Jews of Iraq*. Jerusalem: Ben-Zvi Institute [Hebrew].

Ben Yehuda, Eliezer. 1908–1958. *Thesaurus totius hebraitatis et veteris et recentioris*. Jerusalem: Ben-Yehuda. 16 vols. Reprinted 6 vols. New York: Yoseloff, 1960.

Blau, Joshua and Simon Hopkins. 2006. "On Aramaic Vocabulary in Early Judaeo-Arabic Texts Written in Phonetic Spelling." *Jerusalem Studies in Arabic and Islam* 32:433–471.

Blau, Joyce and Veysi Barak. 1999. *Manuel de Kurde: Kurmanji*. Paris: L'Harmattan.

Brauer, Erich. 1993. *The Jews of Kurdistan*, completed and edited by Raphael Patai. Detroit: Wayne State University Press.

Breuer, Yochanan. 1997. "The Function of the Particle 'qā'" in Babylonian Aramaic." *Lĕšonénu* 60:73–94 [Hebrew].

Brockelmann, Carl. 1908–1912. *Grundriss der vergleichenden Grammatik der semitischen Sprachen*. 2 vols. Berlin: Reuther & Reichard.

Campbell, Lyle. 2004. *Historical Linguistics: An Introduction*. 2nd edition. Cambridge, Massachusetts: MIT Press.

Clarity, Beverley E. et al. 2003. *A Dictionary of Iraqi Arabic: English-Arabic, Arabic-English*. Georgetown Classics in Arabic Language and Linguistics. Washington, D.C.: Georgetown University Press.

Cohen David. 1995. *Dictionnaire des racines sémitiques ou attestées dans les langues sémitiques*. Avec la collaboration de François Bron et Antoine Lonnet. Fascicule 5:H-HTT. Paris/Leuven: Mouton/Peeters.

Cohen, Eran. 2008a. "The Copular Clause in Jewish Zakho Neo-Aramaic." *Journal of Semitic Studies* 53:43–68.

———. 2008b. "Focus in the Jewish Neo-Aramaic Dialect of Zakho." *Lĕšonénu* 70:661–678 [Hebrew].

Contini, Riccardo. 1998. "Considerazioni sul presunto 'dativo etico' in aramaico pre-Cristiano." In *Études sémitiques et samaritaines offertes à Jean Margain*, 83–94. Histoire du texte biblique 4. Edited by Christian-Bernard Amphoux, Albert Frey, and Ursula Schattner-Rieser. Lausanne: Editions du Zèbre.

Correll, Christoph. 1974. "Ein Vorschlag zur Erklärung der Negation čū (ću) in den neuwestaramäischen Dialekten des Antilibanon." *Zeitschrift der deutschen morgenländischen Gesellschaft* 124:271–285.

Dalman, Gustaf. 1905. *Grammatik des jüdisch-palästinischen Aramäisch*. 2nd edition. Leipzig: J.C. Hinrichs.

Dobbs-Allsopp, F.W. 1995. "Ingressive *qwm* in Biblical Hebrew." *Zeitschrift für Althebraistik* 8:41–54.

Elihay, J. 2005. *The Olive Tree Dictionary: A Transliterated Dictionary of Conversational Eastern Arabic (Palestinian)*. Jerusalem: Minerva.

Epstein, J.N. 1960. *A Grammar of Babylonian Aramaic*. Jerusalem: Magnes [Hebrew].

Fassberg, Steven E. 1985. "Determined Forms of the Cardinal Number 'One' in Three Pentateuchal Targumim." *Sefarad* 45:209–215.

———. 1997. "Translations of 'Water' in Targum Pseudo-Jonathan." *Massorot: Studies in Language Traditions and Jewish Languages* 9–11:483–494 [Hebrew].

———. 2005. "Lexical Investigations in Jewish Palestinian Aramaic: Is There a Shift of 'Aleph to 'Ayin?" In Bar-Asher and Florentin 2005:243–256 [Hebrew].

———. 2008a. "The Forms of 'Son' and 'Daughter' in Aramaic." In Gzella and Folmer 2008:41–53.

———. 2008b. "The Jewish Neo-Aramaic Dialect of Čalla." In *Neo-Aramaic Dialect Studies: Proceedings of a Workshop on Neo-Aramaic held in Cambridge, 2005*, 65–74. Edited by Geoffrey Khan. Piscataway, NJ: Gorgias.

Fellman, Kadia. 1978. *Catalogue of the Recordings in the Tape Archives.* עדה ולשון ג. Jerusalem: Hebrew University of Jerusalem Language Traditions Project.

Fitzmyer, Joseph A. 1979. "The Phases of the Aramaic Language." In *A Wandering Aramean: Collected Aramaic Essays*, 57–84. Society of Biblical Literature Monograph Series 25. Chico, California: Scholars.

———. 1995. *The Aramaic Inscriptions of Sefire.* 2nd edition. Biblica et Orientalia 19/A. Rome: Pontificio Istituto Biblico.

Fleisch, Henri. 1961. *Traité de philologie arabe.* Vol. I : Préliminaires, phonétique, morphologie nominale. Beirut: Imprimerie Catholique.

Fox, Samuel E. 1997. *The Neo-Aramaic Dialect of Jilu.* Semitica Viva 16. Wiesbaden: Harrassowitz.

———. 2002. "A Neo-Aramaic Dialect of Bohtan." In Arnold and Bobzin 2002: 165–180.

———. 2007. "The Story of Mem u Zine in the Neo-Aramaic Dialect of Bohtan." In Miller 2007:69–79.

Garbell, Irene. 1965. *The Jewish Neo-Aramaic Dialect of Persian Azerbaijan.* Janua Linguarum Series Practica 3. The Hague: Mouton.

Goldenberg, Gideon. 1993. "Otto Jastrow, *Der neuaramäische Dialekt von Hertevin (Provinz Siirt)*—A Review Article." *Journal of Semitic Studies* 38:295–308. Reprinted in Goldenberg 1998:630–643.

———. 1995. "Attribution in Semitic Languages." *Langues orientales anciennes: philologie et linguistique* 5–6:1–20. Reprinted in Goldenberg 1998:46–65.

———. 1998. *Studies in Semitic Linguistics.* Jerusalem: Magnes, 1998.

Greenfield, Jonas C. 1970. "*HAMARAKARA > ʾAMARKAL.*" In *W.B. Henning Memorial Volume*, 180–186. Edited by Mary Boyce and Ilya Gershevitch. London: Lund Humphries.

———. 1972. "Three Iranian Words in the Targum of Job from Qumran." *Zeitschrift der deutschen morgenländischen Gesellschaft* 122:37–45.

Gzella, Holger and Margaretha L. Folmer, editors. 2008. *Aramaic in Its Historical and Linguistic Setting.* Veröffentlichungen der Orientalischen Kommission 50. Wiesbaden: Harrassowitz.

Halevy, Rivka. 2004. "The Function of the Construction 'Verb + *l-* + Personal Reflexive Pronoun' in Contemporary Hebrew." *Lěšonénu* 66:113–143 [Hebrew].

Hashiloni, Aḥiya and Yosef Hashiloni. 1985. "חכם יעקב (אחיה) השילוני זצ״ל" התחדשות: כתב-עת של יהודי כורדיסטאן בישראל 5:129–132.

Hasselbach, Rachel. 2007. 'External Plural Markers in Semitic: A New Assessment." In Miller 2007:123–138.

Heinrichs, Wolfhart, editor. 1990. *Studies in Neo-Aramaic.* Harvard Semitic Studies 36. Atlanta: Scholars.

———. 2002. "Peculiarities of the Verbal System of Senāya within the Framework of North Eastern Neo-Aramaic (NENA)." In Arnold and Bobzin 2002:237–268.

Henkin, Roni. 1994. "On the Narrative Imperative in Negev Arabic and in Russian." *Journal of Semitic Studies* 39:245–283.

Hoberman, Robert D. 1988. "The History of the Modern Aramaic Pronouns and Pronominal Suffixes." *Journal of the American Oriental Society* 108:557–575.

———. 1989. *The Syntax and Semantics of Verb Morphology in Modern Aramaic: A Jewish Dialect of Iraqi Kurdistan.* American Oriental Society 69. New Haven: American Oriental Society.

———. 1990. "Reconstructing Pre-Modern Aramaic Morphology: The Independent Pronouns." In Heinrichs 1990:79–88.

———. 1997. "Modern Aramaic Phonology." In *Phonologies of Asia and Africa,* 1:313–335. Edited by Alan S. Kaye. Winona Lake, Indiana: Eisenbrauns.

———. 2007. "Semitic Triradicality or Prosodic Minimality? Evidence from Sound Change." In Miller 2007:139–154.

Hony, H.C. 1957. *A Turkish-English Dictionary.* 2nd edition. With the advice of Fahır İz. Oxford: Clarendon.

Hopkins, Simon. 1989a. "Neo-Aramaic Dialects and the Formation of the Preterite." *Journal of Semitic Studies* 34:413–432.

———. 1989b. "A Tale in the Jewish Neo-Aramaic Dialect of Naγada (Persian Azerbaijan)." *Jerusalem Studies in Arabic and Islam* 12:243–281.

———. 2002. "Preterite and Perfect in the Jewish Neo-Aramaic of Kerend (Southern Iranian Kurdistan)." In Arnold and Bobzin 2002:281–298.

Hozaya, Younan and Anderios Youkhana. 1999. *Bahra: Arabic—Assyrian Dictionary.* 2nd edition. Arbil: Assyrian Aid Society of America.

Huehnergard, John. 1983. "Asseverative *la and Hypothetical *lu/law in Semitic." *Journal of the American Oriental Society* 103:569–593.

Jaba, Auguste. 1879. *Dictionnaire kurde-français publié par Ferdinand Justi.* St.-Pétersbourg : l'Académie Impériale.

Jastrow, Otto. 1990. "Personal and Demonstrative Pronouns in Central Neo-Aramaic: A Comparative and Diachronic Discussion Based on Turoyo and the Eastern Neo-Aramaic Dialect of Hertevin." In Heinrichs 1990:89–106.

———. 1993. *Laut- und Formenlehre des neuaramäischen Dialekts von Mīdin im Ṭūr ʿAbdīn.* 4th edition. Wiesbaden: Harrassowitz.

———. 1994. *Der neuaramäische Dialekt von Mlaḥsô.* Semitica Viva 14. Wiesbaden: Harrassowitz.

———. 1997. "The Neo-Aramaic Languages." In *The Semitic Languages,* 344–377. Edited by Robert Hetzron. London: Routledge.

Kamil, Murad. 1963. *Beiträge zur Entstehung der vierradikaligen Verben in den gesprochenen semitischen Sprachen.* Memoires de l'Institut d'Egypte 57. Le Caire: L'institut française d'archéologie orientale.

Kapeliuk, Olga. 1997. "Spirantization of ṯ and ḏ in Neo-Aramaic." *Massorot: Studies in Language Traditions and Jewish Languages* 9–11:527–544 [Hebrew].

———. 2008. "The Perfect Tenses in Urmi Neo-Aramaic." In Gzella and Folmer 2008:313–334.

Kaufman, Stephen A. 1974. *The Akkadian Influences on Aramaic.* Assyriological Studies 19. Chicago: University of Chicago Press.

Khan, Geoffrey. 1999. *A Grammar of Neo-Aramaic: The Dialect of the Jews of Arbel.* Handbuch der Orientalitisk 47. Leiden: Brill.

———. 2002. *The Neo-Aramaic Dialect of Qaraqosh.* Studies in Semitic Languages and Linguistics 36. Leiden: Brill.

———. 2004. *The Jewish Neo-Aramaic Dialect of Sulemaniyya and Ḥalabja*. Studies in Semitic Languages and Linguistics 44. Leiden: Brill.

———. 2007. "The Morphology of Neo-Aramaic." In *Morphologies of Asia and Africa*, 1:309–327. Edited by Alans S. Kaye. Winona Lake, Indiana: Eisenbrauns.

———. 2008. "The Expression of Definiteness in North-Eastern Neo-Aramaic Dialects." In Gzella and Folmer 2008: 287–304.

Krotkoff, Georg. 1982. *A Neo-Aramaic Dialect of Kurdistan: Texts, Grammar, and Vocabulary*. American Oriental Series 64. New Haven: American Oriental Society.

———. 1985. "Studies in Neo-Aramaic Lexicology." In *Biblical and Related Studies Presented to Samuel Iwry*, 123–134. Edited by Ann Kort and Scott Morschauser. Winona Lake, Indiana: Eisenbrauns.

Kutscher, Eduard Yehezkel. 1964. "Aramaic Calque in Hebrew." *Tarbiz* 33:118–130 [Hebrew].

———. 1967. "Jewish Palestinian Aramaic." In Rosenthal 1967, I/1:51–70.

———. 1976. *Studies in Galilean Aramaic*. Translated by Michael Sokoloff. Ramat-Gan: Bar-Ilan University.

———. 1982. *A History of the Hebrew Language*. Edited by Raphael Kutscher. Jerusalem: Magnes.

Lane, Edward William. 1863–1893. *Arabic—English Lexicon*. 8 vols. London: Williams and Norgate.

Leander, Pontus. 1928. *Laut- und Formenlehre des Ägyptisch-Aramäischen*. Göteborgs högskolas årsskrift 34.4. Göteborg: Elanders boktryckeri aktiebolag.

Lidzbarski, Mark. 1898. "Semitische Kosenamen." In *Ephemeris für semitische Epigraphik*, 2:1–23. Giessen: J. Ricker.

MacKenzie, D.N. 1981. *Kurdish Dialect Studies*. 2 vols. London Oriental Series 9. London: School of Oriental and African Studies.

Maclean, Arthur John. 1895. *Grammar of the Dialects of Vernacular Syriac*. Cambridge: Cambridge University Press.

———. 1901. *Dictionary of the Dialects of Vernacular Syriac*. Oxford: Clarendon.

Macuch, Rudolf 1982. *Grammatik des samaritanischen Aramäischen*. Studia Samaritana 4. Berlin: Walter de Gruyter.

Malik Yaqu. 1964. ܐܬܘܪ̈ܝܐ ܘܬܪ̈ܝܢ ܦܠܫܐ ܬܒܝܠܢ̈ܝܐ [= *The Assyrians and the Two World Wars*]. Tehran.

Mann, Jacob. 1931. *Texts and Studies in Jewish History and Literature*. 2 vols. Cincinnati: Hebrew Union College Press.

Meehan, Charles and Jacqueline Alon. 1979. "The Boy Whose Tunic Stuck to Him: A Folktale in the Jewish Neo-Aramaic Dialect of Zakho (Iraqi Kurdistan)." *Israel Oriental Studies* 9:174–203.

Miller, Cynthia L., editor. 2007. *Studies in Semitic and Afroasiatic Linguistics Presented to Gene B. Gragg*. Studies in Ancient Oriental Civilization 60. Chicago: Oriental Institute.

Morag, Shelomo. 1988. *Babylonian Aramaic: The Yemenite Tradition. Historical Aspects and Transmission, Phonology, The Verbal System*. Jerusalem: Ben Zvi Institute [Hebrew].

Morrison, Craig. 2008. "The Function of *qṭal hwā* in the *Acts of Judas Thomas*."
In Gzella and Folmer 2008:257–285.

Mutzafi, Hezy. 2000. "The Neo-Aramaic Dialect of Maha Khtaya dBaz: Phonology, Morphology and Texts." *Journal of Semitic Studies* 45:293–322.

———. 2002. "On the Jewish Neo-Aramaic Dialect of Aradhin and its Dialectal
Affinities." In Arnold and Bobzin 2002:479–488.

———. 2004. *The Jewish Neo-Aramaic Dialect of Koy Sanjaq (Iraqi Kurdistan)*.
Semitica Viva 32. Wiesbaden: Harrassowitz.

———. 2005. "The Reflexes of the Word אדנא ('Ear') in Eastern Neo-Aramaic:
Etymology, Diversification and Innovation." In Bar-Asher and Florentin
2005:243–256 [Hebrew].

———. 2006a. "On the Etymology of Some Enigmatic Words in North-Eastern
Neo-Aramaic." *Aramaic Studies* 4:83–99.

———. 2006b. "An Eighteenth Century Poem on David and Goliath in Jewish
Neo-Aramaic and Hebrew." *Massorot: Studies in Language Traditions and
Jewish Languages* 13–14:125–162 [Hebrew].

———. 2007. "The Sound Change *ṭ > š in Ṭyare Neo-Aramaic." *Le Muséon*
120:351–364.

———. 2008a. *The Jewish Neo-Aramaic Dialect of Betanure (Province of Dihok)*.
Semitica Viva 43. Wiesbaden.

——— 2008b. "Trans-Zab Jewish Neo-Aramaic." *Bulletin of the School of Oriental
and African Studies* 71:409–431.

Nehama, Joseph. 1977. *Dictionnaire du judéo-espagnol*. Avec la collaboration
de Jesus Cantera. Madrid: Consejo Superior de Investigaciones Científicas,
Instituto Benito Arias Montano.

Nöldeke, Theodor. 1868. *Grammatik der neusyrischen Sprach am Urmia-See und
in Kurdistan*. Leipzig: T.O. Weigel.

———. 1875. *Mandäische Grammatik*. Halle an der Saale: Buchhandlung des
Waisenhauses.

———. 1910. *Neue Beiträge zur semitischen Sprachwissenschaft*. Strassburg: Karl
J. Trübner.

Odisho, Edward Y. 1997. "A Comparative Study of Pet Names in English and
Assyrian." In *Humanism, Culture, and Language in the Near East: Stud-
ies in Honor of Georg Krotkoff*, 319–333. Edited by Asma Afsaruddin and
A.H. Mathias Zahniser. Winona Lake, Indiana: Eisenbrauns.

Pat-El, Na'ama. 2008. "Historical Syntax of Aramaic: A Note on Subordination."
In Gzella and Folmer 2008:55–75.

Pennacchietti, Fabrizio A. 1997. "On the Etymology of the Neo-Aramaic Particle
qam/kim-." *Massorot: Studies in Language Traditions and Jewish Languages* 9–
11:475–482 [Hebrew].

Polotsky, Hans Jakob. 1961. "Studies in Modern Syriac." *Journal of Semitic Studies*
6:1–32.

———. 1967. " Eastern Neo-Aramaic: Zakho." In Rosenthal 1967, II/2:104–111.

———. 1979. "Verbs with Two Objects in Modern Syriac (Urmi)." *Israel Oriental
Studies* 9:204–227.

Rabin, Chaim. 1969. "The Nature and Origin of the *Shafʿel* in Hebrew and
Aramaic." *Eretz-Israel* 9:148–158 [Hebrew].

Redhouse, James W. 1890. *A Turkish and English Lexicon Shewing in English the Significations of the Turkish Terms*. Constantinople: A.H. Boyajian.

Ritter, Hellmut. 1990. *Ṭūrōyo: Die Volkssprache der syrischen Christen des Ṭūr ʿAbdîn, C : Grammatik : Pronomen, "Sein, Vorhanden Sein", Zahlwort, Verbum*. Stuttgart : Franz Steiner.

Rivlin, Yosef Yoel. 1959 = שירת יהודי התרגום: פרקי עלילה וגבורה בפי יהודי כורדיסתן. Jerusalem: Bialik Institute.

Rollinger, Robert. 2006. "The Terms 'Assyria' and 'Syria' Again." *Journal of Near Eastern Studies* 65:283–287.

Rosenthal, Franz, editor. 1967. *An Aramaic Handbook*. Wiesbaden. Porta Linguarum 10. Wiesbaden: Harrassowitz.

Rubin, Aaron D. 2005. *Studies in Semitic Grammaticalization*. Harvard Semitic Studies 57. Winona Lake, Indiana: Eisenbrauns.

Sabar, Yona. 1974. "First Names, Nicknames, and Family Names Among the Jews of Kurdistan." *Jewish Quarterly Review* 65:43–51.

——. 1975. "The Impact of Israeli Hebrew on the Neo-Aramaic Dialect of the Kurdish Jews of Zakho: A Case of Language Shift." *Hebrew Union College Annual* 46:489–508.

——. 1976. *A Neo-Aramaic Midrash on* Beshallaḥ *(Exodus): Introduction, Phonetic Transcription, Translation, Notes and Glossary*. Wiesbaden: Harrassowitz.

——. 1982. "The Quadriradical Verb in Eastern Neo-Aramaic Dialects." *Journal of Semitic Studies* 27:149–176.

——. 1983. *The Book of Genesis in Neo-Aramaic in the Dialect of the Jewish Community of Zakho*. עדה ולשון ט. Jerusalem: Hebrew University Language Traditions Project.

——. 1984. *Homilies in the Neo-Aramaic of the Kurdistani Jews on the Parashot Wayḥi, Beshallaḥ and Yitro*. Jerusalem: Israel Academy of Sciences and Humanities [Hebrew].

——. 1990. "General European Loanwords in the Jewish Neo-Aramaic Dialect of Zakho, Iraqi Kurdistan." In Heinrichs 1990:53–66.

——. 2002a. *A Jewish Neo-Aramaic Dictionary: Dialects of Amidya, Dihok, Nerwa and Zakho, Northwestern Iraq*. Semitica Viva 28. Wiesbaden: Harrassowitz.

——. 2002b. "*Mah Nishtannah*: A Comparison of the Neo-Aramaic Translations and the Hebrew Text of Two Kurdistani Passover Haggadot: A Historical-Linguistic Study, Including Remarks on Kurdistani Passover Folklore." *Lěšonénu* 64:73–91 [Hebrew].

——. 2002c. "Ad *Lěšonénu* 64, pp. 73–91." *Lěšonénu* 65: 95–96 [Hebrew].

——. 2004. "*Mi Khamokha* in Jewish Neo-Aramaic." *Ben ʿEver la-ʿArav: Contacts between Arabic Literature and Jewish Literature in the Middle Ages and Modern Times* 3:95–120 [Hebrew].

——. 2005. "Yona Gabbay, A Jewish Peddler's Life Story from Iraqi Kurdistan as Narrated by Him in His Jewish Neo-Aramaic Dialect of Zakho (Four Episodes)." *Mediterranean Language Review* 16:167–220.

——. 2006. *The Five Scrolls in Jewish Neo-Aramaic Translations: Dialects of ʿAmidya, Dihok, and Urmiya*. עדה ולשון כו. Jerusalem: Jewish Oral Traditions Research Center.

Soden, Wolfram von. 1995. *Grundriss der akkadischen Grammatik*. 3rd edition, unter Mitarbeit von Werner R. Mayer. Analecta Orientalia 33. Rome: Pontificio Istituto Biblico.

Sokoloff, Michael. 1990. *A Dictionary of Jewish Palestinian Aramaic of the Byzantine Period*. Ramat-Gan: Bar Ilan University Press.

———. 2002. *A Dictionary of Jewish Babylonian Aramaic*. Ramat-Gan: Bar Ilan University Press; Baltimore: Johns Hopkins University Press.

Spitaler, Anton. 1938. *Grammatik des neuaramäischen Dialekts von Maʿlūla (Antilibanon)*. Abhandlungen für die Kunde des Morgenlandes 23. Leipzig: Deutsche Morgenländische Gesellschaft.

———. 1967. "The Aramaic Dialect of Maʿlūla." In Rosenthal 1967, II/2:82–96.

Steiner, Richard C. 1987 "*Lulav* vs. **lu/law*: A Note on the Conditioning of **aw > u* in Hebrew and Aramaic." *Journal of the American Oriental Society* 107:121–122.

———. 1995a. "Linguistic Features of the Commentary on Ezekiel and the Minor Prophets in the Hebrew Scrolls from Byzantium." *Lĕšonénu* 59:39–56 [Hebrew].

———. 1995b. "The Words מאה '100' and מאתין '200' in *Derashot* Based on Popular Dialects of Aramaic." *Tarbiz* 65:33–36 [Hebrew].

Talay, Shabo. 2008. *Die neuaramäischen Dialekte der Khabur-Assyrer in Nordostsyrien*. Semitic Viva 40. Wiesbaden: Harrassowitz.

Tezel, Aziz. 2003. *Comparative Etymological Studies in the Western Neo-Syriac (Ṭūrōyō) Lexicon*. Studia Semitica Upsaliensia 18. Uppsala: Uppsala Universitet.

Vollers, Karl. 1896. "Beiträge zur Kenntniss der lebenden arabischen Sprache in Aegypten: II. Ueber Lehnwörter. Fremdes und Eigenes." *Zeitschrift der deutschen morgenländischen Gesellschaft* 50:607–657.

Weiss, Raphael. 1979. *The Aramaic Targum of Job*. Tel-Aviv: Tel Aviv-University [Hebrew].

Yona, Mordechai. 1999א. *Aramaic-Kurdish—Hebrew Dictionary*. Jerusalem: n.p.

———. 1999ב. *Hebrew—Aramaic-Kurdish Dictionary*. Jerusalem: n.p.

———. 2003. *Kurdish Jewish Encyclopaedia*. 3 vols. Jerusalem: Bialik Institute [Hebrew].

Studies in Semitic
Languages and Linguistics

3. Corré, A.D. *The Daughter of My People*. Arabic and Hebrew Paraphrases of Jeremiah 8.13-9.23. 1971. ISBN 90 04 02552 9

5. Grand'Henry, J. *Les parlers arabes de la région du Mzā b (Sahara algérien)*. 1976. ISBN 90 04 04533 3

6. Bravmann, M.M. *Studies in Semitic Philology*. 1977. ISBN 90 04 04743 3

8. Fenech, E. *Contemporary Journalistic Maltese*. An Analytical and Comparative Study. 1978. ISBN 90 04 05756 0

9. Hospers, J.H. (ed.). *General Linguistics and the Teaching of Dead Hamito-Semitic Languages*. Proceedings of the Symposium held in Groningen, 7th-8th November 1975, on the occasion of the 50th Anniversary of the Institute of Semitic Studies and Near Eastern Archaeology of the State University at Groningen. 1978. ISBN 90 04 05806 0

12. Hoftijzer, J. *A Search for Method*. A Study in the Syntactic Use of the H-locale in Classical Hebrew. With the collaboration of H.R. van der Laan and N.P. de Koo. 1981. ISBN 90 04 06257 2

13. Murtonen, A. *Hebrew in its West Semitic Setting*. A Comparative Survey of Non-Masoretic Hebrew Dialects and Traditions. Part I. *A Comparative Lexicon*.
    Section A. *Proper Names*. 1986. ISBN 90 04 07245 4
    Section Ba. *Root System: Hebrew Material*. 1988. ISBN 90 04 08064 3
    Section Bb. *Root System: Comparative Material and Discussion*. Sections C, D and E: *Numerals under 100, Pronouns, Particles*. 1989.
    ISBN 90 04 08899 7

14. Retsö, J. *Diathesis in the Semitic Languages*. A Comparative Morphological Study. 1989. ISBN 90 04 08818 0

15. Rouchdy, A. *Nubians and the Nubian Language in Contemporary Egypt*. A Case of Cultural and Linguistic Contact. 1991. ISBN 90 04 09197 1

16. Murtonen, A. *Hebrew in its West Semitic Setting*. A Comparative Survey of Non-Masoretic Hebrew Dialects and Traditions. Part 2. *Phonetics and Phonology*. Part 3. *Morphosyntactics*. 1990. ISBN 90 04 09309 5

17. Jongeling K., H.L. Murre-van den Berg & L. van Rompay (eds.). *Studies in Hebrew and Aramaic Syntax*. Presented to Professor J. Hoftijzer on the Occasion of his Sixty-Fifth Birthday. 1991. ISBN 90 04 09520 9

18. Cadora, F.J. *Bedouin, Village, and Urban Arabic*. An Ecolinguistic Study. 1992. ISBN 90 04 09627 2

19. Versteegh, C.H.M. *Arabic Grammar and Qur'ānic Exegesis in Early Islam*. 1993. ISBN 90 04 09845 3

20. Humbert, G. *Les voies de la transmission du Kitāb de Sībawayhi*. 1995. ISBN 90 04 09918 2

21. Mifsud, M. *Loan Verbs in Maltese*. A Descriptive and Comparative Study. 1995. ISBN 90 04 10091 1

22. Joosten, J. *The Syriac Language of the Peshitta and Old Syriac Versions of Matthew*. Syntactic Structure, Inner-Syriac Developments and Translation Technique. 1996. ISBN 90 04 10036 9

23. Bernards, M. *Changing Traditions*. Al-Mubarrad's Refutation of Sībawayh and the Subsequent Reception of the *Kitāb*. 1997. ISBN 90 04 10595 6
24. Belnap, R.K. and N. Haeri. *Structuralist Studies in Arabic Linguistics*. Charles A. Ferguson's Papers, 1954-1994. 1997. ISBN 90 04 10511 5
25. Talmon R. *Arabic Grammar in its Formative Age. Kitāb al-'Ayn* and its Attribution to Ḥalīl b. Aḥmad. 1997. ISBN 90 04 10812 2
26. Testen, D.D. *Parallels in Semitic Linguistics*. The Development of Arabic la̱- and Related Semitic Particles. 1998. ISBN 90 04 10973 0
27. Bolozky, S. *Measuring Productivity in Word Formation*. The Case of Israeli Hebrew. 1999. ISBN 90 04 11252 9
28. Ermers, R. *Arabic Grammars of Turkic. The Arabic Linguistic Model Applied to Foreign Languages & Translation of 'Abu ayyān al-'Andalusī's* Kitab al-'Idrāk li-Lisān al-'Atrāk. 1999. ISBN 90 04 113061
29. Rabin, Ch. *The Development of the Syntax of Post-Biblical Hebrew*. 1999. ISBN 90 04 11433 5
30. Piamenta, M. *Jewish Life in Arabic Language and Jerusalem Arabic in Communal Perspective*. A Lexical-Semantic Study. 2000. ISBN 90 04 11762 8
31. Kinberg, N. ; Versteegh, K. (ed.). *Studies in the Linguistic Structure of Classical Arabic*. 2001. ISBN 90 04 11765 2
32. Khan, G. *The Early Karaite Tradition of Hebrew Grammatical Thought*. Including a Critical Edition, Translation and Analysis of the Diqduq of 'Abū Ya'qūb Yūsuf ibn Nūḥ on the Hagiographa. 2000. ISBN 90 04 11933 7
33. Zammit, M.R. *A Comparative Lexical Study of Qur'ānic Arabic*. ISBN 90 04 11801 2 (in preparation)
34. Bachra, B.N. *The Phonological Structure of the Verbal Roots in Arabic and Hebrew*. 2001. ISBN 90 04 12008 4
35. Åkesson, J. *Arabic Morphology and Phonology*. Based on the Marāḥ al-arwāḥ by Aḥmad b. 'Alī b. Mas'ūd. Presented with an Introduction, Arabic Edition, English Translation and Commentary. 2001. ISBN 90 04 12028 9
36. Khan, G. *The Neo-Aramaic Dialect of Qaraqosh*. 2002. ISBN 90 04 12863 8
37. Khan, G., Ángeles Gallego, M. and Olszowy-Schlanger, J. *The Karaite Tradition of Hebrew Grammatical Thought in its Classical Form*. A Critical Edition and English Translation of *al-Kitāb al-Kāfī fī al-Luġa al-'Ibrāniyya* by 'Abū al-Faraj Hārūn ibn al-Faraj. 2 Vols. 2003. ISBN 90 04 13272 4 (*Set*), ISBN 90 04 13311 9 (*Vol. 1*), ISBN 90 04 13312 7 (*Vol. 2*)
38. Haak, M., De Jong, R., Versteegh, K. (eds.). *Approaches to Arabic Dialects*. A Collection of Articles presented to Manfred Woidich on the Occasion of his Sixtieth Birthday. 2004. ISBN 90 04 13206 6
39. Takács, G. (ed.). *Egyptian and Semito-Hamitic (Afro-Asiatic) Studies in Memoriam W. Vycichl*. 2004. ISBN 90 04 13245 7
40. Maman, A. *Comparative Semitic Philology in the Middle Ages*. From Sa'adiah Gaon to Ibn Barūn (10th-12th C.). 2004. ISBN 90 04 13620 7
41. Van Peursen, W.Th. *The Verbal System in the Hebrew Text of Ben Sira*. 2004. ISBN 90 04 13667 3
42. Elgibali, A. *Investigating Arabic*. Current Parameters in Analysis and Learning. 2004. ISBN 90 04 13792 0
43. Florentin, M. *Late Samaritan Hebrew*. A Linguistic Analysis of Its Different Types. 2004. ISBN 90 04 13841 2
44. Khan, G. *The Jewish Neo-Aramaic Dialect of Sulemaniyya and Ḥalabja*. 2004. ISBN 90 04 13869 2

45. Wellens, I. *The Nubi Language of Uganda.* An Arabic Creole in Africa. 2005. ISBN 90 04 14518 4
46. Bassiouney, R. *Functions of Code Switching in Egypt.* Evidence from Monologues. 2006. ISBN 90 04 14760 8
47. Khan, G. *Semitic Studies in Honour of Edward Ullendorff.* 2005. ISBN 90 04 14834 5
48. Mejdell, G. *Mixed Styles in Spoken Arabic in Egypt.* Somewhere between Order and Chaos. 2006. ISBN-10: 90 04 14986 4, ISBN-13: 978 90 04 14986 1
49. Ditters, W.E. and Motzki, H. (eds.). *Approaches to Arabic Linguistics.* Presented to Kees Versteegh on the Occasion of his Sixtieth Birthday. 2007. ISBN 978 90 04 16015 6
50. Zewi, T. *Parenthesis in Biblical Hebrew.* 2007. ISBN 978 90 04 16243 3
51. Baalbaki, R. *The Legacy of the* Kitāb. Sībawayhi's Analytical Methods within the Context of the Arabic Grammatical Theory. 2008. ISBN 978 90 04 16813 8
52. Peled, Y. *Sentence Types and Word-Order Patterns in Written Arabic.* Medieval and Modern Perspectives. 2009. ISBN 978 90 04 17062 9
53. Al-Wer, E. and R. de Jong. *Arabic Dialectology.* In honour of Clive Holes on the Occasion of his Sixtieth Birthday. 2009. ISBN 978 90 04 17212 8
54. Fassberg, S.E. *The Jewish Neo-Aramaic Dialect of Challa.* 2010. ISBN 978 90 04 17682 9
55. Kahn, L. *The Verbal System in Late Enlightenment Hebrew.* 2009. ISBN 978 90 04 17733 8
56. Marogy, A.E. *Kitāb Sībawayhi.* Syntax and Pragmatics. 2010. ISBN 978 90 04 17816 8